THE
DEAD
PLEDGE

COLUMBIA STUDIES IN THE HISTORY OF U.S. CAPITALISM

COLUMBIA STUDIES IN THE HISTORY OF U.S. CAPITALISM

Series Editors: Devin Fergus, Louis Hyman, Bethany Moreton, and Julia Ott

Capitalism has served as an engine of growth, a source of inequality, and a catalyst for conflict in American history. While remaking our material world, capitalism's myriad forms have altered—and been shaped by—our most fundamental experiences of race, gender, sexuality, nation, and citizenship. This series takes the full measure of the complexity and significance of capitalism, placing it squarely back at the center of the American experience. By drawing insight and inspiration from a range of disciplines and alloying novel methods of social and cultural analysis with the traditions of labor and business history, our authors take history "from the bottom up" all the way to the top.

For a complete list of titles, see page 291.

THE
DEAD
PLEDGE

The Origins of the Mortgage
Market and Federal Bailouts,
1913–1939

JUDGE GLOCK

Columbia University Press
New York

Columbia University Press
Publishers Since 1893
New York   Chichester, West Sussex
cup.columbia.edu

Library of Congress Cataloging-in-Publication Data
Names: Glock, Judge, author.
Title: The dead pledge : the origins of the mortgage market and federal bailouts,
    1913–1939 / Judge Glock.
Description: New York : Columbia University Press, [2021] | Series: Columbia
    studies in the history of U.S. capitalism | Includes bibliographical
    references and index.
Identifiers: LCCN 2020039985 (print) | LCCN 2020039986 (ebook) |
    ISBN 9780231192521 (hardback ; alk. paper) | ISBN 9780231192538
    (paperback ; alk. paper) | ISBN 9780231549851 (ebook)
Subjects: LCSH: Mortgages—United States—History—20th century. | Farm
    mortgages—United States—History—20th century. | Mortgage banks—
    United States—History—20th century. | Bailouts (Government policy)—
    United States—History—20th century. | Loans—United States—Government
    guaranty—History—20th century. | United States—Economic policy.
Classification: LCC HG2040.5.U5 G577 2021 (print) | LCC HG2040.5.U5 (ebook) |
    DDC 332.7/2097309043—dc23
LC record available at https://lccn.loc.gov/2020039985
LC ebook record available at https://lccn.loc.gov/2020039986

Columbia University Press books are printed
on permanent and durable acid-free paper.
Printed in the United States of America

Cover design: Milenda Nan Ok Lee
Cover image: Library of Congress

CONTENTS

ACKNOWLEDGMENTS

M y former adviser, Jennifer Mittelstadt, has been an incomparable help in turning this project from a few inchoate ideas into something in which I hope she can take some small measure of pride. I was always impressed by her thoughtful advice and close attention, which went above and beyond the call of duty. I likewise appreciate the help of David Greenberg, T. J. Jackson Lears, and Eugene White, all of whom enriched my time and my work at Rutgers University. I am grateful as well to the many other professors in both the History and the Economic Departments at Rutgers, who enlivened what is often a solitary enterprise.

The Mellon Foundation provided generous support in both the early and the later periods of my work. The Herbert Hoover Presidential Library and the Roosevelt Institute and Presidential Library provided me with funds and time for research, which enhanced the final product. Brian Balogh and the Miller Center at the University of Virginia provided me with a lovely academic home for two years to work on the project.

My later colleagues at the Department of Economics at West Virginia University, especially Joshua Hall and Eric Olsen, offered new ideas and insights. Likewise, my current colleagues at the Cicero Institute, especially Joe Lonsdale and Clay Spence, have helped keep my historical research grounded in the contemporary world. The editors at Columbia University Press, including Bridget Flannery-McCoy and Stephen Wesley, and the editors of the Histories of Capitalism series, including Louis Hyman and Julia Ott, have worked to improve the manuscript from the moment it landed in their inboxes.

The many archivists at numerous libraries deserve more time and credit than I can provide here. Without their support, this project would have been greatly diminished, perhaps to the point of nonexistence.

Thanks is also due to the *Business History Review* for allowing some selections of chapters 3 and 4 to appear in the article "The Rise and Fall of the First Government Sponsored Enterprise: The Federal Land Banks, 1916–1932," 90, no. 4 (Winter 2016): 623–45, and to the *History of Political Economy* for allowing some parts of chapters 5 and 8 to appear in the article "The 'Riefler-Keynes' Doctrine and Federal Reserve Policy in the Great Depression," 51, no. 2 (April 2019): 297–327. Both of these articles, however, contain substantially different material and have different focuses than the text here.

My parents have always been understanding of my rather atypical career path and my winding way along it. I hope the completion of this book helps justify some of their faith in me.

Most of all, I thank my wife, Sophia, for putting up with my years of archival absences, solitary study, and, inevitably, discussions about mortgage finance. My debt to her can never be cleared. As a meager down payment, I dedicate this work to her.

THE
DEAD
PLEDGE

INTRODUCTION

I n Willa Cather's novel *O Pioneers!* (1913), the fierce and independent
Alexandra Bergson convinces her brothers, Lou and Oscar, to place
a mortgage on their Nebraska homestead in order to buy some neigh-
boring land. Yet the very thought of a mortgage terrifies all of them. They
remember the burden a mortgage placed on their father when he first came to
the country, and they are loath to place such a weight on themselves. "Mortgage the homestead again?" Lou cries out. "I won't slave to pay off another mortgage. I'll never do it. You'd just as soon kill us all, Alexandra, to carry out
some scheme!"[1]

In fact, it was at exactly this time that the stresses imposed on such families
by high-stakes, high-interest mortgages inspired a new political movement, a
movement that hoped both to alleviate the burden of mortgage debt and, ironically perhaps, to make mortgages a part of the broader financial world. In this
period, farmers such as Alexandra Bergson made alliance with once-reviled
bankers to sell America on a new mortgage scheme.

This book traces the history of that movement and of its consequences for
American life, economics, and politics. At its heart, the new movement declared
it the government's duty to keep all sectors of the economy in a grand balance
with one another, most importantly by supporting cheap mortgages and financing to those sectors, such as agriculture, that lagged behind. The book explains
how this idea was embraced by wide swaths of farmers, politicians, intellectuals, builders, and, of course, bankers. Though little understood today and
seemingly tangential to the main currents of American thought, the dream of

economic balance through finance was at the center of many early twentieth-century debates and had profound ramifications for American capitalism and American government. Most importantly, the movement for balance shaped the modern banking system of the United States, which became ever more focused on mortgage debt and ever more bolstered by government guarantees.

The commonplace plea to restore "balance"—to people's lives, to the national budget, to the political system—has been so omnipresent that it is hard to conceive of a time when it carried rhetorical weight. Balance is, after all, no more than a metaphor, with amorphous yet positive connotations, used to invoke reason and fairness. Perhaps the very banality of the term has obscured its importance in earlier thought.

Yet the call for a balanced economy once stirred political passions. That call began, as so many calls of this era, with the farmers.[2] Ever since the birth of capitalism, farmers had grumbled that banks catered only to merchants and manufacturers. Banks had long accepted money from these groups and loaned the money back to them, usually to finance goods traveling from one place to another or raw materials going through manufacturing. At most banks, these loans lasted for only a few weeks or months. Attempts by farmers to create "land banks," or banks that loaned for the long term on mortgages, the types of loans farmers needed most, met with opposition and failure. By the turn of the twentieth century, farmers faced insuperable barriers to securing the cheap, long-term loans they needed. As the financial system grew in importance, farmers' exclusion from it became an ever more salient issue.

In the early twentieth century, farmers, bankers, and many intellectuals began to argue that the declining fortunes of agriculture, along with the declining proportion of the population devoted to farming, was a threat to the entire economy. They formulated the inchoate outlines of an ideology, one that argued that an economy needed some sort of stability between all its producing sectors. If one sector, such as farming, fell behind, the rest of the economy was sure to follow. In this light, farmers' failure to finance themselves sapped their productivity and purchasing power, drove them into the cities, and posed a threat to the urban world as well.

New politicians in this era, such as Senator Henry Hollis of New Hampshire, joined hands with rural bankers, new farm groups such as the Farmers Union, and "rural-credits" experts such as David Lubin to plead that special government privileges to some banks could help balance the stagnant farm sector with the buoyant industrial sector. Beginning in 1913, these advocates transformed the new and nominally private Federal Reserve System by giving it special government privileges and demanding it support longer-term loans to farmers. More significantly for this story, in 1916 these groups created the Federal Land Banks, which relied on the government's implicit backing to package farm mortgages into mortgage-backed bonds. These two systems began a new era in government-supported finance.

In the following decades, the federal government would use the powers of these semipublic banks to become an overweening figure in the financial world. And these new institutions, despite their continuing nominal concern for farmers, would be dominated by bankers, who would use them to succor an increasingly precarious banking system. The supposed means, government credit to banks made in order to support farmers, quickly became the ends, with the government using its new power to buttress banks.

In the 1920s, however, during an era of drastic declines in crop prices, rural partisans began to form a more complex theory of economic balance. They became concerned about the problem of low farm prices. Advocates of this theory, such as George Peek, Hugh Johnson, and Bernard Baruch, thought that a new imbalance between low agricultural prices and high industrial prices meant the two grand sectors of the economy could not "trade" with each other. They argued that low farm prices prevented farmers from buying industry's goods, which threatened the general economy. These reformers gave birth to the "price-parity" movement, which demanded that the government ensure an equitable price for farm crops. Yet as these ideas of price balance were implemented in the Herbert Hoover administration and later in the Franklin Roosevelt administration, through new agencies such as the Federal Farm Board, they also were used to support banks and their mortgages. In practice, the new administrators of price supports understood that higher crop prices helped farmers pay down their loans to the banks. Such ideas about price balance eventually became another addendum to the ideology of balance through finance as well as another means to support banks.

The ideology of economic balance eventually spread beyond the farm to the cities. During the Great Depression, certain sectors of the economy, such as home construction and the heavy industries, such as lumber, that depended on it, were exceptionally sluggish. New advocates of balance, now including professional economists such as Wesley Clair Mitchell and Winfield Riefler, and urban bankers already involved in mortgage debt, such as the managers of "building-and-loan" banks, argued that only government support for urban mortgages could bring these sectors back to equality with the rest of the economy and thus restore prosperity. Herbert Hoover and then Franklin Delano Roosevelt brought the ideology of economic balance from the rural to the urban sphere and into the forefront of national policy. Both administrations eventually made subsidizing urban mortgages the quintessence of both recovery and reform in the Great Depression. Both also spearheaded the creation of new semipublic mortgage corporations and agencies, such as the Federal Home Loan Banks in 1932 and the Federal National Mortgage Association (also known as

Fannie Mae) in 1938. At the same time, they pressed for several reforms of the Federal Reserve and the national banking system, all directed at encouraging long-term loans and cheap mortgages, which further tied the government into supporting the financial world.

Although the first half of the twentieth century is often called the "Age of Reform," and innumerable historians have traced the new programs, from minimum-wage legislation to food inspection to Social Security, that reshaped American economic and political life in this era, the government reforms to ensure balance through finance rivaled or perhaps surpassed in scale the more well-known programs.[3] By the beginning of World War II, the government was surrounded by an array of semipublic financial institutions unimaginable just thirty years earlier. The government now supported the Federal Reserve Banks, the Federal Land Banks, the Intermediate Credit Banks, the Reconstruction Finance Corporation, the Federal Home Loan Banks, the Home Owners Loan Corporation, the Federal Farm Mortgage Corporation, the Federal Deposit Insurance Corporation, the Federal Housing Administration, the Federal Savings and Loan Insurance Corporation, the Federal National Mortgage Association, as well as a host of other programs, subsidies, and guarantees—all designed to cosset the banking world and to entice banks into making more risky loans and mortgages.

These new semipublic financial institutions exceeded in size other, better-known political innovations of the era, such as the Federal Trade Commission and the Social Security Administration. In fact, by 1939 government corporations and credit agencies owned or guaranteed more than $12 billion in financial assets, the majority of which involved financing farm and home mortgages. The entire federal budget that year, at the end of the New Deal, was only $9 billion.[4] Thus, the most significant and extensive government safety net to emerge from the first half of the twentieth century was the net protecting banks and lenders.

One reason why these Brobdingnagian institutions were and are not better known, both then and now, is that their spending, lending, and guarantees were off the books and did not appear in most reports of the government budget. These corporations were only "semipublic," relying on the government's implicit support if they ever got in trouble. They provided politicians a means to support certain industries without having to directly call on taxpayers. Funds for the subsequent bailouts of these institutions would be required only of future politicians, sometimes generations later.

Thus, the U.S. government birthed by the Age of Reform was largely a government that subsidized mortgage loans and supported finance through new corporations and agencies. By the end of this period, many reformers understood that even if they had not achieved a grand balance between farm and industry or among all industrial sectors, they had made the federal government the greatest investment partner and mortgage banker in the world.

Viewing the politics of the early twentieth century through the lens of economic balance and government finance should reshape our understanding of that era in several ways. First, despite a mass of literature examining the ideologies behind the Progressive Era and the New Deal, there is almost no discussion of the ideology of "economic balance" or how it competed with an older understanding of government, which was defined by opposition to special privileges to one economic sector or class, what was then known as "class legislation."[5] This book describes a battle of ideas between those who continued to attack class legislation and those who celebrated economic balance and new privileges. It demonstrates why older politicians and intellectuals, especially in the Democratic Party, once embraced the idea that government should strive to ensure "equal protection of the law" to all economic groups. These politicians thought the government should eschew all special privileges for any one class but most particularly for the corrupt banking world. By contrast, new farmer, builder, and banker movements argued that in the inherently unjust world of contemporary capitalism, special privileges for some groups were necessary. They worried instead about an economy unfair in its marrow and thought only government support, especially financial support, could restore that balance.

This book shows that although the methods and language of economic balance sometimes changed, the basic idea remained consistent. The balancing ideal stated that the economy was best conceptualized as a collection of large economic sectors, such as agriculture and industry, or light and heavy industry, that traded with one another and that needed to share equally in prosperity if that trade were going to continue. The government's duty was to ensure a rough equality among sectors, using financial guarantees or price supports, so each sector could purchase the goods produced by the other sectors. Although the focus on abstract sectors or classes in the economy, as opposed to a focus on aggregate measures of the economy, has fallen into desuetude, such analysis was once a political commonplace.[6] This book also shows the surprising continuity of this balancing ideology throughout the era and across different politicians and political parties, which were often assumed to be at loggerheads.[7] Whether Democrat or Republican, whether during the Progressive Era or the subsequent "normalcy," whether during Herbert Hoover's New Era or Franklin Roosevelt's New Deal, the desire to balance economic sectors through finance was the sine qua non of American political economy. The old ideology of class legislation eventually became a forgotten relic, but the idea of balance through finance permeated American government and reshaped it for the rest of the twentieth century and into the twenty-first. Even after the ideal of economic balance faded, the financial reforms inspired by it remained.

The book explains how diverse economic interests, even those often thought to be at loggerheads, touted these reforms and ideas. Bankers, farmers, and builders became political bedfellows to argue for financial balancing.[8] The book also shows how often politicians and government officials did not just respond to these interest groups but were continuing members of them. Investors inhabiting the halls of Congress and bankers running the new semipublic corporations used government both to pursue their groups' ends and to reap their own rewards. They used government funds, government agencies, and government publicity to shape the debates around these ideas and to encourage confidence in the banks that they owned as well as to encourage sales of their investment products. They used what would later be known as the "revolving door" to continue reaping their rewards after leaving government office. Instead of viewing the increased intertwining of the political and banking world as an aberrational corruption that bedeviled reformers in this period, one should see the mixture of politics and banking as an explicit goal of these reformers, who hoped to involve government more explicitly in the banking world and vice versa.[9]

This book does not, however, treat ideology as a mere scrim for such interests. The struggle between the dying idea of class legislation and the emerging idea of economic balance was one of the central ideological struggles of the era. It reshaped both the government and the economy in ways no single interest group fully anticipated. After all, these interest groups had to convince many politicians and voters who had no connection to farming or banking that financial support to these groups was necessary. At the same time, many intellectuals, economists, and those most nebulous of creatures, reformers, embraced the ideology of economic balance out of sincere belief and were often the strongest promoters of it. Although the interests behind the ideology were obvious, ideas had their own motive power and helped shape the nature of American politics in ways no interest group could predict.

One, perhaps surprising, result of foregrounding the ideology of economic balance is that it challenges the now common view that most economic reforms in the early twentieth century aimed to redistribute income to consumers. This book demonstrates that Progressive and New Deal policies aimed more often at stimulating certain industries than at stimulating the consumers who purchased from them.[10] For instance, from the 1920s through the 1930s, many politicians hoped to charge consumers higher prices for food even though they understood that such high prices lowered consumers' income. They knew, however, that high food prices assisted producing farmers and the banks that made loans to them. The book also demonstrates how both the Hoover administration and the New Deal aimed to lower construction worker wages in order to encourage more profitable building. The consistent goal of these policies was increasing profits in certain sectors to encourage more investment in them. Contrary to those who argue that a modern mass-consumption "Keynesianism," premised on deficit spending, came to define American economic policy, this book shows that economic theorists of the time, including John Maynard Keynes himself, thought achieving prosperity meant ensuring profitability in certain stagnant industries.[11] When consumers and workers came into conflict with financiers and businesses in this period, the latter typically triumphed, not as part of a conservative reaction but because of original and powerful currents of "reform."

Finally, this book explains how the expansion of government financial guarantees restructured the relationship between the American state and banking and remade American capitalism. Most histories of American "state building" have ignored how the government expanded its influence through expanding its financial supports in this period,[12] and many banking historians have slighted the importance of ever-increasing government support in the reshaping of this industry.[13] In the literature on the history of capitalism, the political encouragement of debt is often seen as a way to entice more consumer spending, in the mold of mass-consumption Keynesianism or as a substitute for direct redistribution, as opposed to a way to support certain businesses.[14]

This book shows how the government used its new financial guarantees to restructure banks, pushing them away from their older customers and loans and directing them toward new types of riskier lending. Before the Progressive Era, bankers tended to lend money only to merchants and manufacturers, and their loans tended to last for just a few weeks. From the time of Adam Smith, these habits were embodied in banking laws and regulations and became known as the "real-bills doctrine" after the short-term merchants' bills on which banks made loans. Mortgages and other long-term loans were illegal for most banks and discouraged by most bankers.

The new believers in economic balance aimed to encourage banks to make longer-term loans to both the agricultural industry and the housing industry. They forced the government to support months-long loans for the planting and harvesting of crops, years-long loans on livestock and home repairs, and, most especially, decades-long mortgages for farmers and builders. These reformers understood that only by covering lenders with government guarantees could investors feel confident in making and then trading these long-term mortgage debts as part of a new mortgage market. To use the modern term, the government used its guarantees to make long-term loans and mortgages "liquid" or always capable of being sold and transformed into cash.[15] In this new conception, if mortgages could be made as easily tradable and liquid as short-term paper, those parts of the economy that depended on land could be brought into balance with other parts that did not. Thanks to these reformers' efforts, banking was transformed to make once-excluded mortgages the centerpiece of the banking world. Bankers once defined themselves as investors in short-term debts who avoided mortgages at all costs, but by the modern era the majority of bank assets would become mortgage debt. Thanks to government support, the American banking world became the mirror image of its former self.[16]

Some of the new government guarantees to banks in this era were explicit, some were implicit (as in the creation of the first implicitly guaranteed government-sponsored enterprises, such as the Federal Land Banks), and some were merely a promise to keep up a market in mortgages or other debts if trading in them slowed. The government sometimes bought bad banking debts, sometimes gave loans or deposits to banks in troubled times, sometimes gave tax exemptions to banks, and sometimes purchased their stock. Often, too, government loans to farmers or businesses were just thinly disguised ways for these groups to pay back their bankers. By the end of the period, almost every type of financial institution received some type of direct or indirect government assistance. At the same time, almost every risky investment had a potential home in one of the era's new semipublic corporations or government agencies.

All of these state supports expanded the power of banking and finance in the economy. The supposed "financialization" of the economy, which putatively emerged in the 1970s and 1980s, actually began in the first part of the twentieth century as part of a general ideology of balancing real economic sectors. In fact, the earnings of the banking and finance industry grew throughout this period and attained a temporary peak in the New Deal at about 6 percent of total gross domestic product, a level the industry would not reach again until the 1980s. At the same time, an increasing proportion of those profits came from an ever-growing number of mortgages. Whereas in 1890 the nation's mortgage debt was barely $68 per person, after World War II it increased to almost ten times that level. Similarly, in the 1890s the majority of that mortgage debt was loaned and owned by local individuals, yet by the postwar period almost all of it was in the hands of rapidly expanding banks backed by the government.[17] This synchronized expansion of the American state and American finance was one of the most important transformations in the first half of the twentieth century and arguably the one with the most long-lasting consequences. In the savings-and-loan crisis of the 1980s, the financial crisis of 2008, and the coronavirus crisis of 2020, the government would use its expanded powers to provide trillions of dollars of bailouts to both bankers and the businesses who borrowed from them.

A brief illustration helps show the combined revolution of American government and banking. In 1910, amid a heated national debate about reforming American finance, an economics professor at Northwestern University, Murray Wildman, wrote an article ridiculing a then lonely proposal to lend government money to failing banks. "There is no more reason why the members of the banking profession should stand before the public treasury hat in hand than that any other group of business men should do so." He noted that the Populist Party had recently begged the government to fund mortgage loans to farmers and that most Americans had derided this idea. Wildman asked his readers if it would "be any more preposterous" for the government "to have a special fund" to support tottering banks than to give them a special fund to loan on questionable mortgages?[18] Yet in a little more than twenty years, the U.S. government would be loaning on or guaranteeing billions of dollars of American mortgages, and at the same time it would use these loans and guarantees to bail out the banks and investors making those mortgages. Thus, two propositions about federal assistance for mortgages and for banks, which in 1910 were regarded as equally ludicrous, would soon come to define much of American government.

This book's first chapter traces the roots of the land bank idea that came to inspire American farmers, reformers, and bankers. It describes how the rise of merchant-focused banking in the 1600s, "commercial banking" as it was called, provoked frustration among farmers. These concerns sparked a centuries-long, transatlantic discussion on how to create a new type of bank, a "land bank," based on farmers' most important piece of wealth. The chapter describes the birth of the land bank idea in the mystical group known as the Spiritual Brotherhood as well as three failed attempts to implement it: first, purely government-owned land banks; second, purely private land banks; and, third, cooperative land banks. Finally, it demonstrates how reformers in the early twentieth century settled on the possibilities of a new type of semipublic land bank that seemed to combine the best of previous ideas. The semipublic land bank would include both cooperative and for-profit features but also government guarantees to investors. By the early 1910s, these new semipublic banks became the most popular international solution to farmers' financial problems. Chapter 1 places the land bank idea in a long tradition of transatlantic reform and demonstrates in a way not discussed in the historiography of banking how normal banking and mortgage banking shaped each other as they both evolved.

Chapter 2 explains how a still incipient idea of economic balance, focused on the balance of population among different sectors, arose during the early twentieth century and how that ideology led to new forms of federal support for finance. It describes the battle between the Wilson administration, which held to the old Democratic Party ideals of equal protection of the laws and opposition to class legislation, and new banker and farmer groups, such as the Farmers Union, which demanded financial support for agriculture. The latter groups' pleas had a profound though unacknowledged impact on the shape of the Federal Reserve Act of 1913, which granted several concessions to farmers and their debts. Their pleas also led to the creation of the Federal Land Banks in 1916 as the first of what would later be known as government-sponsored enterprises, nominally private financial companies that relied on the implicit backing of the federal government. The chapter helps reimagine our understanding of the Progressive movement in the Democratic Party by showing how the movement struggled against older ideas of class legislation and how it came to focus on federal financial reforms.

Chapter 3 shows how bankers and investors pushed the Federal Land Banks to provide support for floundering banks and how the Land Banks became ever more divorced from the interests of farmers. Even as the ideology of agricultural balance became clearer, the Land Banks became increasingly devoted to salvaging not farmers but banks, all as part of an increased government focus on finance. Previous historians have pointed to changes between the "reformist" Wilson administration and the supposed "normalcy" of his Republican successors, but this chapter shows the continuity of federal support for rural finance through both parties and several administrations.

Chapter 4 explains how declining farm prices in the 1920s led to a new type of balancing ideology, known as the price-parity movement, which pushed the government to use new forms of credit to support both farm prices and farm debts. The chapter shows how the government enlisted both the new Federal Farm Board, which loaned federal money to raise crop prices, and the older Federal Land Banks to support a version of this parity ideology and to support banks whose problems were exacerbated by the fall in crop prices. It describes how both of these institutions became overextended and collapsed. It investigates the eventual bailout of the Land Banks, Congress's first official bailout of a financial institution. This chapter supplements the meager literature on the price-parity movement and demonstrates how the movement was tied into wider hopes for agricultural, industrial, and financial balance.

Chapter 5 describes how ideas of economic balance migrated from their origin in the agricultural sector to the industrial sector and began to focus on the problems of "illiquid" urban mortgages. It shows how President Herbert Hoover and his economic advisers formulated a new theory in which the cost of urban mortgages determined the cycles of boom and bust in the economy through its influence on construction. The most important financial reforms of the Hoover presidency therefore aimed at lowering urban-mortgage costs. These reforms involved using the Federal Reserve and other institutions to support banks that held bad mortgage debts and creating the nation's second implicitly backed mortgage corporation, the Federal Home Loan Banks, based on the recently bailed-out Land Banks. This chapter thus reframes the U.S. government's response to the Great Depression. Unlike previous histories of this crucial period, it shows that the government thought that making urban mortgages cheap, liquid, and safe should be the cynosure of economic recovery.

Turning to the New Deal, chapter 6 describes how the Franklin Roosevelt administration continued and expanded the policies of the Progressive reformers and earlier Republican administrations in farm finance. It shows that from the beginning of his presidential campaign Roosevelt focused on creating a balance between the agricultural economy and the industrial economy, using both price and financial supports. It shows how economists and advisers around Roosevelt perceived the collapse of the financial system during the Hoover administration as a result of the failure of rural–urban balance and especially of the failure of farm mortgages. The Roosevelt administration thus extended the agricultural price and financial supports created by Hoover and vastly increased the use of the revived Federal Land Banks. Whereas previous histories of the New Deal have slighted the importance of farming and especially farm finance in its original vision, this chapter demonstrates their centrality.

Chapter 7 describes how advisers in the Roosevelt administration, including some economists carried over from the Hoover administration, such as Winfield Riefler, returned again to the issue of balance in the industrial sector, especially in regard to home construction. Their renewed focus on balancing stagnant housing production with other resurgent industries led to the passage of the National Housing Act of 1934. This act created new means to protect banks from mortgage losses and laid the foundations for two semipublic institutions, the Federal Savings and Loan Insurance Corporation and Fannie Mae, both of which were later bailed out by the government. Unlike histories that claim the National Housing Act aimed at encouraging suburban development, this chapter highlights the financial motives behind the act and shows its importance in the New Deal's recovery efforts.

Chapter 8 describes how the ideology behind the National Housing Act came to shape the entire Roosevelt administration and especially Roosevelt's reaction to the recession of 1937. In this period, Roosevelt and his advisers pushed the Federal Reserve System to fully support banks stuck with unsalable mortgages and drastically extended the ambit of the National Housing Act. At the same time, the administration began assaults against high housing costs and high wages in construction unions in order to encourage more residential lending and building. By the beginning of World War II, the New Deal had transformed American banking to make mortgages a permanent part of it, even while surrounding the banking system with ever more government guarantees. This financial revolution in the latter years of the New Deal has not been previously discussed, but this chapter argues that it remains perhaps the most significant legacy of that era.

The conclusion explores how institutions originally designed to balance sectors carried on into the postwar period and how they shaped the nature of our modern financial bailouts. It shows that although the farmer, building, and banker movements did not fundamentally rebalance the economy, as many had hoped, they nevertheless gave birth to the financial industry of today, an industry buoyed by federal guarantees, especially for mortgage debt. The conclusion shows how in myriad ways the United States is still dealing with the consequences of its forgotten quest for balance through finance.

CHAPTER 1

MAKING THE LAND LIQUID

The Roots of Land Banking

T he Air Bank ("Bankers in Air" its banknotes unpropitiously said) opened its doors in 1769 in the Scottish parish of the same name.[1] At the bank's inauguration, its patron, the duke of Buccleuch, and some of his fellow landed nobles flaunted their supposed altruistic motives for creating the bank and their dreams of development for the Scottish countryside. They especially celebrated the cheap mortgage loans the bank would give to farmers. In the following three years, the bank and its book of mortgages grew rapidly, and its banknotes soon made up the majority of the currency of Scotland. Yet in 1772 a run by noteholders, who wanted to reclaim the original gold and silver coins they had deposited at the bank, led to the bank's collapse, which in turn caused an unprecedented financial panic in London. The Scottish author James Boswell wrote, "War, famine, and pestilence, used formerly to fill up the number of the general calamities of mankind," but now financial panics added something new to man's woes. Boswell fretted that "all Scotland has been shaken by a kind of commercial earthquake, while, like a company connected by an electrical wire, the people in every corner of the country have almost instantaneously received the same shock."[2] After the panic, banking fell into disrepute.

One man who witnessed this collapse divined a moral in it, a moral he thought would allow people to distinguish between good banks and bad banks. The absent-minded bachelor Adam Smith had once been a tutor to the young duke of Buccleuch and had sailed with him to Europe. While in France he had met some of the continent's earliest economists, the Physiocrats, who believed that land was the source of all wealth and who spurred Smith's interest in economic philosophy. After his return to Scotland and the failure of his benefactor's bank, however, Smith attacked the very landed conception on which the bank was founded. His friend the philosopher David Hume knew Smith was working on a new book on economics at the time of the panic, and he wrote to him asking if "these events any-wise affect your theory? Or will [they] occasion the revisal of any chapters?"[3] They would.

In *An Inquiry Into the Nature and Causes of the Wealth of Nations* (1776), written while Smith was still on the duke's annuity, Smith conceded that the Air Bank's "design was generous" and that it was instituted for "public spirited purposes." Yet he thought that the bank had a major defect. Its loans were based on "improvements [for] which the returns are the most slow and distant, such as the improvements of land. To promote such improvements was even said to be the chief of the public spirited purposes for which it was instituted."[4] Smith worried that such long-term loans on land were inappropriate for a bank. He made a stark distinction between what he called "real bills," which would suit a bank, and "slow" loans, which would not. Real bills were short-term loans given by banks to commercial traders that were backed by real physical merchandise and could be quickly recovered if the borrower failed to pay. "Slow" loans, such as loans on land, also known as mortgages, lasted for long periods of time, and they could not be collected easily if the bank were in a pinch. Smith said that banks should ignore such slow loans entirely and leave mortgages to wealthy individuals.[5]

Smith argued that banks could not support long-term mortgages because of the way that banks were funded. Most of a bank's funds came from gold and silver coins temporarily "deposited" at the bank by customers. In exchange for these coins, bank customers then received notes from the bank, which they or anyone else who acquired the notes could bring back to the bank counter at any time. In a panic, all of these noteholders could flood the bank with demands for coins that usually were being loaned out to others. Smith said that if bank loans were based on short-term real bills, the loaned money would come back before the flood of notes had reached full tide, and the bank would be safe. If those loans were on long-term mortgages or other slow debts, however, the bank would be unable to satisfy its noteholders and would go underwater.[6]

Although Smith did not use the modern term *liquidity*, he offered a liquid metaphor for what he considered proper banking. He said, "The coffers of the bank, so far as its dealings are confined to such customers, resemble a water pond, from which, though a stream is continually running out, yet another is continually running in, fully equal to that which runs out."[7] The goal, in Smith's conception, was to keep both banks' notes and loans flowing like water, to make both the money emitted by the banks and the loans of the bank "liquid," or capable of being quickly transformed into cold, hard cash.

Nothing was less liquid, both financially and metaphysically, than land.[8] William Playfair, the famous Scottish polymath, elaborated on Smith's observations in this regard. He argued that so long as banks confined their loans to real bills, they would keep themselves and the whole banking system liquid and stable. He wrote that "it is one essential thing in every Bank that the sums advanced by it should be for temporary purposes. This is one of the principals laid down by Mr. Smith, and, a proof thereof, is that the bank of A[i]r in Scotland, which was a Land Bank, was ruined principally by lending to men of landed property. . . . The agriculture of the country was benefited, but the borrowers were unable to pay."[9]

In time, Smith's theory that banks should limit themselves to only short-term commercial lending would be known as the "real-bills doctrine" and would define the practice, laws, and regulations of modern banking. It eventually became a ubiquitous refrain among bankers that the very "first duty of banking" was to "distinguish between a mortgage and a [real] bill" and to loan only on the latter.[10] Banking in a sense was *defined* by its avoidance of mortgages. Yet where did this doctrine leave those whose wealth was tied up in their land and who now had no way to transform that land into money?

Although the idea of a land bank, a bank explicitly made to loan on mortgages, is often relegated to the status of a historical oddity touted by eccentrics, the idea exerted a powerful pull over the Western imagination for centuries. In its earliest years, land banks promised an alternative to the commercial banks that became the norm of Western finance. Although historians have occasionally noted the idea's appearance in certain periods, they have ignored how and why it became a recurring dream in agricultural circles for generations. In fact, as Adam Smith's story shows, regular banking and land banking evolved in tandem and influenced each other throughout their respective histories. The evolution of the land bank idea and of its contrast, the modern "commercial bank," was the result of an ongoing transatlantic conversation on the nature of banking, the nature of mortgages, and the nature of government.[11]

The driving motivation for land bank believers was the seeming inequity between an urban world awash in finance and a rural world excluded from it. The land bank was not yet conceived as an exercise in overall economic balance but rather as the landholders' attempt to achieve financial equality with the rest of a growing economy. Yet the problems Smith identified continued to bedevil land bank promoters. There remained the insoluble dilemma of making long-term loans on hunks of immovable land when banks could lose their deposits at a moment's notice. Fitting land and mortgages into banks would be a circle difficult, maybe impossible, to square.

Promoters of land banking made three separate attempts to discover the solution to the dilemma, each of which ran aground. The first efforts to make land banks mere extensions of the government led to rampant inflation; later attempts to allow private commercial banks, such as the Air Bank, to invest small portions of their loans in land led to panics and collapses; attempts to allow cooperative groups to loan on land encountered insuperable dilemmas in trying to expand. By the early twentieth century, these failures meant modern banking was ever-more defined by its opposition to mortgage loans.

After years of effort, the seeming solution to the problem of illiquid land in both Europe and America was found in a new type of quasi-public, quasi-private corporation. These new corporations would rely on the support of the government but would be owned by private shareholders or cooperatives. This solution seemed to give the stability of government guarantees and oversight while allowing private groups to retain control, and, of course, profits.

This chapter examines how the goal of liquid land became a recurring theme in the West from the seventeenth century through the early twentieth century. The chapter also shows how, long before theorists elaborated on what would later be called "economic imbalances," the land bank was tied into the dream of financial equality for agriculture. The land bank idea gave birth to a new type of semipublic bank that would soon reshape both banking and politics in the twentieth-century United States.

Government Land Banks in the Age of Revolution

In England, land had long been the focus of government and law. As one historian has said, in England "the law of the land was principally land law."[12] Yet English barons used the law to prevent the hasty disposal of land and thus the dissipation of their power and wealth. Their "common law" placed tight restrictions on selling, trading, or lending on land. More entrepreneurial landowners, however, struggled to dodge these limitations, and as early as the fourteenth century they and some clever lawyers invented the "mortgage." Under a mortgage loan, the land remained nominally in the hands of the lender, while in fact the borrower owned and used the land at his or her pleasure. The lender pretended to receive a sort of rent from the borrower instead of the forbidden interest. The actual title to the land transferred only on the final day when the debt was paid off, when the contract thus "died," and the land was supposedly conveyed for the first time. The death of the debt gave the instrument its French name, *mort gage*, or the "dead pledge."[13]

During the English Civil Wars of the seventeenth century and during what became known as the Financial Revolution after the wars, new classes began to displace the landed aristocracy at the center of English life and lending.[14] Goldsmiths began to offer their customers, who were frightened by royal and revolutionary confiscations, a safe place to deposit their gold and silver coins.

In return, their customers got paper notes, or IOUs, which promised to return the coins whenever the customers asked. The goldsmiths soon realized that they could lend out most of these deposited coins to others because all their customers did not desire the coins back at the same time. The goldsmiths kept just a fraction of those coins at their shops in reserve for customers' requests, even while their notes circulated like the coins. Goldsmiths' notes became a new kind of money, which people used to pay for all types of goods. One contemporary report noted that "severall persons being Goldsmiths and others by taking or borrowing great summes of money and lending out the same for extraordinary lucre and profitts have gained and acquired themselves the Reputacon [sic] and Name of Bankers," based on the wooden board or "bank" on which they conducted business.[15] The modern banker was born.

Some intellectuals concerned with the position of agriculture hoped to make land and mortgages a substantial or maybe fundamental part of the new banking system. Among them was a mystical club of agricultural obsessives known as the Spiritual Brotherhood. This group combined new ideals of scientific discovery with alchemical dreams of spiritual and environmental improvement. They were radical democrats and freethinkers, and they, like the goldsmiths, flourished during the English Civil Wars. As one historian notes, however, "their primary focus . . . was to find ways to enhance the productivity of plant and animal husbandry." Most notably, they were "advocates for the improvement of all available land."[16]

Tying the new world of banking to the old world of land was an essential part of the Spiritual Brotherhood's vision and inspired its invention of the land bank idea. In 1650, just one year after the execution of the English king for high treason, a young brotherhood member with an expansive investment portfolio, William Potter, wrote a lengthy pamphlet called *The Key of Wealth*. Potter offered a parable about a hitherto undiscovered "Myne of Gold *in this Land.*" The mine was the land itself, not transformed into money and thus not sufficiently used. Potter suggested that if a group of people could together mortgage the land they owned as individuals and together guarantee their own debts, they could create notes based on this durable, double security, and these notes could circulate throughout the country just liked the goldsmiths' notes.[17] The term *key* was alchemical language for the Philosopher's Stone, which could transform base metal into gold. In this new alchemy, the land bank could transform old land into fresh paper money.[18] Sir Cheney Culpeper, a wealthy landowner and member of the Spiritual Brotherhood, converted Potter's vague alchemic mummeries into a more concrete "Bank of Lands" plan. Culpeper said that basing a new currency on land would mean "land would rise much in price," while the bank would "furnish the Landed man with Bank-credit."[19]

The pamphlets by the alchemic brotherhood found fertile soil, but the brotherhood was not thrilled with those who reaped the fruits of its ideas. Its original goal had been to take money out of the hands of those whom it called "covetous princes," yet all of the earliest land banks would be formed as addendums to governments.[20] After the Glorious Revolution of 1688, the triumphant Whig Party composed of merchants and financiers encouraged the new king, William, to charter the Bank of England, one of the world's first "central banks," a bank to lend to other banks and to the government itself. This Whig financial ascendency and its new bank attracted the attention of gimlet-eyed landholders and Tories, who warmed to the once-revolutionary idea of a land bank.[21] One aristocratic Tory bemoaned that "the present Royal Bank refuses to supply Mortgagers," and therefore the already indebted "Landed-Men" could not get new loans, which meant "the Merciless Money'd Man takes the Advantage of him."[22]

A few landed Tories proposed to the king a new government land bank, which they argued could also provide the monarchy with loans.[23] Desperate for cash, King William chartered the bank and subscribed the majority of the original investment. But the opposition of the Bank of England and those same "Money'd Men" meant that the land bank could not raise sufficient funds, and it folded even before it could open its doors.[24] The land bank failure caused many of the Tories, later transformed into the group known as the Country Party, to cement their opposition to the new Whig regime. Opposition leaders such as Lord Bolingbroke continued to lament the ties between the new moneyed aristocracy far from the land and the corrupt government. They urged an economy whose credit was based more on land than on gold or government debt. The Country Party men and their criticisms of corrupt and monied government became the principal inspiration for later American revolutionaries,[25] yet their impact on incipient land banks in the American colonies came first.

The American colonies were land rich and cash poor, and to the early farmers of the American wilderness the land bank idea exerted a pull as nowhere else on earth. As early as the 1650s, the Massachusetts Puritan leader John Winthrop corresponded with a Spiritual Brother on land banks, and his library held Potter's pamphlet *The Key of Wealth*. In the 1660s, one Puritan divine who had talked to Potter before leaving England proposed a "Fund of Land . . . in the nature of a Money-Bank" for the Massachusetts Bay Colony.[26]

The new American colonies formed a series of land banks, the first ones to come into existence. These banks supplied almost all of the paper money of the budding American economy and were extensions of the colonial governments. South Carolina established the first land bank in 1712, followed by Massachusetts in 1714 (after a particularly heated battle), Rhode Island in 1715, New Hampshire in 1717, and Pennsylvania and New Jersey in 1723.[27] New Jersey's bank was typical. The New Jersey government set up a public-loan office in each county, which promised loans of up to one hundred pounds of new paper currency to anyone who mortgaged his land to the government for up to half the land's value.

The notes the borrower received in exchange would be legal tender everywhere in the colony.[28] In Pennsylvania, a young Benjamin Franklin engaged in one of his first political campaigns by lobbying for a state land bank. He later won a state contract to print the new land bank currency, which he called "coined land."[29]

Although some of these public land banks acted conservatively, many colonies used them recklessly to print excessive notes. The consequent inflation stirred the British government, which worried that the cheapened notes robbed British creditors and merchants. Beginning in 1740, the American land banks would collapse under the weight of a British campaign against them. John Adams later said the British suppression of land banking was one of the first causes of the colonists' break with England, comparable to the effect of the later and better-known Stamp Act.[30] Samuel Adams, whose father was one of the most important advocates for the Massachusetts Land Bank and who was ruined by its demise, would swear revenge on the British government and inspire some of the first colonial actions against it.[31] After moving to England, Benjamin Franklin continued his fight for land banking and suggested that the Seven Years War be paid for by an America-wide land bank system. The British government instead passed the Stamp Act to raise funds and the Currency Act to ban all colonial paper money once and for all. Both acts sparked immediate rebellions, leading to the American Revolution.[32]

On the other side of the ocean, another revolution seemed to discredit government land banking forever. In 1789, the revolutionary French government created its infamous *assignats* currency. These notes were backed by confiscated and mortgaged Catholic Church lands. In 1790, Edmund Burke warned that to "establish a current circulating credit upon any *Land-bank . . .* has hitherto proved difficult at the very least. The attempt has commonly ended in bankruptcy." He predicted that the new money was only a means for the French government to inflate the currency and cheat its creditors.[33] Within five years, the overprinted *assignats* depreciated until they became a byword for inflation down through the ages.[34] The belief that a government could run a currency based on "coined land" fell into desuetude, as did the dreams of a landed class even further from finance.

Private Mortgages in the New United States

The American Revolutionary War, much like the English revolutions, encouraged the rise of a new commercial and financial class, and this class squelched efforts to revive the old land banks. When the financier Robert Morris founded the country's first private bank, the Bank of North America, in Philadelphia in 1782, he explicitly said that its banknotes would be a substitute for old land banks' notes. Its bylaws forbid it from lending long term on mortgages or farm land.[35] One farmer writing to a Philadelphia newspaper complained that the new bank discriminated against his class and argued that a "great source of discontent would have been avoided had this institution been made . . . a bank of mortgage, for accommodating landholders with loans," instead of a bank "*altogether commercial.*"[36] The new elites ignored such pleas. Alexander Hamilton, a devoted reader of Smith, helped establish the second bank in the young nation, the Bank of New York, in 1784, and this bank also refused to lend money on mortgages. In a jest at land bank counterproposals, Hamilton mocked those who were "persuaded that the land bank was the true philosopher's stone that was to turn all their rocks and trees into gold." The Bank of United States, also designed by Hamilton and chartered by the U.S. Congress in 1791, carried the same restrictions against land lending.[37] Morris, Hamilton, and others succeeded in creating a viable and commercial alternative to the old colonial land banks. Their efforts made private commercial banks based on merchant's real bills the center of finance in the young American nation. The new financial aristocracy was ascendant in American, as it was in England.[38]

Yet farmers continued to demand more mortgages. In the fractious new union, many states found ways to accommodate farmers' debts.[39] Especially after President Andrew Jackson vetoed the rechartering of the national Second Bank of the United States in 1832, states began to allow purely private, for-profit banks to invest in mortgages even as they tried to avoid the problems of illiquid land that Smith and others had pointed out. They did this by allowing private banks to invest just a small portion of their loans in land while keeping the rest of their loans short term and "liquid."

For instance, a new banking law in New York state in 1838 allowed a limited mortgage backing (or "collateral") behind 10 percent of private banks' notes.[40] A farmers' magazine of the period celebrated that the law meant the "landholder can raise any reasonable amount" from the banks, which would make mortgages "favorite objects of investment."[41] A commercial newspaper, by contrast, lamented that the new law ignored the fundamental truths about banking. It mocked "this alchymistic process" by which "the vitality of landed property is to be extracted" and argued that banks "should be restricted in their operations to the discounting of [lending on] business paper. It is for the private capitalist to make long loans. . . . This is among the elementary principles of banking."[42] In 1842, Louisiana, with one of the largest banking sectors in the world in New Orleans, created a distinctive new banking system that allowed private banks to be divided into two parts. One part would act like a regular commercial bank, with short-term loans on merchant debts funded by notes and deposits payable upon a customer's demand. Another part of the bank could make investments for long terms and on mortgages, but that part had to be funded by stockholders, who could not ask for the immediate return of their money. Before then, every bank was funded in part by a purchase of stock or "capital" by its owners and in part by notes and deposits, but Louisiana recognized that these different sources of funding could support different types of loans. Because the investment in "stock" could never be removed, it seemed the perfect type of fund to support long-term mortgages.[43]

A similar strategy emerged in some state-chartered "trust companies," such as the Ohio Life and Trust Company, founded by a New York banker named Isaac Bronson. As the historian John Denis Haeger notes, Bronson once believed along with his contemporaries that a bank's "credit should be lent only on short-term, most often no longer than sixty days, and only on the best security—the actual goods in transit."[44] Yet after some personal success in loaning on mortgages, Bronson tried to combine both long-term and short-term loans in one bank, similar to Louisiana's plan. As Haeger argues, this new "company represented a workable compromise among the merchant's need for credit, [and] the farmer's need for long-term capital."[45] Yet when the Ohio Life Insurance and Trust Company boomed and then busted, it inaugurated the Panic of 1857, which brought a sharp collapse in the U.S. economy. The *Chicago Daily Tribune* said the company's failure astonished the nation because "capitalists placed perfect confidence in its soundness," and everyone assumed it had loaned only on "the best of real estate at a low appraisement."[46] The company's failure seemed a black eye for land-and-mortgage banking even when provided by private banks.

The Civil War gave those who witnessed the panic a chance to reshape the American banking system again and to keep land out of it. Among those who harbored this goal was Senator John Sherman, a financial wizard but an unlikely politician known as the "Ohio Icicle," who coldly viewed the war as a financial battle. (He said that "the problem was not whether we could muster men, but whether we could raise money."[47]) Sherman pushed for a national banking system and a uniform national currency to help fund the war. Under his plan, this currency would be provided by any number of private "national banks" that were chartered by the federal government, which would keep only federal bonds to back the limited number of notes the banks were allowed to issue.[48] These national banks could still, however, accept coin deposits and allow customers to write checks on those deposits and to use these deposits to fund other types of loans. (Deposits and checks had recently increased in importance relative to banknotes and would increase even more after the creation of the new national system.)[49]

Sherman, however, also saw the failure of the Ohio Life and Trust Company in his home state as irrefutable evidence against mortgage banking, and he tried to end it. In his memoirs, he lamented the parlous situation of the state banking systems, which were "sometimes secured. . . . . . by real estate." He noted that "whenever a failure occurred, such as that of the Ohio Life Insurance and

Trust Company, it operated like a panic in a disorganized army."[50] In congressional debates, Sherman found supporters for his ban on mortgages. Congressman James Brooks of New York said that experience taught him "that the use of real estate in banking was unsafe."[51] In fact, in the wake of the Panic of 1857, his state had eliminated mortgage banking entirely because the New York bank regulator argued that banks that loaned on mortgages were particularly likely to fail.[52] With this political support as well as a little legerdemain, Sherman slipped an amendment into the National Banking Act of 1864 forbidding mortgage loans in the new national banks.[53] A final National Bank Act by Sherman in 1865 taxed state banknotes out of existence, meaning national banks were the only ones in the country with circulating currency.[54]

The new national banks' influence after the Civil War was vast, and the clause forbidding mortgages, slipped in almost unawares, became the definite standard for the nation. A popular banking textbook from the era repeated the truism that it "has been said to be the first duty of the banker to learn to distinguish between a [merchant's] note and a mortgage, his business lying with the former." This same textbook further argued that "real estate, of course cannot be regarded as a banking security, however desirable it may be as an investment of individuals, for it is not only subject to great fluctuations in value, but is at times unsalable; and the law of the United States therefore wisely prohibits investments in it."[55] A typical article in the new *Bankers Magazine* reiterated and updated the arguments Adam Smith had made a century earlier. Its author, the renowned finance expert Charles Conant, said that "short-term commercial paper gives the assets of a bank an essentially liquid character. Every day in times of normal business should bring into the bank nearly as many persons having paper to pay as it brings persons asking the redemption of notes or the payment of deposits." Yet if money were loaned upon a mortgage for a number of years, the bank's funds "would be 'locked up' in banking parlance," and the bank would fail.[56] With the state banks for the moment pushed almost entirely into the new national system, the real-bills prohibition against land and mortgage banking was stronger than ever before—to the rage of many farmers.

Cooperative Land Banks and the Populists

Because of the new national banking laws, farmers had to rely on a chaotic and fractured system for mortgages. In the postbellum period, individual lenders provide almost all farm mortgage loans, as Adam Smith had argued they should. As late as 1890, when the government did its first national survey of mortgages, individuals made 70 percent of all mortgages.[58] For wealthy neighbors or relatives, a mortgage was a safe way to get a high interest rate with little risk. The investor could see the local house or farm he or she was loaning on and could keep close tabs on its owner. Individuals generally loaned no more than 50 per-cent of the value of the land, with any higher amount provided by a more expensive second mortgage at higher interest. These mortgage loans were gen-erally only for five years at most and had large "balloon payments" at the end of the term, which had to be rolled over, with extra commissions, if they were not paid off. Because of the lack of capital in the West and the South, interest rates on these individual mortgages could approach 10 percent a year or more. Economists at the time noted the "rigid and local character of mortgage bank-ing in America," which put American landholders essentially in the same situ-ation as British landholders before the Financial Revolution of the seventeenth century.[58]

The major alternative to the local mortgage mogul was cooperative financ-ing, a proposal tracing back to the Spiritual Brotherhood. Just as the brother-hood two hundred years earlier had recommended that groups get together to guarantee payment of their debts and mortgages, now William Raiffeisen, a German burgomaster, recommended that Europe's rural villagers do the same. He midwifed a number of cooperative or communal banks in his country that made mortgage loans to farmers who cooperatively promised to mortgage their land together. As was typical of many European financial reforms, Raiffeisen proposed these cooperatives as explicit antidotes to Jewish moneylenders, and anti-Semitic tropes littered much of their early publicity. Nonetheless, his Euro-pean cooperatives were lauded around the globe as the solution to farmers' ills.[59]

In America, similar cooperative credit systems arose. In 1890, more than half of all mortgages not held by individuals were held by the two main types of cooperative groups, mutual savings banks and "building and loans," which, despite their name, often loaned on farms. These cooperative banks demanded that customer deposits be kept in place for months or years, so they were more stable than typical bank deposits. These groups often made mortgage loans up to 80 percent of the value of a farm and for up to twenty years, with the princi-pal of the mortgage gradually paid off, or "a-mortized" ("killed off"), by the bor-rower.[60] The other great cooperative source of funds in this period was life insurance companies, which at the time were largely mutuals owned by their policyholders, who obviously invested for the long term. By 1875, more than half of all life insurance funds were in mortgages.[61]

In the 1870s and 1880s, cooperative mortgage groups expanded rapidly. They became more national and profit oriented and lost their local and cooperative features. National buildings-and-loan associations, to many a contradiction in terms, began to lend eastern money on new western farm mortgages. They often transformed these mortgages into mortgage-backed bonds, with up to a hundred different mortgages as their backing or collateral. After Connecticut and New York allowed their insurance companies to make mortgage loans out of state, a host of new "mortgage brokers" sprouted up in the West to send mortgages back east to swelling insurance company balance sheets. Mortgage debt ceased to be a mere local thing and began to be traded and moved across the country and even sold internationally as part of an incipient mortgage market.

By the end of the 1880s, these cooperative groups, many of which shed their cooperative forms for corporate charters, began to seem like new and dangerous behemoths, worse than the old local mortgage lender. The mortgage itself, once seen as a desperate necessity for farmers, became a heavy burden in a time of postwar deflation, high interest rates, and distant eastern money lenders.[62] Many commentators began trading the quip that "credit supports agriculture, as the cord supports the hanged."[63] An epic poem written at the turn of the century, *The First Mortgage*, even analogized Adam's sin in the Garden of Eden to a weighty mortgage: "And then a mortgage Adam gives / On every soul that ever lives," but "when that mortgage was arranged / How quickly everything changed." The poem contrasted Adam's mortgage note with Christ's mission on earth, which "released [man] from the mortgage and debt."[64]

High-priced mortgages also became a political bugaboo and inspired unprecedented activism, especially by the new Populist Party. One Populist song of the era warned:

> The farmer is the man
> Lives on credit till the fall
> With the interest rate so high
> It's a wonder he don't die
> For the mortgage man's the one
> That gets it all.[65]

The Populists agitated for a different type of mortgage: cheaper and provided directly from the government. Their "sub-treasury plan," announced in the party's Ocala Platform in 1890, demanded that the government loan money not only "on non-perishable farm products," as many historians have noted, but "also upon real estate," which has often been forgotten.[66] The Populist Party platform of 1892 lamented "homes covered with mortgages . . . and the land concentrating in the hands of capitalists," and it demanded a government land bank as a solution.[67] As one journalist said, the Populists and their eventual presidential candidate, William Jennings Bryan, also demanded inflation to make "it easier for debtors in general to pay their obligations, and in particular for farmers to get rid of the burden of their mortgages."[68]

Yet no mortgage reforms were enacted. In the aftermath of the Panic of 1893, the entire burgeoning mortgage market based on enlarged cooperatives crumbled. Mortgage-backed bonds proved insufficiently backed, mortgage brokers and national building and loans collapsed, and the nation's faith in a mortgage market ebbed.[69] After new gold discoveries and consequent inflation began in

THE NEW UNCLE SAM.

How the Farmers' Alliance propose to have the Government run when they get the power.

1.1 Cartoon mocking Populist land bank plans, which used anti-Semitic tropes common at the time when discussing moneylending. *Judge* magazine, 1891.

Source: Library of Congress.

the late 1890s, the demand for cheap government mortgages and inflation faded as well. Individuals and smaller cooperative groups again captured the mortgage market. Attempts to make cooperatives the basis for cheap and widespread mortgages, just like previous attempts by government-backed land banks and private mortgage banks, had apparently come to naught. The philosopher's stone that would unleash the power of coined land remained hidden.

Semipublic Land Banks Abroad

Americans interested in a different model for land banking needed only to look abroad again to the newest and at long last seemingly successful iteration of the idea. It was this final version that would provide the basis for most American mortgages for the next hundred years. Beginning in the mid–nineteenth century, European governments supported and subsidized the creation of new mortgage banks, but they left control and profits in the hands of either investors or cooperatives. In the new conception, public support would provide investors the confidence they needed to make long-term investments, while supposedly preventing the government from interfering too explicitly with operations. It seemed an obvious and fruitful compromise between all of the earlier visions.

The new semipublic banks appeared first in France, where Emperor Napoleon III created the Credit Foncier to ameliorate what some called a "mortgage leprosy" in the nation. Napoleon gave a public subsidy to the bank and kept the right to appoint some of the top officials of the bank, but the bank's general policy remained in the hands of an assembly of private shareholders, who provided the majority of the funds.[70] By 1863, the Foncier had helped inspire a *Boden Kredit*, or land bank, in the Austrian Empire.[71] This bank acquired special tax exemptions, and, as one historian states, "derived its privileged position among the Viennese banks from acting as the banker of the imperial family and the Court." In 1870, Prussia founded the Central Bondenkredit by royal order, with similar goals. Despite its private shareholders, its president and senior executives required confirmation by the Prussian king. Similar German land banks, such as the Central Landschaft of Prussia, founded in 1873, helped commercialize the bonds of early cooperative institutions known as Landschaften. As one later commentator argued, mortgage "co-operation in Germany was originally founded on the principle of self-help, but the State finally came to its aid."[72] Britain in the 1880s tried a similar strategy abroad. It set up an agricultural land bank in Egypt after conquering that country and gave its private investors a state guarantee of profits.[73]

The attraction of the new land banks was the same as in the era of the Spiritual Brotherhood: to bring agriculture into the new economy. As one historian points out, in Germany "the domestic political appeal of the [*Boden Kredit*] project from Bismarck's point of view was obvious: here was a way to reconcile the East Elbian landowners to the new liberal era—through cheap credit."[74] Yet the combination of public support and private profit was original.

These semipublic banks would be the model for America's first modern land bank, which it instituted abroad, in the Philippines. William Howard Taft, the jovial former judge and now governor of the new U.S. colony, knew the islands needed financial reform. Taft's first task on the islands was to create a new gold currency. With the assistance of several international "money doctors," as they were known at the time, especially journalist Charles Conant, he succeeded in replacing worn, old silver coins with a national gold standard.[75] Yet Taft, Conant, and others knew such pricey gold currency was of little use to the mass of poor peasants, or campesinos, who grew barely enough food to sell. They also knew that such peasants were suffering. A virulent plague had infected their cattle, and the corpses of their cows littered the island. The rebellion against the Americans by Emilio Aguinaldo and the violent repression of it had also left scorched fields in its wake.

The Philippine peasants and local leaders proposed a solution to the problem of degraded land, seemingly more pressing than degraded currency. Taft said that during his first sweltering tour of the islands the one reform that was "most strongly and repeatedly" urged was the creation of an agricultural bank. Indeed, everyone from mayors to small farmers said "again and again" that the government should extend aid to farmers through cheap mortgages. "No public gathering of any sort . . . is ever held in the islands that emphasis is not put on the importance of an agricultural bank." Even Aguinaldo, who had recently been captured by the Americans and then pensioned into peace, wrote to Taft that the new government should create an agricultural protection bank, which would draw funds from the U.S. Treasury and make mortgage loans at 4 percent annual interest.[76]

The new colonial overlords and money doctors were not interested in a pure government bank. In *A Special Report on Coinage*, Charles Conant diverted attention to the advantages of a semipublic land bank.[77] Conant later said that "Governor Taft was very much interested in this subject, and it was at his suggestion" that he (Conant) turned to focus on the issue because "in nearly every province the need of mortgage banks was represented to him."[78] When the U.S. government sent Edwin Kemmerer of Princeton University, another money doctor, to administer the new currency, Taft redirected him to report on mortgages as well.[79] Kemmerer's report detailed the three older models of mortgage banks: a "purely governmental institution," an "agricultural bank conducted by private capital," and a "cooperative association." When discussing these options, he believed one had to consider the supposed racial tendencies of Filipinos. He thought a purely government institution, although most desired by the islanders, would "encourage the already too prevalent proclivity of the native population to depend upon the government for financial aid and support. It would tend to encourage dependence and laziness." He believed that a private bank was unlikely because the "risks are at present too great for the enticement of private capital," no matter the capital's source. A cooperative bank would not work, because he thought Filipinos lacked the "intelligence, foresight, honesty, self-control" necessary for the system.[80]

The solution seemed to offer itself to Kemmerer, a fourth option that straddled the other three: a "private institution . . . with liberal government guarantees and concessions, as for example, the Agricultural Bank of Egypt."[81] The Egyptian semipublic, semiprivate colonial hybrid (an "unqualified success," according to Kemmerer) would be his model, but Kemmerer's report featured more than one hundred pages detailing the "special assistance and concessions" for mortgage investors among the governments of "nearly all civilized countries." He then asked how "if state assistance is necessary in the more advanced countries of the world, how much more imperative is it in a backward country like the Philippines?"[82] Kemmerer's plan had the Philippine government guarantee dividends of at least 4 percent upon any invested stock in the new agricultural bank to entice new investors, even as it supervised the bank's operation.[83] Taft, in his annual governor's report, supported the public–private hybrid. He said his administration was "not prepared at present to recommend the establishment of a mortgage bank, owned and conducted by the Government, and it recognizes the danger of locking up the assets of a commercial bank in landed securities. There appears to be no reason, however, why a mortgage bank, organized according to the methods which have been thoroughly tested in Europe, should not be established in the Philippine Islands," with similar public and private interests involved.[84]

In 1906, the Philippine Commission governing the islands, and Taft, now the U.S. secretary of war, endorsed their semipublic land bank plan to the U.S. Congress.[85] Before the hearings on the bank, the chairman of the House of Representatives Committee on Insular Affairs said that "Secretary Taft thinks that this is one of the most important subjects ever before the committee."[86] Jeremiah Jencks, the third in that era's triumvirate of money doctors and Kemmerer's former mentor, testified in its favor.[87] The final House committee report noted that the bank and its special government supports were "a departure from the financial methods of the American people, but conditions in the archipelago are exceptional and can not be determined by the standards of this country."[88] The act passed easily. Jeremiah Jenks declared that the creation of the farm mortgage bank was the "greatest single thing" that America had done for the islands.[89]

Despite the enticement of guaranteed returns, private investors were reluctant to fund the untested institution, and despite ever-increasing public subsidies, the bank raised little money and trusted the islanders with few loans.[90] In February 1916, the agricultural bank was bought out and dismantled by another local bank.[91] Meanwhile, the Egyptian bank that Kemmerer had declared an "unqualified success" descended into bankruptcy.[92] Despite such failures, the semipublic model would inspire America's own mortgage bank idea, which was percolating just as the Philippine bank was faltering.

Bringing the Semipublic Land Bank Home

In his book *The Farm Mortgage Handbook* (1916), the investment adviser Kingman Robins noted that that there had been a recent surge in interest among Americans in mortgage reform. Robins said that "'rural credits,'" as the topic was now called, "became a 'problem' in the popular sense about 1910" and ever since had occupied a prominent space in public debate. The heightened attention to mortgages was the work of a new group of reformers and politicians.[93] In this era, three prominent intellectuals would attach themselves to three prominent politicians, each of whom would identify with one of the three major parties to run in the heated presidential elections of 1912. Each would also draw on one of three previous land bank plans (ignoring the Populists' more extreme government land bank). The new Republican president William Howard Taft would lean on Cleveland banker Myron T. Herrick, who emphasized the benefit of purely private mortgage banks for America. Bull Moose candidate Theodore Roosevelt would rely on a prophet of Irish collectivism, Horace Plunkett, who emphasized cooperatives as a type of progressive but private reform. Democratic senator Duncan Fletcher would rely on the peripatetic farmer-intellectual David Lubin, who advocated German state-supported banks as a new ideal. Their contrasting visions reflected the divisions between the parties and would shape how Americans saw the new possibilities of land banking.

For obvious reasons, Myron Herrick was a believer in private banks. He was a successful Cleveland lawyer and later governor of Ohio, where he worked with the Ohio politicians and future presidents William Taft and Warren Harding.[94] After leaving the Ohio governor's office, he became the head of a large "mutual," or cooperative, savings bank in Cleveland, which invested a significant amount of its money in farm mortgages. At the meeting of the American Bankers Association in 1911, he demanded a study of how bankers and farmers could work together on mortgages. He worried that bankers had for too long ignored the great possibilities of the farmers' market, which had caused the two groups to remain at loggerheads.[95] He later published a short book on the topic, *How to Finance the Farmer: Private Enterprise—Not State Aid* (1915).[96] In 1912, Herrick accepted now President Taft's offer to become ambassador to France, which, Taft said, "will be a good holiday for you."

Herrick insisted that he use the opportunity to study land banking in Europe. Herrick's advocacy helped place a crucial plank in the Republican Party platform of 1912, which stated, "It is as important that financial machinery be provided to supply the demand of farmers for credit as it is that the banking and currency systems be reformed in the interest of general business."[97] In an era when the party's platform was described as "a covenant with the people and a sacred pledge," this plank carried real weight.[98]

The Progressive or Bull Moose Party, which formed after Teddy Roosevelt bolted from the Republicans, also had its own mortgage intellectual. Horace Plunkett was a knighted landlord in Ireland and a fervent believer in the possibilities of rural cooperation. Partially at Plunkett's instigation, in 1908 Roosevelt had formed the Country Life Commission, which examined the forces causing farmers to flee the land. Its final report lamented the "lack of any adequate system of agricultural credit" and called for a "method of cooperative credit" similar to that which had succeeded in other countries.[99] With Roosevelt and Plunkett's advocacy, the Progressive Party platform of 1912 stated: "We pledge our party to foster the development of agricultural credit and cooperation" (and "to re-establish the Country Life Commission").[100]

The Democratic Party would have the most influence on future rural-credit reform. In 1912, the Democratic senator Duncan Fletcher of Florida was looking for a cause to bring back to his constituents, and he found one that he would press for decades. Fletcher, who sported a broad forehead and an even broader mustache, had practiced law for a few years before entering local political offices for more than two decades. Since arriving in the Senate, he had been carrying on a correspondence with David Lubin, the American founder of the International Institute of Agriculture in Rome. He invited Lubin to the annual Southern Commercial Congress in Nashville, Tennessee, in April 1912 to talk about mortgage banks in Europe.

Lubin, who according to one friend had the bearing of a "Minor Hebrew Prophet," was enamored of the German method of cooperative but state-directed credit, the *Landschaften*, which combined communal rural mortgages into mortgage-backed bonds. Despite many of those groups' anti-Semitic tendencies, he believed they offered a vision of a cooperative future.[101] In the Prussian tradition, the state was heavily involved in such enterprises. He noted that the officials of the *Landschaften* were declared "indirect public officials" who had to take an oath of office upon appointment. The king appointed the banks' top officials and had special powers of control and examination.[102] Lubin celebrated the special tax and legal benefits given to the groups as well as the "semi-government officials" who ran them. He argued that "it is the safeguarding, the rigorous safeguarding, of this system by the Prussian Government that gives the bonds the high value they have in the open market." He said that without this safeguard "such a bond would not be liquid; it can not be liquid."[103] Lubin proposed that the solution to American's farmers' ills "is not to be found in a non-governmental agency, nor is it to be found in a governmental agency, but it is to be found in a semi-official governmental agency."[104] Lubin also thought the *Landschaften* explained why "political life of Germany is more sound to the core . . . than the political life of other countries."[105]

After a rousing speech by Lubin to the Southern Commercial Congress in Nashville, the group submitted planks to the Democratic platform demanding semipublic mortgage banks.[106] In the Democratic platform of 1912, following the plank that called for new banking legislation, which would soon be embodied in the Federal Reserve Act, the party stated that "of equal importance with the question of currency reform is the question of rural credits or agricultural finance. Therefore, we recommend that an investigation of agricultural credit societies in foreign countries be made."[107]

The Democratic Party platform demanded a new type of investigative commission for rural credits, one appropriately involving both private and public support. The Southern Commercial Congress agreed to fund a massive delegation, as many as two people from each state in the union, to go to Europe and conduct a thorough study of agricultural credit on that continent. They began a fund-raising drive involving mailings and door-to-door requests as well as the advocacy of the two main farmers' lobbies, the National Grange and the Farmers Union. Fletcher and Lubin also looked to state legislatures, which provided funds to send their own state officials along with the delegation. The new rural-credits commission swelled to an unprecedented size just as political concerns about mortgages hit their peak in the presidential election campaign of 1912.[108]

President Taft attempted the make the mortgage issue an important part of his reelection.[109] A note from an assistant told Taft that "cheap and easy borrowing for farmers would be a thing that would appeal greatly to the agricultural vote and should be exploited in the campaign book, as it is mentioned in the party platform."[110] In October, Taft published Myron Herrick's new report from France on private mortgage banking, finished just in time for the election, and distributed it to all the state governors of the nation, with a laudatory foreword by himself.[111]

After Taft lost the three-way race, however, he devoted the last days of his presidency to pursuing rural-credit reform.[112] He called Herrick back from Paris to speak at the Governor's Conference in Richmond, Virginia, and the conference promulgated a private mortgage-banking law that states could adopt.[113] Taft then invited the state governors to the White House, where he told them that pushing rural-credits reform was the most important thing they could do for the country.[114] Herrick got a further leave of absence from his post to testify in front of Congress on the subject and to ask for federal funding for the investigatory commission traveling to Europe.[115] He found surprising support from the new president elect, Woodrow Wilson, who spoke out on rural credits for the first time. In an open and widely published letter to Roosevelt's intellectual, Horace Plunkett, Wilson said the proposed rural-credits commission had his "entire and cordial" approval.[116]

In the lame-duck congressional session, Senator Fletcher stumped for the commission.[117] He passed a bill invoking for the commission the diplomatic consideration of the countries it visited. In the last minutes of the session, a conference committee snuck $25,000 into the Agricultural Appropriations Act to send seven officials appointed directly by the federal government.[118] Taft signed these bills on his last day in office in March 1913 and had his secretary of state send instructions to all European embassies stating that the U.S. government took a "deep interest" in the forthcoming investigation.[119]

This new Rural Credits Commission, which left for Europe just two months later, would be a watershed not just in land bank history but in Progressive reform. It would also be the culmination of more than two hundred years of transatlantic discussion on mortgage banking. Its dozens of members would travel a total of eighteen thousand miles; interview hundreds of state officials, private bankers, and cooperative groups about different means of providing farmers with cheap mortgages; and compile thousands of pages of evidence. The historian Daniel Rodgers claims the commission was the single "most extraordinary of the era's institutions of transatlantic policy inspection."[120] Lubin and his *Landschaft* ideal, however, became its guiding light, and he would subtly direct the commission and its final report into endorsing the semipublic banks he had wanted all along.[121]

By the end of the election and the inauguration of the Rural Credits Commission, it seemed as if a new type of American mortgage banking, the transmogrified remnant of the old land bank ideal, was finally on its way to realization, with crucial government assistance. Rural advocates' centuries-old dream of a land bank catering to their needs was coming to fruition, with a new model of semipublic support. The hope for liquid land and agricultural plenty seemed within reach. Yet even among farmers and Progressives there was opposition.

CHAPTER 2

THE SPECIAL PRIVILEGES OF
THE FEDERAL BANKS

In the early twentieth century, many banking debates revolved around an event that had taken place almost a hundred years earlier. In 1832, President Andrew Jackson vetoed the act rechartering the Second Bank of the United States, severing the connection between the U.S. federal government and the American banking system. The veto not only was a pivotal moment in financial history; it would also become a touchstone of Democratic Party ideology for almost a century. In his veto message, Jackson elaborated on his and his party's grievances against the bank, but the complaints orbited around one central problem: the bank was the grant of a special privilege by the government to one group of men. Jackson used the term *privilege* twenty-seven times in his veto. He especially lamented that the charter had given the bank the exclusive privilege of issuing paper currency anywhere in the nation, a privilege denied to all others.

In Jackson's view, the central desideratum of government was to provide equal protection of the laws to all and to abjure special privileges to any. In a soon-to-be famous line in the veto, Jackson said that if government "would confine itself to equal protection, and, as Heaven does its rains, shower its favors alike on the high and the low, the rich and the poor, it would be an unqualified blessing." In Jackson's vision of American government, the president had a special duty to protect the public from the grasping pleas of special interests and the congressional representatives who kowtowed to them. His veto, he said, protected "the humble members of society—the farmers, mechanics, and laborers—who have neither the time nor the means of securing like favors to themselves" from Congress.[1]

Jackson's veto message became the defining ideology of the Democratic Party, its Nicene Creed, repeated endlessly over the years. One Democrat said that the veto "deserves to be written in letters of gold, for neither in truth of sentiment or beauty of expression can it be surpassed."[2] The Democratic Party in the years to come defined itself by its support of equal protection of the law, at least for economic groups, and its opposition to "class legislation," or laws that privileged one economic group or class. The party especially became the advocate for a complete divorce of government and banking, or what was called "the separation of bank and state."[3]

Yet by the early twentieth century, something changed in the Democratic Party and the ideology that animated it. Although the party in the years of Woodrow Wilson continued to celebrate Jackson and his struggle against the privileged bank, two of its most important reforms would be the creation of two privileged, government-supported banking systems: first, the Federal Reserve Banks and, second, the Federal Land Banks. How Jackson's and the Democratic Party's ideology of equal protection and opposition to privilege, especially for banks, transformed into an ideology that celebrated the granting of government privileges to new semipublic banks is the story of this chapter.

Debates about special privilege and equal protection have attracted attention from historians interested in legal history, but these debates have not penetrated the political and economic history of the early twentieth century.[4] This chapter shows this ideology's centrality in political discourse, but it also shows how groups of bankers, farmers, and politicians teamed together to overthrow it and replace it with the beginnings of a new ideology. In these years, certain interest groups and intellectuals began to claim that the old idea of equal protection would still leave some groups behind. They advocated that the government act as a force intervening directly for the benefit of certain classes in order to "balance" different economic sectors. Stagnant agriculture and booming industry especially needed to be brought into some new sort of equality. Advocates claimed the best way to do this was to create government-supported, or semipublic, banks with special provisions for farmers.[5] In this vision, both farmers and bankers would be given special privileges in order to rebalance an economy that was already unbalanced and unfair at its core. In an era of depopulated farms and overcrowded cities, these advocates thought equal protection was not enough to ensure equal opportunities and outcomes.

Other historians have described the shift in the Democratic Party in this period as one from laissez-faire to activist, embodied in a shift in legislation in the later years of the Wilson administration.[6] Yet conflating the warring ideologies of equal protection and economic balance with laissez-faire and activist, respectively, has caused endless confusion about the changes in the party. This chapter shows that the Democratic Party did not shift from a classical liberal to a modern liberal party but shifted how it saw the manner in which government could be involved. The party that once believed government intervention was legitimate only as long it protected all classes began to assert that the government's job was to bolster certain class interests and balance them in a fundamentally unbalanced world. The chapter describes how newly assertive groups in agriculture and banking pushed traditionalist Democrats, including President Wilson and his allies, to compromise on their beliefs and to grant new special privileges to both farmers and bankers.

Democrats and the War Against Privilege

Although both the Democratic Party and the Republican Party attacked the supposed scourges of class legislation and special privileges in the nineteenth and early twentieth centuries, the ideal of equal protection found its most comfortable home in the Democratic Party.[7] The party's first official platform in 1840 argued that "justice and sound policy forbid the government to foster one branch of industry to the detriment of any other."[8] Such statements crescendoed over the years. In 1889, George Vest, Democratic senator from Missouri, said that the Democratic Party had always been "the inveterate foe of class legislation."[9] The Democratic platform of 1892 denounced the recent Republican tariff as the "culminating atrocity of class legislation" because it protected the manufacturing class and taxed the farming class, and the platform of 1896 said the government should "not discriminate between class or section."[10] In 1900, the National Association of Democratic Clubs said one of its main objectives was to "oppose class legislation[,] . . . [t]o maintain inviolate the fundamental principle of Democracy—'Equality before the Law.'"[11] In 1904 and 1906, the party's *Campaign Text Book* would put the statement "Equal rights to all, special privileges to none" right next to the book's title on the cover and on the first page.[12] The *Democratic Campaign Book for 1910*, quoting a Democratic congressman, argued that "the Democratic party stands to-day where it always stood and where it always will stand—for equal rights to all and special privileges to none . . . for equal and exact justice to all men—no class legislation; no caste."[13] The language of class legislation became ever more common in political discourse. By the 1910s, according to an analysis of all published texts at that time, the phrases *special privilege, equal protection of the laws,* and *class legislation* attained a peak in usage that they would never attain again.[14]

In the late nineteenth and early twentieth centuries, opposition to class legislation had a special appeal to farmers. The first major farm interest group, the National Grange, formed with the help of federal agriculture officials in the

1860s, attacked class legislation continuously. A typical resolution of the Grange assembly said, "It has ever been the principal and teaching of the Grange to avoid anything that tends to class legislation."[15] The national Farmers Alliance created in 1889 stated that its two main aims were to educate farmers and "to demand equal rights to all and special favors to none."[16]

Two particular federal privileges elicited farmers' scorn. First, farmers opposed tariffs as pernicious legislation benefiting manufactures and urbanites at the expense of rural consumers and exporters. Second, farmers fought the government privilege of allowing only a limited number of national and largely urban banks to issue currency, the system Republicans had created during the Civil War.[17] Although the Great Commoner and farmers' advocate William Jennings Bryan is more often noted for his proposal to freely coin silver, in 1896 he ran on a Democratic platform that cited Jackson's veto and argued that national banks should not have an exclusive right to issue paper currency. Bryan said that to "empower national banks to issue circulating notes is to grant a valuable privilege to a favored class."[18] These farm advocates hoped that eliminating the special privileges of the tariff and the banking system would be enough to restore farming to its rightful place in the nation's economy. In 1912, these traditionalist Democrats found a champion in their new presidential candidate, Woodrow Wilson.

In Democratic Party theory dating back to Jackson, the president was the keeper of the torch of equal protection, especially for the excluded poor and farmers. In this ideal, only the president could comprehend the whole of the country and protect it from the appeals of special interests in the legislative branch. As Democratic president James K. Polk explained in 1848, the president represented "the whole people of the United States, as each member of the legislative department represents portions of them."[19] Woodrow Wilson would seem to embody the fondest of these Democratic hopes.

The importance of executive authority manifested itself to Wilson at an early age. Wilson's father, a Scotch Irish Presbyterian minister, forced his once recalcitrant and possibly dyslexic boy to bend to his studies, and Wilson was ever after grateful to him for it. One need not be a Freudian to assert that such a strong father had an impact on Wilson's vision of executive authority. Yet Sigmund Freud argued in a critical study of Wilson published posthumously that Wilson's "passionate love of his father was the core of his emotional life."[20] (It was an emotionally turbulent life, and, despite his placid exterior, Wilson once wrote, "I have the uncomfortable feeling that I am carrying a volcano about with me."[21]) Under his father's spurs, Wilson tried law and then studied political science at Johns Hopkins University, where his dissertation, later published as *Congressional Government* (1885), was an extended lament on the boundless ambitions of a Congress infected with special interests, which had come to overawe the presidency. He dedicated the book, of course, to his father.[22]

Wilson, in line with his executive, Jacksonian vision, viewed equal protection as the cynosure of good government.[23] He argued that the "true object of government is justice; not the advantage of one class."[24] During his whirlwind campaign in 1912, then governor Wilson of New Jersey told the American people, "I understand it to be the fundamental proposition of American liberty that we do not desire special privilege, because we know special privilege will never comprehend the general welfare. This is the fundamental, spiritual difference between [Democrats and Republicans]." In his more poetic moments, he imagined a future world where unborn children would "open their eyes in a land where there is no special privilege."[25]

After his election and inauguration, Wilson's first task was to attack that particular bugbear of class legislation for generations, the tariff. To implement this reform, he called Congress into a special session and became the first president to address them in person since John Adams.[26] Wilson told the gathered representatives that the tariff "had built up a set of privileges" that benefitted particular manufacturers and that the representatives' task was to "abolish everything that bears even a semblance of privilege."[27] With forceful rhetoric and abundant public support, he succeeded in getting the lowest tariff rates through Congress in generations and in passing a new income tax to replace the lost revenue. It seemed to many that Congress had responded to Wilson's bold assertion of authority and had taken the bit in its mouth with cheerful acquiescence. The dream of a disinterested Democratic president battling entrenched privilege had become flesh. Yet the Democratic unity in the tariff fight was to prove the exception. When Wilson stepped to the next plank in the party platform, currency reform, the splits in the party opened wide.

New Banking Privileges

Despite Wilson's strong convictions, he was also a believer in a unified Democratic Party, which meant he was willing to compromise those convictions to hold it together.[28] Compromise became necessary when he saw his beloved party divided on what exactly special privilege meant for banks. Wilson's willingness to compromise between the party's factions ironically ended up creating new and unprecedented privileges for banks.

Almost all Democrats saw the current national banknote system, limited in amount and issued mainly by urban banks, as an invidious privilege. Yet some in the party, such as William Jennings Bryan, thought that creating money was an inherent duty of government. In their conception, if the government simply printed and distributed notes without discrimination, there would be no danger of class legislation, only a beneficent government that showered its blessings on all sellers and buyers alike. The party had endorsed pure government paper, or greenback, currency in two earlier platforms, and its farmer members had long supported the position. The National Grange claimed that "the issue of currency is fundamentally a government function which should . . . not be surrendered as a special privilege to any set of individuals."[29]

Other members of the party were leery of government control. They fretted about the inflation that bedeviled former government currencies. These reformers' solution to the currency problem was to charter private banks that would issue currency only under strict rules and only when lending on bankers' "real bills," or short-term commercial loans, as Adam Smith had once recommended. They believed that the amount of currency in circulation would then respond only to real trade and real debts. Although the currency-issuing banks would be private, they would respond naturally to changes in business conditions and therefore would evoke no special privilege. As one proposal stated, the "increase and decrease [in currency] should be automatic," or, as it was also called, "elastic."[30]

As chairman of the powerful House Banking and Currency Committee, Carter Glass became the most influential advocate of the so-called real-bills doctrine in Congress. He would shape the currency-reform bill and much of American banking for decades. Glass admitted he "had no special qualification for the work" except for "a reasonable amount of common sense acquired as a practical paper and successful newspaper publisher" in his hometown of Lynchburg, Virginia. The small but pugnacious Glass would be Wilson's bantam fighter in the congressional ring. He forthrightly called Wilson his leader and remained in awe of the man and his fight for what Glass called "financial freedom."[31] His belief in equal protection was also in line with Wilson's. A biography cowritten by one of his aides said that Glass believed a "Democrat is one who holds to the historic principle of his party, 'equal rights to all and special privileges to none.'"[32]

Glass's original currency plan, written with his assistant H. P. Willis, a preeminent real-bills theorist, tried to create a decentralized, automatic, and private banking system. They proposed several regional "Federal Reserve Banks" (the number would eventually be twelve), whose capital and officers would come from contributions by national and state "member banks" in their region. The Reserve Banks would be purely private and would operate for the benefit of these banking members. The twelve banks would help spread the benefit of banking more widely, away from what Glass called the "financial cancer" of Wall Street and New York City.[33] The notes the Reserve Banks provided to banks in exchange for their real bills would constitute the country's new currency. Aside from chartering the Reserve Banks, the government would stay away from them. These banks' currency would not even be legal tender; it would float on its own bottom, with people accepting it as they chose.[34]

2.1 Representative Carter Glass.

Source: "Carter Glass," in *Men of Mark in Virginia: Ideal of American Life, a Collection of Biographies of Leading Men in the State*, vol. 1, ed. Lyon Tyler (Washington, DC: Men of Mark, 1906), 310.

To the Bryan wing of the party, these private banks were a privileged abomination and an insult to the party's greenback traditions. Wilson used his powers of compromise to bridge the gap between the factions. First, at a meeting in his governor's mansion in Trenton, New Jersey, on a snowy day after Christmas in 1912, a bedridden Wilson asked Glass and Willis to place a government "capstone" over the private banks. He wanted a central regulatory board to coordinate the Reserve Banks' activities and keep at least some control in the hands of the people. Glass was forced to concede and thus the government-staffed Federal Reserve Board was born.[35]

Other members of Wilson's inner circle wanted more public control. Wilson's hyperkinetic secretary of the Treasury, William McAdoo (soon to marry Wilson's daughter), and his new secretary of state, William Jennings Bryan, would be satisfied with nothing less than publicly printed greenbacks. McAdoo and Bryan got the crusading lawyer and already famous investigator into the "Money Trust," Samuel Untermeyer (a Lynchburg, Virginia, native, like Glass), to write up a government-currency plan. On the other side of the Capitol building from Glass, another greenback plot was brewing. The Senate had just created, for the first time, its own Banking and Currency Committee to deal with the impending financial reforms. The Democratic Party caucus appointed as its head an unreconstructed Bryanite, Senator Robert Owen of Oklahoma, who, oddly, had also been born in Lynchburg. He enlisted Untermeyer to draft his government currency bill as well.[36] When Glass saw the new greenback proposals, he was horrified. He asked McAdoo if they were serious about having the government control the money supply for the nation. "Hell, Yes!," McAdoo replied.[37]

Wilson was forced to resolve the disagreement between these groups of warring Lynchburgians (he had been born nearby in southwestern Virginia). At a late-night White House conference with the two committee chairs, Glass and Owen, on June 18, 1913, Wilson split the difference. He promised to keep the private Federal Reserve Banks Glass wanted but to back all notes issued by the banks with the complete faith and credit of the U.S. government—in other words, to have the government guarantee the notes' full value.[38]

Wilson's promise of a government guarantee inspired a rabid conservative reaction. Some claimed the clause, along with the new public Federal Reserve Board, made the Reserve Banks government loan offices, as in the old colonial days. The *New York Sun* said that the "provision for a Government currency and an official board to exercise absolute control over the most important of banking functions is covered all over with the slime of Bryanism."[39] In reality, there was little chance the government guarantee would be necessary because all Federal Reserve notes would be backed by both pledged real bills and member banks' capital, but the symbolism was important. Wilson admitted as much to Glass, saying that the government guarantee, after all, "*is* a mere thought.

And so, if we can hold to the substance of the thing and give the other fellow the shadow, why not do it, if thereby we may save our bill?" As so often in the history of American banking, the shadows were an important consideration. Glass, at first dismayed, saw Wilson's political wisdom. "And this was the man they called a dreamer! This was the man they insisted had no political sense!" Glass claimed the actual guaranty would not be needed "in ten thousand years."[40]

Yet the compromise was more significant than Wilson or Glass knew. The federal guarantee established a precedent. Although in the pre-Jackson era the government had invested in some private corporations and had later loaned money and land to railroads and other groups, it had never before given its complete credit to a private or semiprivate organization.[41] Yet more special privileges followed. Wilson, in a compromise to the bankers who worried about too much government control through the Reserve Board, agreed to set up a Federal Advisory Council composed of bankers who would advise the Reserve Banks. It was the first of what would become innumerable industry advisory councils that would shape government in the following decades and that gave a special voice to privileged classes.[42] More importantly, Senator Owen made the Reserve Banks the first corporations exempt from the new income tax law, which would be a powerful precedent for future tax-exempt corporations.[43]

Glass seemed oblivious of the new privileges in his bill. He continued to attack the Republican Party's currency proposal, which he said created a national bank with "important privileges and accorded [it] certain governmental exemptions. It was likewise invested with unusual powers for a privately owned enterprise."[44] This attack, in fact, could perfectly describe his own plan. The Democrats had taken an important step almost unawares. They now planned to use the government to organize banks and provide new types of special privileges for them. In the years to come and in the debates over mortgages, farmers would cite these precedents with increasing fervor.

Special Privileges for Underprivileged Farmers

Despite traditional Democratic opposition, government privilege became acceptable to large numbers of the party faithful in the early twentieth century. Around this time, new intellectuals, rural Democrats, and "progressive" bankers came to believe that mere equal protection and opposition to class legislation would not revive farmers' precarious way of life. They declared the very nature of modern society to be unbalanced, most importantly between thriving industry and stagnant agriculture, and said that government's job was not to remove itself from the struggle but to rectify those inequities through "rebalancing" the economy, especially through supporting farm finance. Under their

conception, farmers and other disadvantaged groups should receive fundamentally *unequal* benefits from government because society as it existed was
fundamentally unequal. In effect, they believed in the poet William Blake's quip
that "one law for the lion and ox is oppression."[45]

Of course, the desire to improve the situation of agriculture and concerns
about agriculture's poverty relative to urban life were as old as history itself.
Such concerns motivated many of the land bank ideas described in the previous chapter. But in the early twentieth century, a more coherent ideology about
the relationship between the rural and urban worlds began to coalesce. The first
sprouts of this idea emerged from fears about unbalanced urban and rural populations. Many farm groups in the early twentieth century believed that the
greatest problem facing the nation was the ongoing flight from farms to the cities, caused not by any government favoritism to industry but by the tendencies
of modern life. As late as 1880, almost 50 percent of all workers were in agriculture. By 1900, however, that proportion was barely 30 percent.[46] New advocates of a balanced economy thought that prosperity emerged from the trade
between the two distinct groups of farmers and workers and worried that the
trade was now breaking down as the relative size of the farm economy and farm
population continued to shrink.

These farmers found their first, unlikely advocate in James J. Hill, a railroad
magnate and financier who was refashioning himself as an economic prophet.
In 1906, Hill demanded "national revolt" against the flight of people from the
farms to the cities and said that "government ought not to hesitate" to provide
special benefits for farmers to encourage them to stay on the land.[47] In an
address to the American Bankers Association, Hill warned of the "disturbance
of the balance between one form of industry and another upon which prosperity and stability depend." He spoke of overcrowded cities with insufficient food
and of untilled fields and rotting, unharvested crops. He said each sector needed
to have nearly equal numbers of workers if each were to thrive. He thought
bankers specifically should focus on how to revive "agriculture; and [to main-
tain] a proper economic relation and balance between it and all other [groups]."[48]
Some people, such as Theodore Roosevelt and Taft's secretary of agriculture
James Wilson, said Hill's jeremiads pointed to a fundamental problem in the
economy that government needed to rectify.[49] President Roosevelt formed his
Country Life Commission to address the very same concerns about depopulating farms, and it, too, recommended more rural credit for farmers.[50]

Some thinkers began pointing to other examples of unbalanced rural and
urban population as warnings of America's fate. Myron Herrick, the banker
advocate for rural credits, argued that England's current economic inequities
came from the growth of large cities at the cost of the declining country, which
meant "England is all out of balance."[51] Many attributed the fate of the Roman
Empire to parasitic cities sucking people and resources from the countryside,

and, as always, this invocation of Rome added further urgency to the appeals. As one historian testifying before Congress on a rural-credits bill lamented, "overurbanization" was always a curse. "The ablest living historians claim that this wrought the destruction of Rome," and yet we in America "have developed our industries in a lop-sided fashion, without the proper poise and balance to insure [sic] general and permanent prosperity."[52]

New farm interest groups proclaimed that in the face of the declining farm population, they needed more than simply an end to class legislation. Groups such as the Farmers Union, formed in 1902, conceived themselves as advocating explicitly for the farmer class and demanded that "legislatures and congresses do for them what they have done for others—pass laws that will be beneficial for their interests." When they argued that government had to help "bring the farmer up to the same standard as that of other classes," they were proclaiming an end to the anti-class-legislation position of groups such as the Grange.[53] Another new farmer organization, the American Society of Equity, expressed in its name the need for government to equalize sectors and, as one historian has pointed out, became "a class organization, openly appealing for support on the basis of class interest."[54] Farm groups understood, however, that mere self-interest was not a sufficient plea to triumph in politics. They and their intellectual allies predicted the dangers of unbalanced development for the prosperity of the urban world, too.[55]

At the time, the farmers' foremost wish was financial reform. The Farmer Union's first demand was "to discourage as much as possible the present mortgage and credit system."[56] The popular writer and farm advocate Thomas Cushing Davis stated in his book *The High Cost of Living: Cause–Remedy* (1912) that the root of rural imbalances was high-cost mortgages. He claimed that the "American farmer, if he has a loan upon his property, is kept in a continuous state of uncertainty," which "depresses his spirits and robs him of that hope which is absolutely necessary to success or the proper enjoyment of life. Under such conditions, is it at all surprising that men are *leaving* the *farm*, and the *cities are being overcrowded*?" He thus proposed a new semipublic "Government Bank of the United States" to make agricultural loans.[57] In one congressional hearing, a Farmers Union official pointed to a potential model but put a racial interpretation on it: "The United States Government in the Philippine Islands, as I understand, has established a bank over there whereby they help the yellow man directly. They help the farmers build their homes and improve their farms." And if the "United States Government can go 10,000 miles . . . and help the yellow farmer, I see no reason why they cannot help the farmer in this country."[58]

Although some farmers continued to rail against greedy bankers, others recognized in the bankers a potential ally in their struggle for equality. The National Grange began celebrating the American Bankers Association's efforts

VOL. LIV. No. 1385.   PUCK BUILDING, New York, September 16, 1903.   PRICE TEN CENTS.
Copyright, 1903, by Keppler & Schwarzmann.

Puck

"What fools these Mortals be!"

Entered at N. Y. P. O. as Second-class Mail Matter.

THE AGE OF PROSPERITY.

UNCLE JOSH.—The boys won't stay on the farms no more.
UNCLE SILAS.—No; an' you can hardly expect 'em to. Nowadays, even the mortgages don't stay on the farms

2.2 On the cover of the Democratic magazine *Puck*, September 6, 1903, "Uncle Josh" and "Uncle Silas" discuss mortgages held by outside interests. "Uncle Josh—The Boys Won't stay on the farm no more. Uncle Silas—No: an' you can hardly expect 'em to. Nowadays even mortgages don't stay on the farm."

Source: Library of Congress.

to "create a [new] system of farm finance," and an American Society of Equity newspaper had a banker explain to its readers that "there should be no antagonism between these two classes," banker and farmer.[59]

Many enterprising bankers indeed bristled at their exclusion from farm loans and mortgages and tried to find a new banking model that would allow them to make such loans. Although they worried that normal commercial banks, with their flighty deposits, could not supply farmers' long-term needs, a semipublic mortgage bank with long-term financing might. A *New York Times* article from the period was headlined "How the Bankers and the Farmers May Get Together on Loans" and explained how both could support new types of financing. One article in the *Bankers Magazine* argued that there was a need for "some form of government land bank best adapted to American conditions."[60] Many bankers presented such plans as an exercise in rural–urban balance. Charles Conant, one of the founders of the Philippine land bank, told the American Bankers Association that he worried that because of depopulating farms "the demand for food products is more than overtaking supply" and that a "central organization for the issue of mortgage bonds, recognized by the Federal Government, like the Credit Foncier [in France], would probably be required" to stabilize the economy.[61] The managing director of the Southern Commercial Congress, in arguing for public financial support, stated the balance metaphor most vividly: "We are rapidly losing the balance between country and city. If we lose the balance, the country tips over; if we find a means of maintaining the balance, we strengthen the life of the country for all time to come."[62]

Both the farmer and the banker advocates for balance found powerful allies in the U.S. Congress, which tended to listen to groups Wilson dismissed as mere "special interests."[63] Despite longtime Democratic appeals for executive dominance and equal protection, Congress had always thrived on weighing different interest groups' claims and catering to them. One congressman famously argued that in Congress one learns that "all major interests in society are equally legitimate" and that "representatives of the great legitimate interests are equally honest."[64] Unlike the president and his Jacksonian ideology, Congress tried to represent distinct groups, not a singular public interest.

A newly expanded and rambunctious Congress had emerged at the beginning of Wilson's presidency in 1913, and in this Congress special interests had new avenues to press their pleas. Under the just completed census, the House had increased from 394 to 435 members, where it has remained ever since. Many at the time worried the House's larger size did much to "destroy its decorum" and break down the control of the House leadership.[65] The Senate also expanded by four when Arizona and New Mexico were admitted to the union in 1912, which size it would keep for almost fifty years, while the new Seventeenth Amendment mandating direct election of senators also made senators more responsive to their constituents. Congress's increased physical size necessitated a new and expansive architecture, which manifested the increased importance of Congress as an independent force. Congress had just erected two majestic, marble-faced office buildings, one for the House and one for the Senate, its first official structures outside the Capitol. These buildings were designed by that era's most famed neoclassical architects, John Merven Carrère and Thomas Hastings, and included Turkish baths, lavish cafeterias, and colonnaded committee rooms.[66]

President Wilson had earlier prayed that Congress's leaders would "substitute statesmanship for government by mass meeting" and a single public interest for pleas by individual congressmen.[67] Yet the new Congress members had their own demands. In the previous Congress, both houses had voted to overthrow the internal leaders Wilson had hoped would corral them, including the Speaker in the House of Representatives and the president pro tempore in the Senate. The center of power in this new Congress moved from the congressional leaders to the totality of the congressmen, especially among representatives in the Democratic Party. One analyst of the time said that the "unwieldy size of the house [sic], as well as the exigencies of party" led the Democrats to create a new organization in both houses known as the "party conference" or, less euphemistically, the "party caucus."[68] When either of the two chambers' Democratic caucuses voted by two-thirds to state a principle on legislation, the decision was binding on all members at the threat of expulsion from the party. The man considered the first Senate majority leader, John Worth Kern of Indiana, said he wanted to create a Senate "Democratic not only in name but in practical results"—in other words, one that listened to each senator.[69] The Senate Democrats also created a "'whip' so-called," as the caucus notes said, to give the caucus's decisions heft.[70] In the House, the caucus created a new "steering committee" to appoint members to each of the legislative committees, a power that had previously been held by the Speaker. Cordell Hull, a member of the steering group, said its members tried to "mold" the House committees so they would get "maximum recognition by legislative action for classes of American citizens who had been long neglected" by the government.[71] In other words, the new Congress would heed the calls of all groups.

These internal transformations meant the Democratic Party in Congress would be subject to all the sectional logrolling and back-scratching that worried longtime Democrats such as Wilson. The new Congress and caucus offered their own vision of government, one where special interests could secure their just place in an inequitable political and economic world. In this new Congress, farmers' and bankers' advocates had a receptive forum.

A Federal Reserve for Farmers

The Democratic House caucus, the new instrument of collective congressional power, would decide the fate of Glass's refashioned Federal Reserve bill. The caucus's meetings on the bill became a watershed in the organization of farmers and bankers for privileges. They would force more concessions and privileges on Glass's already compromised plans. Years later Glass would remember the caucus as "lively" and "memorable.... No such scenes were ever witnessed before, nor have they been enacted since."[72] It was lively because, as the *Wall Street Journal* said at the time, "all is not harmony in the Democratic caucus."[73] Although intended to last no more than a few days, the Democratic caucus debate, conducted in the House chambers, continued throughout most of a sweltering August.

The subject that most attracted farmers' attention in the caucus was the seemingly mundane issue of "discounting." In Glass's original plan, the state and national member banks that joined the Federal Reserve system would get one major benefit from the new system: they could sell to the Federal Reserve their real bills, their own commercial loans with no more than forty-five days until due, and receive new Federal Reserve notes for them. In exchange, the Federal Reserve would take a slight "discount" from the bills' full value for its trouble. This was, in effect, a loan on the banker's previous loan, which allowed the banker to secure ready cash in case of an urgent need. The discounts also allowed the Federal Reserve Banks to earn a tidy profit. Although the subject could seem esoteric, the ability to discount certain kinds of debts and not others was of immense importance. As H. P. Willis later wrote, the ability to define what loans could be discounted "was a power of the first magnitude," which meant "the authority to determine the distribution of credit in the United States and in a certain sense to fix the cost of such credit. The importance of this power could not be overestimated."[74] Loans that could be discounted by the Federal Reserve could easily be turned into currency and would be encouraged. Loans that could not be discounted would become more expensive and discouraged.

Limiting such discounting to only short-term, forty-five-day bills would seem to make the nation's banking system ever more commercial and ever more divorced from farmers. Even loans to farmers for planting and marketing crops, processes that lasted for months, were thus excluded from the Federal Reserve System. The farmers argued that despite any explicit rule against farm loans, the short-term rule *in effect* discriminated against them. One rural congressman said that although farmers "did not believe that agricultural paper should be allowed any special privileges, [they] yet were of the opinion that the [Glass] bill ... would in practice result in a discrimination of agricultural interests."[75] Like some critics of the ideology of class legislation, he still refused to explicitly demand privileges for his own group, yet he understood that some laws that seemed to apply equally in reality had disparate impacts.

In the caucus, Glass had to parry attacks from what he called the "economic guerillas," who demanded the Federal Reserve discount long-term loans on farmers' crops stored in warehouses before sale.[76] Glass privately told the farmers' leader, Robert Lee Henry, that he would see him in hell rather than let such a measure pass. With the support of Wilson and even William Jennings Bryan, Glass was able to beat back the guerillas' attacks in a caucus vote.[77] In the history of the Federal Reserve, written largely by Glass and his supporters, the defeat of the crop loan plan is usually described as the end of the rural insurgency.[78]

Yet after the defeat, rural congressmen pressed to allow the Federal Reserve to discount medium-term loans for the planting and selling of farmers' produce. During one caucus meeting, the rural insurgents met with their opponents in the lobby outside the House chambers and got them to agree to a longer, ninety-day limit for discounting loans on planted crops, exactly double the time given to commercial debts.[79] When the caucus agreed, one farm rebel claimed that "we have won all we have contended for," and Robert Lee Henry even declared that this agreement "came practically to the amendment I have advanced during the last three months."[80] Glass denied such claims, but he later pushed the limit of all rediscounted paper up to ninety days. Such a move was a clear example of ideology at work because it blunted the charge of privileges for an agricultural special interest, even at the cost of longer-term and supposedly less-real or liquid loans. In the Senate, the more radical Robert Owen later increased the limit for farm loans to 180 days, again a clear privilege, and this limit was retained in the final bill.[81]

The rural insurgents' second demand was a clause allowing national banks to make mortgage loans, even if these loans could not be discounted at the Federal Reserve. Long before the caucus, farmers groups swamped the bill's drafters with demands for allowing farm mortgages in national banks, which had been illegal since the Civil War.[82] A member of the Farmers Union complained to Congress that banks should be allowed to make "long-time loans suitable for poor men to buy land and pay for it by amortization," so farmers like him could purchase property.[83] Many bankers also complained to Congress about the exclusion of farm mortgages from their banks.[84] Sol Wexler, a southern banking magnate, testified that, despite laws against it, "[n]ational banks are almost compelled in certain sections of the country to lend a certain amount of money on real estate" because that was the only valuable asset many farmers had. In some states, such as Mississippi, "all the banks are lending money upon mortgages." Wexler and others described the extensive subterfuge they used to get around the existing laws, including setting up semilegal banking subsidiaries with special savings deposits kept for long-term loans.[85] An exasperated H. P. Willis, speaking for Glass and other real-bills advocates, asked one banker if "you merely want your acts legalized?"[86]

Unfortunately for Glass, the Democratic Party platform of 1912 had already stated that national banks should be able to loan on farm mortgages.[87] When Glass conceded and allowed mortgage loans on farm land for just a few months, the Democratic caucus extracted another concession and increased the limit on farm real estate loans to twelve months. Robert Owen in the Senate again acted to further farmers' privileges and increased the term to five years.[88] Glass later lamented that "there was such an insistent demand to have additional loans made on farm lands" that he agreed to the mortgage provision only as a sop "to tide over" the farmers until they could consider a rural-credits bill.[89] For the first time since the Civil War, mortgages became part of the national banking system.

The final and perhaps the most important issue confronting the House caucus was how to deal with the party platform on rural credits. The plank declared that a rural-credits bill was of "equal importance" with currency reform, and many rural Democrats refused to let their colleagues forget it. William Murray of Oklahoma, known as "Alfalfa Bill Murray" for his insistent invocation of his farm, proposed an amendment to fuse a new semipublic mortgage banking system with the Federal Reserve. To Glass's and his allies' horror, the proposal passed the caucus.[90] This amendment forced the president to wade into the swamp of the caucus and make a clear statement of his principles. He told the Democrats on August 13, "Again and again during the discussion of the currency bill it has been urged that special provision should be made in it for the facilitation of such credits as the farmers of the country most stand in need of— agricultural credit as distinguished from ordinary commercial and industrial credits." He complained that the bill and the new Federal Reserve System "could not be made to reach as far as the special interests of the farmer required." He promised, however, to consider a more thorough rural-credits bill in the future if advocates would drop the current one.[91] Wilson's implied veto threat ended any hope for a combined bill. The caucus made a promise to consider rural mortgage banks in the next session, and for now this promise placated the rebels.[92]

The Federal Reserve Act that emerged from the caucus and then the Senate inaugurated a new age in American finance. Glass hoped he had created an automatic or elastic currency that would cement his real-bills dream. Yet the bill had moved far from Glass's original vision. It was now riddled with the very types of special privileges he claimed to detest. The government was directly liable for the Reserve Banks' debts and exerted control over them through the Federal Reserve Board; the banks had to make special allowances for farmers' loans, and for the first time since before the Civil War the nation's banks could now invest in farm mortgages. Almost as important, the Democratic caucus was on record demanding a comprehensive plan for rural-credit banks. Glass worried that "a lot of bunk was being handed out to the farmer" in the process of the act's passage, but he and Wilson thought the plan was worth the compromises.[93] Despite the best wishes of many of its proponents, the nation's banking system was already beginning to move away from the real-bills doctrine and toward special privileges to bankers and farmers.

Precedented Privileges for Land

President Wilson wanted to stick to the ideal of equal protection and anti–class legislation for the proposed new rural-credit system. In his State of the Union Address in December 1913, he celebrated the Federal Reserve Act as a system fit for all classes but lectured that for the Democrats' promised mortgage bank the farmers "should be given no special privilege, such as extending the credit of the Government itself," despite the obvious and unmentioned precedent of the Federal Reserve Act.[94]

When the conservative Democratic representative F. W. Moss proposed a mortgage bank plan soon afterward, it was to Wilson's tastes. Moss argued that "the farmers are not asking for any special privilege" in his rural-credit bill and said, "I deny that the Government has any moral right to advance public money to finance the industrial operations of any class of its citizens."[95] His bill allowed the government to charter any number of private cooperative banks, owned by their borrowers, which could make long-term mortgages, up to forty years, in the model of the building-and-loan associations. These loans would be limited to only 50 percent of the value of the farm, to keep the loans safe, and would be amortizing, where the borrower would gradually pay off the principal of the debt as well as the interest each year. The cooperatives would raise money by issuing mortgage-backed bonds.[96] Guy Huston, a prominent Chicago banker, asked Moss to allow for-profit, noncooperative mortgage banks to get national charters, too, and Moss agreed.[97] Moss said the charters for two types of banks made it a "purely competitive bill . . . not only between different institutions, but between different types of institutions." The different types of banks also helped satisfy those reformers such as Horace Plunkett, who wanted cooperatives, and Myron Herrick, who wanted regular shareholder-owned banks.[98] In a letter to House majority leader Oscar Underwood in early 1914, Wilson enthused over the new bill and said it should be the second most important bill pushed in the Democratic caucus for the coming year, behind a new antitrust act.[99]

One part of the mortgage bill, however, could only be construed as a special privilege and thus caused consternation for its sponsors. The bill provided an exemption from federal, state, and local taxes for all of the new mortgage banks and their bonds. In Moss's testimony before Congress, the congressman admitted that no part of the bill so troubled him as this feature. The main problem was that in this era local property taxes not only reached the farmers' land but also the mortgages made on that land (the mortgage debts were a kind of "property") and finally the bonds based on those mortgages (another kind of "property"). If the banks, mortgages, and bonds were not exempt, the taxes would be compounded into double or triple taxation. Moss thought no mortgage bank could sustain such taxation, "so that the system itself rises and falls with this one paragraph of the bill." Without it, he said, "you had just as well throw the bill in the wastebasket."[100]

Moss, with his traditional Democratic inclinations, still worried that if Congress included this tax exemption, other "corporations will then ask to have their income exempted." In the end, "recognizing the fact that I was not creating a new precedent," Moss copied the language exempting the banks from taxation from the Federal Reserve Act. Nevertheless, he recognized that his act went much further, exempting the income of everything from the littlest cooperatives to the for-profit banks to even the bonds they would sell.[101] The exemption was an incredible privilege to the new mortgage banks, but he thought it a necessary compromise and importantly one with a precedent in recent reforms.

As Moss suspected, this concession did spur more demands. One Oklahoma representative asked why there could not be at least be a "contingent provision" for government aid, considering that, after all, the Federal Reserve Banks received exactly that in the form of their guaranty. The representative said, "While I do not believe in giving special favors to the farms or special benefits to any class, they certainly ought to be on the same basis of Government favoritism as commercial banks, it seems to me." Senator Henry Hollis of New Hampshire, the cochairman of the joint committee conducting the rural-credits hearings, said, more rightly than he knew, "I imagine this Government help will turn out to be one of the fighting points of this measure."[102]

Senator Henry Hollis would become the most important legislator in the story of the federal land banks. He was senator for only one term, during Wilson's first six years, but he was an essential part of the new Democratic coalition. He was a Progressive lawyer who had become involved in a local mutual-savings bank and whose financial expertise secured his appointment to the new Senate Banking and Currency Committee.[103] Hollis, however, was also the senator most clearly opposed to the old Democratic ideology of equal protection and anti-class legislation. At one committee hearing in 1914, he said, "I occupy a peculiar position on class legislation. I do not think there is any objection to class legislation, and I have [so] said."[104] Later, when another senator claimed he would not favor class legislation for anyone except farmers, Hollis said the whole idea of class legislation was "a bogy that is conjured up now and

2.3 Senator Henry Hollis of New Hampshire.

Source: Library of Congress.

then by constitutional lawyers who want to scare somebody. We are passing class legislation all the time. The only question is, Is such legislation sound; is it wise class legislation?"[105]

Like others', Hollis's opposition to the idea of class legislation was tied to his hope for a balanced population. Hollis said that the "tendency to abandon agriculture and seek the larger centers of population has become a national menace in this country and in Europe. It increases the cost of living and causes a one-sided development."[106] He confessed later to "serious alarm" at the "rapidly increasing city population[;] . . . we must turn the tide of population from the cities to the country, and to do so we must offer the farmer an equal opportunity with the banker and the business man."[107] Equal opportunity, however, required more than equal benefits from the government.

In congressional hearings on Moss's bill, Hollis discussed benefits to farming families, but he focused on the benefits of enticing investors with the tax-exempt bonds. He attracted witnesses who shared this interest. One large landowner from Florida, in fact an aristocratic relative of Otto Von Bismark, F. J. H. Engelken, told the committee, "I have tried, in considering this bill, to eliminate myself as a farmer and put myself in the place of an investor, because you gentleman are really, in the last analysis, holding a brief not for the farmers but for the investor." Engelken said that only by securing "the immediate confidence of the investor" could the farmer himself get money through bond sales.[108] When Hollis asked him, "Can you think of any way in which the Government help out this system?," Engelken responded that the government might establish a central board of financiers to help organize the banks and market the bonds "because the farmer must be led."[109]

In Hollis's committee, the interest in the measure soon shifted from the supposed ends, cheap loans to farmers, to the means, abundant and secure bonds based on such loans. Many bankers testified that they saw the virtues of government support in making these bonds safe and lucrative. A banker from Denver, Colorado, said that the government could help make "our country banks financially interested in these land-mortgage banks" by giving the banks' special guarantees.[110] The New York banker S. D. Scuder said that, despite his conservative inclinations, he had concluded, "after much thought, that 'some Government help' to start this thing is absolutely necessary."[111] The *Bankers Magazine* said that if large mortgage banks were formed with federal support, "the farm mortgage might be standardized and given greater currency in the investment markets."[112]

Many members of Congress expressed their own interest in these new bonds, both for themselves and for the financial institutions they ran. Representative Everis Hayes of California said, "I do not know how it will affect other people, but . . . I sometimes have a little money to invest, and I have made up my mind that I would buy some of these bonds in my home bank."[113] Hollis said that in his home bank "we can not get as many first-rate real estate loans . . . as we would like," but "I think our bank would be very glad to have a line of these bonds."[114] Herbert Myrick, head of the largest farm newspaper publishing company in America (not to be confused with the banker Myron Herrick), privately told Hollis a couple of years later, "I fancy your ambition is my own—to have these bonds become the one universally popular investment among all the people."[115]

The financial focus was evident in the redrafting of Moss's rural-credits act. The joint rural-credits committee run by Hollis and Representative Robert Bulkley, a Cleveland lawyer who also ran a mutual savings bank, employed H. P. Willis, drafter of the Federal Reserve Act, to rewrite the bill. Almost all of the important revisions in the act were done to inspire more confidence in the financial world and, as Hollis said, to make the new act "harmonious with the Federal reserve act [sic]," which it mirrored in many respects.[116] There would be twelve regional Federal Land Banks, which would be owned by the local cooperatives and would sell bonds based on the cooperatives' mortgages. They would be jointly liable for each other's debts. The regional banks were necessary because, as one banker said during the hearings, "there has got to be some big organization that people will respect, not in Dakota, but that they will respect in Washington or California or Michigan or any other place—something that when it is mentioned it is not open to doubt whether a debenture [bond] is good."[117] There would also be a new Federal Farm Loan Board, not to ensure government control but to inspire confidence in investors and "lead" the farmers, as Engelken suggested. The board's members would be paid $10,000 a year because, as Hollis explained later, they had to "have the salary high enough to attract at least two first-class financial men in whom the moneyed institutions of the country have confidence."[118] Most significantly, the joint committee also voted to have the federal government buy up to $50 million in Federal Land Bank bonds annually, giving a direct government subsidy to the banks but without a complete guarantee. Hollis claimed that this was a "middle ground" bill, one that had the government giving "indirect aid of a substantial character."[119] (The Joint-Stock Land Banks, the noncooperative private banks created by Moss, would be supervised by the Federal Farm Loan Board and would enjoy tax exemption but would not receive direct support.)

For longtime believers in equal protection, the bill was a scandal, especially its provision to purchase private bank bonds.[120] T. C. Atkeson, a prominent member of the Grange, claimed that the bill "is the rankest kind of special privilege." Representative Ellsworth Bathrick said with some frustration, "I have said that this bill is not agricultural, but is financial."[121] One farmers' petition from rural Illinois attacked the act as "rank class legislation" made to assist the "money power" in selling the bonds, not the farmers who needed loans.[122] Another farmer said that the proposed Hollis plan was a "fake rural credits bill" that "would benefit only established money-lending agencies." It "is not a farmers' bill. Far from it. It is simply another bankers' bill."[123]

When the joint subcommittee on rural credits presented its final bill to Wilson, the president said he was "unalterably opposed to the government aid provision."[124] On May 12, 1914, Wilson sent Carter Glass a letter to read at the gathering House Democratic caucus. He said it was his "very deep conviction that it is unwise and unjustifiable to extend the credit of the Government to a single class of the community" and that such a conviction "has come to me, as it were out of fire."[125] The implied veto threat and invocation of the bogey of class legislation ended the bill in this session of Congress but elicited outrage. In two different front-page stories, the *New York Times* called the Democratic caucus "one of the stormiest meetings ever held by the majority party in Congress." Rural congressman Willard Ragsdale gave an impassioned speech in which he accused the president of "breaking faith" with the Democratic Party and its platform for rural credits. Others hurled invective at the party and its supposed leader.[126] Endless filibusters shut down the House chamber.[127] In the November midterm election, congressional Democrats suffered a devastating defeat, whittling their House majority to almost nothing, which did nothing to calm the divisions.

Wilson's hold on his party, on Congress, and on the old Democratic shibboleths about class legislation and equal protection seemed ever more tenuous. Yet Wilson continued to sound his long-held creed. In an open letter to Secretary of the Treasury William McAdoo soon after the election, Wilson argued that his administration had already brought about a kind of constitutional and economic Arcadia. Before his administration, he said, "groups and classes were at war with one another, [and] did not see that their interests were common." Now, with new equitable laws, "suspicion and ill-will will pass away." In the same vein, he celebrated the new Federal Reserve as an "instrumentality by which the interests of all, without regard to class, may readily be served," which was a subtle poke at advocates of federal support for farmers.[128] In December, Wilson told the lame-duck session of Congress that the Democratic Party's economic program was "virtually complete" and required no major new legislation.[129] Most of his own party disagreed.

The Public Battle for Rural Credits

The open opposition to Wilson proved how heated the discussion on the mortgage bill had become. People on every side of the issue and in all parts of government soon mobilized to make the debate on mortgages a public one. The result was a massive publicity campaign from all sides of the issue that proved how money, organization, and mobilization mattered to the interest groups Wilson pledged to keep out of government.

The National Grange, once the bastion of equal protection, began to relent on its dogma and concede that some special privileges could be beneficial as long as farmers were in charge of those privileges. It argued that if a bank "shall receive any special privileges . . . [the bank] should be composed of farmers and not by [*sic*] capitalists of high finance."[130] As early as January 1914, the Grange had promised to send out sixty thousand letters to its members demanding some kind of government support for farmers and their loans.[131] The members of one tiny Grange group from Plainfield, Connecticut, wrote to their congressman that their farms "are encumbered by mortgages," enough to "discourage the b[r]avest tillers of the soil," so they needed some financial help. They also noted that government aid to the farm banks "is not class legislation," without specifying why.[132] Another rural petition conceded that Congress should provide some form of aid to help "in establishing a market for the bonds."[133] The largest farm-press publisher, Herbert Myrick, wrote innumerable editorials and articles on the need for a national mortgage system, which helped mobilize farm supporters across the nation.[134] The Southern Commercial Congress, through Senator Duncan Fletcher, also continued to push for land bank legislation through meetings and printed publicity.[135]

Those opposed to the bill also organized and publicized their efforts. In May 1914, a group of fifty brokers who made and sold farm mortgages met in the Astor Hotel in New York. The group styled itself the Farm Mortgage Bankers Association of America, which in time would become the Mortgage Bankers of America, one of the most powerful trade associations in the country. As the *New York Times* said, the subject "chiefly in the minds" of these men was opposition to rural-credits legislation. Although many banks and investors stood to benefit from rural-credit reform, these mortgage brokers, who mainly sold western mortgages to eastern insurance companies, saw the system as government-funded competition. Yet even they could support some variations on the plan, such as the private Joint-Stock Land Banks, which they hoped would market mortgage bonds "with the prestige attached to Government institutions."[136] (This group helped keep larger lobbies, such as the American Bankers Association and its new magazine the *Banker Farmer*, divided on the proposed bill.[137])

In this era, however, much of the national debate took place in and through government forums and government institutions. The Government Printing Office was a central tool used by Congress and rural-credit supporters in shaping that debate. Although the Printing Office is today a little-considered appendage of Congress (and in this digital age is called the Government Publication Office), in 1914 it was a behemoth, another material representation of increased congressional power. That year its appropriation, at almost $5.9 million dollars, made it significantly larger than the Department of State, the Department of Commerce, the Forest Service, the Public Lands Service, and the White House. It also had more employees, at almost four thousand, than the Department of Justice, the Department of Labor, the Office of Indian Affairs, and a host of other better-remembered government organizations.[138] As Congress took ever more advantage of its franking privilege to send its documents free of charge through the mail, the Printing Office emerged as a powerful force in public discourse that could counter the president's own bully pulpit.

As chairman of the Senate Committee on Printing, the rural-credits advocate Duncan Fletcher had a particular advantage. He used his position to inundate the nation with printed material on mortgage reform.[139] He said, "My office has been instrumental in building up the literature on this subject." He sent President Wilson a list of seventeen Senate documents totaling thousands of pages of material that he had helped print, such as *People's Banks in North America*, *Systems of Rural Cooperative Credit*, and *Land and Agricultural Credit in Europe*.[140] Senator Hollis got into the act, too, printing nine thousand copies of his mortgage bill to distribute.[141]

The rural-credit printing extravaganza provoked complaints. One senator took the floor in late 1913 to demand new printing committees in both houses because he thought the current committees "are in danger of abusing the privilege," citing rural-credit pamphlets as an example.[142] A Republican Senate opponent of the mortgage bill argued that Hollis and others "have had enough matter printed to inform all the world as to the rural-credit system of every country on Earth," and a Democratic senator had to agree with the statement.[143]

Beyond issuing scads of printed material, advocates of the rural-credits system were also successful in using government money to continue investigations favorable to the system.[144] Just as Wilson was blocking the rural-credits bill in the early summer of 1914, the Senate Agricultural Committee inserted an appropriation for $40,000 for the Department of Agriculture to study mortgage reforms, hoping to provide more empirical backing for the enterprise.[145] In early 1915, Congress also gave to the rural-credits commission sent to Europe, with Fletcher still at its head, government funds to continue operating, studying, and publicizing the issue and the need for government-supported land banks.[146] The mortgage debate, fueled by both private and public funds, peaked in the presidential election year of 1916.

The New Age of American Finance

The combined public and private pressure made some kind of rural-credits bill inevitable by 1916. Wilson and his conservative allies knew they could not oppose all reforms if they were going to get the farmer vote, and so they allowed a new bill to come up in Congress.[147] At Wilson's insistence, Hollis removed the provision for the purchase of bonds by the federal government, but then he inserted a clause forcing the government to purchase some temporary stock in the twelve Federal Land Banks. The federal government had not purchased stock in a private corporation since the age of Andrew Jackson, who had ended a practice he thought especially redolent of privilege. Yet Wilson agreed to the compromise because the investment was to be retired gradually as the private cooperatives grew and bought more of the twelve Federal Land Banks' stock on their own.[148] Agricultural Committee chair Frank Lever told Wilson that with this stock-buying provision "we can bring in line a lot of the radicals and pass the bill." The fact that the federal government would exert some owner-ship control over the banks also comforted some traditional farm lobbies. They conceded that the proposed bill was their only hope for cheap mortgages in the foreseeable future, and so they swung into support for the act.[149]

Yet Hollis also made the momentous decision to *imply* that federal support for the banks was even more substantial than it at first appeared to be. Hollis's act declared the banks and bonds "instrumentalities" of the federal govern-ment.[150] The term *instrumentality* was as ambiguous then as it is now, but to many it implied more expansive government support. The banker Myron Her-rick claimed the term "instrumentalities . . . is mere subterfuge." These banks, "empowered to use the cash, good faith, and credit of Government[,] are Gov-ernment institutions to the extent that investors in their shares and bonds would have a moral, if not a legal right, to look to the United States for return of their money."[151] Others saw such support in a positive light. North Dakota senator Asle Gronna said that with such implied backing these "farm-loan bonds will be absolutely as good as Government bonds." Therefore, he would like to buy them.[152]

Against Wilson's wishes, Hollis also had the Senate place other provisions in the bill for government support. The bill allowed new government trust funds, such as the Postal Savings Fund (created in 1910 to back small, banklike deposits at federal post offices), to invest in the land bank bonds. These trust funds had previously invested only in purely government debts, and thus this investment made the two types of bonds appear synonymous. Hollis also allowed the government to deposit money in the land banks for short periods. He explained that under the latter provision the government "will advance to a land bank money if it gets in temporary difficulty," what others might see as a bailout. He hoped that with these provisions "the Government should put itself back of this system to a reasonable extent."[153]

In the House of Representatives, agricultural representative Frank Lever also pushed for these privileges. He supported them as measures to protect inves-tors, arguing, "The system will be only just as strong as this connecting bridge—this bond. The system will succeed or fail just in proportion as the bond is strong or weak." He said government bank deposits would comfort bond inves-tors especially. Representative James Byrnes, later secretary of state and a Supreme Court justice, praised the implicit guarantee inherent in such a clause, saying that if "Congress goes to the people of this Nation and invites them to become purchasers of these bonds . . . then it becomes a duty on the part of this Congress to take such action as makes absolutely sure this interest will be met annually, and this is the only way we can guarantee it, as I see it."[154] One opponent complained about the government support and tax exemption and said this was the first time he had heard "any real, true, honest, sincere 'friend of the farmer' plead for the investor. According to the gentleman from South Carolina [Byrnes] and others, we ought to pass this bill in order to protect the man whose money is to be invested in these bonds. In other words, we will drop the farmer for the moment, to look after the Rockefellers; we will take care of the Carnegies now."[155] Nonetheless, the tie between the farmers and their potential investors was cemented. A House vote for government deposits in the banks won 80 to 66, to great roars and general applause.[156] One congressman noted after the vote that he heard a gentlemen say that "he would purchase these bonds since the Government would back them up."[157] Hollis's demand for what he felt was wise class legislation for both bankers and farmers had triumphed on both sides of the aisle and in both chambers of Congress.

Despite Wilson's opposition to government support for the bonds, he was trapped by the popularity of the bill. It would have been political madness to veto a bill boosted by a publicity campaign in a presidential election year, a year in which the farmers would most likely be the determining vote. The constructive ambiguity of the implicit guarantee in the bill also allowed Wilson to claim he was not going back on his principles. On Monday July 17, 1916, at 10:00 a.m., in a crowded White House room, with official photographer in tow, the president signed the Federal Farm Loan Act into law.[158]

The Federal Farm Loan Act inaugurated a new era in American government and American finance. Most importantly, it created a new type of banking institution whose implicit government backing would help market its bonds to the investing public. Along with the Federal Reserve Banks, the

2.4 President Woodrow Wilson signing the Federal Farm Loan Act, July 17, 1916.

Source: Farm Credit Archive, http://www.farmcreditarchive.org/.

Federal Land Banks also began a new era of government-privileged banks. Although many Democratic politicians had fought throughout Wilson's presidency for the ideals of equal protection and continued attacking special privileges and class legislation, the Democratic Party had begun to reshape itself and to move away from these old ideals. The party's support for farm finance would, it was hoped, help farmers and their banks create a new economy balanced between rural and urban sectors, with more balanced populations. To secure investment in these new institutions, however, farmers had agreed to give bankers special privileges. In the following decade, bankers would take advantage of the opportunity.

CHAPTER 3

THE FEDERAL LAND BANKS AND
FINANCIAL DISTRESS, 1916–1926

When Secretary of the Treasury William McAdoo called the Democratic lawyer George Norris at his stately Philadelphia home in mid-1916 and asked him to join the new Federal Farm Loan Board, Norris was stunned. He admitted he knew almost nothing about the board or the Federal Farm Loan Act that had created it. He had never had any particular connection to or interest in farming. McAdoo, however, waxed lyrical about the importance of the new position and claimed that its "dignity and responsibility" could be inferred by its high salary, $10,000 a year. Such a plea resonated with Norris, whose friends had said of him, "Public spirit can seldom do its work well on an empty purse." As a self-starting lawyer, Norris had already acquired a tidy fortune pitching railroad bonds, and as a current deputy chairman of the Federal Reserve Bank of Philadelphia he had already been a part of President Woodrow Wilson's financial reforms. After reflection, Norris thought he might be of service to the new farm system, "notably in the financial end." He later said he was excited to be part of "the establishment of an entirely new governmental function."[1]

The Federal Land Banks were indeed a new government function. Although the banks were nominally private and were supposed to be operated for the benefit of farmers in local cooperatives, they were also a federal "instrumentality" with an implicit guarantee from the government. During the first decade of their existence, the government's fixation with protecting the banks' bonds and the financial markets that relied on those bonds meant control remained in the hands of the new Federal Farm Loan Board and of the bankers who populated it. The board would encourage the growth of the Federal Land Banks. By the late 1920s, their combined assets would make them the largest bank in the United States.

Yet the Federal Land Banks were but one part of the federal government's increased focus on protecting finance. With the rise of both the Federal Reserve Banks and the Federal Land Banks and then the increasing financial demands of World War I, the federal government made unprecedented efforts at succoring the private investing world. Later, when the postwar deflation prompted a slew of rural-bank failures, the government used its new financial powers to augment the countryside's wobbling banking system and continued creating new semipublic financial institutions to assist in the endeavor. Although the ideology of a balanced economy blossomed in this era and politicians claimed financial supports were necessary to maintain the farm economy, the link between farms and finance became ever more tenuous, and bankers' backing for such reforms more obvious.

The expansion of government's responsibility for financial stability represented a new and significant role for federal politicians and officials, which continued through the administrations of both parties and throughout the decade from 1916 to 1926. Whereas many researchers have noted the split between a reformist Wilson presidency and the supposed Republican "normalcy" of the postwar years, this chapter demonstrates the continuity of political support for banks that ran through both parties and through their relationship to the expanding Land Banks.[2] The result of such efforts was a continuous intertwining of bankers, politicians, and government officials.

Many officials seemed oblivious to the new relationship. George Norris, without a hint of irony, later celebrated his time with the Land Banks but wrote in regard to another proposed financial scheme, "If there are any two things that will not mix without the most disastrous consequences, those two things are politicians and any form of banking or moneylending."[3] Yet that is precisely the task Norris and his nation were embarked upon.

The Merger of Politics and Banking

Despite earlier petitions to allow farmers to manage the banks, all except one of the four new Farm Loan Board members appointed by the administration would be intimately attached to the banking industry. After Norris, who would become the board's executive head or farm loan commissioner, the most influential member was the tough and gregarious Judge Charles E. Lobdell, its Republican standard-bearer. In a speech before the Mortgage Bankers Association, he referred to "we bankers, and I use the term 'we' with justification."[4] Before joining the board, Lobdell was president of at least three banks and one

3.1 Members of the original Federal Farm Loan Board in front of the Treasury Building, c. 1917. *From left to right*: Herbert Quick (a rural-credits expert), W. S. A. Smith (a rural banker), Charles Lobdell, and George Norris.

Source: Library of Congress.

building-and-loan association and had recently been president of the Kansas Bankers' Association. He continued to own stock in at least two of those banks during his time on the board and rarely missed an opportunity to feather his own nest.[5] When President Wilson met the board members at their swearing-in ceremony, his only question concerned their financial skills: "Do you think the bonds can be sold?" Norris knew they had just the group to do it.[6]

The titular chair of the Federal Farm Loan Board was the secretary of the Treasury, William McAdoo, who had already acquired enhanced power in the administration. Like Wilson, McAdoo was the son of a southern Scotch Irish Presbyterian and he also was a former lawyer. Wilson called McAdoo "attractive and dynamic." The president's daughter agreed and married him soon after he joined the administration. McAdoo's marriage cemented the tie between the two men.[7]

Wilson also had immense respect for the office of the secretary of the Treasury. In a later edition of his most famous work, *Congressional Government*,

Wilson regretted he had not earlier "give[n] sufficient weight, I now believe, to the powers of the Secretary of the Treasury," who "has proved at many a critical juncture in our financial history—notably in our recent financial history—of the utmost consequence."[8] Wilson referred to the fact that for years the secretary of the Treasury had deposited federal money in national banks in order to assist the financial system during a panic. The Treasury had not tried to put deposits in specific failing banks; rather, the goal had been to move money into or out of the federal Treasury vaults and into the banking system in general in order to manage total bank lending.[9] Although Wilson typically opposed such discretionary government benefits for certain groups, he claimed that the secretary historically "has exercised, not political, but business power. He has helped the markets as a banker would help them. He has altered no policy."[10]

Wilson's blind spot to the supposed political nature of such banking intervention manifested as McAdoo took on new powers.[11] During the banking panic at the outbreak of World War I, McAdoo provided government insurance to private shippers in order to export more crops and thus import more gold. The goal was not farmers' earnings but monetary stability. As the economist William Silber states, "McAdoo had suspected all along that the solution to the financial crisis lay in agricultural exports," which would bring hard currency back to American shores.[12] McAdoo later inaugurated the wholly federally owned U.S. Shipping Corporation with the same end to encourage more gold imports. He also began to deposit government money in specific southern banks to help finance cotton-crop movements, a departure from the broad government deposits of earlier years.[13] From early in his tenure, McAdoo became the most interventionist and active secretary of the Treasury in the nation's history. He had the health of the nation's financial system very much at heart.

McAdoo also became a prominent salesman for the new Federal Land Banks and their bonds. When the Federal Farm Loan Board conducted hearings in August 1916 to decide where to place the twelve new Federal Land Banks, McAdoo used the hearings to interest the investing public. Thus, the board started its hearings not in farming regions in the West and South but in towns in the Northeast because, as Norris noted, that was "where there is a large amount of capital available." While there, the board members felt "inclined to dwell upon advantages of those bonds as investments."[14] At one hearing, McAdoo said the bonds represented "a prime character of credit, safe, thoroughly desirable, and attractive."[15] McAdoo added to that credit by hinting at the bonds' implicit guarantee. To a large crowd in Augusta, Maine, he noted that the bonds were "printed in the Bureau of Printing & Engraving in Washington, with the same care and skill as is exercised in printing the currency of the United States[,] . . . [and] these are the only bonds issued by any bank or quasi-public institutions or private institutions which are given the protection of the Secret Service of the United States." Although these statements celebrated the hardiness of the farm loan bonds against counterfeiters, McAdoo's main point was to imply, as he would time and again, that they were just as good as official U.S. debt.[16]

When the board members returned to Washington, DC, they were confronted with an avalanche of mailed material from the towns they had visited, all trumpeting their benefits as a location for a new Federal Land Bank. A pamphlet from Petersburg, Virginia, noted the city was within "easy reach of the Federal reserve bank [in Richmond] and of the largest member banks in the Federal Reserve System . . . through which many of the farm loan bonds will be marketed."[17] Some of the cities' arguments were explicitly political. Columbia, South Carolina, sent a package of colored maps, notes, and politicians' letters of support. In a note entitled "Congressman Lever's Interest," the city began by stating, "We know the Board to which we address this argument is not a political body," but "you cannot, any more than we can, be insensible to the fact that this district, of which Columbia is a part," is represented in Congress by "the chairman of the most important committee in the House of Representatives— the committee on agriculture," and that the chairman, Frank Lever, had an essential part in drafting the act.[18] Norris said later that one very important "controlling influence in our decisions" on locating the banks was to avoid "locating a bank in a state capital," which is "necessarily a political hotbed." Yet Columbia, the capital of South Carolina, got its bank. Lever, soon after leaving Congress, was appointed to the Farm Loan Board. He later admitted that he thought the position was "something that would let me rest a little bit, after six years of hard labor" in the House of Representatives.[19]

The Farm Loan Board encouraged political appointments throughout the system.[20] Board member W. S. A. Smith wrote to one Land Bank president in July 1917 that "it is extremely necessary of the Farm Loan Board to have friends in Washington, and if the Senators or Congressmen give us the names of good men capable of filling any positions which may come, we are very, very, very much in favor of obliging them in this."[21] Senators in particular received board attention. As Norris wrote later, "We were a Bureau of the Treasury Department and Treasury appointments are regarded as 'Senatorial Patronage.'" After Senator Duncan Fletcher demanded a local Land Bank appoint his brother, the bank president wrote to the board that "this bank is already in possession of one of Senator Fletcher's relatives as an appraiser," and it wanted no more of "Senator Fletcher's kin forced on us." Appointments as appraisers, who evaluated the land that the banks loaned on, were a particular source of political envy.[22]

Many appointees to the Federal Land Banks happened to be local bankers with political heft, but appointments were not the only way to give bankers favors. The Land Banks did not hold public deposits, so they had to keep their money in private commercial banks. These banks understood the necessity for political pull in attracting funds. In one case, Secretary McAdoo forwarded Norris a telegram from a national bank president in Chattanooga, the city where McAdoo had made his first fortune, who asked if his bank could be selected to hold Federal Land Bank funds. On April 4, 1917, Norris told the local Federal Land Bank president that he "presume[d] that he is himself a friend or acquaintance of Secretary McAdoo" and asked him to provide the national bank in Chattanooga some consideration.[23] Three days later the Land Bank sent a check for $30,000 to be deposited in the Chattanooga bank.[24] The Land Banks also required outside title insurance for their loans. To this end, the president of the Berkeley (California) Federal Land Bank had his friends organize the Oakland Title Company to inspect land titles for mortgage loans. The company's prospectus declared that the Land Bank needed hundreds of thousands of dollars' worth of title inspections, and "we confidently expect to be able to procure and control a large portion of it" because the company had "among our stockholders and directors those in touch with and having influence over these very transactions."[25]

For the Land Banks' first bond offering, Norris knew he needed allies in the financial world. "I realized that if we attempted to sell our bonds in competition with the municipal, railroad, and utility bonds offered by the established Bond Houses, we could not expect any co-operation from those Houses." He wanted to pull the country's financial powerhouses close to his banks and simultaneously to move his new banks into their orbit.[26] B. Howell Griswold, a member of the established Baltimore firm Alexander Brown & Sons, had helped lobby for a Land Bank in his city with the promise that he would help sell the bonds.[27] With the Baltimore bank in place, Norris asked for his assistance. Griswold quickly replied, "I am a Democrat, Mr. Norris," and he wanted to help the banks "both for party reasons and because I believe that this is a sound and helpful measure." Griswold then cajoled what he later called a few of the "most conservative investment houses" in the nation to add stature to the bond sales, including such luminaries as Lee, Higginson and Company of Boston and Brown Brothers and Company of New York. The group would underwrite and guaranty the sale of all farm loan bank bond issues for most of the next two decades. It turned out to be one of the most lucrative deals in the group's history.[28] To demonstrate bipartisan political support, Griswold employed former Supreme Court justice Charles Evan Hughes, just months removed from his failed Republican presidential run against Wilson, to write an opinion that the bonds' implicit guarantee was "binding on the conscience" of Congress. Thus, the bonds "must be regarded as obligations having the support of the good faith and credit of the United States." Hughes's statement was widely advertised.[29]

The Farm Loan Board worked to spread the bonds to all parts of the financial system. Although the government postal savings trust fund at first refused to invest in the bonds, the trust fund had to deposit the money it collected in local banks, as provided for in the law, and these banks had to put up collateral to protect the deposited funds. Norris wrote to the postmaster general to ask that he allow farm loan bonds as collateral for these deposits, which was done. The board also asked the Federal Reserve Board to classify bank investments in farm loan bonds as a normal bank loan and not as an investment in farm real estate, which was still legally limited, and the Federal Reserve did so.[30]

The Farm Loan Board also campaigned in state legislatures to make the bonds legal investments for the safest and most highly regulated financial institutions. The goal was not only to open up new sources of funds but also to give the states' official imprimatur to an untested asset. As the *Wall Street Journal* later reported, the board felt that "it would be good advertising and a long step toward popularization of these securities" if states allowed insurance and trust companies to buy them.[31] Norris went to his home state of Pennsylvania, where his friend the state attorney general wrote several bills making the bonds legal investments for banks, insurance companies, and trustees of widows' and orphans' funds. Norris hobnobbed and drank with the political panjandrums and helped the bills sail through. He wrote later, "It was in a perfectly proper cause, but I could not help thinking that it was a beautiful example of what Theodore Roosevelt called 'invisible government.'"[32] By the end of the Federal Land Banks' first year, twenty-two states passed laws allowing farm loan bond investments in the most regulated institutions.[33]

The Farm Loan Board harvested the fruits of its efforts in its first bond sale in July 1917. The sales provided more than $10 million to the Land Banks to offer mortgages to farmers across the country at about 5 percent interest. Norris called the sale an "unqualified success."[34] He could also be content that the handful of bond houses that sold the bonds enlisted an ever-growing horde of smaller firms to market them to the public. Almost one thousand firms throughout the country would eventually help sell the farm loan bonds, which together employed almost ten thousand salesmen on the ground to market them. Norris thus helped create a veritable army of farm loan bond believers to support the new investment.[35]

The gains from this investment redounded to the politicians who had made it all possible. McAdoo told Norris that although they should not publicly discuss politics, the act "was a Democratic measure, passed by a Democratic Congress and signed by a Democratic President, and that as the Party would have to bear the odium if it proved a failure, [the Party] was entitled to whatever credit attached to its enactment." That credit was increasingly tangible to bond purchasers.[36] As one Federal Land Bank president said in early 1917, the increasing "popularity of this act" was due not to the fact that farmers would get more loans but to the fact that "the real estate security is going to be for the first time commercialized" and thus could bring gains to investors.[37] Investors now had the government to thank for their tax-exempt and liquid mortgage bonds. Through the land bank system, the government's popularity became tied to its ability to bring capital gains.

The "Financial Front" in World War I

Even while the government solicited investors to support the new banks, it began enlisting those same investors to support an unprecedented world war. On April 2, 1917, in a fiery speech before Congress Woodrow Wilson requested a declaration of war against Germany. Congress overwhelmingly obliged. One result was a demand for funds unparalleled in U.S. or world history. To meet this demand, Congress gave Secretary McAdoo the power to offer billions of dollars of Liberty Bonds at his discretion to the public.

From his experience selling farm loan bonds, McAdoo realized that bond sales had the dual advantage of raising money and building political support. He argued that government bond salesmen had "to capitalize on the emotion of the people," which would both help sell the bonds at a lower rate and help people identify with the war effort.[38] McAdoo said a "man who could not serve in the trenches in France might nevertheless serve in the financial trenches at home," what he grandiloquently called the "financial front."[39] In his soon to be infamous Liberty Bond drives, McAdoo strove to make the American citizen synonymous with the American investor, and he employed all the methods of propaganda and popular pressure at his disposal to do so. He enlisted popular singers and movie stars and staged massive parades. Anyone refusing to buy "liberties" became politically suspect.[40]

To encourage banker investment in the war, McAdoo supported and Congress passed the War Finance Corporation Act in April 1918. The act created a new semipublic corporation that guaranteed bank loans to necessitous war industries. McAdoo argued that the corporation "should be regarded primarily as a measure to enable the banks . . . to continue to furnish essential credits for industries and enterprises." But this corporation also had to sell bonds. Benjamin Strong of the New York Federal Reserve Bank argued that "although the Government did not guarantee" the new bonds, people would buy them because of the government's implicit association. He thought this association "would have a strong sentimental effect" on usually unsentimental bond buyers.[41] Senator Henry Hollis, who had so recently created the implicitly backed Federal Land Banks, wondered, "Why is it that socialism to help the well-to-do is sound and respectable, while socialism to help the poor is unsound and disreputable?" But he, too, said he would vote for the act.[42] The War Finance Corporation thus became another implicitly backed government enterprise that aimed to support banks and investors.

The flood of liberties and bank loans, however, posed a threat to the Federal Land Banks, which now faced more competition for investors' cash. To reinforce the Land Banks, McAdoo deposited hundreds of thousands of federal dollars in them. Yet he knew that the banks needed even more and that they might be forced to close without sufficient funds. He decided that Congress had to buy the Land Banks' bonds directly, as Senator Henry Hollis had once demanded they do.[43] Norris, still attached to the old Democratic creed of equal protection, was conflicted about the move. He worried that giving federal money to the banks would mean "giving to one class an advantage to which it is not fairly entitled."[44] He complained that he "had not come to Washington to be a mere conduit for passing out Government money to farmers," thus showing himself seemingly oblivious to his task. Yet he agreed to follow McAdoo's lead.[45]

The public debate on direct support for the Land Banks commenced on the reconvening of Congress on January 4, 1918, and it is significant that the proposal was considered on the day the administration furthered its financial control of the country. Earlier that day President Wilson stood in the House's rostrum over a joint session of Congress and in stentorian tones exclaimed that he had taken complete control of the nation's railroads. He said that protecting the "owners and creditors of the railways, the holders of their stocks and bonds," was an essential goal of his takeover. "Indeed, one of the strong arguments for assuming control of the railroads at this time is the financial argument. It is necessary that the values of railways securities should be justly and fairly protected." Railroad stocks and bonds "constitute a vital part of the structure of credit, and the unquestioned solidity of that structure must be maintained." (In a tellingly appropriate move, Wilson placed Treasury Secretary William McAdoo in charge of the nationalized railroads.) Furthermore, in what could only be a subtle explanation for his abrupt shift on the upcoming farm loan bond debate, Wilson said one reason the government needed to take control of such large organizations was that "all great financial operations should be established and coordinated with the financial operations of the Government. No borrowing should run athwart the borrowings of the federal treasury."[46]

The Land Bank bond measure, introduced by a reluctant Representative Carter Glass, would both secure the safety of the bonds and allow the government to synchronize all financial offerings. Representative Joseph Cannon, the erstwhile boss of the House, rose on that same day to say that the act confirmed Charles Evan Hughes's opinion that the government was "morally back of these bonds." He asked why the government should not just guarantee the bonds and have it spelled out in "black and white"? Congressman Louis McFadden, a conservative Republican who had always claimed the system would need government aid, said that he "might assume an attitude today of 'I told you so.'"[47] The bill easily passed, ending the battle around direct federal support for the Land Banks, which had occupied most of Wilson's first term, less than a year after the banks had opened.[48] After the amendment's passage, when one newspaper tried to explain "why U.S. Land Bank bonds are booming," it could provide a simple answer: "Uncle Sam is behind the bonds."[49]

As the war ground to its conclusion, the Land Banks faced another existential crisis that would further federal support for the system. The Farm Mortgage Bankers Association of America, which had been formed to fight the original Federal Farm Loan Act in Congress and which organized the one locus of financial opposition to the banks, began a legal suit against them in early 1919.[50] In public mailings, the association argued that the banks represented "unfair discrimination in favor of a certain class."[51] The banks were "purely for the farmers. . . . That is why the law is correctly termed class legislation." The suit said that such an act of class legislation and the extension of the inherently government privilege of tax exemption to one group made the banks unconstitutional.[52] The *Wall Street Journal* said the group based its argument "in opposition to what it considers class privilege."[53]

The Land Banks, in turn, hired the best legal team to make a defense. William McAdoo had just resigned as the secretary of the Treasury, citing, in a surprisingly forthright letter, the "inadequate compensation" of a cabinet officer and his desire to "retrieve my personal fortune."[54] Toward his goal, McAdoo was hired as a special assistant attorney general for the Land Banks' case, with an unspecified compensation. The Chicago Joint-Stock Land Bank, one of the for-profit but still tax-exempt corporations that were just starting to organize, also put him on its payroll. It was McAdoo's first legal case in almost a decade, and it was to defend the system he helped organize.[55] The farm loan system also hired George Wickersham, Taft's former attorney general, and Charles Evan Hughes, former Supreme Court justice, Republican presidential candidate in 1916, and a previous defender of the act. It was one of the most powerful legal teams ever assembled. The team's counterarguments against the mortgage brokers centered on the federal government's constitutional duty to control the currency, which they said gave the government a special right to direct the nation's financial system.[56]

After an intense oral argument before the Supreme Court in January 1920, however, the Court stalled on its decision for thirteen months. Yet the continued existence of the lawsuit petrified bond buyers and made the sale of the bonds impossible.[57] The new Treasury secretary, Carter Glass, pled for more funds, and Congress quickly and almost unanimously allowed the Treasury to buy Land Bank bonds for another year.[58] One Iowa banker wrote to Glass saying he thought that farmers were "very grateful to you for your efforts on their behalf" in protecting the Land Banks. But he noted his own interest by saying that extra funds provided by these purchases would help farmers pay off their loans to local banks, including his own.[59]

When the Supreme Court finally decided in favor of the Land Banks in February 1921, it stated that the federal government had almost unfettered authority to organize any system to assist with currency and finance. The Federal Land Banks were a necessary and proper exercise of that authority under the Constitution.[60] By that time, the Treasury had purchased almost $180 million in federal farm loan bonds, a not insignificant sum considering that the entire federal budget before the war was barely $700 million.[61] The twin crises of the war and the lawsuit tied the Land Banks ever closer to the federal government, even while the Land Banks and the government provided ever more explicit support to bankers and investors.

HELP AT LAST!

—Thiele in the Sioux City *Tribune*.

3.2 Cartoon celebrating the U.S. Supreme Court decision upholding the Federal Farm Loan Act.

Source: Reprinted in *Literary Digest*, March 26, 1921.

Republican Balance and the New Agricultural Lobby

By the time the Supreme Court upheld the Federal Farm Loan Act, agriculture in America faced an extraordinary crisis. The wartime boom in farm commodities was ending. Numerous government agencies and public corporations created during the war to support food prices, often organized by the former engineer Herbert Hoover, such as the Food Administration, the Grain Corporation, and the Sugar Equalization Board, finally shut down in the summer of 1920.[62] The War Finance Corporation had been modified under its new chief, the stockbroker Eugene Meyer, to subsidize export credits for farmers, but it, too, ran out its time-limited authority. Along with the Federal Reserve's efforts to wring the wartime inflation out of the economy and the arrival of a bumper harvest season in 1920, crop prices collapsed in what became known as a "price panic."[63] Mortgage debts, so freely given by both the Land Banks and private banks during the boom and based on inflated crop and land prices, now proved burdensome. One Oklahoma farmer wrote to the secretary of agriculture demanding a total moratorium on all mortgage payments. The farmers had supported the war, he said, so "why should we all have our homes taken from us?"[64] The new Republican administration of Warren G. Harding, backed by a solidly Republican Congress, rode into office on the pleas of farmers oppressed by the panic.

During the 1920s, the demands of ever more radical rural congressmen and their banker allies would cause the Republican Party to fully embrace the ideology of balance.[65] As a consequence, almost all of the significant legislative reforms passed and implemented by the Republicans in the 1920s came in the agricultural sphere and as part of an explicit ideology of balance. Henry C. Wallace, the editor of *Wallace's Farmer* and Harding's future secretary of agriculture, would become a prominent voice for this movement.[66] In June 1920, he put a plank in the Republican Party platform that argued that "national greatness and economic independence demand a population distributed between industry and the farm, and sharing on equal terms the prosperity it holds is wholly dependent upon the efforts of both. Neither can prosper at the expense of the other without inviting joint disaster." In this vein, the platform advocated for furthering the new farm loan system and for placing an actual farmer on the Farm Loan Board.[67] Harding, in his first annual message to Congress in December 1921, said he took these pleas to heart and hoped Congress could help "restore the proper balance between city and country."[68]

Just like the Democrats, the Republicans would try to support agriculture by supporting banks. One new reason for this focus, however, was the parlous state of rural banks after the war. The postwar price panic had been disastrous for farmers, but it had also been disastrous for the banks that loaned to them.

The banks' distress, like that of the farmers, would not soon pass. In the 1920s, more banks would fail than in any previous decade in American history, the vast majority of them in small, rural communities. Out of twenty-eight thousand banks existing when the decade began, almost eight thousand would fold by its end.[69] One study at the end of the decade by economist O. M. W. Sprague declared that "the great majority of banks failed" because of the stress of lower farm prices after the war, "stress that was particularly severe because . . . [of] a large increase in the number of farms mortgaged and the amount of mortgage indebtedness."[70] The simultaneous bust in both crop and land prices meant bad farm loans would bedevil these banks and the entire banking system up through the Great Depression. Bankers demanded the government do something about what they now termed "frozen assets," debts that banks could neither collect on nor sell, especially the new farm mortgages allowed under recent reforms.

The Land Banks, even if they had helped inflate the previous boom, provided a potential remedy for both banks and borrowers.[71] Thus, in a special congressional session Harding called early in 1921 to address the farm crisis, his administration demanded more mortgage loans as a way to pay off old ones. The stiff Scotch Irish Presbyterian industrial and banking mogul Andrew Mellon, now secretary of the Treasury, went before Congress in June 1921 to testify for a bill that allowed him to deposit up to $50 million of federal cash in the Land Banks to make new loans. Mellon justified his retreat from free-market orthodoxy by stating, "If ever the situation required the aid of the Government to the Federal land banks, now is the time," seemingly unaware that these banks had been receiving support almost since the moment of their founding.[72] Republican congressmen who had recently denounced the Democratic interventions now saw the virtues of such support.[73] One Republican banker, J. H. Allen, who would soon start his own mortgage bank, had recently argued that the "use of subsidies has been and is an established custom or function of this government." Of course, "those of us who are Republicans know that for many generations" the party had supported subsidies for manufacturers and railroads. Now the farmer needed subsides, too, and Republicans should oblige.[74]

Charles Lobdell, the voluble Republican Farm Loan Board member, now appointed the new farm loan commissioner, testified that these mortgage loans would help banks first. He had personal reasons to hope so. He said that "from my personal relation with the banking business" and as "the principle holder in two country banks," he knew most farmers were "anxious to put a mortgage on [their] clear farm[s] to relieve the local bank[s]," a somewhat surprising motive. When one representative asked Lobdell if "the commercial banks of this country would be largely benefited by . . . having that loan of farm-land credits now in their portfolios cleaned up and taken care of by these farm loans?," Lobdell agreed.[75] Congress passed Mellon's special-deposit bill.

The Republican administration's early efforts were insufficient, however, because a new and more powerful farm lobby began pressuring the administration. The original farmer organization, the National Grange, emerged from its conservative slumber to open a congressional lobbying office in Washington in 1919 (although its hired lobbyist pleaded that he was not "seeking class interest or advantage.")[76] More significantly, the American Farm Bureau Federation coalesced as a powerful political force at the beginning of the Harding administration, largely through the organizing work of the Department of Agriculture. And the Farm Bureau, unlike previous groups, was almost entirely focused on political lobbying. Gray Silver, a wealthy apple grower and Maryland bank president, headed the bureau's powerful new Washington office, from where he was credited with originating the technique of flooding congressmen with telegraphs and mail right before an important vote. He also sent baskets of his apples to top congressmen, senators, cabinet officials, banking regulators, and even the president, all of whom provided grateful thank you notes.[77] In May 1921, Silver organized a meeting in his lobbying office with Frank Lever of the Federal Farm Loan Board, the lawyer Chester Morrill of the Department of Agriculture, and nine senators from both parties who agreed to work together to push agricultural reform. The group soon grew to include more than thirty senators and began holding regular meetings.[78] These bipartisan senators formed the Farm Bloc or Agricultural Bloc, the first explicitly single-industry group in Congress, which would vote across party lines to protect its interests.

Rural representatives also formed an agricultural bloc in the House, and this bloc helped them maintain disproportionate representation in that chamber. After the census of 1920, which showed that urban areas for the first time held the majority of the country's population, as many advocates of balance warned they would, agricultural congressmen refused to reapportion the seats to meet the new population, a first in American history. This refusal gave farmers additional power in the House throughout the 1920s.[79]

Senator Arthur Capper of Kansas, the leader of the Senate group, said in his book *The Agricultural Bloc* (1922) that the group's members organized in order "to establish a proper balance between the agricultural and other industries" and that their main desire was to "preserve the balance between agricultural and industry." Capper, of course, noted that mortgage demands remained central and that the "high cost of money for agriculture has been the cause of increasing difficulty for farmers for a number of years."[80] The Farm Bloc formed its own Rural Credits Committee and commissioned agricultural publisher Herbert Myrick to write and publish a book on the issue. The book argued that more finance was needed to counteract the "underlying economic conditions that drive people from country to cities."[81]

At the end of the special congressional session in the first half of 1921, by which point Congress had passed only three relatively minor bills to relieve the farm crisis, Harding asked Congress to adjourn, but there was a revolt. Buoyed by thousands of telegrams sent by Gray Silver and the Farm Bureau, the Senate voted twenty-seven to twenty-four against the motion to adjourn and pledged to pass more bills for farm relief. Silver described a hectic period, with committee meetings almost every day and "evening meetings with the agricultural 'blocs' in the Senate and the House almost every night" in the Farm Bureau's office.[82] The Farm Bloc succeeded in passing the Highway Act, which focused on "farm-to-market" roads to deliver produce, and the Grain Futures Act, which put a tax on short-selling grain that the dealer did not possess. But the bloc also encouraged financial reforms. An amendment to the Farm Loan Act allowed bonds to be sold at up to the maximum of 5.5 percent interest, above the former 5 percent limit, in order to attract more investment, all while keeping the maximum mortgage to farmers at 6 percent.[83] Though this reduced margin would squeeze the Land Banks' income and even threaten their solvency, it enhanced the reach of the system and the profit for bond investors, who now included both private banks and individuals.

To placate the Farm Bloc, the Harding administration, at the request of the suave political powerbroker and financial panjandrum Bernard Baruch, also recommended extending the life of the War Finance Corporation. The new bill would allow the corporation to loan or discount $1 billion dollars to banks to support farm producers on one- to three-year loans. This was so-called intermediate credit between the short term offered by the Federal Reserve and the long term offered by the Federal Land Banks.[84] Eugene Meyer, the War Finance Corporation's head, noted that the bill was not focused on relief for farmers but was "intended to provide relief for banks, particularly small country banks." Yet the bloc supported the effort and helped pass the bill.[85] After this flurry of class legislation passed, Congress finally adjourned. It would never be the same.

The nation was astounded at the influence wielded by the farm lobby, a new class organization directly organized inside Congress. The Washington tell-all *Behind the Mirrors* (1922), published anonymously, described the Agricultural Bloc as by far the most powerful group in Congress. It said that Gray Silver was "a lobbyist with the power of a dictator, or a dictator with the habits of a lobbyist." It argued that Silver's American Farm Bureau "rules the Senate" and was "forcing it to extend credits to farmers."[86] (Silver would benefit from this activism. Although he was on the verge of bankruptcy in the early 1920s, he would soon acquire both Joint-Stock Land Bank and Federal Land Bank mortgages on his farm.[87]) One contemporary observer noted that formation of the "'Agricultural Bloc' was symptomatic of the striking tendency which had been observable toward the enactment of class legislation" and worried that such "government by groups would be contrary to the basic principles of American government, a menace to the constitutional structures."[88]

Yet some argued that the country should celebrate the new movement and its goal of class equality. The popular writer Grover Clark wrote in the *Atlantic Monthly* in mid-1921 that modern thinkers "condemn class legislation and special privilege as severely as did our predecessors. Modern industrial and social development, however, has forced us to a new conception" of these categories. "Real equality, not only before the law, but in all men's relations, will be secured by making sure, through legislation or otherwise, that a balance is maintained." He believed equal opportunity required special government support for some sectors. Thus, the nation "must take active steps to achieve a balance. Negative effort for taking away the advantages from the few will no longer suffice."[89]

Farm blocs soon began sprouting in state legislatures. In February 1922, the *New York Times* noted that an "agricultural bloc is forming at the [New York State] Capitol" around a bill allowing savings banks and trust companies to buy land bank bonds.[90] Three midwestern state legislatures even organized their own "rural-credits bureaus" to loan state money directly on farm mortgages.[91] Within the first year of the new Republican regency, the political forces behind balancing the farm economy through finance were stronger than ever.

The Banking Beneficiaries

Despite the support from farmers, the new federal financial institutions focused their efforts on saving tottering rural banks burdened by now "frozen assets." According to a survey conducted by the Federal Farm Loan Board, more than 90 percent of borrowers claimed they used their money to pay back previous mortgages or other loans. Thus, the Land Banks' mortgages were not used to purchase new land or convert tenants into property owners, as some of the political rhetoric had once argued, but to pay off bank debt.[92] At one point in 1922, the Farm Loan Board took a survey of all mortgage loans given by all Land Banks in a seventeen-day period. It was pleased to find that $3 million of the $4.3 million in loans provided went either through loan repayments or simple deposits into the funds of local banks.[93] The Investment Bankers Association of America noted this statistic in arguing that the Land Banks had helped "reimburse country banks" and assisted in "alleviating the rural credit situation."[94] In congressional testimony on President Harding's first land bank bill, Lobdell explained the process to Representative Henry Steagall of Alabama: "Here is what happened in the last three years in your State, Mr. Steagall: Your cotton farmers lost money and went broke, and they had indebtedness in the bank that was incurred for every household purpose," and now that bank, too, was in trouble. He explained how Federal Land Bank loans helped the cotton farmer repay the bank.[95]

The Federal Reserve system also reached out to support rural banks. The Reserve Banks, although nominally devoted to only short-terms loans, began renewing discounted loans at rural banks again and again for months or even years, in effect supporting long-term loans, especially to farmers.[96] The Farm Bureau lobby celebrated that it had helped organize this "long-time credit" for farmers through the Reserve Banks.[97] In early 1921, the Federal Reserve Bank of Atlanta reached out to work with the Federal Land Banks, too. In view of "the unparalleled need for real estate farm loans," it urged the Land Banks to extend as many mortgages as it could. It promised in turn to exert all its efforts "in developing and stimulating a market for Federal Farm Loan bonds."[98]

With these institutions' obvious solicitude for finance, it is not surprising bankers became more vocal supporters of the farm loan system. The *Journal of the American Bankers Association* argued early in the decade that the association's member banks should encourage the "greatest use of the facilities of the Federal farm land bank system," which could help release funds in rural banks that were now illiquid or frozen.[99] The association's members sent letters to the journal demanding that the government "speed up the farm loan system" or "give land banks free reins." They insisted that the "government should strengthen Land Banks," "broaden [the] farm loan system," and "legislate to save the Land Banks."[100] These bankers' voices were heard in the halls of power. When in 1924 Republican politicians finally discussed filling the "farmer spot" on the Federal Farm Loan Board promised by the administration years earlier, the debate, as Senator Charles Curtis of Kansas explained, revolved around whether they should appoint a "farmer banker" or a "banker farmer."[101]

The Joint-Stock Land Banks, which at first developed more slowly than the Federal Land Banks, also began to expand in the 1920s under the Republican administration. Their explicitly noncooperative and for-profit charters were more in line with Republican orthodoxy, but they also provided another lucrative way for bankers to benefit from the Farm Loan Act.[102] The Federal Farm Loan Board ruled that officers of Joint-Stock Land Banks could remain in position as officers in other financial institutions, despite federal laws banning interlocking directorships at banks. When Judge Lobdell announced this ruling to the Farm Mortgage Bankers Association, he was met with wild applause. One mortgage banker said that after the stormy relationship between the Farm Loan Board and the mortgage brokers, the announcement was like a ray of sunshine. Another said Lobdell's statement "gave me a new light and a new hope." Yet another member said that "our institution will not take an antagonistic attitude" to the system now that they could form such banks. This ruling represented an important rapprochement between the land bank system and the one formerly recalcitrant sector of the financial world.[103]

The Joint-Stock Land Banks could also, like the Federal Land Banks, help support endangered rural banks. J. H. Allen, the Republican president of one of the new joint-stock banks, told Congress that he and his fellow land bankers had altruistic motives: "We are willing to sacrifice our profits in order that we can relieve these country bankers who are struggling to-day to keep their doors open."[104] Allen did not mention that he had already taken a personal loan of $24,000 from his own joint-stock bank and used it to pay off his heavy debts to a commercial bank that he also partially owned, which was in the same building and run by the same officers. (Allen would soon become the second most powerful officer in the joint-stock bank lobbying association.)[105]

The Joint-Stock Land Banks allowed politicians and officers in the farm loan system to cash in on their political pull. Frank Lever, one of the authors of the original act and then a member of the Farm Loan Board, announced he would resign his board position to head the First Carolinas Joint-Stock Land Bank. Lever claimed that "he would have to forgo his political ambitions in order to do justice to his family by engaging in private business."[106] Still-sitting Democratic senator Joseph Robinson of Arkansas, who would go on to be the Senate's powerful majority leader during the New Deal, organized another Joint-Stock Land Bank in Little Rock. A former director of a Federal Land Bank left his post to assist Robinson in the effort.[107] In 1922, M. L. Corey, a relatively fresh Republican appointee to the Federal Farm Loan Board, resigned and within four months told the Treasury he had been "retained by several bond houses" that sold Joint-Stock Land Bank bonds. W. H. Joyce, another one of the board's recently appointed but now former members, began a job as a lobbyist for another group of Joint-Stock Land Banks.[108] Farm lobbyists got involved in the Joint-Stock Land Bank system, too. Louis Taber, secretary of the American Association of Joint-Stock Land Banks, agreed to become master of the National Grange only if he could keep his top positions at three separate joint-stock banks and their lobbying shop. The Grange agreed.[109]

Many progressives, including those in the Farm Bloc, however, justified the even greater government benefits to the Federal Land Banks as the means to create a more "cooperative" financial system. Many had hoped that the national farm loan associations, the cooperative groups that nominally ran the banks and to which the Land Banks officially gave their loans, would form the nucleus of a new "cooperative commonwealth." But these associations, too, became tools of finance. The farm loan associations' secretary-treasurers, who were the "life of the farm-loan association," according to reports, began using their offices to push outside banking interests. Farm Loan Board member Herbert Quick complained that in most cases the "secretary-treasurer is [also] the local banker. He uses the association for the purpose of making it advisable for people to come into his bank. . . . [T]he fellow who is not a depositor in his bank is not getting as good service as the fellow who is."[110] Farm loan commissioner Lobdell complained that a secretary-treasurer in one local association was actually "the president of the biggest bank and he has other money to loan." (He did note, however, that another association, "where I have my own farm and have a loan under this system," was working fine.)[111]

Many of the offices of these supposedly cooperative associations were in fact located in a local bank and run by its employees.[112] Other secretary-treasurers used their position as a political base. Laura Ingalls Wilder, the famed writer of the *Little House on the Prairie* series, worked as secretary-treasurer of a Missouri farm loan association from 1917 until the early 1930s. She later ran, unsuccessfully, for local office on the basis of her work there. Her daughter, Rose Wilder, said at the time that Laura Wilder's local political office "will go in nicely with her Farm Loan work."[113]

Farm Loan Board member Herbert Quick complained to a congressional committee that it was hard to get actual farmers as opposed to bankers (or politicians) interested in these supposed cooperative groups "unless you give them hoods, masks and a ritual," which elicited a burst of laughter from congressmen who knew the resurgent power of the Ku Klux Klan.[114] In reality, most farm loan associations also excluded black or minority farmers, despite sporadic attempts by the Farm Loan Board to push their inclusion. H. R. Ellis, a black farmer from Virginia, for instance, wrote that the local association in his area was "white and do not want us with them." He asked the Federal Farm Loan Board to issue a separate charter for a "colored" association. The board, however, preferred to have a single farm loan association in each area and thus effectively sanctioned these lily-white groups' denial of loans to black farmers.[115]

The Farm Loan Board soon stopped pretending that these associations, which technically owned the Land Banks, should control them. Lobdell told Congress that the Federal Land Banks should not be subject to the whim of local cooperatives because the banks' "bonds are endowed with qualities that are not similar to any other instrumentality under the sun. . . . They are the moral obligation of the United States." He aimed jibes at the very idea that ill-educated farmers in these associations could run a banking system. He and the board recommended giving themselves complete control of all twelve Federal Land Banks and taking away the cooperatives' votes on bank directors. When Representative Henry Steagall asked if the local cooperatives could run the system, Lobdell responded, "The owners of the system, no."[116] Congress gave the board near total power over the local Federal Land Banks. It was now the banks' regulator, their salesman, and their owner, all in one.

Reforming the Banks for Their Beneficiaries

Some financiers wanted the federal government to move beyond supporting just mortgage loans to farmers. Bernard Baruch had been pitching the need for an expansion of the War Finance Corporation's authority to discount intermediate-term (one- to three-year) loans from banks.[117] Yet the incongruity of a "war" corporation continuing five years after the armistice was obvious to all. The corporation's chair, Eugene Meyer, asked Congress to create Intermediate Credit Banks instead, to be run by the Federal Land Banks. The twelve Intermediate Credit Banks would be capitalized at $5 million each, entirely given by the federal government, and would have the ability to issue their own tax-exempt bonds. Fred Bixby, the head of the American Live Stock Association, which needed loans for up to three years to raise full-size cattle, admitted he wrote the bill along with Meyer.[118]

The creation of the Intermediate Credit Banks helped cement the bond between farmers and bankers. The first head of the American Farm Bureau Federation, James Howard, a former bank cashier, advocated the Intermediate Credit Banks at the American Bankers Association annual meeting in White Sulpher Springs, West Virginia, in May 1922. Howard remembered that he spent three days buttonholing bankers at hotel lobbies and on golf courses, even caddying for some of them, in an almost too-perfect metaphor for their political relationship.[119] Such kowtowing bore fruit when that Bankers Association meeting came out completely for the proposal. In an argument for economic balance, the association said that "before the general business of this country can be restored to a prosperous condition the American farmer must be prosperous." Therefore, it urged the new intermediate-credit bill to assist farmers and ranchers "establish credit through their respective banks."[120]

The new bill for intermediate credit passed at the end of the first Republican Congress in early 1923. Unlike the Federal Farm Loan Act, the Agricultural Credits Act explicitly denied that the government had any legal obligation for the new intermediate banks, and some argued that the contrast between this act and the continued silence on the Federal Land Banks made the latter's support from the government clearer.[121] The Washington representative of the Farm Bureau Federation, Gray Silver, wrote to Bernard Baruch that this act achieved his goal of broad government support of finance, and Baruch soon bought $1.1 million of the new banks' bonds.[122] Silver began advising state farm bureaus on setting up their own corporations to take advantage of the act and thus helped transform them into combined lobbyist-financiers.[123] He also wrote later to one state banking association to say that the creation of the Intermediate Credit Banks had "lifted all need of friction between farmers and bankers."[124]

The new banks demonstrated that the federal government felt a responsibility to maintain all parts of the loan market to farmers. From the short term at the Federal Reserve to the medium term at the Intermediate Credit Banks to the long term at the Federal Land Banks, the government would be responsible for debts at every point of time in the farmers' lending market. All of these reforms also helped push commercial banks farther away from their short-term real-bills origins. One farm group argued that the advantages provided to banks in these acts were given as a "liberal concession to bankers in agricultural and livestock communities, and not as class legislation," but they failed to elaborate the distinction.[125] The Treasury Department explicitly adopted the language of balance to describe its new reforms. Its annual report for 1923 noted it was "evident that with fairly balanced relations between our own industries this country may enjoy a good degree of prosperity." Thanks to recent financial legislation, "agriculture is regaining its position."[126]

Threats to the System

The dangers of having government officials encourage private profits was demonstrated soon after the new Agricultural Credits Act passed. Judge Lobdell, never one to pass up his own self-interest, resigned his post as farm loan commissioner, which paid $10,000 a year, to become a full-time bond salesmen for the Federal Land Banks at $25,000 a year. Lobdell asked Treasury Secretary Mellon to sign off on the switch. Mellon shrugged. "Men are daily leaving the public service and taking advantage of the information that they acquired in public service for private gain adverse to the Government," but at least Lobdell was using his connections to make money while still working with the government.[127] Numerous senators denounced the arrangement, but the approbation given by Mellon and former farm loan commissioner George Norris, now again a member of the Federal Reserve Bank of Philadelphia, quieted the outrage.[128] According to insiders, the new farm loan commissioner, R. A. Cooper, a former South Carolina governor, was sponsored for the position by a group of South Carolina banks to whom Cooper owed a personal debt of $10,000 and who hoped that the commissioner's salary would be enough to pay them back.[129]

Another source of Land Bank profits elicited even more outrage. The Land Bank bonds were entirely exempt from taxes, which meant they were bought largely by wealthy individuals in high tax brackets to escape the "confiscatory" taxes of up to 70 percent first imposed during the war. The head of the Brookings Institution, the economist Harold Moulton, noted that a "Federal Farm Loan bond is a much better investment for people with large incomes than is any other security" and wrote that the "truth is that these bonds are being purchased in wholesale quantities by men of very large means, who thereby escape the payment of a substantial portion of their federal taxes."[130] These exemptions led many fiscal conservatives and populists to oppose the entire idea of tax-exempt investments, which had spread exponentially since the creation of the Land Banks. One professor of finance had pointed out years earlier that although every form of tax exemption is "a system founded on special privilege . . . the weakest stronghold of that policy lies in the tax-exemption clauses of the Federal Farm Loan, and it is here that attacking forces should first be concentrated."[131]

When Treasury Secretary Andrew Mellon proposed a constitutional amendment to ban all future issues of tax-exempt bonds, the constituency around the farm loan bonds fought him with zeal. America's wealthiest investors and its farmers demonstrated their new alliance. In the House debate in early February 1924, rural representative James Begg argued against the amendment by saying that "if it was right to create long-time securities and cheap money for the farmers, then it is wrong to vote for this, and there is no other conclusion," a pronouncement met by much applause.[132] Representative Thomas Harrison said that if this amendment passed, "the farm-loan banks are virtually doomed."[133] After one of the sharpest debates in recent memory in the House, the amendment fell short of the two-thirds needed by just seven votes.[134] Political support for the Land Banks was a major reason for this narrow defeat, a defeat that shaped the nature of taxation in the United States for generations.[135]

A more concrete reason for congressional support for the Land Banks can be divined from a confidential report compiled a decade later by the Farm Loan Board, which listed every Land Bank loan that went to a senator, congressman, or one of their relatives. The report showed hundreds of thousands of dollars' worth of such loans. Many of these individuals, including Senator "Cotton Ed" Smith of South Carolina and a few members of the prominent Bankhead family of Alabama, had multiple loans, despite restrictions on borrowing only on a primary residence. Many, again including Smith and the Bankhead family, owed thousands of dollars in delinquent payments but had not been foreclosed upon.[136] One farm loan association understandably complained to Congress that "the favored Politicians are getting loans larger in proportion to the Farmer who has no Political Influence."[137] Yet the benefits provided by the farm loan system to the banking, farming, and political worlds made the Land Banks inviolable.

The Faltering Land Banks

After President Harding died suddenly in August 1923, the administration of the new president, Calvin Coolidge, embraced the ideology of balance and the financial means to achieve it. In Coolidge's State of the Union Address the following year, he said his government would work for the "permanent establishment of agriculture on a sound and equal basis with other business."[138] When Coolidge ran for reelection in 1924, the Republican Party platform promised "to take whatever steps are necessary to bring back balanced conditions between agriculture, industry and labor."[139] Coolidge's Federal Reserve Board argued that although the "economic balance as between various industries and sections of the country is not yet fully restored," efforts by the nation's credit agencies were helping approach that goal.[140]

The president was privately less sanguine about government's prospects for helping farmers. Coolidge told farm loan commissioner R. A. Cooper, "Well, farmers never had made money. I don't believe we can do much about it. But of course we will have to seem to be doing something."[141] Coolidge's first biographer, William Allen White, however, would note that Coolidge had a longtime connection to mortgagors providing funds to these farmers. He said that in Coolidge's hometown of Plymouth, Vermont, a "classic Plymouth reply" to any question about their economic situation would be, "'Twould be a hard life if 'twa'n't for our Iowa six per cent mortgages which help some!" Plymouth's investments in western mortgages had provided the margin to keep the sluggish town afloat and prosperous for years. White thought Coolidge had brought the perspective of farm mortgage investors into the White House.[142]

The agricultural drought and depression in the northwestern states in 1924 gave the Coolidge administration an opportunity to test its ideology of financial balance. This region had already suffered more than most since the war, and the Spokane Federal Land Bank had already received the most sustained political pressure for loans. Idaho senator Frank Gooding asked Andrew Mellon in early 1922 to open up the spigots of funds in his state. The senator threatened to go public with his concerns and said, "Every day, I am getting appeals for relief through the Federal Farm [Loan] Board, and our people out there are suffering from bank failures." Mellon conveyed these concerns to the board and bade its members to listen.[143] As the Treasury noted later, the area's distress was "rendered the more acute by a considerable number of bank failures in those sections."[144] The area, in fact, had become inundated with bad debt and debt collectors. One reporter described the "great invasions" of collectors that rolled over these states like "swarms of grasshoppers." He found collectors crowding the trains and the hotels and lying in wait at livestock markets and grain threshings to catch unwary farmers. One Federal Land Bank collector estimated that three thousand debt collectors were scouring North Dakota alone, absorbing the few crops the drought hadn't yet taken.[145]

The drought also happened to hit states that were an essential battleground in the upcoming presidential election. Thus, on January 23, 1924, Coolidge sent a special message to Congress asking them to allow the last remnants of the War Finance Corporation to make loans to the livestock industry in the area and to assist in the "restoration or strengthening of the capital resources of the country banks and financing institutions necessary to the proper service of the farmer." He called a conference in Washington, DC, with leading bankers and farmers, the Federal Reserve Board, and the Federal Farm Loan Board to attack the problem. At the conference, Coolidge told the attendees that "agriculture cannot stand alone. The banks cannot stand alone," and asked them to cooperate. Private groups, with the official support of the Federal Reserve and the Federal Land Banks, organized the semipublic Agricultural Credit Corporation to buy the frozen assets on local-bank balance sheets.[146] One reporter said that in his travels through the region he "found no less than seven paternalistic institutions—governmental, semi-governmental and private—that were working to save the rural banks and the farmers in these four states."[147]

Yet the rapid expansion of the Federal Land Bank loans eventually cost the Spokane Federal Land Bank. The Farm Loan Board created a special committee in 1925 to investigate the bank's situation, and what it found was alarming. The committee said the condition of the region "is one which must be seen to be understood" and had "no precedent in the history of the country anywhere." Many borrowers were "struggling to retain their homes in the face of a seventy-five per cent abandonment of the neighborhood."[148] More concerning, the committee found that the Spokane Land Bank was lying about its finances. It claimed that whereas the bank's earnings on paper were "in the neighborhood of $800,000 per annum," they were in fact half that if reckoned "on the basis of monies actually collected."[149] The committee complained likewise of the bank's excessive expenses, presumably including an elaborate new building it had constructed. They thought the bank was on the edge of failure.[150]

As a result of these findings, the Farm Loan Board put the Spokane Land Bank into a kind of bankruptcy or conservatorship. It appointed a "Spokane Commission," made up of officers of the other Land Banks, which advanced $4 million from the rest of to buy defaulted Spokane mortgages. In return, the other banks received euphemistically titled "Spokane Participation Certificates," which entitled them to whatever could be recovered from foreclosed farms. The Spokane Commission's public report put the situation in the most flattering light, claiming that the lands would be "taken over on a basis which guarantees the contributing banks against ultimate loss."[151] A private investigative committee under Paul Bestor, president of the Saint Louis Land Bank and later farm loan commissioner, was less optimistic. Its report included photographs of bleak, desolate farms with little sign of vegetation or cultivation, fruitlessly encumbered with mortgages. One woman farmer, a former schoolteacher from New York and one of the last residents of a neighborhood of abandoned farms, told the investigative committee that the Spokane Land Bank officials should be "strung up" for their reckless behavior in providing bad loans and then foreclosing on them. The report thought that it "would be unworthy of a farm loan system to even give these farms away." The committee argued that the losses on the mortgages had gone from the $4 million originally estimated "to $8 million [and] now almost $15 million." The committee said it "seems evident that the contributing banks can never be repaid from the sale of farms" unless there was some "miraculous change."[152]

At the same time as the Spokane Land Bank was collapsing, the most prominent Joint-Stock Land Banks were imploding as well. Guy Huston was a Chicago banker who had been the main impetus behind the clause allowing Joint-Stock Land Banks in the original Farm Loan Act. Not surprisingly, he also received one of the earliest charters for his Chicago Joint-Stock Land Bank, which became the largest in the country. For eight years, Huston also was president of these banks' trade lobby, the American Association of Joint-Stock Land Banks.[153] One Wall Street firm called him "unquestionably the outstanding figure in the Joint Stock Land Bank system."[154] Yet the Guy Huston group of banks was having problems with delinquent mortgages. Instead of suggesting that Huston write them off as a loss, though, farm loan commissioner Cooper encouraged Huston to set up a dummy corporation, what became Farmers' Fund, Inc., to buy the bad mortgages at full value. This shell game was necessary because, as Cooper later admitted in a deposition, the board thought it was important that banks in trouble should continue lending; otherwise, the "impression gets out" the bank is going to fail.[155] Cooper admitted that encouraging such skullduggery was not usually appropriate for an independent bank regulator, but he said his Farm Loan Board was as much a cheerleader for the banks as a supervisor. He said that the board was required to "assist the banks" by trying "to persuade, if I may use that word, the public to invest in the securities. That we tried to do."[156] Such "persuasion" occasionally meant covering up the banks' true situation. The board was so attentive to these needs that outside bond investors began to question its veracity. One investor wrote to Mellon that "it is commonly being said among investors that government supervision is a joke."[157] Mellon, too, complained to President Coolidge that the Federal Farm Loan Board was not conducting the "independent supervision" that he had hoped.[158]

The board's subterfuge could not paper over the real problems in the land bank system. By mid-1926, Secretary Mellon wrote to President Coolidge that at least three Joint-Stock Land Banks were insolvent. Commissioner Cooper, he urged, should "be held largely responsible for what appears to be a collapse" in the system because he "has been in frequent personal contact with the principal officers under investigation and has in many instances with his colleagues and assistants undertaken to set up a defense for them." Mellon thought Cooper's activities in defending the banks were "such as to give cause for questioning the motives influencing his official acts."[159] The same day Mellon sent his letter, Cooper offered his resignation to President Coolidge under the weak excuse of his health.[160] Confirming Mellon's concerns, Cooper would quickly be hired as a lobbyist for one of the Joint-Stock Land Banks.

After Cooper's retirement, the denouement of the land bank system came fast. Within the next year, three Joint-Stock Land Banks, two of which were associated with Guy Huston, collapsed. Huston was sentenced to nine years in the Federal Penitentiary at Leavenworth for mail fraud and other crimes involved with hiding his banks' assets and liabilities. Both the president and the former secretary of the Kansas City Joint-Stock Land Bank, also associated with Huston, were sentenced to six years and one year, respectively, at Leavenworth. A secretary-treasurer of one joint-stock bank in South Carolina committed suicide and left a note confessing to thousands of dollars of shortages in his account.[161] As for the Federal Land Banks, an employee of the Berkeley bank also committed suicide when it was revealed that he had embezzled $16,000 from the bank.[162]

Even the new and largely quiescent Intermediate Credit Banks got caught in a scandal when they lost hundreds of thousands of dollars on loans to insolvent local banks in North and South Carolina. Cooper later testified to Congress that he had pushed these bad loans in order to help failing private banks: "I will state to you gentlemen, frankly, that the banks and the board have approved rediscounts that we knew were hazardous, because with the breaking down of banking facilities in a community, and the distress of agriculture, we have felt that we should go to the very limit."[163] Again, the attempt to salvage banks had redounded back on the rural-credit system. Meanwhile, some states that had created their own government-funded mortgage banks to assist the Federal Land Banks encountered similar dilemmas. North Dakota's state land bank system collapsed after it revealed tens of thousands of dollars in unrecoverable or seemingly odious debt. The state attorney general, William Lemke (who later resurrected himself as a prominent congressmen), had used a loan from the system to buy a $22,000 house. Other state systems, such as Minnesota's Rural Credit Bureau, met the same fate.[164]

The insolvency and distress of these new semipublic financial systems, now intimately intertwined with the country's private finances, threatened to bring down those structures they had helped protect for years. There was the danger that they would throw the entire economy they had hoped to balance into a new form of imbalance. The attempt to merge government and banking, to the supposed benefit of both, was imperiled. Coolidge and the Republican Party knew drastic action was necessary, but they disagreed about what that action should be.

CHAPTER 4

FALLING PRICES AND MORTGAGE CRISIS, 1926–1933

In the early 1930s, after more than a decade of low or falling prices for farm products, the Cornell agricultural economists George Warren and Frank Pearson divined a seeming truth about the differing politics of inflation and deflation. They noted that "when prices rise, the government's activities are primarily for the protection of the consumer." But when prices fall, "strenuous efforts are put forth to protect producers and creditors." Creditors especially demanded help in such a deflation: "Since debts cannot be paid, the government is called on to take over private debts of banks, railroads, farmers, and home owners."[1] The problems of agriculture in the 1920s and early 1930s would be defined by falling crop prices, and so, as Warren and Pearson argued, the U.S. government made every effort to protect farm producers and the creditors who lent to them.

The decline in crop prices after World War I made American farmers aware of prices in a way they were not when Congress created the Federal Land Banks. Wheat prices, which had peaked at $2.16 a bushel in 1919, fell to 92 cents by 1923. Corn prices fell from $1.51 a bushel in 1919 to 52 cents as early as 1921. A number of other crop and livestock prices followed these trends downward, only to bump along at a lower level for most of the following decade. Agricultural prices fell faster and further than prices elsewhere after the war, and they stayed lower, leading to new protests from farmers as the rest of the economy entered a peerless prosperity.[2]

Although the original advocates of the Land Banks thought that the imbalance between agriculture and industry could be attributed to differences in access to finance, in the 1920s a new movement for balance arose. This movement claimed that the greatest difference between the two sectors was in the prices they received for the products they sold. In this new conception, low prices for farm goods were the root of all the ills and imbalances in the economy, and bringing farm prices up to the level of industrial prices was the only means to restore equality. The "price-parity" movement crescendoed during the Coolidge and Hoover administrations, bringing a new language of balance into both popular and academic prominence.

Although this new price-balance ideology formed as an addition to the ideology of financial balance that inspired the Federal Land Banks, it was also understood as a means to restore financial health. Higher prices, advocates such as Warren and Pearson argued, would help farmers pay off their long-standing farm debts, especially their burdensome mortgages, inherited from earlier, inflated times. In fact, from the late 1920s until World War II, the government's increasing desire to control the relationship of different sectors' prices became an important part of the overall goal of stabilizing the financial sector, including the new federal "instrumentalities," such as the Federal Land Banks, which supported that sector. As the Hoover administration instituted a version of the price-parity plan, it used new federal instrumentalities and new kinds of federal lending to do so.

Although there is a small literature on the price-parity movement, historians have not analyzed how similar but still distinct ideas about a balanced economy shaped both that movement and the movement behind the Federal Land Banks and how they interacted. Historians have instead remained focused on the rise of a cooperative or "associationalist" farm policy in which the government, especially under Herbert Hoover, helped organize cooperatives to fight for farmers' interests.[3] These writers have ignored the importance of both the price-parity movement and the Federal Land Banks in the economic history of this era and have failed to show why the government remained determined, as in earlier years, on using government credit to support private creditors. Even after the twin crises of a price collapse and an explosion in farm foreclosures in the Great Depression, the government fixated on using credit to rebalance and sustain the increasingly fragile farm finance system. Such efforts would culminate in the first explicit bank bailout by the federal government, the bailout of the Federal Land Banks. Although this period began with a new focus on balance through price controls, it ended with the ever-increasing use of federal credit to support banks.

The Purchasing Power of the Farmer's Dollar

At first glance, George Peek and Hugh Johnson might seem odd prophets of a new farm movement. Peek was a slick and peripatetic midwesterner who climbed up the rungs of the John Deere plow company to become a wealthy

executive.[4] Johnson was a frenetic army lawyer who began his public life assist-
ing the draft in World War I.[5] Both became protégés of the financier Bernard
Baruch at the War Industries Board. After the war, Peek moved over to the long-
suffering Moline Plow Company and hired Johnson as his general counsel. At
the plow company, the dangers of a depressed farm market to industrial success were painfully obvious.

In 1922, influenced by their experiences in government, finance, and industry, Peek and Johnson wrote their manifesto *Equality for Agriculture* under the
aegis of the new American Farm Bureau Federation. Their pamphlet was a plea
for an economy balanced between agriculture and industry, the fulcrum of that
balance being a fair price for each group's products. They claimed that the rural
population bought some "40% to 60% of domestic commerce, which is 90% to
95% of all our commerce." Without the purchases by the farm economy, the
industrial economy, which traded with farmers, was doomed. They argued that
"industry and labor cannot survive the absence of half the population from the
market without destructive collapse."[6]

Peek and Johnson said that in order to keep both sides of the economy trading, the government had to set a fair price for depressed farm products relative
to industrial goods. Using a recent publication on prices by the Cornell agricultural economist George Warren, they showed that farm prices had fallen further than other prices in the economy and thus had to be brought up to "equality," what would later be known as the "parity price" of the period right before
World War I. To maintain this price, the government should ship surplus crops
overseas until domestic prices rose. Johnson later argued that "if only we could
give the agricultural half of our population a fair price for its products, we
could create—in our own backyard—one of the richest markets for industry
in the whole world."[7] *Equality for Agriculture* also noted another benefit of
their proposal: higher prices would help lighten the "enormous burden" of
rural debt contracted during the war inflation and thus protect both lenders
and borrowers.[8]

Ideas about the need to balance prices had already begun to percolate in this
period and were tied into increasingly forthright attacks on the older idea of
class legislation. Bernard Baruch explained in an *Atlantic Monthly* article that
special price legislation for farmers was necessary due to their troubled situation. He said that "farmers are not entitled to special privileges; but are they
not right in demanding that they be placed on an equal footing with the buyers of their products and with other industries?" If the economic world were
inherently unequal, as it then seemed to be, it was no privilege merely to bring
farmers up to the new American standard. Baruch said, "American democracy
is unalterably opposed alike to enacted special privilege and to *the special privilege of unequal opportunity that arises automatically from the failure to correct
glaring economic inequalities.*"[9] Like earlier promoters of balance, he thought

equal opportunity in an unequal world demanded more than equal benefits from government. He became an advocate of his pupils Peek and Johnson's ideas and contributed thousands of dollars to their educational campaigns.[10]

National Grange master Louis Taber, in a speech to its annual convention later in the decade, also argued for equality for agriculture and against older ideas of class legislation. He said that the "city is the farmer's best customer. Conversely, agriculture consumes, directly or indirectly, from twenty to thirty per cent of the manufactured goods of the nation." He said a price-parity plan was not "class legislation or special favor to any one group" because it attempted only to equalize benefits between existing groups such as those benefits granted by the tariff. Of course, this was precisely the further extension of class legislation the Grange once denounced.[11] The journal *Wallace's Farmer* joked that many urbanites "denounced what they call class legislation. . . . They seem to think this is a criminal novelty in legislative chambers" now that it was farmers' turn to get part of it.[12] To these new advocates, class legislation was just an inevitable aspect of politics and should be pursued most forcefully by those groups left behind.

Henry A. Wallace, son of Harding's incoming secretary of agriculture, Henry C. Wallace, and editor of *Wallace's Farmer*, found statistical evidence to buttress farmers' arguments. The younger Wallace's book *Agriculture Prices* (1920) provided evidence going back hundreds of years that crop prices were "inelastic"—that is, they changed rapidly with small changes in demand or supply relative to other parts of the economy. These rapid price changes caused problems for farmers dealing with fluctuating returns and prices relative to industry. With the farm price rise and collapse following World War I, these problems were more acute than ever. Wallace hoped the government would thus help farmers "meet the other classes of society on equal terms" and get the appropriate prices for their products.[13]

Ideas about balancing crop prices were soon broached in the highest halls of government. President Harding called the National Agricultural Conference in 1921 to support his plan for increased rural financing, yet the conference's final report argued that low farm prices were the root of most of the nation's economic ills. It declared "that no revival of American business is possible until the farmer's dollar is restored to its normal purchasing power."[14] Secretary of Agriculture Henry C. Wallace pushed these ideas in the next administration. President Calvin Coolidge later complained, "At every Cabinet meeting . . . Secretary Henry Wallace used to be grumbling and complaining about the price of corn and was always wanting the government to do something about it."[15] As one historian has said, in the 1920s Secretary Wallace became "doubtful that more liberal credit for the farmer would narrow the disparity" between the two groups and found price supports to be a solution. Equality for agriculture became Secretary Wallace's guiding star, for salvaging both farmers and credit. As his paper *Wallace's Farmer* explained, "Thousands of mortgaged land owners are dependent for their future prosperity on the course of prices."[16]

In the 1920s, writers and politicians described their price campaigns as an attempt to increase the farmer's "purchasing power." Yet their understanding of the term is divorced from the modern one. In much of the modern and historical literature, "purchasing power" is described as something analogous to the consumer's ability to purchase goods. The historian Meg Jacobs states that in this period, "'purchasing power' was shorthand for redistributive economic policies designed to enable the working and middle classes to buy basic necessities."[17] Many have connected the phrase to John Maynard Keynes's later idea of the "marginal propensity to consume"—that is, the amount of income devoted by households to buying consumer goods instead of to saving. Keynes's idea seemed to necessitate redistribution toward the lower classes, who spent as opposed to saved more of their income.

Yet "purchasing power" in this era was merely a measure of how many goods one could get in exchange for money or credit. Such purchasing power came from businesses and investors just as much as from consumers.[18] When the term was used in the 1920s, it most often referred to the "purchasing power of the farmer's dollar" or of the "farmer's product." This was the amount of money farmers acquired from the rest of the economy in exchange for their crops.[19] The new price-parity movement was not directed at increasing purchasing power on the whole or as part of a purely income-based redistribution but at keeping it balanced across different producing groups. And the movement considered the farmer as a producer rather than a consumer. Most obviously, price-parity advocates understood that high crop prices meant increasing the prices of many goods paid for by consumers, especially low-income consumers, but they considered this burden worth it so that certain producers would have more income. As Warren and Pearson said, during a deflation it was producers who attracted attention.

As the price-parity idea gained adherents, the Coolidge administration attempted to fight it. Coolidge's aide and future vice president Charles Dawes scoffed that Peek and Johnson pushed their plan simply because it helped "these fellows sell plows."[20] The administration hewed to what was already an older idea of balance. The Treasury's annual report for 1923 argued that it was "evident that with fairly balanced relations between our own industries this country may enjoy a good degree of prosperity." It said that although "the farmers as a class are below the workers of other industries in purchasing power," the new Intermediate Credit Banks provided the best hope for restoring them.[21] Coolidge even supported a new plan to lend $100 million in government money to farm cooperatives.[22] Other groups opposed to price parity redoubled their efforts. Members of an American Bankers Association committee "pledged ourselves, as American bankers," to assist farmers marketing their products, "the prices of which have been ruinously low for the past two years," but in this vein they trumpeted only more credit through their own banks and the Intermediate Credit Banks.[23]

After the Intermediate Credit Banks' failure to stanch the flow of troubles in the agricultural economy, Peek and Johnson's plan became the polestar of attempts to revive agriculture. The growing Agricultural Bloc in Congress tried to pass a version of the plan, known as the McNary-Haugen bill after its Senate and House sponsors, in 1924 and then again in 1926 but failed in the face of anti-class-legislation opposition. By early 1927, however, the *New York Times* noted that the "farm question has reached the footlight of the national stage—politically and economically. Farm relief is to be the leading question for Congress."[24] The Agricultural Bloc, along with what one magazine later called the "lash and whip of the farm lobby," pushed the bill over the top at the end of the lame-duck session of Congress that year, but the president stood in the way.[25] In his veto message, Coolidge conceded that "no one can deny that the prices of many farm products have been out of line with the general price level for several years." He promised to work to afford "agriculture a just and secure place in our economic scheme," but he could not endorse government price support.[26]

If Coolidge intended to run for president in 1928, he needed the farm vote, and such a veto did not help him. He thus had to do something that would relieve the misery of an increasingly vocal farmer class. Eugene Meyer, then head of the slowly liquidating War Finance Corporation, said that as "an alternative to the McNary Haugen bill, [Coolidge] was brought around to the farm credit system as his chosen instrument of relief, and to the need to strengthen that instrument while using it."[27] Yet the goal of improving the struggling farm loan system even while providing more relief for farmers would prove daunting.

The Savior of the Land Banks

Many Americans thought that if anyone could save the farm loan system, that person would be Eugene Meyer. After all, Meyer was one of the outstanding private and public actors of his generation. The first son of a successful German Jewish immigrant and financier, Meyer made his own fortune trading on the New York Stock Exchange. While at the exchange, he led a campaign to bring transparency to companies' public balance sheets and thus made stock investing something more than a blind gamble.[28] Yet Meyer always yearned for public service. At an early age, he had written himself a "map of life" that had him first earning a fortune and then entering public service at age forty. In 1917, one year ahead of schedule, he went to Washington to work at the War Industries Board as a "dollar-a-year" man with Bernard Baruch, who would godfather many of Meyer's successes.[29] With Baruch's help, Meyer was appointed to the new War Finance Corporation, which was continuously intertwined with the Federal Land Banks and became incorporated in them, in a fashion, as the Intermediate Credit Banks.

As a manager and officer in semipublic corporations, Meyer became a true believer in balance through finance. He argued in the *Banker Farmer* magazine in late 1922 that "the vibrations of distress in any of the important agricultural section are promptly felt in the manufacturing and industrial centers. When the buying power of the Middle Western farmer is diminished, it may mean the closing of shoe factories in New England or lumber mills in the South." Therefore, "agricultural is not a sectional or class interest. It is, in the broadest sense, a national interest. Adequate financing for the farmer and stockman . . . would go far toward stabilizing the whole business machinery of the country."[30] However, Meyer personally identified with the lenders rather than with the borrowers. He declared himself to be "a banker lending the public's money."[31]

At first glance, Meyer could seem unassuming, slight, and paunchy, but his staffers tended to worship him, with one celebrating his "extraordinary ability . . . his very generous attitude . . . his courtesy" and remembering a "sort of loyalty that I can't explain which grows up between the men who work under Meyer and Meyer himself."[32] Outsiders had a different reaction. One individual called him "one of the vainest people I've ever seen."[33] His wife, Agnes, a noted art scholar and an important Washington socialite, understood his pride and was grateful it could not go further. When someone proposed that Eugene could be president of the United States, Agnes noted in her diary, "I am profoundly thankful that E is a Jew for this will effectively protect him from the lure of that fata morgana."[34] Others kept the prospect alive.

After the forced resignation of farm loan commissioner R. A. Cooper in 1926, Treasury Secretary Andrew Mellon, another financier turned government nabob, came to ask Meyer to lead the board. Mellon explained the situation of the Land Banks, which Meyer remembered later as "an unrelieved tale of negligence, nepotism, and outright violations of the law." Meyer said that if the situation were as bad as Mellon intimated, he would need to fire at least two members of the four-member board, but Mellon refused to push out members of a supposedly independent agency.[35] In mid-1927, however, the Kansas City Joint-Stock Land Bank, which Farm Loan Board examiners had just declared healthy, fell into an ignominious bankruptcy. As Meyer said, with "this giant collapse momentarily silencing all voices to the contrary, I was given a recess appointment." At his request, the Coolidge administration, seemingly released from its scruples, forced three members off the board.[36]

4.1 Eugene Meyer.

Source: Federal Reserve History, http://www.federalreservehistory.org/People/DetailView/37.

Meyer assumed the helm of the Farm Loan Board with the understanding that if the land bank system were going to be of service to both bankers and farmers, it first had to protect itself. Meyer began his salvage efforts by transferring much of his successful War Finance Corporation over to the farm loan system. Floyd Harrison and George R. Cooksey, two other War Finance board members, became members of the Farm Loan Board. Meyer's chief secretary and general counsel Chester Morrill, who had worked briefly on drafting the original Federal Farm Loan Act and who had helped form the American Farm Bureau, also moved over from War Finance.[37] Morrill said their collective task was "to do a housecleaning job," and so they embarked on airing the Augean Stables with vigor. Morrill estimated that almost 80 percent of those employees directly under the board were "weeded out . . . as fast as we could."[38] In the field force, which Meyer described as a "howling wilderness" of incompetents and patronage seekers, they removed examiners, land appraisers, and other officers. Forced resignations went down to the level of file clerks, stenographers, and typists, whose seats were filled by loyal War Finance Corporation personnel, some of whom continued pulling checks from the corporation in addition to their checks from the Farm Loan Board.[39]

Besides his administrative reforms, Meyer endeared himself to the public and Congress by admitting the failures of the farm loan system for the first time. In his official appointment hearing in 1927, he told the congressional committee, "The system is new. Mistakes have been made."[40] (Former commissioner Cooper used a similar passive voice in a letter to the same committee, admitting that "mistakes were made" during the system's expansion.[41]) In response to Meyer's forthrightness and reforms, Congress increased the Farm Loan Board's appropriations and expanded its force of examiners and appraisers. In two years, the board's total expenses almost doubled. And Meyer pushed his expanded staff harder. In May 1928, the Wall Street Journal investigated the Old Land Office Building in Washington where the board was located and noted that although 4:30 p.m. was once the usual check-out time, now there was "an extraordinary amount of night work," and electric bulbs continued burning long past sundown.[42]

With Meyer's background, it was not surprising that he wanted to use this improved force to improve the market for Land Bank bonds. The board began printing detailed quarterly statements of the financial condition of all twelve Federal Land Banks, a process that "met with the approval of the banks, investment bankers, and others interested."[43] Meyer also increased the "spread" between the interest rate provided on bonds and the interest rate on loans to farmers to a full one percent, from three-quarters of one percent, which meant that although farmers had to pay higher interest, the Land Banks themselves would have more funds.[44] Such efforts bore fruit, and for the first (and only) time in their history the Land Banks made a public bond offering at 4 percent, acquiring the cheapest money yet for the system. Coolidge even mentioned this low rate as an administration success story in his State of the Union Address in December 1927.[45]

Not everyone was happy about Meyer's transformations, though. Senator Duncan Fletcher of Florida, who had long considered himself the keeper of the rural-credits flame, accused the new Farm Loan Board members of "representing New York financial interests" instead of farmers' interests.[46] The *Progressive Farmer* called the new appointments a "[k]idnapping" of the board, which "has now been turned over to Wall Street."[47] As one farm press editor told Meyer privately, "Their accusation is that you are trying to operate the Federal Farm Land Banks and the Federal Intermediate Credit Banks to create a good market for bonds instead of to actually help farmers." Meyer did not deny it.[48]

Hidden Problems

Within a year, the public believed that Meyer had completed the housecleaning job he set out to do and had secured financial stability for the Land Banks. Meyer understood privately, though, that his success rested on hiding damning facts about the banks. As he later said, he chose not to "parade in public all the weaknesses in the administration of the bureau and of the system" because airing all the damage would have been "very disadvantageous to the credit of the system." He asked that much of his congressional confirmation hearings for his appointment to the Farm Loan Board be conducted in private and that material that reflected poorly on the banks be removed from the record.[49]

The financial statements Meyer released to the glee of bond markets were more extensive than the old ones, but they also contained more evasions. The Farm Loan Board stopped "charging off" the total value of defaulted loans and of foreclosures from their assets. In a word, it pretended the defaults would not cost any money. In order to encourage more loans, the board told the Land Bank appraisers to be more generous. Meyer wrote that they should make their appraisals "intelligent and liberal" and told them the main danger was that they "undervalue farm lands."[50] This upbeat talk prevailed despite the board's own numbers showing that its appraisals were not stingy. Even with the very high 50 percent down payment required for a Federal Land Bank loan, the banks were losing on average more than 10 percent of the mortgage on each farm sold after foreclosure, and this number was rising.[51] The private reports Meyer received about individual Land Banks were more troubling than he let on in public. One examiner of the Federal Land Bank of Columbia, South Carolina, reported to Meyer in late October 1927, "I predict untold 'grief' for the institution."[52] In the next year's report on this bank, an examiner said, "All seem to recognize that the bank is in a bad condition," but none had any plans to right it.[53]

Another politically dangerous problem was also swept under the rug. Although former farm loan commissioner Charles Lobdell was comfortably ensconced at his $25,000 a year job as bond salesmen for the Land Banks, a confidential board report in mid-1928 found uncomfortable discrepancies in his financial statements. The report said Lobdell was engaged in "juggling prac-tices" and was "juggling bonds" between different accounts to avoid reporting losses. More incriminating, the report found that Lobdell took a $15,000 loan from one of the bond companies with which he was negotiating to support a Montana property scheme and that he asked for $50,000 from another bond house for the same lands (he told the latter he could double their money).[54] The report indicated that one of the paragons of the system, a Farm Loan Board member since its inception and a former commissioner, was corrupt. Lobdell resigned under duress, but publicly the board only said that the position of bond salesmen had been "discontinued."[55]

Meyer's obfuscations meant the public remained oblivious to these cascad-ing problems in the system. When Meyer retired from the Farm Loan Board in May 1929, there was near universal praise for his work, and his political star had risen higher than ever.[56] The new president, Herbert Hoover, for whom Meyer had campaigned, thanked him profusely for all the assistance he had given the country and its banks.[57]

Herbert Hoover and the New Price Parity

More so than any of his presidential predecessors, Herbert Hoover was a believer in the ideology of balance, and he embraced both its price and financial variet-ies. As early as 1920, Hoover worried about "a tendency to ill balance between the agricultural and general industry" and demanded a "careful balance of gen-eral industry to agriculture."[58] Hoover was a former mining engineer who became the food administrator under Woodrow Wilson during the war, from whence he learned the importance of agriculture to the nation's economy. Despite his alternatively frenetic and phlegmatic disposition, during his time as secretary of commerce in the 1920s he became one of the most respected poli-ticians and thinkers in the nation. He used his popularity to encourage agri-cultural reform and to promulgate the necessity of balance.

After his election to the presidency in 1928, Hoover organized the Commit-tee on Recent Economic Changes as a proto–think tank or transition team for his presidency. The committee was led by the Columbia University economist Wesley Clair Mitchell, who had once also worked at the War Industries Board with Bernard Baruch.[59] The committee's final report, issued in 1929, empha-sized above all the need for the government to ensure a balanced economy: "All parts of our economic structure from the prime processes of making and of marketing to the facilitating functions of finance, are and have been interde-pendent and easily affected" by each other. But, it continued, "therein lies the danger." The report warned that the interdependence of sectors meant that inequalities between them threatened everyone. If "any group develops a method of artificial price advancement which puts one commodity out of balance with other commodities . . . to this extent equilibrium will be destroyed, and destroyed for all."[60] The final section of the report was titled "Economic Balance" and said that to "maintain this balance" between different sectors, "great industries, such as agriculture," which had lagged, must be brought up to equality by the federal government.[61]

In fact, the earliest draft of the report was even clearer about the dangers of imbalance. It argued that "with each successive advance [in the economy], there has remained a farm problem somewhere in the rear." That "there exist unbalanced and unbalancing elements in the present situation of the United States," it noted, "is fairly obvious, and that therefore the accustomed unpleasant readjustment must close these prosperous years is to be expected." This final forewarning of disaster is thickly crossed out in pencil, with a heavy X mark placed next to it, most likely by Hoover himself, and did not appear in the published version.[62] Yet the message of the economic report stuck with Hoover. He later stated in his memoirs that at the beginning of his presidency "agriculture had been out of balance with the rest of the economic system for some years." He was determined to right it.[63]

Others in Hoover's administration echoed these themes. Hoover's undersecretary of the Treasury, Ogden Mills, eventually to replace Andrew Mellon as secretary, argued that "even during recent years of high prosperity, agriculture failed to advance to the high level attained by other industries. Well-balanced national economy requires the placing of agriculture on an equality with other industries."[64] He explained how imbalanced sectors were a general economic threat: "a reduction in purchasing power [in one sector] immediately affects the market for goods produced by other groups. A nicely adjusted balance is disturbed." He said the government needed to right this balance to prevent collapse.[65]

As the concerns of Hoover's economists and advisers suggested, farm balance would be his almost singular focus in his early presidency. His first significant action as president was to summon a special session of Congress to pass new farm-price legislation. In place of the McNary-Haugen plan, which raised prices by funding exports, Hoover proposed a new type of federal lending to bolster prices. His Federal Farm Board (Meyer unsuccessfully complained about the similarity of the name to the Federal Farm Loan Board) would be given $500 million of federal funds, which it could loan to farmers' marketing cooperatives so that they could hold crops off the market until better prices resulted or arrived. The plan thus used federal credit to balance prices, happily uniting the two ideologies, at little immediate cost to the taxpayer.[66]

The agricultural lobbies gave their full-throated support to Hoover's cooperative plan, partially because they had a direct interest in it. Since the early 1920s, these lobbies, including the National Grange, the Farmers Union, and the American Farm Bureau Federation, had begun funding and managing a host of cooperatives, including cooperative grain elevators, cooperative insurance funds, cooperative coal-purchasing groups, and cooperative fruit-, wool-, cotton-, and tobacco-marketing groups. The Grange and the Farm Bureau had already helped pass an act in 1922 shielding such farm cooperatives from antitrust laws as well as an act creating the Division of Cooperative Marketing in the Department of Agriculture. They had for years been asking for direct government loans to such cooperatives.[67] Hoover's proposed federal credit supported not only the lobbies' constituents but also the lobbies, which became, in effect, eager business enterprises.[68]

Hoover also enlisted financial interests behind the bill. To guide his Federal Farm Board bill through Congress, he tapped a banker from Newark, New Jersey, Congressmen Franklin Fort, who had a long history of rural-credit advocacy. (Fort's father had been the head of President Taft's committee on rural credits in 1912.)[69] In Hoover's first speech on the newly passed Agricultural Marketing Act of 1929, he lamented the "heavy indebtedness . . . inherited by the industry from the deflation processes of the 1920s." Higher crop prices would help pay back that debt.[70] The chair of the new Federal Farm Board embodied the interests of economic balance. Alexander Legge was recently chairman and president of the International Harvester Company. Like Peek and Johnson's work at Moline Plow Company, his work was a perfect example of the interconnection of farm and industry. Legge had also worked, like Peek, Johnson, Meyer, Mitchell, and so many others in this movement, with Bernard Baruch as vice chairman of the War Industries Board.[71]

Not long after the Federal Farm Board's creation, it had to confront the stock market crash and a rapid deflation of all prices, especially crop prices. As Henry A. Wallace had pointed out, crop prices tended to be the first to rise or fall. The program was thus born into the swirl of the Great Depression, and its early loans to cooperatives defaulted as prices for their products continued dropping.

Yet one of the Farm Board's foremost concerns was that the collapse in prices would endanger rural banks, and it moved to protect them. In November 1930, a day after dozens of rural banks shut their doors, the Farm Board began its most expansive loans to date, in this case to wheat cooperatives. Legge later said that "the day this action was announced was 'black Monday' for rural banking," and without Farm Board help for wheat "similar disaster threatened many grain-growing sections."[72] Another member of the Farm Board said support "was necessary because of the 'frozen' condition of many country banks."[73] The board's annual report for 1931 said helping farmers "was only one reason for stabilization." Another reason was that "lenders of every sort had made advances on grain. . . . Banking and mercantile credit throughout the Wheat Belt was conditioned to a considerable extent on wheat prices."[74] Franklin Fort, the banker behind the Agricultural Marketing Act, argued that although the Federal Farm Board did not save farmers or prevent a wider collapse in farm prices, it stopped a "complete disruption of the nation's banking and business structure." The board's wheat actions were "necessary to stabilize wheat prices or banks would have been forced to close." He said a similar lending program for the cotton industry had "prevented many bank failures" in the South.[75]

The Federal Farm Board became ever more involved in supporting bankers. It made a special deal with southern bankers, with the assistance of Bernard Baruch, to keep cotton off the market and thus protect cotton's price, which the bankers hoped would protect their loans to cotton farmers.[76] The new chair of the Farm Board even attended the conference of the Mortgage Bankers Association to ask how he could help them.[77] The board eventually gave up trying to stabilize crop prices, which continued dropping, and argued that the country should focus instead on readjusting the nation's farm debts. With corn prices down from 51 to 32 cents a bushel, and with wheat down from 92 to 38 cents a bushel, there seemed little else the board could do.[78] In the Federal Farm Board's final annual report for 1932, after it noted the hundreds of millions dollars lost in defaulted loans, it argued that "at the present level of prices, fixed-charge burdens—notably tax and mortgage debt payments—have become excessive. Some equitable means of readjustment of these burdens must be worked out."[79] Hoover, like Coolidge, was forced back to the power of the Federal Land Banks and their mortgages as the best hope for solving the combined problems of farmers and bankers.

The Nation's First Bailout

Herbert Hoover had had a strained history with farm mortgages. In his memoirs, he recalled that the "mortgage upon Uncle Allan's farm," where he had lived after being orphaned, was "a constant source of anxiety and a dreadful damper on youthful hopes." In one campaign speech, he remarked that because of his impoverished childhood "the word 'mortgage' became for me a dreaded and haunting fear from that day to this."[80] Despite this fear, he had worked during his teenage years as a clerk in his uncle's Oregon Land Company. When he later worked in the Department of Commerce, he researched new ways to provide cheap mortgages.[81] Hoover recognized the Federal Land Banks as both a means to ease this mortgage burden and a perfect example of his peculiar brand of government-led associationalism because of the supposed the cooperative groups at their base.[82]

Yet after the stock market crash and a Supreme Court decision threatening Joint-Stock Land Bank special protections in bankruptcy, Hoover argued that credit of the joint-stock system had to be protected first. He proposed a bill that would force Joint-Stock Land Bank stockholders to provide extra funds to those banks in case of failure. Many in Congress blanched at dunning the banks' investors.[83] Representative Henry T. Rainey of Illinois, an up-and-coming firebrand in the House who would become Speaker in the first Congress of the New Deal, painted his rural constituents not as borrowers of the joint-stock system but as investors in it. He claimed he had "a great many farmers in my district who have invested in the stocks as well of the bonds of these banks that are now in receivership, and I have been hearing from them" about the danger of new payments. What Rainey did not mention was that he was a stockholder in the Joint-Stock Land Bank started by former congressman and former Federal Farm Loan Board member Frank Lever and that this bank, too, was in danger. Other congressmen were more explicit about their connections. Representative Roy Fitzgerald of Ohio testified that he was "intensely interested" in the bill because "I face financial ruin in this situation." He had bought $35,000 of Kansas City Joint-Stock Land Bank stock, which amount he would have to pay again to support the bank if Hoover's bill passed. He described himself as a "victim of this law," and his lugubrious complaint received sympathetic responses from an assembled House Banking and Currency Committee.[84] Congress thus shouted down Hoover's attempt to ask for more support from investors.

Hoover appointed H. Paul Bestor as the new chair of the Federal Farm Loan Board and gave him the task of again saving the whole land bank system. Bestor, like Hoover, had been born into a poor farm in Iowa, and he, too, remembered the "terrible years" when it was "impossible for us to pay the mortgage on our farm."[85] Although in May 1930 he proposed accounting rules that obscured the extent of the losses in the system, he knew such legerdemain was not sustainable.[86] On the same day he released his new rules, Bestor met with the president in the White House. He expressed concern about a pending visit by the leaders of several farm lobby groups, including the National Grange, which was headed by Louis Taber, who happened to be president of his own Joint-Stock Land Bank.[87] Bestor worried these groups would lobby for even more obfuscation and even more extensions of the Federal Land Banks loans. He thought this was the last thing the government should do. They had to face facts and recognize that all the banks were near failure and needed direct federal support to survive.[88] Hoover was not yet ready for such a move, but over the next year he met with Bestor at least eight more times in the White House.[89] Hoover requested and received weekly accounting statements from Federal Land Banks detailing their financial situation and the growing number of delinquent loans, but he kept these numbers from the public.[90]

Investors realized, however, that the government was not telling the whole truth about the land banks, and the land banks' bonds continued dropping in value. The bonds' decline was in turn hurting the balance sheets of already troubled commercial and investment banks, which had invested in the bonds. One contemporary scholar, Raymond Goldsmith, noted that "the depression in bond values . . . reached foreign bonds and land bank bonds in the course of 1931, [and] began to endanger the whole banking structure."[91] A later Federal Reserve study of failed national banks in 1931 showed that Federal Land Bank and Joint-Stock Land Bank bonds were prominent on the list of fifty bond issues "contributing the greatest depreciation to the portfolios" of the banks and caused the banks to lose more money than almost any other investment they made.[92] The ongoing collapse of the two farm loan systems was thus an important additional cause of the collapse of the banking system as a whole, which the farm loan systems had once hoped to sustain.

In September 1931, Bestor wrote a stilted and pained nine-page letter to the president explaining why the government needed to bail out the Land Banks. He said that 17 percent of all Federal Land Bank mortgages were delinquent. In the Spokane Land Bank, 26.1 percent were delinquent, in the Columbia Land Bank 35.9 percent. When farms were finally foreclosed, they were "usually in a run-down condition" and impossible to sell. Bestor said they should ask Congress for up to $100 million to buy stock in the banks, which would rejuvenate "confidence in the bonds of the Federal Land Bank system" without having to officially "guarantee their payment."[93]

Bestor's plan proposed the first explicit bailout of a financial institution by the federal government. Instead of merely lending money or temporarily buying bonds, the government would become a part owner of the new system in order to prevent its collapse. The necessity of the plan became apparent four days after his letter, when Britain's departure from the gold standard caused a global meltdown in financial markets. Few have since noted that Hoover's announcement of a private credit pool to support the banking system coincided with his request to Congress on October 7 to pass Bestor's land bank bill.[94] The day after Hoover's announcement, the farm loan bonds shot up in price three to five points, and the *New York Times* reported the bonds' "strongest advance . . . seen in many weeks." The National Grange, with its Land Bank connections, celebrated Hoover's "splendid and far-reaching move" to protect them.[95]

In the public hearings on the bailout bill, Bestor denied that the banks were truly in danger of collapse. He claimed the money was only temporarily necessary to "restore confidence in the market."[96] Congress, unaware of the extent of the problems and believing that it was providing only temporary support to a solvent institution, passed a bill that provided $100 million in new capital, with an extra $25 million given to help farmers facing foreclosure. The *New York Times* trumpeted, "New Capital Lifts Land Banks' Bonds."[97]

The government threw other supports around both the Federal Land Banks and the Joint-Stock Land Banks. The Reconstruction Finance Corporation (RFC), a new public financial corporation created by an act passed the day before the Land Bank bailout, also came to the Land Banks' aid. The head of the new corporation was former farm loan commissioner Eugene Meyer, and, according to law, one member of its board needed to be the current farm loan commissioner, now Paul Bestor. Two of the five other directors of the corporation also had connections to the system. One was Judge Wilson McCarthy, whose first recommendation from a senator cited his Joint-Stock Land Bank experience and who was not surprisingly endorsed by Senators Joseph Robinson, Duncan Fletcher, and others involved in that system.[98] The other director was Harvey Couch, an Arkansas Utility executive who also happened to be a director at Senator Robinson's Joint-Stock Land Bank.[99]

Prominent politicians demanded the RFC provide government largesse to the Federal Land Banks. Everett Sanders, head of the Republican National Committee, and Angus McLean, former North Carolina governor and friend of Meyer's at the War Finance Corporation—incredibly, both of them presidents of their own Joint-Stock Land Banks—demanded more federal aid. As Sanders wrote to the White House on his Republican National Committee letterhead, it would "be very unfortunate indeed if we should begin to have some joint stock land bank failures" so soon before the election, which might cost Hoover some farm states.[100] In October 1931, Sanders even published his own pamphlet titled *The Government's Obligation to the Joint Stock Land Banks*, arguing that Congress had the moral responsibility to remedy the all-too-apparent defects in the system. He said the " 'good faith and credit of the sovereign' requires that it come to the aid of [both] the joint stock and Federal land banks, which from their inception have been nothing but Federal instrumentalities."[101]

The RFC allocated millions to both the Federal Land Banks and the Joint-Stock Land Banks.[102] With the help of Philadelphia's Federal Reserve Bank president and former Farm Loan commissioner George Norris, the Federal Reserve system, now under the Federal Reserve Board's new chair, Eugene Meyer, bought or loaned on millions more in Federal Land Bank bonds, despite the fact that they were not the usual government bonds eligible for purchase by the Fed. The purchases provided investors with more evidence of the bonds' official backing.[103] Farmers working to protect their land from foreclosure, however, hardly noticed the effort.

Foreclosed

In the early 1930s, the farm-foreclosure crisis, which had attracted sporadic attention in the 1920s, emerged as a national scandal, becoming for many Americans the defining feature of the Great Depression. Farm foreclosures, which had been a mere 3 per 1,000 farms in the 1910s, increased to 16 per 1,000 by the end of 1920s and then reached almost 28 per 1,000 in 1932, with some states reaching almost 50.[104] As one farmer remembered, "If you incur a debt, when, say, corn is 80 cents a bushel, and you try to pay for it when it is 2 cents a bushel, it doesn't make any difference how hard you work, you can't do it."[105] When the farmers couldn't meet the old payments, the mortgage lender usually foreclosed, and the sheriff came to the farm to conduct an auction on its front steps. As one child of the time remembered, people in the early days of the Depression would come to watch the foreclosure sales "partly out of morbid fascination." These auctions would sell everything a family owned, down to their treasured family photos, for as little as a nickel or dime.[106] As the Depression wore on, though, the witnesses became more rebellious. One foreclosing judge, working not too far down the road from Hoover's childhood home in Iowa, was driven out of town with a rope around his neck, and a bystander remembered that they almost "were gonna string him up in old horse thief fashion." Other judges were threatened or had their courtrooms disrupted by groups of angry farmers desperate to prevent foreclosure sales.[107]

In early 1932, the soon-to-be infamous Farmers Holiday Association organized at a grand meeting in Des Moines, Iowa, as a radical offshoot of the Farmers Union, and farm foreclosures were squarely in its sites. The group was led by the firebrand Milo Reno, a rangy former Populist remembered by one congressman as "a rabble-rouser de luxe!"[108] Although many today emphasize the association's desire for farm-price increases, the first of Reno's four-point demands was for state-mandated moratoriums or "holidays" on all mortgage payments.[109] The holiday movement began participating in the fight against foreclosures on the ground, through "direct action," including using "ropes under their coats" and threatening violence against foreclosing creditors and judges. A historian of the holiday movement later noted that "farmer protest [took] its most militant form in the drive to resist mortgage foreclosures."[110]

Many politicians supported the burgeoning antiforeclosure rebellion. On the floor of the House of Representatives, Fiorello La Guardia said, "The farmers of Iowa who resisted to protect their homes will take their place in history with the Boston Tea party [sic]." He said the farmers had been pushed against the wall and were near revolution, and so "the interest rate will have to be brought down to 3 per cent to save the republic."[111] In this period, mere points of interest on mortgages attained an existential importance. Senator Henrik Shipstead, too, said the attacks on farm foreclosures were equivalent to the beginning of the American Revolutionary War and its "shot heard round the world."[112] When midwestern governors held a conference on farm mortgage relief in Des Moines in the summer of 1932, some governors, such as Floyd Olson of Minnesota, expressed sympathy for Milo Reno's radical plan for a mortgage moratoriums.[113] The governor of North Dakota, William Langer, even ordered out the state militia to *prevent* sheriffs from conducting foreclosure auctions. He told people to "shoot the banker if he comes to your farm. Treat him like a chicken thief."[114]

Federal Land Bank foreclosures attracted particular political condemnation. Milo Reno said, albeit with little evidence, that in Iowa "the Federal Land Bank is the most hard-boiled of the farmers' creditors" and "leads all private institutions in demanding its pounds of flesh."[115] One Farmers Holiday Association member who faced a Land Bank foreclosure said the "Federal Land Banks at the time were worse than the insurance companies."[116] The press also began attacking the farm loan foreclosures, supposedly the one type of foreclosure directly under government control. The national investigative magazine *Collier's* published a devastating critique of the Land Bank foreclosures complete with a cartoon of a massive pig labeled "Federal Land Banks" uprooting a family home.[117]

Besides the financial collapse of the farm loan system, Hoover thus had to contend with wave of foreclosures and growing resistance to them, especially those at his beloved semipublic banks. Hoover's colleagues reminded him of the political value of action against the banks. A letter from an Iowa member of the RFC told Hoover that "nothing would be so helpful politically in Iowa at

4.2 Cartoon attacking the Federal Land Banks, 1932. The caption reads "Quasi-governmental financing has perverted 'farm-relief' into a thing of disaster."

Source: Owen P. White, "Helping the Farmer Out," *Collier's*, October 8, 1932.

this time as a 'softening of the arteries' on the part of some of these institutions which are supposed to be relieving the farmer" but "whose only activity at the present time seems to be confined to foreclosing of mortgages."[118] Iowa's governor wrote Hoover that stopping Federal Land Bank foreclosures would "swing the farm states into line" in the coming election.[119] Whereas Hoover had at one time made a chilly response pleading constitutional inability to those who asked for leniency from the land bank system, in late October 1931 he convinced Bestor to send a letter to all the Land Banks counseling ease.[120]

When Hoover decided a year later to make his major presidential campaign speech on farm policy in Des Moines, the navel of the farm rebellion, he had to confront the foreclosure crisis. Right before the speech, he summoned a conference of private mortgage lenders to Chicago and elicited a promise to stop "needless foreclosures" on farms. Hoover then forced the Federal Land Banks to publicly pledge ease on collections and foreclosures. He likewise received a promise "that the whole power of the Reconstruction Finance Corporation is to be thrown back of the agencies who lend money and receive farm mortgages."[121] Nonetheless, on his train ride to Des Moines, Hoover looked from his presidential rail car to see crowds of angry Farmers Holiday Association protestors lining the route.[122]

At the teeming Iowa Coliseum in Des Moines on October 4, 1932, surrounded by chaos and protests, Hoover explained how glad he was, "as a son of the soil of this State, to come back to where I was born." He also reminisced about the hard times he had endured as a child, where there was so little joy because he was told "everything must be saved for the mortgage." He told them "the mortgage situation—that is, long-term credits—is one of our most difficult problems." He could only promise, however, to ask the next session of Congress, after the election, to refinance some of the farmers' Federal Land Bank mortgages.[123]

Hoover's opponent in the campaign, New York governor Franklin Delano Roosevelt, expounded endlessly on the horrors of these foreclosures. Roosevelt said that under Hoover "practically nothing was done toward removing the destructive menace of debt from farm homes." He claimed that Hoover did not care about ending foreclosures, only about protecting the banks that made the mortgages. To Roosevelt's "sneers," as Hoover called them, that he was only protecting banks, he responded that Roosevelt "knows full well that the only purpose in helping a bank is to protect the depositor and the borrower. He knows full well that the only purpose of helping a farm-mortgage company is to enable the farmer to hold his farm."[124] Despite Hoover's own efforts to stop foreclosures, his appeal to trickle-down assistance did not appeal to the public.

In the period between Roosevelt's landslide election and his inauguration, farmers' battles against foreclosures reached their peak. In December 1932, a national conference of all major farm lobbies proposed as their first demand

4.3 Protestors at farm foreclosure auction in Iowa in the early 1930s.

Source: Library of Congress.

a national mortgage moratorium and a refinancing of all existing mortgages through the Federal Land Banks. On the ground, angry farmers now crowded foreclosure sales and threatened to assault anyone who bid more than a penny, forcing the mortgagors to relinquish their claims. The Farmers Holiday Association blocked courthouse steps so attorneys could not submit their foreclosure papers. It shunted mortgage holders to barnyard judges or "Councils of Defense" consisting of Holiday members, who decided what they thought the mortgagee owed.[125] One lender was de-pantsed and had his tires slashed before being driven out of the area. A Kansas City realtor was found murdered just after he foreclosed on a property.[126] At the same time, "Pretty Boy" Floyd was becoming a folk hero not just by robbing banks but by burning mortgage documents in them. It seemed as if all of Hoover's efforts had been for naught, as the nation's farmland spiraled ever closer to anarchy.

Hoover and his allies had wanted to balance agriculture with industry, using both price and credit support, which they hoped would restore the overall economy and end farmers' suffering. Yet the continuing deflation in the Great Depression and the resulting foreclosure and banking crises made such efforts

4.4 National Guard troops called to protect a judge in Iowa during a foreclosure, c. 1933.

Source: *New York Times*, https://lens.blogs.nytimes.com/2009/05/18/from-the-archive-how-we-used
-to-deal-with-foreclosures-in-this-country-1933/.

seem irrelevant. Federal credit once provided as a gift now seemed a burden.
The price-and-credit collapse led Hoover and Congress to bail out the Federal
Land Banks and extend ever more guarantees and support to financiers, all to
little success. Yet from early in his administration Hoover had worried that economic imbalances had spread far beyond the farms. From his second year in
office, he had begun using similar ideas and similar methods to rescue the rest
of the economy.

CHAPTER 5

HERBERT HOOVER AND THE URBAN-MORTGAGE CRISIS IN THE GREAT DEPRESSION

I n March 1930, President Herbert Hoover pondered how to steer the nation out of the economic doldrums that already threatened his presidency. He had been considering one route of escape with some of his advisers, and finally he wrote to the chairman of the Federal Reserve Board with a plan. Hoover thought that something had to be done to secure full employment: "It seems to me that the one direction which is always economically and socially sound is in home building, in which there is a large consumption of labor directly and indirectly through both producers' and consumers' goods." The problem, as Hoover saw it, was that the "conditions by which home building is financed today are the most backward segment of our whole credit system" because it was difficult to invest money in "isolated and small sized mortgages."[1]

Hoover's concerns about home-building and mortgage finance were noteworthy, but so was the institution to which he addressed them. Thus far in its history, the Federal Reserve had had little to do with long-term debts such as mortgages. From its inception, it had hewed to the belief that it should "discount" (or loan money on) only short-term debts backed by goods that could be easily sold. Hoover asked, however, if the Federal Reserve Banks would discount longer-term mortgages for home building. This was a radical move, but he went further. Hoover described the benefits of the semipublic Federal Land Bank system for agriculture and wondered if the Federal Reserve could encourage a similar system for urban mortgages.[2] After the Federal Reserve Board refused to pursue Hoover's suggestions, he replaced two of its members with more sympathetic individuals, including one who would be his economic consiglieri for the remainder of his time in office, the former Federal Land Bank chief Eugene Meyer. With these commands and actions, Hoover opened a new front against the Depression, one that he would push for the remainder of his presidency. He hoped to bring the Federal Land Bank mortgage plan into the urban sphere and thus halt the greatest economic and financial collapse in American history.

When Hoover identified home building as the single best path for economic recovery, and when he identified cheap mortgages as the best way to bolster building, he was drawing on changes in economic thought that had emerged over the previous decade, some of which he had encouraged. The problem, as Hoover and others saw it, was similar to that which had once bedeviled farm mortgage borrowers. Commercial banks, where most of the nation's wealth was located, tended to invest in only short-term loans on goods, known as real bills, which could always be quickly sold, and they thus avoided long-term mortgages.[3] This problem had supposedly been ameliorated for farmers through the Federal Land Banks, but there was no equivalent system for urban mortgagors.

At this time, many economists also came to believe that home building and attached "heavy industries" (also known, confusingly, as "producer goods," "durable goods," or "fixed-capital goods" industries), were particularly sensitive to financing costs. They thought a weakness or imbalance in home construction relative to the rest of the economy was an essential factor causing the ups and downs of the business cycle. Rather than provide a continual hand up to a struggling sector that had been left behind, as many advocated in theories of urban–rural balance, these economists thought that the government had to provide targeted financial support to construction in the midst of economic downturns and withdraw that support later when the economy recovered, thus keeping the economy on what they called a balanced path.

This chapter reveals that, to an extent unrecognized by previous historians, most of Hoover's major economic reforms during the Depression were devoted to providing new government guarantees and support to home mortgage finance. Although in the first year of his presidency Hoover had attempted to support farmers, and although he would later use federal farm mortgages as a means of relief, for most of his presidency it was the urban mortgage that attracted his attention. With this motivation, Hoover first pressed the Federal Reserve to loosen monetary policy to spur more mortgage loans. He later succeeded in opening the Federal Reserve to lend on mortgages and other long-term debts directly. Hoover and his new Reserve Board governor, Eugene Meyer, also pushed Congress to create the Reconstruction Finance Corporation to purchase failing or "frozen" mortgage debts. Finally, Hoover secured the creation of the nation's second semipublic mortgage institution, the Federal Home Loan Banks, which were based on the Federal Land Banks and would support the small urban mortgages made by banks and "building and loans " (B&Ls). Although Hoover failed spectacularly in his attempt to save the economy, the American financial system was completely transformed in the attempt. Now almost every financial asset had a potential public home in the Federal Reserve, the Federal Land Banks, the Federal Home Loan Banks, or the RFC. By the end of Hoover's presidency, the government had become an almost universal guarantor of investors and of the financial sector.

In the vast literature on the Great Depression, the collapse of the banking sector and the inadequate response by the federal government to this collapse have long retained pride of place.[4] Though many writers have discussed the misunderstandings and policy mistakes behind these failures, none of them has analyzed how contemporaries, including President Hoover, understood the banking collapse as a result of bad mortgages and failures in related sectors such as home construction.[5] This chapter shows how Hoover and his administration perceived urban-mortgage failures as the most pressing problem of the Great Depression and how they hoped to use new financial guarantees to revive and balance certain moribund sectors of the economy, whose collapse threatened both the banking system and the nation.

Home Loans in the Early Twentieth Century

Expensive farm mortgages had long excited grievances, but expensive urban mortgages began to spark similar complaints and outrage at the turn of the twentieth century. One urban mortgage broker admitted that the common conception of the "mortgage holder was of a man with black mustache and beetling brow, who turned out the poor widow and her sick child into a wintry world."[6] For many, Upton Sinclair's novel *The Jungle* (1906) cemented this stereotype. The novel cast its jaundiced eye not only on the meatpacking industry but also on the woeful state of home financing. The book describes how rapacious lenders deceive Lithuanian immigrant Jurgis Rudkus and his family into purchasing slum housing near the Chicago stockyards at a high interest rate. The family admit that they heard "cruel stories of people who had been done to death in this 'buying a home' swindle," but they thought they were different. After years of making oppressive payments, Jurgis returns home one day to find his family has been thrown out by their lender: "Why, they had put their very souls into their payments on that house, they had paid for it with their sweat and tears—yes, more, with their very lifeblood." It is a climactic moment of disillusionment for Jurgis, after which he nearly loses his mind. "Ah, God, the horror of it, the monstrous, hideous, demonical wickedness of it! . . . That first lying circular, that smooth-tongued slippery agent! That trap of the extra payments, the interest, and all the other charges that they had not the means to pay."[7]

Horror stories such as the Rudkuses' meant most urban families did not bother buying homes at all. In 1900, less than 40 percent of urban families owned their own home, and in large cities such as Chicago that portion was less than 30 percent. Those who bought often avoided the heartaches of loans by paying for most of the house out of pocket, so only one-third of homes were encumbered by any debts at all.[8] Many of those remaining debts, like the Rudkuses', were not actually mortgages but "land contracts," which allowed lenders to avoid the legal baggage of mortgages and move for speedy foreclosures outside of courts.[9]

The reason most home loans were either onerous or impossible to obtain in this era was that few institutions granted them. Just as with farm mortgages in the early twentieth century, it was illegal for most commercial banks to make home loans, so most mortgage money came from local, wealthy individuals, who loaned on only the first 50 percent of a home's value. The rest had to be funded by even higher-interest second mortgages. Both first and second mortgages had to be renewed, along with pricey new brokers' commissions, or paid off in a large "balloon payment" after five years. But just as farmers organized in cooperatives to fund their own cheaper mortgages, so did urban workers. The working class organized groups known as mutual banks, savings banks, or B&L associations, all of whose main assets were small home loans. These cooperative groups furnished about a third of all mortgages, and reformers identified them as the enlightened alternative to the local mortgage lender. And just as in farm cooperative banks, their loans were more generous. They lasted up to twenty years, with "amortizing" payments gradually paying off the principal, and were for up to 80 percent of the value of the home. All these sources of mortgage funds, however, were dependent on local money and were only rarely supplemented by mortgage loans from national insurance companies or other financial groups. Thus, despite expanding income and more Americans moving to cities, the national homeownership rate dropped from the 1890s through the 1910s.[10]

Urban mortgages became a political issue at the same time agricultural debt began to attract the federal government's special solicitude. Despite vociferous complaints about government discrimination against agriculture during the original debate on the Federal Farm Loan Act in 1916, that act's proponents conceded that their plan excluded urban borrowers. Not a few urban representatives brought up this point in the debate. Representative William Howard of Atlanta said that if the government were going to assist farm mortgagors, "by what process of reasoning can you deprive the industrial toiler from bringing up his security, his little house and lot he owns in the city, and getting his money"?[11] Although Congress did not allow Federal Land Banks to make urban mortgages, that year it did finally allow national banks to make loans on urban homes, though with the constraint of holding the loans for only one year.[12] Although this measure was barely a toe in the door, for the first time since its creation America's national banking system would include home financing. It was a momentous step and tied the country's banking industry into urban real estate's speculations and fluctuations.

During World War I, however, the government rationed credit as it rationed other goods. Urban-mortgage credit was hit hardest of all, leading to stalled construction, overcrowding, government rent controls, and antirent and anti-eviction riots.[13] The demands for mortgage reform crescendoed. After the war, the burgeoning United States Building and Loan League, the national organization for cooperative B&L associations, got Woodrow Wilson to draft and introduce an urban-mortgage plan in Congress. As one housing organization said, the plan was "modeled somewhat upon the Federal Farm Loan Act."[14] At the Democratic National Convention in 1920, the vice presidential nominee Franklin Delano Roosevelt asked for a plank in the Democratic platform that would call for the "energetic and intensive development of the Farm Loan policy and the extension of the same principle to urban home builders." In the face of postwar retrenchment, though, these bills and plans went nowhere.[15]

Hoover Adopts a Cause

When Herbert Hoover accepted the position of commerce secretary in President Warren Harding's cabinet in early 1921, he knew what he wanted to focus on. "When I came to the Department," he later remembered, the economy was still in shambles after the war. "I was convinced that a great contribution to reconstruction and a large expansion in employment could be achieved by supplying the greatest social need of the country—more and better housing."[16] Hoover requested and received appropriations for the creation of a special Housing Division underneath him. He placed John M. Gries, a Harvard economist who appropriately held the "Chair of Lumber" there, as its new head.[17] Hoover explained to the public that "construction is the balance wheel of American industry" because "if building falls off, there is bound to be a slackening in many other lines of industry, resulting in unemployment, decreased purchasing power of employees, and further depression. The ebb and flow in the demand for construction . . . thus to a large degree affects our economic stability."[18] Hoover's postwar Conference on Unemployment, filled with sympathetic economists, made the same argument. Its final report said that the "greatest area for immediate relief of unemployment is in the construction industry, which has been artificially restricted during and since the war. We are short more than a million homes."[19]

Just as farmers fretted about the low prices of the crops they sold after the war, Hoover worried about the price of construction. Yet his concern, and that of other economists, was about the excessively *high* prices of the goods and labor that went into construction. His Conference on Unemployment said that whereas "agriculture has reached an unduly low plane . . . some branches of the construction industries are of the highest. If the buying power of the different elements of the community is to be restored, then these levels must reach nearer a relative plane."[20] In this vein, Hoover helped create the American Construction Council to standardize building and lower costs. The man chosen to head it was one of Hoover's erstwhile participants in Woodrow Wilson's war administration, with whom Hoover had a pleasant history, Franklin Delano Roosevelt.[21] At the council's inauguration in 1922, Roosevelt, soon after being stricken with polio, wrote to Hoover thanking him for presiding in his absence and for continuing research on housing and building cycles.[22]

Mortgage issues, however, loomed largest in Hoover's mind.[23] Although Hoover argued that most construction problems were local, he told one senator, "There is one problem that has [a] distinctly national character . . . that is, the mobilization of finance for home building. We have mobilized the commercial capital of the country through the Federal Reserve Banks. We have mobilized the farm mortgage capital through the Farm Loan Bureau. . . . The country badly needs a mobilization of the home building capital based upon building and loan associations, insurance companies, and savings banks."[24] Hoover got into the weeds on mortgage issues, writing about individual company mortgage plans, second-mortgage interest rates, and specific amortization schedules.[25] As early as 1921, he told Senator William Calder, who had sponsored Wilson's earlier B&L plan in Congress and who was, not coincidentally, a prominent home builder: "My own thought is that we could build upon the foundation of such [B&L] associations together with other types of mutual or limited profit institutions by organizing some method of central mobilizations of their resources," a sort of separate Federal Land Bank system for home mortgages.[26]

Other groups with ties to Hoover and to the old Federal Land Banks took up urban-mortgage reform. The Brookings Institution, run by the economist Harold Moulton, who worked on Hoover's economics committees, created its own committee to analyze urban real estate financing. Its chairman was Charles Lobdell, the former chief of the Federal Farm Loan Board who had been fired for graft and manipulations of accounts. Lobdell's committee argued that the country's "experience with farm mortgages seems to indicate that in the absence of a considerable degree of organization, real estate mortgages" could not be offered cheaply. His report argued that "what is needed is some institution or institutions with abundant resources, high credit, strong business connections," such as the Land Banks, to market new urban-mortgage bonds to the public.[27]

Hoover failed to secure much more than hortatory support for mortgage reform, but home building did surge after the war. From barely 150,000 units constructed in 1918, the housing industry would build more than one million homes in each of the peak years of 1925 and 1926. The infamous Florida land boom (and later bust) in this same period inspired the Marx brothers' film *The Coconauts* (1929), in which Groucho Marx's character tells potential homebuyers: "You can have any kind of a home you want to; you can even get stucco! Oh, how you can get stuck-oh!"[28]

Home financing also boomed after the war. Mortgages went from 1.7 percent of all commercial bank assets in 1920 to 5.4 percent in 1926. Real estate increased faster than any other type of banking asset in those years.[29] Meanwhile, B&L associations almost quadrupled their assets over the decade, becoming substantial banking organizations in their own right as opposed to mere local cooperatives. Even while expanding their focus on mortgage lending, they began offering more short-term deposits and resembling their banking competitors.[30] There was also an explosion in what one investor called a "peculiarly happy and comparatively modern development": real estate bonds backed by mortgages, usually on large buildings, pitched to investors across the country.[31] Whereas real estate bond issues totaled less than $100 million a year immediately after the war, by 1925 they had soared past a billion dollars per year and soon constituted almost 15 percent of all mortgage debt.[32] The Investment Bankers Association of America created a Real Estate Securities Committee and hyped the virtues of the new mortgage-backed bonds to small investors, especially women and mothers seeking safe savings.[33] These changes in the financial system meant that for the first time in history American mortgages owned or supported by financial institutions outnumbered those held directly by individuals. Hoover managed in press releases and his memoirs to take some credit for this expansion in home building and financing.[34]

In 1926, though, there was a housing crash and a brief recession, which some blamed on the previous housing boom. The government's first response to this collapse was not to restrict banks' access to mortgages but to expand that access again with the hopes of spurring home building. In 1927, bankers pushed for the passage of the McFadden Act, authored by Pennsylvania representative and bank president Louis McFadden, which allowed banks to invest in urban mortgages for up to five years and as a larger percentage of their assets than they were previously allowed.[35] It also gave national banks the right to openly invest in securities subsidiaries, which politicians hoped could market the new mortgage bonds.[36] There were, of course, objections. Congressman Robert Luce of Massachusetts worried that in a period "when frozen credits due chiefly to real-estate loans have brought so much disaster to so many banks," it was "incomprehensible that this [investment in mortgages] would be extended further." Senator Carter Glass of Virginia expressed similar concerns.[37] Yet Herbert Hoover and the American Bankers Association pushed the McFadden Act through Congress in early 1927.[38]

Bankers responded to the federal vote of confidence in mortgage debt. After the passage of the McFadden Act, the *Bankers Magazine* celebrated the "growing market for first mortgages" and defended urban mortgages' increased "marketability" for regular commercial banks.[39] In 1928, a Federal Reserve committee said it was comforted that new money from the lower interest rates it encouraged "had gone into the construction of buildings," which was important because such "uses of credit are a factor in business recoveries from recessions."[40] Home building stabilized at about 750,000 homes a year as the economy boomed again.[41] It seemed as if mortgages and building were responding directly to the government's pushes and pulls in the banking world, which in turn were steadying the ups and downs of American business.

Long-Term Interest Rates and the Business Cycle

Beyond the pressure of interest groups and politicians, heightened attention to mortgage finance emerged from a new intellectual debate on the nature of finance and the business cycle.[42] New economists in this era, often attached to Herbert Hoover and to the "institutionalist" school of economics, which looked at the social and legal structures of the economy, began to focus on the seemingly esoteric issue of long-term interest rates as the central issue in the ups and downs of business. These theorists tried to show that interest rates on long-term loans—that is, loans for years or even decades—had a significant effect on "fixed capital" and construction investment. They also argued that such investment in turn was the crucial determinant of the state of the economy. Earlier advocates of farm financing, most often independent writers, farmers, and bankers, had argued that mortgage loans to farmers would ensure a stable and enduring balance of sectors. These new theorists, by contrast, who tended to be professional economists in university departments, argued that helping regular banks make long-term loans, especially for building, would help pull the economy out of its periodic depressions.

In 1913, the same year as the creation of the Federal Reserve Banks, Wesley Clair Mitchell of Columbia University released his magnum opus *Business Cycles*, which was reprinted dozens of times over the following decades. Amid a welter of financial and corporate data, Mitchell noted that the interest rates on short-term loans, which were the focus of the Federal Reserve and most banks, were a relatively small cost for most businesses. Thus, an "advance of the rate by 1 or 2 per cent may make so small a fraction of the whole cost as not to deter men from borrowing."[43] Long-term rates, however, *were* significant. High interest rates on loans lasting five or ten years would cause businesses to "hesitate" in a way that high short-term rates would not and could thus deter investment. In the section "Critical Point," on the turning point of the business cycle, Mitchell noted in particular the fact that "in construction work the volume of new contracts declines when the rise in long-term interest discourages borrowing," thus leading a cyclical downturn [44] Mitchell implied that if long-term interest rates could be reduced in a recession, construction work might help pull the country out of it. Yet Mitchell offered no obvious way for policy makers to lower such rates.[45]

The institutionalist economist Harold Moulton, soon to be president of the Brookings Institution and a participant with Mitchell on some of Hoover's economic committees, offered a way for the government to assist long-term lending.[46] Whereas many banking theorists, still cleaving to the belief in the "real-bills doctrine," argued that commercial banks and the Federal Reserve should stick to short-term loans, Moulton argued that any bank should be encouraged to make any type of loan, of any length. In the process, he made the most sustained attack on the real-bills doctrine in its history. Moulton complained that before Mitchell most studies of banking were "devoted solely . . . to what is called 'commercial' banking" and that the more important subject of permanent, long-term investment was ignored.[47] In a series of four well-publicized articles in the *Journal of Political Economy* titled "Commercial Banking and Capital Formation," Moulton said that despite theorists' and regulators' demands, most commercial banks in practice ignored the real-bills doctrine and already loaned money on long terms, often by renewing short-term loans indefinitely. He said that more than half of all loans provided by commercial banks were in fact "devoted to investment uses" on the long term and that most of these loans were used to create "fixed" or permanent capital, such as buildings.[48] Moulton implied that the legal restriction on mortgage and other types of lending were for naught and that so-called commercial banks were already lending for all sorts of purposes in a single national "money market." In a later book with the grandiloquent title *The Financial Organization of Society* (1921), Moulton said that banks' long-term lending meant the powers of the Federal Reserve were much greater than most analysts recognized: "By a policy of very low discount rates, together with the release of all restrictions on credit extension," the Federal Reserve could ease funding for commercial banks, which would then expand the number of their long-term loans. This expansion would "increase profits and wages, give steady employment to all who care to work, and facilitate the marketing of investment securities."[49]

Moulton's ideas about a unified money market for all types of loans were radical for their time, but they were taken up and extended by others.[50] Waldo Mitchell (no relation to Wesley Clair Mitchell), working off of ideas incipient in Moulton's work, pioneered what he called the "shiftability" theory of commercial banking. He agreed with Moulton that commercial banks already made many long-term loans, and he further argued that these loans were just as "liquid," or capable of being turned into cash, as real bills. Unlike Adam Smith, who argued that liquidity came from short-term loans coming due and being paid off quickly, Waldo Mitchell thought all loans could be liquid if they could be sold to another investor or a "stronger bank" for cash. He quoted one of Moulton's commercial banking pieces that said that "*liquidity is tantamount to shiftability.*" Therefore, the government should feel comfortable encouraging such long-term loans in the banking world, which would expand the ability to shift the loans to other banks and make them even more "liquid."[51] In his article "Interest Rates as Factors in the Business Cycle" (1928), Waldo Mitchell also followed Wesley Clair Mitchell in emphasizing the importance of long-term loans to recessions and recoveries by showing how certain businesses that tended to lead the business cycle were also most affected by changes in these rates. "Heavy industries" with lots of fixed capital, such as lumber, public utilities, and construction, responded most to changes in such rates and tended to be the first industries to collapse in a downturn, whereas "light industries," such as food processing and textiles, did not respond to such changes and tended to be stable across the business cycle.[52]

These economic ideas were synthesized by the genial Winfield Riefler, who would come to have a profound influence on U.S. monetary and mortgage policy over the next three decades. "Win," as he was known, studied under Harold Moulton's wing at the Graduate School of the Brookings Institution at the same time as he worked at the Federal Reserve's Research Division.[53] His research culminated in his book *Money Rates and Money Markets in the United States* (1930). Riefler had compiled years of data on both long- and short-term interest rates, and he noted a striking correlation that seemed to support his adviser's theories. The book said that "the same monetary conditions which affect the banks" making commercial loans are reflected "also in the securities market and contribute to the similarity of rate movement in the long and short-term money markets." His charts and tables furnished "striking evidence of the existence of a national unified money market which responds throughout to changes in the demand and supply of funds." Thus, short- and long-term rates moved in synchronicity. Money anywhere affected the "dearness" of money everywhere. Riefler agreed with Waldo Mitchell and others that although short-term rates seemed to have little effect on investment, for loans "involving long-term commitments[,] . . . such as housing and public utility projects, the cost of interest" had an important effect.[54] From his position inside the Federal Reserve Board, Riefler seemed to show that the Reserve Banks, through their control of short-term rates, actually had more power over long-term rates, mortgages, and the entire economy than many recognized. If the Federal Reserve could increase rates during booms and lower rates during busts, they could keep the economy on a steady path.[55]

Riefler argued that controlling such rates was as an essential means of ensuring balance between different sectors, or economic "equilibrium," as he called it. "In a society resting basically upon specialization of function, the primary problem of economics is the problem of equilibrium. In such a society the ability of the average individual to consume is determined by the presence of a market for his products as a producer."[56] Therefore, the "lack of equilibrium" between different sectors was a continuous danger for a modern economy. Keeping interest rates low in a depression, especially for sectors that tended to vary with the business cycle, such as home building, would ensure that different producers' incomes were equal and therefore that they could keep buying and trading with more stable sectors. The Federal Reserve, just by controlling interest rates, could balance the whole economy. There would be ample opportunities to test such a theory in the turbulent years ahead.

The Federal Reserve and Long-Term Interest Rates in the Great Depression

In 1928, the Federal Reserve began raising interest rates to prick the stock market bubble, but, influenced by Riefler's and others' work, Fed officials worried about the other effects of high interest rates. One Federal Reserve report noted that higher interest rates "had been followed frequently by a recession in business activity after an interval of six months to a year, attributable mainly to curtailment of building activity."[57] In April 1929, George Harrison, the stolid lawyer and new chief of the all-important New York Federal Reserve Bank, worried that higher interest rates had contributed to "difficulty in obtaining second mortgage money and loans for building operations, and also difficulty in selling real estate bonds."[58] In September 1929, as the stock market approached its collapse, Harrison still focused on reports about how "high rates of interest are having a serious effect upon new building projects."[59]

Even after the stock market burst in the fall of 1929, the Federal Reserve continued to focus on mortgage issues. Harrison argued the Federal Reserve needed to act aggressively to lower interest rates, not in order to support stocks but to "open the bond and mortgage market" to new funds, as economists in the institutionalist tradition argued should be done in a downturn.[60] A couple of months later Harrison worried again that "mortgage money in particular is not yet freely available."[61] In March 1930, the Open Market Investment Committee of the Federal Reserve Banks, which helped control interest rates by buying or selling government debt in the open market, said that in "both 1921 and 1927 business was supported in recession by a continued substantial volume of building construction . . . [but] in the past few months building has continued at a low ebb without any indication of substantial recovery."[62] Harrison argued that one reason for the now global downturn was continuing high long-term interest rates. He said that central banks everywhere "should do all they can toward rehabilitating the long term money market." These concerns helped inspire the reduction of the New York Federal Reserve Bank's crucial rate on discounting bank loans from 6 to 4 percent in early 1930.[63]

In the new Hoover administration, there were similar concerns. Although many historians have focused on Hoover's efforts at spurring public works, Hoover himself believed that private construction was more crucial for recovery. He argued that "possible expansion of construction in these private industries is about four or five times that in public works."[64] He saw the Federal Reserve Banks and their control of interest rates as an essential instrument in encouraging building. In addition to his contacts with the institutionalist economists, Hoover often met with George Harrison at the president's weekend camp in Rapidan, Virginia, and absorbed Harrison's views on the economic calamity. One of Hoover's assistants even noted that Harrison sometimes "comes mightily close to being the 'top man'" in the administration. Hoover thought the Reserve Banks were a fitting tool for fighting the crisis because they mimicked his "associationalist" vision of government-directed cooperation. He called the Reserve Banks "a widespread cooperative organization, acting in the broad interests of the whole people."[65]

After the stock market crash, Hoover explained to the nation the importance of the Federal Reserve's efforts. One day after "Black Thursday," October 24, 1929, Hoover made his famous statement that the "fundamental business of the country . . . is on a sound and prosperous basis," yet few noted the one cloud Hoover saw on the horizon. He said that although most of the economy was strong, "construction and building material industries have been to some extent affected by the high interest rates." Lower interest rates by the Federal Reserve, he hoped, could improve the situation.[66] A couple of weeks later, on November 5, Hoover said that due to lower Federal Reserve rates "there will be more capital available for the bond and mortgage market. That market has been practically starved for the last 4 or 5 months." He hoped those markets would now lead the recovery.[67] At a news conference in March 1930, he celebrated the Federal Reserve's efforts to lower rates but worried that money "for mortgage purposes in business and agriculture has lagged behind the other segments of credit." He still hoped that "the measures taken by the Federal Reserve System should stimulate the availability of credit for mortgage purposes and enable the resumption of residential construction, which has been lagging behind the other categories." Thus, the "worst effects of the crash on employment will have been passed during the next 30 to 60 days."[68] Hoover's infamous failed prediction of recovery was thus premised on a revival in mortgage lending. The economist Wesley Clair Mitchell celebrated Hoover's efforts to stimulate downtrodden sectors with increased financing, claiming that "a more significant experiment in the technique of balance could not be devised than the one which is being performed before our very eyes."[69]

The idea that central banks could control long-term interest rates and therefore the economy also acquired new currency on the other side of the Atlantic. In Cambridge, England, John Maynard Keynes, already the world's most famous economist, added his voice to the chorus of those demanding a reduction of all types of interest rates. In the two-volume *A Treatise on Money* (1930), by far his most extensive work to date, Keynes said it was odd that interest rates on short-term loans, which lasted for only a few months, "should have any noticeable effect on the terms asked for loans of twenty years or more." Yet "up-to-date material has recently become available in Mr. W. W. Riefler's *Money Rates and Money Markets in the United States*" that showed that the effect of the "short-term rate of interest on the long-term rate is much greater than anyone who argued on the above lines would have expected."[70] Keynes spent pages discussing Riefler's work and made clear what to do with this information. He said that almost "the whole of the fixed capital of the world is represented by buildings, transport, and public utilities; and the sensitiveness of these activities to even small changes in the long-term rate of interest . . . is surely considerable."[71] He noted in particular that "house-building is probably larger than any other one kind of investment" and thus most important in leading the economy in and out of depressions.[72] In a public lecture at the time *Treatise* was published, he said that in "the long run [at least, to note an earlier Keynes slogan, the long run in which most people were still alive] I rely on a fall in the long-term rate of interest more than any other factor" to alleviate the current slump.[73] Keynes gave Riefler's and the institutionalists' ideas extra intellectual heft. One book review from the era offhandedly mentioned "the Riefler–Keynes theory of the relation between the long and short term money rates" and the possibility of controlling these rates as a means of ending depressions.[74]

It was in this period that Eugene Meyer returned to the political stage with similar concerns. Like Hoover, Meyer had once focused on the problems of agricultural mortgages and balance but now became more concerned about urban problems.[75] He had begun talking to the Federal Reserve Research Division about urban mortgage interest rates, and in early 1930 he sent one of Hoover's associates a graph, most likely from Riefler, that he said "shows the relation between money and building contracts in an interesting way."[76] Meyer also began sending to Hoover's commerce secretary weekly statistics on building contracts from the *Engineering News-Record*.[77] He later said that it was foolish to try "to restore employment and prosperity and improve business through helping consumer activity, instead of [through] durable goods activity, such as restoring building," which he thought was the only way to bring about a recovery.[78]

Hoover, already primed by Wesley Clair Mitchell, Harrison, and others to focus on construction and mortgages, was intrigued by Meyer's ideas and decided to enlist him again in his administration. In August 1930, he called Meyer at home and explained that the current Federal Reserve Board governor, Roy Young, was retiring. Hoover said, "I'm going to appoint you a member of the board and then governor. I won't take no for an answer," then hung up without waiting for one.[79] In fact, Hoover had pushed Young and another Federal Reserve Board member into early retirement to open spots for supposedly more activist individuals.[80] Whereas earlier in Hoover's presidency his secretary could tell one person that the "president has refused to discuss the [Federal Reserve] Board even with its members in his desire not to interfere with what must be an independent agency," such niceties became moot in the Depression.[81] Meyer's Fed appointment received shining reviews. The power broker Bernard Baruch told the *New York Times* that "if the President had taken a thousand good men and rolled them into one," he would not have a better individual than Meyer for the job.[82] Hoover soon called him "the most valuable man I've got."[83]

Just as Meyer had moved his War Finance Corporation loyalists over to the Federal Farm Loan Board, he now moved members of that board over to the Federal Reserve. He hoped that he could reorganize the Federal Reserve in the image of the farm mortgage system. With Hoover's help, he placed two members of the Farm Loan Board on the Federal Reserve Board. Longtime Federal Reserve Board member Charles Hamlin wrote in his diary that the Federal Reserve was "now dominated by Governor Meyer and two former members of the Federal Farm Loan Board," and he worried about the board's "Hooverizing."[84] Another official complained about Meyer's "pets that he brought in there" from the farm system.[85]

The Federal Reserve Board, once a mere regulator of the Reserve Banks, acquired new power under Meyer. George Norris, once head of the farm loan system and now governor of the Philadelphia Federal Reserve Bank, worried that after Meyer's appointment the "board became an operating rather than a supervising authority."[86] Meyer moved the Research Division, which, as he said, "wasn't even close to [the board] physically," closer to himself and thus acquired even more contact with Riefler and his work.[87] He received an advance copy of Keynes's *A Treatise on Money* from the American publisher, and the Federal Reserve library ordered more copies to be made available to the staff.[88] As Federal Reserve Board governor, Meyer started attending the Open Market Investment Committee meetings, previously attended by just the Reserve Bank governors. He demanded lower rates at one meeting the year after his appointment because the "whole history of investment showed that money would go from short-term into long-term channels."[89]

Real Estate Panics

Meyer worried not only about the effects of high-interest mortgages on construction but also about the dangers of defaulting mortgages for banks. He felt he needed to help relieve banks whose portfolios had swelled with mortgages that no longer paid and real estate that banks could not sell. Meyer later said, "I knew that over-speculation in real estate was a major problem in the country." As bad as the stock speculation was, the "real estate speculation I think was the worse."[90] And, unlike stocks, "in real estate, when the decline comes, there *is* no market." Meyer understood that mortgages and real estate were not yet fully liquid or shiftable to other banks, and therefore their default was especially dangerous.[91] Others noted the same problem. One contemporary writer, Raymond Goldsmith, wrote that defaulting mortgages and "the illiquidity of urban real estate had already attained a really dangerous degree" by 1930 and that the "difficulties in American banks have been proportionate to the ratio of real estate."[92]

As Meyer stated in a later interview, he worried that many "banks were nothing but real estate speculation corporations, like the Bank of the United States."[93] This soon-to-be infamous bank was actually called "Bank of United States," with no "the." New York State bank supervisors had demanded the absence of the definite article in order not to give that bank's mainly Jewish immigrant clientele on the Lower East Side the impression that it was guaranteed by the U.S. government. Nonetheless, the calculated ambiguity still had its effect, as many officially ambiguous guarantees in recent years had shown. Recent immigrants had put inordinate faith in the bank as its book of home mortgages grew rapidly. By late 1930, however, the new governor of New York, Franklin Roosevelt, received reports from a special banking commission led by the builder Robert Moses about the bank's parlous situation.[94] By November of that year, Eugene Meyer, too, was receiving confidential and almost daily reports about the bank and began trying to merge it with a healthier institution[95] When Meyer finally traveled to New York in early December, a chaotic run had started on the bank, with depositors besieging its tellers. When Meyer could find no willing financial suitor, the bank closed its doors.[96]

The collapse of the Bank of United States inaugurated the first of five major banking panics over the next three years that would exacerbate the Depression. Some researchers have pointed to this failure and the subsequent nationwide bank runs as the most significant cause of the Great Depression, even more than the stock market crash a year earlier.[97] In April, when the second bank panic of the Depression began with a series of bank failures around Chicago and the Great Lakes region, many again cited defaulting and "illiquid" real estate loans. One Federal Reserve officer said in June 1931 that "fully 95% of the bank

5.1 The run on the Bank of United States, December 1930.

Source: Associated Press.

troubles in Chicago were predicated on real estate," a conclusion echoed elsewhere.[98]

This financial chaos made low interest rates and improved mortgage lending even more necessary. In Federal Reserve meetings from April through July 1931, Meyer and Harrison kept emphasizing the need for reducing interest rates. Harrison said that in the previous few months the Federal Reserve's goal had been "to reduce short money rates and thus encourage the shifting of funds to employment in longer use."[99]

Yet the theory that reduced short-term rates at the Federal Reserve would encourage more mortgages encountered a snag. The connection between the short-term and long-term interest rates, which Riefler and Keynes had divined from statistics going back over the previous twenty years, broke down.[100] Even though the Federal Reserve had reduced its short-term discount rate from 6 percent to almost 2 percent, long-term rates barely budged.[101] And despite the attempts at mortgage stimulation, the rate of construction dropped further. Housing construction in 1931 was down to 250,000 housing units, 75 percent below its peak, with total construction spending falling twice as fast as spending in the rest of the economy. Residential construction fell fastest of all.[102] The previous economic research had demonstrated the profound effect of long-term interest rates on building and on business, but now it seemed as if the Federal

Reserve was impotent to affect them. The times seemed to demand more radical solutions.

John Maynard Keynes was one of the first to notice that interest rates were no longer moving in synchronicity. He worried that something had "upset the normal relations between short-term and long-term rates of interest." Despite the low short-term rate, the high long-term rates continued to inhibit investment, he said, and "it is here, therefore, that I find the most fundamental explanation of the world slump."[103] Keynes's once unthinkable solution was to have governments and central banks directly buy or loan on longtime assets. He argued that the "drastic reduction of the whole complex of market-rates of interest presents central banks with a problem which I do not expect them to solve unless they are prepared to employ drastic and even direct methods of influencing long-term investments which . . . they had better leave alone in more normal times."[104]

In July 1931, Keynes took his first trip to the United States, where he proselytized for his new belief that the government and the Federal Reserve should buy long-term loans. At a lecture at the New School in New York, he told the crowd that directly lowering long-term rates would stimulate building and that it was "above all of building that we must think . . . when we are considering how to stimulate investment."[105] Keynes also met with members of the Federal Reserve Board in Washington, including Riefler and Meyer, and found a sympathetic audience for his ideas. He reported back to the British government that the Reserve Board "want[s] to reduce the long-term rate of interest . . . and they believe that a revival of the construction industry is probably a necessary condition of the recovery of industry in general." He confirmed that this was his own explanation of the country's troubles and said that in "my mind the proofs are overwhelming that the slump is primarily a slump in construction."[106] Riefler, Meyer, and others at the Fed needed no prompting from Keynes. They wanted to take direct action on long-term loans generally and on mortgages specifically.

New Corporations for Old Mortgages

One method to lower the interest rates on mortgages was to organize new corporations either to buy or to discount those mortgages. Ever since Hoover's time at the Commerce Department, he had hoped some private corporations could try to mimic the Federal Land Banks in the urban world.[107] The Great Depression renewed these hopes.

Hoover privately asked the Federal Reserve to investigate new urban-mortgage plans. In the long and detailed letter in March 1930 described earlier, Hoover explained to the board why it should help create some kind of mortgage bank and why it should discount such mortgages directly.[108] In early May, Hoover made a similar argument in a much-discussed public speech to the U.S. Chamber of Commerce, where he noted that "we shall find one area of credit which is most inadequately organized and which almost ceased to function under the present stress": mortgage lending. "From a social point of view this is one of the most vital segments of credit. . . . Here is the greatest field for expanded organization of capital."[109]

The Federal Reserve delegated Winfield Riefler to investigate the possibilities of a new bank. Riefler argued that "if there is to be a revival in residential building," there would have to be a reduction in costs, both building prices and finance charges.[110] Like the Brookings Institution, where his mentor Moulton had worked, Riefler proposed a private company that could discount mortgages and create new mortgage-backed bonds.[111]

Hoover lobbied private groups to form a mortgage bank on their own, without federal support. In August 1930, he announced a special White House Conference on Home Building and Home Ownership, to be composed of any intellectual or interest group concerned about housing. Yet, despite the broad title, he tried to focus the group on creating new mortgage financing. As Hoover told reporters, the most "important problem, and the one that most deeply affects the whole question today, is finance."[112] Behind the scenes, he pushed the conference's planning committee to study and endorse a private housing bank.[113]

Through most of 1930 and 1931, Hoover remained reluctant to have the federal government do anything except study such mortgage banks. Early in 1931, in response to one businessman who wanted the president's imprimatur on a private corporation to purchase real estate bonds, Hoover had said that the president could not appeal for investment in a private company.[114] As with so many scruples Hoover brought to the presidency, however, he soon shed this one as well. After Keynes's visit and the banking panic around the Great Lakes, Hoover at last organized a meeting of bankers in the White House. He secretly asked them to form their own company to buy up real estate bonds. As he described the proposal in a letter to a supporter in August 1931, "For your confidential information I have requested the leading financial institutions of New York to set up some kind of organization for the protection of building bond holders."[115] He noted to another that in the "flood of despairing correspondence that passes over my desk in relation to people who have invested their money in building bonds, there seems to be a great tragedy for hundreds of thousands of unprotected people."[116]

Of all the tragic stories that crossed Hoover's desk during his presidency, defaulting mortgage bonds was an odd one on which to focus, yet restoring such real estate financing was at the crux of his plan for recovery.[117] When the story of Hoover's meeting with the mortgage bankers leaked at the end of August, the *New York Herald Tribune* called it "a far-reaching plan to lift frozen real estate off the market," inspired by the fact that the "real estate stalemate is a major drawback to business recovery." The paper also noted that the proposed new mortgage bond corporation, "though private, would have the approval and the encouragement of the Federal government."[118] On September 17, Hoover organized another meeting to solicit funds for yet another mortgage bank proposal. He asked the former head of the Hoover for President Real Estate Group to create a new national mortgage bank for small mortgages not covered by the large real estate bond group. He hoped the new bank could be "organized by private individuals, but with a Federal charter operating along the lines of the French or Swiss mortgage banking systems."[119]

Within days of these mortgage meetings, however, the British decoupled the pound sterling from gold, and the corresponding run on the U.S. dollar, which many felt would be the next currency to leave the gold standard, inaugurated the third and so far greatest banking crisis of the Depression. This one, too, was centered around the Midwest, where the highest proportion of bank mortgages were located, as well as in the South, where banks held many agricultural loans.[120]

Hoover knew he now needed a bigger plan, one with more federal support. He called another meeting with bankers, this time at Andrew Mellon's lavish apartment at Dupont Circle in Washington. Hoover told the group that they had to help him stop the collapse of banks, which had been faced with the "inability of farmers and homeowners to meet mortgage requirements."[121] To that end, he asked that they form a large credit pool for discounting all assets, including mortgages, not now eligible for discount at the Federal Reserve.[122] When the bankers balked at Hoover's plan, Eugene Meyer chimed in with his own addendum. He said that if the private corporation failed to get results, he would help create an explicit government-run bank to buy up bad assets, something like the War Finance Corporation. Hoover agreed to this condition, and so did the bankers.[123] The day after this meeting Hoover also organized a group of major insurance chiefs and mortgage company executives, again in Mellon's private apartment. There he told them he needed their help more than ever in creating an explicitly federally backed bank just for small mortgages, those currently not covered by the bankers' plan, and asked them to hold off on all foreclosures until the new corporation could be organized.[124]

On October 8, 1931, Hoover announced that the large New York bankers had already pledged $150 million of a proposed $500 million National Credit Corporation for the "rediscount of banking assets not now eligible for rediscount at the Federal reserve banks [sic]." That day he also proposed recapitalizing (or bailing out) the Federal Land Banks and creating a more permanent general mortgage bank for small urban homeowners and builders—what later became the Federal Home Loan Banks. He also asked Congress to expand the eligibility of long-term assets for discount at the Federal Reserve "to give greater liquidity to the assets of the banks," which the economists in the shiftability tradition had long advocated. Every one of these ideas and actions would work directly to lower interest rates on long-term assets, especially mortgages. He thought these actions could finally offer a way out of the depression that was savaging the nation he now led.[125]

Reconstructing the Financial System

The first part of Hoover's plan, the privately run National Credit Corporation to purchase bad bank debts, accomplished little in its short life and soon folded.[126] Hoover then endorsed Meyer's public corporation to buy what would later be known as toxic assets in the bank system. In his State of the Union Address to the new Congress in early December 1931, Hoover argued that the recent credit "paralysis has been further augmented by the steady increase in recent years of bank assets invested in long-term securities, such as mortgages and bonds," which "tend to lose their liquidity in a depression." Instead of forbidding banks from making such illiquid loans, in the old real-bills tradition, he advocated making them safer and more liquid through the proposed Reconstruction Finance Corporation, or RFC.[127]

By luck, Meyer had friends in Congress to push the new public bank. Democratic senator Joseph Robinson, who had already dealt with Meyer when the senator was head of his own Joint-Stock Land Bank, told him that he would "let [Meyer] write the act and lead the agency." Meyer happily penciled in his draft that the Federal Reserve Board chairman would also be the new head of the RFC.[128] Meyer recalled Chester Morrill, who had been his secretary at both the War Finance Corporation and the Federal Farm Loan Board, to be his new secretary at the Federal Reserve, with the goal of midwifing the new program. Meyer considered Morrill, who had once also worked on the Federal Farm Loan Act, "a very good bill drafter" and told him his first job was to draft a new law for the RFC based on his previous experience at all of these agencies.[129] This act, however, had a larger focus, according to Meyer: "We were reaching the whole economy through the agricultural economy in 1921 [with the War Finance Corporation], but this real estate thing was a huge and complicating factor, involving the cities as well as the country, in 1932. It involved the whole economy and the financial structure of the country."[130] Morrill wrote a bill that gave the RFC a broad power to purchase just about any financial asset from any bank or lender.

Meyer made the motivation behind the act clear when he testified before Congress. He said that the RFC idea came from his experience in "relief

work—not relief in the sense of personal subsidies to individuals but in connection with relief to banking institutions and business structures." Meyer said
the RFC would be a godsend for unrelieved bankers with long-term debts
because these assets were "the best in the country. The most fundamental
businesses are financed by securities, notes of farmers, and mortgages, all
kinds of indebtedness which are at the moment called frozen." With proper
assistance from the government, these assets would "thaw out with essential
speed."[131] Others made the same arguments about the RFC's goals with less
charity. Congressman Fiorello La Guardia called the RFC "a millionaire's
dole . . . a subsidy for broken bankers."[132]

Meyer also emphasized to Congress the new corporation's power to increase
construction. He told the House Banking and Currency Committee that
"unsound financing in the real estate field" was the "the most important single
economic factor" in causing the Depression. The new bill would give mortgages
increased liquidity and boost the "most important and fundamental [activity]
in our whole business situation; i.e. construction activity."[133] Meyer pulled out
the charts he had received from Federal Reserve Research Division, which
showed that in the early 1920s there was "a revival in construction that really
was the basis of what proved to be a period of prolonged upward swing" in the
economy. He told the gathered Congress members increasingly desperate for a
solution to the Depression that "nothing increases the movement of goods and
the employment of labor more than construction activity. It affects the mine
and the forest; it employs great quantities of labor in transportation; it adds to
the gross revenue of railroads. It seems to have the most general stimulating
effect."[134]

Due to Morrill's drafting efforts, the RFC was like previous federal financial corporations. It would begin with $500 million in capital from Congress;
it would sell tax-exempt securities "similar to the farm loan system bonds," as
Meyer noted; and its bonds would be eligible for purchase by federal trust funds.
Yet for the first time since the creation of the Federal Reserve Banks, the RFC's
debts would be explicitly guaranteed by the government. Here, unlike in 1913,
the government knew it was taking a significant risk on questionable assets.
Congress passed the act the day before it passed the Federal Land Bank
bailout.[135]

Despite the RFC's new powers, Hoover still wanted the Federal Reserve to
help solve the real estate problem. He had already asked Meyer in December 1931
if the Reserve Banks could discount home mortgages directly.[136] When Meyer
refused to take action, Hoover forced the issue. On a morning in February 1932
in his White House office, he began "talking as fast and as much in earnest as
I have ever heard him talk," according to his legislative liaison James MacLafferty. Hoover claimed that he would take steps that were "almost revolutionary
to try to avert calamity." Soon after his private rant, he invited Eugene Meyer,

Senator Carter Glass, Representative Henry Steagall, Republican Senate majority leader James Watson, and the Democratic Speaker of the House John
Nance Gardner to the White House to discuss a bill that would temporarily
allow the Federal Reserve to discount every financial asset. The group reluctantly agreed to the bill, despite Glass's lament that the plan would "make
William Jennings Bryan turn over in his grave because of his delight."[137] Glass
worried that during the argument about the bill he "was very much afraid that
he swore at the President of the United States."[138]

Meyer went directly from the White House conference to the Treasury building, where the Federal Reserve Board worked, and just as in the case of the
RFC delegated Chester Morrill to draft a bill. The bill allowed the Federal
Reserve to discount or loan its Federal Reserve currency on just about any
asset it chose. During the hearings on the act held two short days after Hoover's
meeting, House Banking and Currency Committee chairman Henry Steagall
pointed out to Meyer that "under the broad language here, you could loan to a
State member bank on real estate security if you saw fit," and Congressman
Robert Luce, waxing incredulous, asked if they could discount anything, "even
to the extent of mortgages?" Meyer confirmed that this was indeed correct. In
fact, it was one of the essential reasons for the bill.[139]

Senator Glass, however, remained devoted to the old real-bills religion and
worried about the transformation of his beloved Reserve Banks into mortgage
lenders. According to Morrill, Glass had been "belly aching even since Wednesday that he had been stampeded into the agreement" endorsing the act. To
limit the damage, Glass insisted on amendments that allowed discounting long-
term assets only in exceptional circumstances and at a higher interest rate and
that limited such discounts to assets from smaller banks. Glass's amendments
passed with the final act.[140]

Hoover worried that Glass's amendments were aimed at preventing one bank
in particular from getting relief, yet it was exactly this bank Hoover hoped to
save with the bill.[141] The Bank of America was then the largest bank in the
nation, and its collapse would be catastrophic economically and politically.
MacLafferty wrote of the California-based bank, "There are even now whisper-
ings going on about their stability. If they were to fail it would be the hardest
blow the Hoover administration could have. . . . I fear such a failure would lose
the Pacific Coast States for Hoover in the coming election."[142] Eugene Meyer
was also concerned about the bank, telling one potential investor that in
"California the principal asset is land. . . . I think I'd examine [the bank] very
carefully from the point of liquidity. Land is not a quick asset."[143] Yet Glass's
restriction on discounts to big banks stood. With the Federal Reserve option
removed, Meyer and Hoover turned to the full power of the new RFC to help
the beleaguered, land-laden Bank of America. Even though Hoover told the
public that the RFC was boosting tiny banks, over its first few weeks more than

half of its total funds went solely to the Bank of America. By the end of March, the bank had received almost a third of all RFC loans.[144]

By the early summer of 1932, it seemed as if the new financial reforms had worked. The banking runs had stopped, and the nation's ever-anxious bankers breathed a sigh of government-supported relief. The success boosted Meyer's standing specifically, and landed him on the cover of *Time* magazine, but this boost elicited Hoover's ire. Hoover's press secretary noted that "there are times when [Hoover] would like to boot Meyer the length of Pennsylvania Avenue."[145] Meyer himself worried about his conflicts with the president and his multiple public jobs. His health was breaking under the strain. The leader of Hoover's recovery efforts, who was running multiple public financial corporations, now had trouble staying awake throughout the day or even walking more than a few blocks without collapsing.[146] Hoover thus had several reasons to place one final new mortgage agency outside Meyer's grasp.

The Creation of the Federal Home Loan Banks and the Failure of Mortgage Reform

The greatest banking run in American cinema is of course in Frank Capra's classic work *It's a Wonderful Life* (1946). It is no coincidence that the run centers on illiquid mortgages. In the movie's climactic scene, the Bailey Brothers Building and Loan Association is besieged by its depositors demanding their money. George Bailey, played by Jimmy Stewart, tries to explain to his irate depositors that "you're thinking of this place all wrong. As if I had the money back in a safe. The money's not here. Your money's in Joe's house . . . right next to yours. And in the Kennedy house, and Mr. Macklin's house, and a hundred others. Why, you're lending them the money to build, and then they're going to pay it back to you as best they can. Now what are you going to do? Foreclose on them?" George's speech and some of his wife's personal cash manage to halt the run, but in the real world other B&Ls weighed down with mortgages had no George and Mary Bailey. The best hopes for these B&Ls were not in the RFC, which dealt with large mortgages and large banks, or in the Federal Reserve System, of which the B&Ls were not members, but in Hoover's proposed federal bank just for small mortgages and cooperative institutions.

Hoover hoped his new Federal Home Loan Banks would be not just an institution for the Depression emergency but a permanent part of American finance. He said that the proposed banks' first goals were "relieving the financial strains upon sound building and loan associations, savings banks, deposit banks, and farm loan banks" and "put[ting] some steel beams in the foundations of our credit structure."[147] Hoover thought the banks would also assist in a revival of construction because a "considerable part of our unemployment is due to stagnation in residential construction."[148] Any benefits to actual home-owners or home buyers went unmentioned.

Hoover's aides, such as the former Harvard professor of lumber John Gries, noted that the new program mimicked the Federal Land Banks, which, ironi-cally, were just then being bailed out.[149] There would be twelve regional Home Loan Banks, which would issue mortgage-backed bonds in exchange for dis-counted small mortgages from cooperatives. The government would temporar-ily buy any stock in the Home Loan Banks not purchased by their B&L "mem-bers." In his State of the Union Address in December 1931, Hoover described the banks to Congress "as a necessary companion in our financial structure to the Federal Reserve Banks and our Federal Land Banks."[150]

Hoover's White House Conference on Homeownership and Home Building, which finally met in December 1931, celebrated his plan. Like so many suppos-edly expert commissions created in these years, the conference largely con-firmed what its organizers had always supported.[151] The conference's final report pontificated about everything from landscaping flowers to road platting, but the only resolution the conference made was to "heartily endorse" the mort-gage system Hoover had proposed a month before the meeting.[152] The bill thus carried a substantial though unearned patina of expertise. Hoover later disingenuously called the plan "the outcome of the national conference on homeownership."[153]

Because the Federal Home Loan Banks were to be a permanent part of the nation's financial structure, Congress took more time molding this bill than it had Hoover's emergency reforms. Massachusetts representative Robert Luce, an expert on congressional politics and history, rewrote Hoover's rough draft with the help of Chester Morrill, the drafter of the Federal Farm Loan Act, the RFC, and recent Federal Reserve reform bills, and moved it through the House.[154] Luce said the basic outlines of his bill were "largely drawn from the farm loan and Federal reserve bills," but "somebody had to decide in the mat-ter of a large number of minor differences between the Federal-reserve and farm-loan machinery. . . . I had to make many decisions offhand." Luce's most important decision was to add to the bill the Federal Land Bank clause declar-ing the banks and bonds "instrumentalities of the United States," thus making them tax exempt. As before, the clause also implied a government guarantee.[155]

The tax exemption, along with the government purchases of bank stock, pro-voked complaints in Congress. When the hearings began in the Senate, James Couzens of Michigan, the obstreperous former partner of Henry Ford, kept ask-ing why the taxpayers should give special support to B&Ls and mortgage banks. Majority leader Senator James Watson, tapped by Hoover to manage the bill in that chamber, responded that he had asked "that very question when they brought up this bill to me to introduce." Watson, a classic Republican standpatter, admitted that such an idea was "abhorrent to my old-fashioned ideas of government." But as a consummate cloakroom compromiser and the man to whom Bartleby's credits the phrase "If you can't lick 'em, join 'em," Watson realized the benefits. He said that once he understood the Home Loan Banks were just another version of the Federal Reserve and Land Banks, the bill didn't seem so radical.[156] When another senator wondered if the bill was designed to "help investment banking instead of current commercial banking," Watson said, "That is it exactly." Couzens perked up at this response: "I thought it was to help the home owner; but you say it is to help the investment bankers." Watson hedged and said that it helped investors in all assets, including homes.[157] Congressman LaGuardia called it merely a "bill to bail out the mortgage bankers," those "bastards who broke the People's back with their Usury."[158]

The financial interests behind the Home Loan Banks bill were obvious. Robert Luce later admitted that he was a shareholder in a cooperative bank in Massachusetts and that his bank recently had become illiquid and had asked him to leave his money there to prevent a run. He also had "been for many years investing a small amount of money in buildings."[159] Luce testified before the House Banking and Currency Committee that in his constituency of Brookline, "one of the wealthiest towns in the world," a well-off citizen had tried to purchase a lavish $10,000 house and was turned down because of the bank's trouble getting funding. Here were the types of horror stories that hit home for many in Congress.[160]

Lobbyists of all stripes mounted a colossal propaganda campaign for the bill. The lumber industry, understanding that two-thirds of its products went into residential construction, became an effective advocate. The National Association of Real Estate Boards set up a Washington, DC, headquarters in what it called "a battle to save the American home." One real estate lobbyist complained that he got what he called "Capitol feet" from tramping up and down "the hard floors in that building" in pressing the bill.[161] Vigorous opposition to the bill did come, however, from the insurance industry, whose many speakers in the congressional hearings worried about the new banks skimming the "cream of the business."[162] When the insurance companies stalled the legislation, Hoover called the B&L leaders to the White House and had them agree to "wage a campaign of education-propaganda" to pass the law.[163]

The insurance industry and other political opposition failed to stop the Home Loan Bank bill, but they did weaken it. As finally passed in June 1932, the Federal Home Loan Bank Act allowed the new banks to discount mortgages at only 50 percent of the value of the house instead of at the 80 percent Hoover had originally recommended. Thus, the new banks did not prevent the second mortgages Hoover so lamented. Also, in a minor sleight of hand, the additional money for the bank stock came not directly from the government but from the RFC, a provision that seemed to comfort those concerned about direct federal contributions to the banks. Hoover placed Franklin Fort, the banker and congressman from Newark, New Jersey, who had helped create the Federal Farm Board, at the head of the Federal Home Loan Bank Board, thus ensuring continuity with the president's earlier efforts.[164]

In June 1932, in fact, Congress and Hoover expanded the powers of all of their semipublic corporations and tried to focus them on building. Congress passed a law allowing the RFC to loan to states and other government entities, especially for construction, and to make loans to special corporations formed to build low-income housing. Tucked inside that bill, they included a clause that allowed the Federal Reserve Banks to lend not just to its member banks but also to any company in "unusual or exigent circumstances." (This clause would later be used decades later to bail out investment banks and private companies outside of the control of the Federal Reserve.[165]) Hoover meanwhile helped organize Banking and Industrial Committees at the individual Federal Reserve Banks. George Norris, who was governor of the Philadelphia Reserve Bank and on the board of a local mutual savings bank, said the committees tried to "do what could be done in averting foreclosures, and reducing unemployment, particularly in the building trades, by stimulating construction and renovation."[166]

Just as the wave of new reforms crested, however, there was another run on Chicago banks, inaugurating the fourth great banking panic of the Depression. This run was again based on frozen real estate. The Home Loan Banks were not organized in time to stanch the bleeding, and the panic sent the economy into another dive.[167] Despite all of Hoover's efforts, house building and construction continued to careen downward in 1932, totaling only about 100,000 units, or one-tenth of their peak level. House values continued collapsing to 20 percent below what they had been at their peak, and foreclosures soared. Hundreds of thousands of Americans were thrown out onto the streets.[168]

After Hoover's defeat at the polls in November, he was confronted with the fifth and final banking panic of the Depression, one that nearly broke the American economy. This final panic, centered around Detroit, Michigan, in early 1933, was once again based on failing mortgages. In Detroit and surrounding cities, the percentage of bank loans backed by real estate was higher than 50 percent.[169] Meyer went to investigate and recounted later, "The Michigan situation was one of those which had many characteristics in common with others. There was a vast amount of real estate speculation in the banks."[170]

The center of the final banking storm was the Guardian Detroit Union group of banks associated with Henry Ford. Some of these banks had more than 70 percent of their assets in illiquid real estate. The head of the group later told Congress that "it was our practice in Detroit to loan on real estate, on homes, and it was our mistake."[171] After Ford failed to come to the banks' aid, the Michigan governor declared a bank holiday, effectively closing all banks in the state, to prevent any further runs. As families in other states rushed to pull their deposits before similar holidays were declared, the crisis spread. Other governors then declared more holidays, and the entire banking structure of the nation unwound. Families could not withdraw small sums to pay for groceries or rent, and much of the nation's buying and selling ground to a halt. Parts of the country began bartering chickens for groceries or yard work for dental service. More often, families already on the brink of starvation simply did without.[172] The failures of the banking and mortgage system had become patently obvious to all. It was also obvious that Hoover's ever-expanding attempts to bail out the banks had come to naught.

In the final days of his embattled presidency, amid an ever-growing panic, Hoover agonized that he had made a crucial mistake. To Meyer's wife, Agnes, Hoover said, "Eugene and I have tried everything on behalf of the bankers but they have fought us, haven't tried to cooperate, haven't even told the truth. They are without ability and without character." Agnes took sympathy with Hoover, noting that he looked old and exhausted. She tried to redirect the conversation, but Hoover would not leave the subject. He bewailed, "It would have been better if Gene and I had never tried to save the banks. If we had let them go, we'd be all over it now."[173] It was too late for such dirges.

Although Hoover's actions failed to prevent bank failures and to create an economic recovery, they did radically reshape the government's relationship to the banking world. In effect, in order to encourage investment in mortgages, Hoover made the government the guarantors of much of the financial system, with myriad new and newly empowered semipublic institutions. Although Congress and others succeeded in limiting the extent of these operations and keeping most of them to the needs of the present "emergency," the government's support for financial stability was plain for all to see, as were the expanded means to accomplish this end. The government had indeed put new "steel beams" in the nation's credit structure, as Hoover had promised. Yet by March 1933 that structure had toppled, anyway, because few actual steel beams had been put up in the real economy. Despite Hoover's frustrations, his successor would take up and expand upon almost all of his ideas on the importance of financial and mortgage reform for economic recovery.

CHAPTER 6

A NEW DEAL FOR FARM MORTGAGES

On a cold March day in 1932, two Columbia professors met outside their adjoining Morningside Heights apartments in New
York City. They were neighbors and colleagues, but they had
never spoken. Before now they had never had a reason.

Raymond Moley was a professor in the Columbia Law School, articulate,
tidy, and self-assured, who hoped to leave his mark on public policy.[1] Rexford
Tugwell was a debonair and radical professor in the Columbia Economics
Department who published left-leaning books on grand themes such as industrial civilization. His radicalism, however, had left him estranged from his colleagues. He complained that professors tended to be "official and correct rather
than interesting."[2] Luckily for both of them, Moley had begun prepping then
New York governor Franklin Delano Roosevelt for his upcoming presidential
run and wanted to organize intellectuals to provide advice. Moley was fed up
with orthodox economic nostrums, so he sought out the unorthodox Tugwell.[3]

When the two met on the sidewalk, Tugwell remembered, "frigid drafts were
blowing up from the river, lifting papers and whirling dust in the doorways and
around the corners." Children and women were milling about them and trying to catch what little winter light remained as the professors started talking.
Surprisingly, amid that dense urban jungle "we discussed the farm problem
first. . . . Their troubles, I said, were obviously involved with the country-wide
depression." Tugwell thought the "farmers' depression had started with falling
wheat and cotton prices as far back as 1921, and all during the speculators' 'new
era' rural problems had got worse. Finally the sickness had spread to industry,

and then to finance." Tugwell knew Roosevelt "had a special feeling for farmers" because of his life on a farm, but he worried that the governor did not understand how the farmers' problems were at the root of the nation's ills. Tugwell would give him an explanation[4]

Tugwell, whose father had made a substantial living canning farm goods, imbibed the connection between agricultural and industrial prosperity at an early age. As he explained his theory later, the nation's central economic problem was that if farmers "could not sell, they could not buy. . . . Thus, closed factories, unemployment, general paralysis!" He said that "it is necessary to note that in 1933 the economic importance of agriculture and industry, of rural and urban interests, was still about equal. This accounts for our preoccupation with the conditions farmers found themselves in."[5] Tugwell thought that only by giving farmers' better prices for their products could the economy be rebalanced and trade between the two great sectors resume, thus spreading prosperity again.

Tugwell's ideas about a rural–urban balance, although by that point common in the public sphere, were still rare in economics departments. The professor provided them with new intellectual weight. Moley was inspired by Tugwell's explanations and agreed that "we merely needed to get the farms prospering again and create a market for the industrial products in the cities."[6] Like their progenitors, Moley and Tugwell also understood the importance of such balancing for the financial sector. Tugwell said that the banking system had collapsed because the "weight of accumulated debt was so heavy, and because assets were so thoroughly frozen. Nothing could lift that weight or thaw the frost but an infusion of buying power" caused by higher farm prices.[7] More directly, Tugwell argued that new government credit provided to farmers and banks, especially cheap mortgages, would both improve farmers' purchasing power and salvage the banking system.

When Tugwell went to the governor's mansion in Albany, Roosevelt was enraptured with his explanation of agricultural balance and its connection to financial confidence. He promised to pursue these ideas in his upcoming campaign. It was then and there that the intellectual edifice of the New Deal was erected.

Most historians of the New Deal describe Roosevelt and the members of his so-called Brains Trust as advocates for a new type of central "planning" that would smooth the business cycle and restore prosperity. Yet historians typically fail to explain exactly what such planning entailed or how it would operate. This chapter shows that from the presidential campaign of 1932 through the first year of Roosevelt's presidency the idea of economic balance shaped all of his economic plans. The early New Deal's foremost goal was to balance the farm economy with the urban economy using both federal price and credit support. Most especially, the New Deal hoped to halt the collapse of the farm mortgage market and create a new type of mortgage that would help rural banks.[8]

The early New Deal's agricultural and financial focus has been slighted in histories of the period. Even in the works on farm policy in the New Deal, mortgage and banking policy receive at best a few stray mentions, even though financial recovery was a significant motivator of farm policy and improving farm finance an important part of such policy. In fact, more money was given as loans to farmers during the New Deal than given out in the more famous grant and subsidy payments.[9] This chapter demonstrates how the New Deal began as an attempt to use agricultural price controls and mortgage credit to restore the battered American economy.

The Brains Trust Finds the Farm Mortgage

Moley and Tugwell were not experts in finance, but a third member of the Brains Trust was. Like Moley, Adolf Berle was a self-assured Columbia University law professor, described by one reporter as a cocky "ball of energy."[10] He, more so than any earlier theorist, made protecting finance central to his proposed economic policy.

Berle's financial ideas emerged out of a work he was just finishing and that *Time* magazine would soon call the "economic bible of the Roosevelt administration,"[11] *The Modern Corporation and Private Property* (1932), which was coauthored with economist Gardiner Means. The book, as is often noted, argued that the divorce of management from ownership made corporations quasi-public entities, something like the quasi-public corporations the government already controlled. Since corporations no longer worked just for their shareholders, they should be under public direction. It is little noted, however, that the book also claimed that property owners were willing to accept the loss of direct control for one reason: their property in the form of stocks or bonds became liquid, or salable, in public markets. Berle said that the modern owner of capital, in effect, made the decision to "exchange control for liquidity."[12]

Berle argued that the economy's new dependence on liquidity meant the "whole future of the present system is inextricably bound to the successful functioning of the security markets." There was a need for constant liquidity of financial assets because if securities were frozen, the liquid finance undergirding the modern economy could stall, as it had after 1929. Berle said, "It should be emphasized that in ordinary times the problem of liquidity is not a problem of maturing loans so much as it is a problem of shifting assets to other banks in exchange for cash." In extraordinary times, like the present, this new shiftability theory, which he embraced, would require the federal government to buy or thaw out those frozen assets.[13] More than any of his intellectual forebearers, Berle emphasized the importance of financial health not just as a side effect of government lending but as the premier reason for such lending.

Berle's financial concerns were reflected in his first memo to the Brains Trust in May 1932. In this memo, Berle said that a renewed confidence in banking and finance was the sine qua non of recovery. (The memo's uncredited author, a friend of Berle's who worked at the Bank of New York, had his own motives for restoring confidence in the banking system.[14]) The cause of the stoppage in credit, the memo said, was that people did not have "confidence in the future permitting them to believe that they can safely entrust such money or resources as they have to the banking system." Thus, "SECURITY OF SAVINGS" was the first step to recovery. The only way the government could support savings was to support investments in four specific credit groups, the two most important of which were farm mortgages and city mortgages. Berle in particular worried about the "extremely bad situation . . . [in] the farm mortgage group." He said that foreclosure of farm mortgages meant more than just the wreck of a home. The questionable farm mortgages were held in thousands of banks, and "these banks first 'freeze' and then fail."[15]

As Berle tried to explain at his first dinner with Roosevelt in the Albany governor's mansion, "Nobody else's credit was good" except the federal government's. Federal credit could be used to undergird the credit of everyone from the "little farmer in Iowa" to the big corporations.[16] As his memo stated, "Credits, both long and short term, are of necessity national in character" and needed to be supported by the nation.[17] Roosevelt was intrigued by Berle's ideas and promised to incorporate them as well as Berle himself in his planning. The governor's reaction left Berle "overjoyed, relieved and happy."[18] His wife wrote in her diary that Berle was having a "frabjous time!"[19]

The three happy warriors—Moley, Tugwell, and Berle—were joined by the final member of the Brains Trust, who had helped invent the modern idea of balance. Hugh Johnson was the cofounder with George Peek of the price-parity movement, and he brought this vision into the incipient administration. Later, as a top official in the administration, Johnson wrote, "If we could have perfect balance among all producing segments—agriculture, capital, industry—there would be almost no limit to our consuming capacity." He thought "the *essence of the New Deal is to point toward that balance.* I think the *essence of what preceded the New Deal was to point away from that balance.*"[20]

Yet the hyperkinetic Johnson, advised by his financier friend Bernard Baruch, also began trumpeting investor confidence as part of restoring balance. In July 1932, he circulated a half-serious "proclamation" by "Muscleinny, Dictator Pro Tem," of the policies needed to ensure recovery. He advocated government loans for such things as "semi-rural self-supporting" housing projects and the writing down of private-debt contracts with new bankruptcy laws. He also said the government should purchase any farm or home mortgage and refinance it at low interest. He hoped these financial reforms would also increase the "buying power of agriculture and remove a considerable part of the deadly disparity between farm and other prices."[21]

The Brains Trust's ideas about rural balance had a personal appeal to Governor Franklin Roosevelt. The governor identified with businesslike farmers because of his long and happy residence on his mother's Hyde Park farm as well as his purchase of a working farm as an investment in Georgia. On official forms, Roosevelt put his occupation as "tree farmer." One of the very first bills he had sponsored as a New York State senator in 1910 was to create a state agricultural credit bank, similar to what became the Federal Land Banks.[22]

Roosevelt was also intimately connected to finance from a young age. His father, with his myriad inherited interests, could be described as a financier, as could his favorite uncle, Frederic Delano, who would soon occupy a variety of advisory positions in his nephew's government. One of the longest and certainly most lucrative jobs Roosevelt ever had was as vice president of the Fidelity & Deposit Company, which insured bonds and other investments. The office of his private law practice, which he maintained at the same time as his Fidelity job in the 1920s, was on Wall Street. As Roosevelt noted, "The two varieties of work seem to dovetail fairly well."[23]

Roosevelt had once assumed that bankers had a particular moral fortitude above that of other businessmen. Yet the legerdemain surrounding the collapse of the Bank of United States in 1930 when he was New York governor sullied that respect.[24] Roosevelt soon told Colonel Edward House, Woodrow Wilson's former confidant, "The real truth of the matter is, as you and I know, that a financial element in the larger centers has owned the Government ever since the days of Andrew Jackson—and I am not wholly excepting the Administration of W. W. The country is going through a repetition of Jackson's fight with the Bank of the United States—only on a far bigger and broader basis."[25]

Yet Roosevelt cared not a whit for the old Jacksonian creed of equal protection or a fight against privileged banks. When Colonel House suggested that Roosevelt give a speech demanding "equality of opportunity for all and special privilege for none," the old rallying cry of anti-class-legislation Democrats, Roosevelt ignored him.[26] Roosevelt paradoxically thought the only way to control bankers was to flood them with more cash, buying their bad assets and boosting their balance sheets. Once the government paid the piper, it could call the tune. As he later told one of his advisers, "There is no doubt in my mind that you and I are being subjected to all sorts of silent pressure by some members of the banking fraternity. . . . They are in a sullen frame of mind, hoping by remaining sullen." Yet there was a solution: "If you and I force these funds on them they will have to act in accordance with our desires."[27] In Roosevelt's mind, controlling finance meant coddling it.[28]

A Presidential Campaign for Mortgage Balance

Roosevelt's campaign for the presidency allowed him to give the most explicit explanation of the ideology of economic balance ever given to the American people. Later historians have claimed that Roosevelt obscured his radical purposes in this presidential campaign or even projected a conservative vision of the future.[29] In reality, Roosevelt was abundantly clear about what he thought had gone wrong with the country and how he was going to fix it. In his campaign, he focused on restoring farm purchasing power and fixing farm mortgages as the means to reestablish prosperity.

Moley said that during the planning of the campaign "agriculture came first" because the "obvious beginnings of our discontents in this country was [sic] the persistence of the delusion that the nation could prosper while its farmers went begging."[30] The deteriorating condition of farmers and rural banks added urgency to the strategy. Besides the foreclosure of almost three out of every one hundred farms in the nation in 1932, the Farmers Holiday Association's violent opposition to foreclosures made banks nervous to collect their debts and exacerbated the ongoing banking panics.[31]

As early as April 1932, Roosevelt explained his ideas about farm balance in his famous "Forgotten Man" speech. The speech left no doubt what class the forgotten man came from. Roosevelt argued that "approximately one-half of our whole population, fifty or sixty million people, earn their living by farming or in small towns whose existence immediately depends on farms. They have today lost their purchasing power. . . . The result of this loss of purchasing power is that many other millions of people engaged in industry in the cities cannot sell industrial products to the farming half of the Nation." Roosevelt thought the first task of his government would be to raise the farmer's dollar to a fair price, but he also made connection between this price reform and finance: "Closely associated with this first objective is the problem of keeping the home-owner and the farm-owner where he is, without being dispossessed through the foreclosure of his mortgage." The farmer's loss of purchasing power led to shaky mortgages, and these bad mortgages then threatened the "little bank and local loan company," which in turned threatened the country's finances. Roosevelt explained that he had three fundamental reforms he hoped to establish as president: "restoring the farmers' buying power, relief to the small banks and home owners," and, finally, tariff reform, a campaign centered on farmers' need for export markets.[32] These three ideas became the leitmotifs of Roosevelt's campaign.

At the Democratic National Convention in July 1932, where Roosevelt made the historic decision of accepting his party's nomination in person, he explained what his administration would accomplish. His speech's stirring peroration, where he said, "I pledge you, I pledge myself, to a new deal for the American people," obscured the more mundane parts of that new deal. Roosevelt told the teeming agents of his election in the Chicago Coliseum that their country was divided into three main groups: the agricultural, the industrial, and "the people who are called 'small investors and depositors.' In fact, the strongest tie between the first two groups, agriculture and industry, is the fact that the savings and to a degree the security of both are tied together in that third group—the credit structure of the Nation." Roosevelt strained to convey to his audience the importance of this abstract credit structure. "Picture to yourself, for instance, the great groups of property owned by millions of our citizens, represented by credits issued in the form of bonds and mortgages—[g]overnment bonds of all kinds . . . mortgages on real estate and cities. . . . We know well that in our complicated interrelated credit structure if any one of these credit groups collapses they may all collapse." Roosevelt briefly discussed the unprecedented levels of unemployment but soon apologized that he had to "go back to this dry subject of finance; because it all ties in together." He also apologized to his audience that he had to "lay emphasis on the farmers" and especially on farmers' debts because "farm mortgages reach nearly ten billions of dollars today and interest charges on that alone are $560,000,000 a year." He argued, "Our most immediate concern should be to reduce the interest burden on these mortgages." In what could only be a first and a last for a presidential nomination acceptance speech, Roosevelt discussed such esoteric issues as mortgage amortization payments and mortgage maturities.[33]

Roosevelt continued to focus on farm finance in other campaign speeches, such as one on the "farm problem" in Topeka, Kansas, in September 1932. Here he uttered his famous echo of Lincoln's "House Divided" speech, turning Lincoln's fight against slavery into a fight for economic balance. He stated, "This Nation cannot endure if it is half 'boom' and half 'broke.'" He made clear that the boom and bust were the city and the farm. He again elaborated on his theory of a seamless web of economic relations and said the country had to recognize "our interdependence in order to provide a balanced economic well-being for every citizen of the country." He thought that if "we would get to the root of the difficulty, we shall find it in the present lack of equality for agriculture." The reforms needed were obvious: "In the first place, there is the necessity, as well all know, for the refinancing of farm mortgages in order to relieve the burden of excessive interest charges and the grim threat of foreclosure." This meant providing more money to bankers. He said, "Specifically, I am prepared to insist that Federal credit be extended to banks, insurance or loan companies . . . on the condition that every reasonable assistance be given to mortgagors."[34]

Roosevelt brought his farm message to urban crowds, too. In his resonant upper-crust accent, he told a Boston group, "I am going to talk to a city audience about farming. I do not make one kind of speech to a farm audience and another kind of speech to a city audience." He argued that "without a balanced economy between agriculture and industry, there can be no healthy national life." He told them "you are poor because they are poor," without noting that he did not think the causality ran in the other direction.[35] He also told the urbanites at the Young Men's Business and Professional League that "whenever income in any great group in the population becomes so disproportionate as to dry up purchasing power within any other group, the balance of economic life is thrown out of order," and explained, "That is why I have so greatly stressed restoring prosperity to our agriculture interests."[36]

As the campaign wore on, and as the foreclosure crisis grew, Roosevelt laid ever more emphasis on the problems of rural credit. In his address in Sioux City, Iowa, in late September, he said, "For more than a year I have spoken in my State and in other States of the actual calamity that impends on account of farm mortgages," and "I do not need to tell you that . . . I realize to the full the seriousness of the farm mortgage situation."[37] By late October, when Tugwell worried that antiforeclosure riots posed a threat to the nation, he convinced Roosevelt to give a speech specifically on farm mortgages in Springfield, Illinois.[38] There, Roosevelt explained that the "Federal Land [B]anks became very important units in our financial life," and Congress should do a complete reorganization of the farm credit system to assist both the farmer and his banker. He said it was a duty of the government "to obtain for [the farmer] the very lowest reasonable rate of interest."[39]

It cannot be said that Roosevelt did not make his intentions with regard to farms and farm mortgages clear or did not emphasize their importance in his overall scheme for economic revival. His landslide election was a resounding mandate for many reforms, but arguably first for creating economic balance between farms and cities and for improving the situation of farm creditors and borrowers.

Crafting a New Deal Mortgage

Roosevelt's speeches gave the nation the broad outlines of his theory of economic recovery, yet he needed to delegate the specifics. For that job, he tapped his Dutchess County farming neighbor. Henry Morgenthau Jr. was the son of a successful German Jewish father who had made a fortune in New York real estate and then, like Roosevelt's family, took that fortune into farming. Roosevelt called the lanky and bald Morgenthau, with his awkward and funereal demeanor, "Henry the Morgue" but remained close to him throughout his presidency.[40] Roosevelt's secretary, Grace Tully, later said that Morgenthau met with the president more than any other member of his cabinet.[41]

6.1 Henry Morgenthau Jr. and his father walking to the Gridiron Dinner, 1937.

Source: Library of Congress.

With Roosevelt's encouragement, Morgenthau took time during the campaign to visit his former college, Cornell University, in tiny Ithaca in upstate New York. Cornell had acquired worldwide renown for its agricultural economics program, and Governor Roosevelt had earlier in 1932 appropriated funds for the construction of a special Cornell Agriculture Economics building there.[42]

On Morgenthau's visit, one particular "ag econ" professor attracted his attention. William I. Myers was a man obsessed with the importance of rural credit. From a poor rural childhood, Myers rose to become Cornell's and the nation's first professor of farm finance. As a professor, Myers continued to work his own farm, even acquiring a mortgage for it from the Springfield Federal Land Bank, after which he said he felt as if he were "really on the way" to success. In the spring semester of 1932, when Morgenthau sought his counsel, Myers was teaching a class on farm mortgages.[43]

At Morgenthau's insistence, Myers began talking with government officials and private bankers on mortgage issues, and not long after Roosevelt won the election, Myers prepared a plan. First, he argued for scrapping the increasingly baroque architecture of federal farm loans and creating a single agency devoted to farm credit. Instead of Hoover's Federal Farm Board for cooperatives, the Intermediate Credit Banks for livestock and medium-term loans, the Federal Land Banks for mortgages, and sporadic seed loans given directly by the Treasury, there would be one farm credit agency with different branches. He also wanted to reduce the rates of Federal Land Bank loans, and he wanted cheap supplemental mortgages to help pay down old mortgages. He said at one meeting with farm groups that in order to get bankers on board with his new plan, "it is necessary to have a little cash to offer these creditors."[44] Thus, Myers's solution to the farm mortgage problem was to provide even more mortgages and more money for lenders, now including the government lenders themselves.[45] As Myers explained later, the government's job "is to put agriculture on a basis of credit equality with corporate industry" through the provision of "constant access to investment markets" for farmers' loans.[46]

At the same time as the credit plan was in the works, Tugwell, Berle, Johnson, and the other Brains Trusters created the outlines of a new farm price plan, known as "domestic allotment." The Brains Trust hoped the government would determine the total amount of land that could be grown for each crop and then "allot" portions of that total to individual farmers. The plan would restrict farm acreage, reduce farm production, and thus, it was hoped, raise the prices of farm products.[47] In February 1933, one economist with the Federal Farm Board, Mordecai Ezekiel, who helped draft the plan, explained the allotment idea in typical balance terms: "If one part of the society has its income cut one-third, and another part has it cut two-thirds, the ability of the two parts to trade with each other is seriously curtailed."[48] Although the Cornell crowd around Myers was not excited about the allotment policy, Tugwell said that "the Cornell group and we did agree on [one thing] and that was that something had to be done about the farm credit situation," most specifically by the "Federal Government on [lowering] mortgage rates."[49]

Farm lobbyists focused on the benefits of the new mortgage plan instead of on allotment. In January 1933, representatives of the Farmers Union, the

American Farm Bureau Federation, the National Grange, and other farm groups met with top Roosevelt officials and agreed that "the farmer must be able to find his credit sources in one place—whether long, middle or short term"—and that the government should provide new mortgage credit to prevent foreclosures.[50] Bankers of course also appreciated the potential benefits. In February 1933, the chairman and president of Chase National Bank, Winthrop Aldrich, said, "Business life goes on well when different kinds of production are in good balance, different types of goods being produced in right proportions." But when "farm products pile up unsold," the "balance among industries must be restored." He said the most important policy the government should implement was "emergency credit relief," especially in the "farm mortgage situation."[51]

During the interregnum directly after Roosevelt's election, the Farmers Holiday Association revolt reached its peak, with violence and riots bedeviling foreclosure auctions. Roosevelt agonized to Tugwell that the antiforeclosure movement "was as near to rebellion as the depression had brought Americans." Tugwell wrote in his diary that Roosevelt knew Americans had been peaceful during the Depression because they all thought "no individual could be blamed. Now, however, minds were being made up. The debtors had centered on foreclosures" as their main enemy.[52] Even in the tranquility of Roosevelt's "little White House" in Warms Springs, Georgia, a group of radical farm protestors interrupted his final vacation before he assumed the presidency. They demanded a new currency based entirely on farm mortgages. Although Roosevelt was not willing to go as far as that, he convinced the marchers that his and their objectives were aligned. He said he would help them get the mortgages they needed. The protestors decamped after declaring themselves "well satisfied with the interview." They promised to support the new president in his financial endeavors.[53]

Halting the Financial Collapse

Roosevelt's speech on his inauguration day, March 4, 1933, will forever be remembered for his ringing declaration against "fear itself." Yet at the speech's center was Roosevelt's continued demand for economic balance. He said, "We must frankly recognize the overbalance of population in our industrial centers." He proposed two ways to achieve balance: first, make "definite efforts to raise the values of agricultural products and with this the power to purchase the output of our cities," and, second, "prevent[] realistically the tragedy of the growing loss through foreclosure of our small homes and farms."[54] Roosevelt's focus now that he had achieved the presidency remained the same as when he had campaigned for it.

Before Roosevelt could do anything to balance different sectors, he had to deal with the fear to which he referred in his speech: the banking panic that had paralyzed the nation. After an earlier series of bank runs, many states had called bank holidays that forbade people from removing cash from their checking and savings accounts. Without the ability to acquire paper currency, much of the country had been reduced to barter, trading wood for eggs or store tokens for groceries. Within days of assuming the office, Roosevelt issued a series of unparalleled executive orders designed to halt the panic. He took the country off the gold standard in order to spur inflation, called a national bank holiday, and made an implicit promise to guarantee all bank deposits, as bankers had recently demanded.[55] In his first fireside chat in March, Roosevelt told the nations' citizens to renew their faith in the banks because banks "keep the wheels of industry and agriculture turning" through their investment in "bonds, commercial paper, mortgages, and many other kinds of loans."[56] His administration officials and holdovers from Hoover's administration wrote a bill that gave the RFC the power to purchase bank stock directly and thus, instead of merely supporting bad loans, to fully bailout endangered banks with new capital. Congress passed this act within hours of reconvening and extended for one more year the Federal Reserve's emergency power to loan on long-term assets.[57]

Roosevelt's financial reforms worked. The end of the gold standard meant prices started rising again after four years of disastrous deflation, and the administration soon began reopening healthy banks. Industrial production grew by 50 percent in just four months, the fastest rate of growth in American history.[58] Roosevelt's actions garnered wide praise and paid some specific political dividends. California senator William McAdoo told Roosevelt officials that he was "overwhelmed with joy" when the administration decided to reopen the wavering California-based Bank of America, which had been heavily involved in speculative mortgage loans and whose chief, A. P. Giannini, had been a heavy financial supporter of McAdoo.[59] To Roosevelt, the crisis and his response further emphasized the importance of finance to the health of the economy and the power of the federal government's credit to restore that health.

New Deal Mortgages in Congress

Luckily for Roosevelt, the new Democratic Congress was filled with farmers, bankers, and investors—all eager to support his financial plans. Both John Rainey of Illinois, the Speaker of the House of Representatives, and Joseph Robinson of Arkansas, the majority leader in the Senate, were major stockholders in Joint-Stock Land Banks.[60] They were also ardent, if self-interested, proponents of federal mortgage support. On the morning of March 23, Roosevelt met with Rainey, Robinson, and nine other congressmen at the White House to explain his farm proposals, and they agreed on Myers's plan for farm mortgage refinancing. According to one report, "President Roosevelt told the conferees that there is no legislation in which he is more deeply interested than this project to lighten the mortgage load of farmers."[61]

Marvin Jones, the chairman of the House Agricultural Committee, became the most important advocate of this plan in Congress. Like many other actors in this drama, he had had the importance of balance and farm credit instilled in him from a young age. His entire life he retained the memory of being a ten-year-old boy and going with his father to the First National Bank in Valley View, Texas, to borrow $250 for ninety days. Jones asked his dad why he had borrowed for only ninety days if he could not pay back the loan for nine months, when his cotton crop came due. His father supposedly told the precocious ten-year-old, "The financial structure of this country is geared to the needs of industry and business and it is kept in what they call 'liquid condition.' There should be a separate credit structure suited to the needs of farm and livestock people." Jones said his father's explanation was "burned into my mind" and forever after inspired his efforts. When he entered Congress, one of his first bills would have forced the Federal Land Banks to provide more and cheaper mortgages. He thought Roosevelt was a perfect vehicle for such plans because Roosevelt "was one of the first men who lifted up his eyes and saw all the way across this broad, big country and, in his grasp of things, was able to visualize a well-balanced country."[62] Jones and William Myers drafted an executive order for Roosevelt, which, under a new reorganization authority that the president used for the first time, centralized all rural-credit programs in a single organization, the Farm Credit Administration (FCA).

Jones and Myers worked with farm and business representatives to draft Roosevelt's larger mortgage-reform bill. Myers said that "the first and one of the most important things" in the bill was to allow the Federal Land Banks to issue the hitherto unimaginable amount of $2 billion in bonds at no more than 4 percent interest, which would in turn allow for billions in cheap mortgages to farmers. This amount was almost double the Federal Land Banks' previous peak of outstanding bonds, and the interest rate was a full percentage point lower. Two members of the American Farm Bureau Federation recommended an explicit government guarantee of the bonds in order to achieve this lower interest rate, even though they admitted that most of the benefits would go to bondholders.[63] Myers objected to an explicit guarantee, but FDR said that his "one important point of difference" with Myers was that he thought bondholders needed support, too. Myers reluctantly rewrote the bill to have the U.S. government guarantee the interest on the bonds but not the principle. Myers argued that confining the guarantee to just the interest "limits the Government's risk," but he would later note that it implied a more complete guarantee as well.[64]

The bill included other handouts to financial interests. It provided the failing Joint-Stock Land Banks $100 million in loans at generous rates to pay off their investors (such as Rainey and Robinson).[65] Myers came up with the amount, as he said, to wind the banks down "in a sympathetic manner protecting the interests of their bondholders" as well as of their borrowers.[66] Louis Taber, the Grange lobbyist and head of his own Joint-Stock Land Bank, helped write the final bill.[67] When Myers floated the bill to Senator Robinson, he said the senator "thought the provisions for the liquidation of the Joint Stock Land Banks were very fair."[68] Shepherded by Jones and his lobbyists, the final mortgage-reform bill made it through Congress with minimal amendments. Jones said the passage of the mortgage-reform plan was his "boyhood dream finally realized."[69]

In the rush of the Roosevelt's first hundred days of legislation, the mortgage-reform bill was attached to the domestic-allotment and crop-restriction bill proposed by Tugwell, and both passed as the Agricultural Adjustment Act. The two bills, for mortgage reform and price supports, were thus two sides of the same attempt at agricultural balance, and restoring financial solvency was central in both. In Roosevelt's first message to Congress in March 1933 urging the price-support program, he had noted higher farm prices would not just help farmers but also work "greatly to relieve the pressure of farm mortgages and to increase the asset value of farm loans made by our banking institutions." And as he described the bill in his next fireside chat, the "prices for basic commodities were such as to destroy the value of the assets of national institutions such as banks, savings banks, insurance companies and others. These institutions, because of their great needs, were foreclosing mortgages," to the detriment of themselves and the farmers. The higher prices of the farm products would bring the banks back to solvency[70] The Agricultural Adjustment Administration, which was run by price-parity ideology founder George Peek, and the allotment scheme it managed have inspired libraries of books and articles, whereas the credit-reform plan and the financial motivations of both plans have attracted almost no attention. At the time, however, the mortgage part of the bill received most of the public praise and press.[71]

Other New Deal acts were conceived in the same balancing spirit. Even the National Industrial Recovery Act of 1933, modeled after the agricultural allotment plan and passed soon after it in order to balance different industrial sectors, was influenced by Roosevelt's ideas of overdeveloped cities. In that act, Congress provided a $25 million revolving fund to loan on mortgages for the purchase of rural homesteads, as Hugh Johnson had demanded in the campaign. As the act said, the fund's purpose was "for aiding the redistribution of the overbalance of population in industrial centers."[72]

By June, at the end of Roosevelt's famous first one hundred days, it looked as if most of the outlines of his plan for economic balance through credit were

6.2 "United," cartoon on the Farm Credit Administration.

Source: Milton Halladay, *Providence Journal*, c. May 1933.

in place. In his fireside chat at the end of the congressional session, in late July, he told the people that the new laws were "not just a collection of haphazard schemes, but rather the orderly component parts of a connected and logical whole." He thought that the most important reforms, besides restoring the government's credit, restored the credit of citizens. He reiterated his earlier metaphor of "a Nation half boom and half broke" and said that if farmers were given

6.3 "By Way of Replacement," cartoon on the Farm Credit Administration.

Source: *Portland Journal*, c. May 1933.

more "purchasing power . . . we shall greatly increase the consumption of those goods which are turned out by industry." He also thought it "a vital necessity to restore purchasing power by reducing the debt and interest charges upon our people."[73] Roosevelt hoped he and Congress had created the instruments to make these plans a reality.

Boosting the Banks

As in previous eras, the supposed means of helping farmers, support to rural banks, often became the new ends of government. After passage of the mortgage-reform bill, the *Wall Street Journal* celebrated that it would "enable small banks in the agricultural regions to put themselves in a more liquid condition."[74] The *Bankers Magazine* argued that under the new bill "the Federal Land [B]anks have an opportunity to be of very great service to banks at the same time they are refinancing farmers" because the Land Banks could take bad assets off the private banks' books.[75]

Morgenthau, who assumed the leadership of the new Farm Credit Administration, understood the need for bank support. Soon after passage of the bill, he announced a special "wholesale" mortgage program, not for farmers but specifically "for reopening closed banks that are weighted down by heavy holdings of frozen farm mortgages."[76] A government report found in November 1933 that 90 percent of the proceeds of all federal farm mortgage loans were used to refinance private mortgages and other debts. The report cheerfully noted that the percentage devoted to refinancing was higher than under the previous administration.[77]

Such credit supports, however, were not enough to revive the farm economy. After a stall in price rises and in the general economy in the summer, the president decided to intensify his inflation push. As his secretary of agriculture, Henry A. Wallace, had shown in his book more than a decade earlier, agricultural commodities were the first to respond to inflation or deflation,[78] and that was precisely Roosevelt's hope. Two other Cornell agricultural economists, George Warren and Frank Pearson, soon to be known as the "Gold Dust Twins," inspired Roosevelt's efforts. Their classic book *Prices* (1933) argued that raising the price of gold specifically led to inflation and benefitted crop sellers and lenders. Warren said in a public speech that considering the current debt burden, there were "only two possible alternatives—either the price level must be raised to the debt level, or the debt level must be lowered to the price level. To complete deflation means completing the process of foreclosure on bankrupt farms and homes." To raise the price level, by contrast, would allow farmers to pay down these debts.[79]

In in his fourth fireside chat in October 1933, Roosevelt explained his gold-buying plan as an exercise in agricultural balance. He said his goal in raising prices was "to restore a balance in the price structure so that farmers may exchange their product for the products of industry on a fairer basis." He said that no one thought "that commodity prices, especially agriculture prices, are high enough yet."[80] After the program began, Roosevelt wrote to Colonel House that the higher crop prices from his gold-purchase program had "stopped foreclosures, saved banks and started people definitely on the upgrade."[81]

Another, more explicit way to save the banks was to make the federal government's mortgage loans more generous and liberal. These loans could then be used to pay back old bank debts. The new mortgage act allowed the Federal Land Banks to loan up to 75 percent of the "normal" value of the farms, and the act allowed the FCA appraisers to determine that "normal" value. Roosevelt talked to Morgenthau about the connection between the inflation and mortgage plans by noting, "I fixed the minimum price of cotton. Can't you adjust your appraisal[s] on that basis?" Morgenthau said they were trying to be as liberal as possible.[82]

These new and more generous loans required a new and expansive bureaucracy. The number of employees under the FCA went from 2,500 at the beginning of the year to almost 15,000 by the end.[83] The FCA in this period became a peerless financial behemoth, with almost $3 billion in assets. The press regularly described it as the "world's largest bank."[84] By almost any measure, it was.

Selling the Public

Despite the Roosevelt administration's best efforts, it, like the Hoover administration, had trouble selling Land Bank bonds to the public. Morgenthau first asked the Treasury secretary to buy some of his bonds, writing in his diary, "I jokingly put it to him, 'I am going to blackmail you into doing it because if you do not buy them, we will have to sell our bonds and may ruin your bond market.'"[85] But the Treasury and after it the Federal Reserve refused to take the strained joke seriously. The revived Land Banks instead began their New Deal career by borrowing $150 million from the RFC, so that one semipublic corporation supported another. The RFC demanded that the funds be used for refinancing mortgages in "impaired or closed commercial banks" as well as to "improve the position of open banks." The FCA, which was of a similar mind, obliged.[86]

Early in 1934 Morgenthau prepared a letter for the president explaining that the original guarantee of only interest payments on the Land Bank bonds was insufficient to attract private investors. "From the common sense point of view everyone knows that the guarantee of interest would, in all probability, be followed by the government making good any deficiency of the principal. This being so, we might as well be frank" and fully guarantee the bonds. He proposed an act whereby the new bonds would be issued through another new, fully public and guaranteed corporation, the Federal Farm Mortgage Corporation.[87]

In a press conference announcing the plan in January 1934, the president admitted that the government had not been completely open about its guarantee of the Land Banks. "Now the question comes up as to whether we should not be honest and face the fact" that if the bonds ever were seriously endangered, "the public and Congress would undoubtedly feel that it was a moral obligation on the part of the Government to make good." He noted that in New York the state government had created quasi-public corporations, and after one of their bankruptcies, the state legislature had recognized "there was a moral obligation—not a legal but a moral obligation—on the legislature to make good the deficiency of the bonds. . . . Now if there is that moral obligation which might arise twenty years or thirty years from now, why, in all common sense, should we not recognize it now?"[88] As the *Wall Street Journal* said after the new bill passed, the act showed that "entering upon the second year of the emergency recovery program the Roosevelt Administration plans to concentrate greater attention on the liquidation of debts through federal financial assistance," of which "first in this field are the farm and home mortgage debts."[89]

In Roosevelt's first State of the Union Address to Congress on January 3, he celebrated his work over the past year in restoring the nation's credit structure. Roosevelt again divided the nation into three parts, noting "the relations of industry and agriculture and finance to each other." After spending time telling the American public to contact the FCA or other agencies if they were in danger of losing their farms or homes, he returned to agricultural balance: "I continue in my conviction that industrial progress and prosperity can only be attained by bringing the purchasing power of that portion of our population which in one form or another is dependent on agriculture up to a level which will restore a proper balance between every section of the country and between every form of work."[90] His first State of the Union included an almost verbatim copy of his campaign promises, but it demonstrated how far he had already gone to achieve them. Through the end of a devastating depression and into the beginning of a sporadic recovery, Roosevelt's first year had contained an enduring vision.

Mortgage Moratoriums and the End of Farm Balance

Events would soon push Roosevelt's focus away from the farm. In January 1934, pressure from traditional financiers caused Roosevelt to stabilize the dollar and thus ended hopes of increased inflation for farm prices. A Supreme Court decision in the same month also ended his plan for a revived farm mortgage system. The case began when a local Minnesota court struck down that state's mortgage moratorium as a "special law and not a general law" and a vicious form of "class legislation" benefitting borrowers over creditors.[91] Yet on January 8, the same day that Roosevelt announced a guarantee of the Land Bank bonds, Chief Justice Charles Evans Hughes read a five-to-four U.S. Supreme Court decision upholding the Minnesota moratorium and thus mortgage moratoriums throughout the nation.[92] The case was the first major Supreme Court decision of the New Deal and gave many Democrats hope that the Court was on the side of the debtors and the activists. Following this decision, three more states passed mortgage moratoriums, and many state supreme courts moved to uphold moratoriums they had once declared invalid.[93] In Congress, the Frazier-Lemke bill for a nationwide farm mortgage moratorium gained a new impetus.[94]

Although these state and federal actions held out hope for farmers, they made a private market for farm mortgage debt impossible. The moratoriums ended any possibility of farmers paying off bonds' investors. The actions thus earned Roosevelt's ire. The president fumed to an adviser about an early version of the Frazier-Lemke bill that it would "wreck [the] recovery."[95] The more limited Frazier-Lemke Farm Bankruptcy Act passed Congress in June 1934, but in signing it Roosevelt showed his pique and said it would require amendment. Many agreed that its five-year moratorium for any farm mortgage payments was too long.[96]

With rampant delinquencies and state and federal moratoriums, the government failed to create a private market for the farm mortgage credit group. Relying ever more on its explicit guarantees, the government instead ended up supporting an ever-larger portion of the farm credit system. By the end of the decade, it controlled more than 50 percent of all farm mortgages in the nation, whereas the older land bank system had never topped 20 percent in the 1920s. No federal urban-mortgage program was ever as extensive in its sphere.[97] In the end, Roosevelt's mortgage policies were largely an expansion of those of earlier administrations. As Myers said in early 1934, the New Deal's work on farm finance "has not been a revolution . . . instead it has been a process of evolution."[98]

Despite the problems, Henry Morgenthau's administration of the farm system impressed Roosevelt enough that he appointed him as his new Treasury secretary. The president told him, "You are one of the two or three people who has made an outstanding success here in Washington, so let's you and I go on to bigger things." As was typical for Roosevelt, he added, "We will have lots of fun doing it together." As was typical for Morgenthau, he told his diary, "I was so dumbfounded when he made this statement that I broke out in a perspiration and sort of mumbled for a few seconds."[99] Yet Morgenthau would remember his work on mortgages as the administration's focus shifted.

The New Dealers' attempt to use price and credit reforms to balance the farm economy with the industrial economy did have a profound effect. The reforms alleviated the mortgage burdens on farmers and helped sustain farmers' incomes. Yet these reforms were even more explicit than previous efforts in their goal of bailing out the banking system, and they, too, failed to bring the economy back into full employment.

Despite Roosevelt's efforts, the focus of the New Deal on agricultural and financial recovery in its first year provoked frustration, just as Herbert Hoover's similar focus had in his first year in office. The inability of the revived farm economy and farm banks to fully resuscitate the industrial economy seemed to require more widespread action. So, like the earlier Hoover administration, the Roosevelt administration switched its attention to the cities.

CHAPTER 7

HOUSING, HEAVY INDUSTRY, AND THE FORGOTTEN NEW DEAL BANKING ACT

On Monday, May 28, 1934, President Franklin Roosevelt met John Maynard Keynes, the world-famous British economist, for the first time, but their conversation in the Oval Office did not go as planned. After Keynes left, Roosevelt expressed his frustration to his secretary of labor, Frances Perkins, the first woman appointed to the U.S. cabinet, "I saw your friend Keynes. He left a whole rigmarole of figures. He must be a mathematician rather than a political economist." Keynes later lamented to Perkins that he had "supposed the President was more literate, economically speaking."[1] Many then considered Keynes's visit a failure, which demonstrated that Keynes's ideology and the ideology of the New Deal would remain at loggerheads.[2]

Yet the day after the meeting, Keynes met with the man Roosevelt called "my economist," the gregarious and genial Winfield Riefler, who was friendly with Keynes. A few years later, Keynes wrote to Roosevelt that he remembered his conversation with Riefler "vividly," especially Riefler's insistence on doing something for housing.[3] In fact, Riefler convinced Keynes to meet with the Senate Banking and Currency Committee, which was considering the administration's new plan for insuring banks directly against losses on individual urban mortgages. At the meeting, Keynes most likely described his belief in the need to lower long-term interest rates in order to stimulate the economy and explained how the proposed mortgage insurance plan would accomplish this end. Keynes's as always sterling arguments seem to have had an impact. Riefler later told Keynes that "your conversations with the Senators had a most salutary effect and may have constituted the turning point in passing the housing legislation.

I can't thank you enough for your help."[4] It was perhaps Keynes's most direct and maybe even his most important impact on the New Deal, and it was done to support home mortgages.

Just as Herbert Hoover had begun his presidency as a believer in balancing the rural and urban sectors of the economy and then moved on to balancing construction and the rest of the economy, Roosevelt's administration trod the same path. Yet the early New Deal housing reforms, especially the National Housing Act of 1934, the result of Keynes's, Riefler's, and others' efforts, have received little attention from writers describing the economic policy of the New Deal.[5] This act and others like it intrigue mainly urban historians who are interested in their impact on the American landscape and who attribute their passage to the influence of suburban developers and real estate interests. To other writers, the National Housing Act is a preeminent example of the New Deal's use of credit to spur consumer spending or to substitute for directly redistributing income.[6] An examination of the act's history, however, shows that the interests behind it were either in the financial industry or among manufacturers in certain heavy industries, along with those intellectuals in the Roosevelt administration concerned about banking and balance. The act is best described, therefore, not as a housing act but as a banking act, which encouraged recovery through supporting particular types of financing.

As in Hoover's time, the administration's urban-mortgage reforms would result in the federal government being liable for potentially billions of dollars of mortgages. In fact, two of the institutions that emerged out of this act, the Federal Savings and Loan Insurance Corporation and the Federal National Mortgage Association, also known as Fannie Mae, would many years later become prominent recipients of federal bailouts totaling in the hundreds of billions of dollars. The National Housing Act was part of a sea change in the New Deal's focus toward balancing heavy industrial production in the urban sector, but it was also yet another expansion of government guarantees to American lenders, whose consequences would reverberate for decades after its passage.

Homes Playing Second Fiddle to Farms

Urban foreclosures, although never as publicly salient as farm foreclosures, had become a national scandal by the time Roosevelt assumed office. In 1932 and 1933, lenders foreclosed on more than half a million urban homes, and the foreclosure rate per home mortgage was more than four times the rate of the 1920s.[7] At the foreclosure sales, many banks had to purchase back the mortgaged houses because there were no buyers. Other banks and owners simply destroyed homes rather than pay increasingly burdensome taxes on them.[8] The

struggles over foreclosures on the ground were often brutal. Groups of Socialist Party members or other activists restocked defaulting renters' or mortgagors' homes after their furniture had been removed. "Home defense" leagues prevented foreclosure auctions through violence and threats. Numerous eviction
riots, some leading to deaths, prevented sheriffs from throwing renters and
owners out on the street.[9]

Franklin Roosevelt's efforts to save urban families from the specter of these
foreclosures have been described as an aspect of his personal-relief program.
Arthur Schlesinger claimed of Roosevelt's first urban antiforeclosure program
that "probably no single measure consolidated so much middle-class support
for the administration."[10] Jordon Schwartz claims, as others have, that Roosevelt "had a passionate interest in home ownership," made manifest in his
numerous housing programs.[11]

Yet Roosevelt never made homeownership the focus of his mortgage programs, and he began supporting urban mortgages as no more than an after-
thought of his farm programs. When he first submitted his bill for refinancing
farm mortgages to Congress, on which his aides had worked for months, he
included a short promise to do something for urban homeowners. His administration, however, had prepared nothing on that issue. The following day Roosevelt sent a hasty letter to W. H. Stevenson, chair of the Hoover-era Federal
Home Loan Bank Board, asking him to draft an urban-mortgage bill "immediately."[12] Baffled as to what the president desired, Stevenson consulted Henry
Morgenthau, who showed him the worked-over bill for farm mortgages. Stevenson and his board copied as much of the farm plan as they could. The new
bill was drafted in a single day.[13]

As was typical in bills of that period, this mortgage reform was aimed not
at debtors but at creditors. Horace Russell, a power in the B&L world and the
general counsel of the Federal Home Loan Bank Board, wrote most of the bill.
It created an emergency corporation named the Home Owners Loan Corporation that would refinance defaulting mortgages, but only if they were held by
existing B&Ls or banks. Like earlier semipublic corporations, the new Home
Owners Loan Corporation was technically not part of the government but
carried only a temporary investment of stock and an implicit guarantee. It
would be managed by the B&L-dominated Federal Home Loan Bank Board.
To further appease the industry, the bill removed a direct loan program from
the Hoover era that the lenders felt competed with their business.[14]

One Treasury official later noted that the B&L people tended to win bureaucratic fights about such programs. He said that Russell and his clique "are
good talkers; [and] know more about the business than we do in the Treasury."[15]
One of Senator Robert Wagner's staff, Leon Keyserling, who worked on the bill
in Congress, agreed that the main benefit of the act was that it "rescued the
banks by taking mortgages." He mentioned no benefits to homeowners.[16] In

Congress, some argued that the bill just created "a sales agency for the build-ing and loan[s]" and that it was "more in the interest of capital than [of] the ordinary citizen." Yet Congress passed the Home Owners Loan Act just ten days after Roosevelt asked for it.[17]

Despite later claims that the Home Owners Loan Corporation provided much-needed assistance to homeowners in the depths of Depression, it was notably slow to start. The total number of foreclosures peaked at 252,000 in 1933 and was only slightly less at 229,000 in 1935, still almost four times the rate of the 1920s.[18] Roosevelt's focus with this bill remained on supporting investors. When in his campaign in September 1932 he had asserted that "every man has a right to his own property," he did not mean a mere house but property as an investment, "which means a right to be assured, to the fullest extent possible, in the safety of his savings."[19] When in the fall of 1933 one woman, Miss Marie Thies of Chicago, told Roosevelt, "Don't forget the poor defaulted real estate bond holders," Roosevelt made the rare gesture of writing back to a personal plea. He said that he felt the need to respond to "your letter in person because of my very deep sympathy for . . . those who invested their savings in real estate mortgage bonds." Like Hoover, whose heart bled at similar tales, he said he hoped to "restore, at least in part, real estate values to a higher level," which made homeownership more difficult to achieve but would help current lenders.[20] With similar motives in mind, in September the Home Owners Loan Corporation created a joint campaign with the FCA to "aid the weaker banks" by purchasing home and farm mortgages and thus to help "institutions in need of building up their assets." The two institutions together promised more than $500 million for the purpose.[21]

The new home program, however, continued to live in the shadow of Roos-evelt's farm programs. At the press conference in early 1934 where Roosevelt announced that the government would fully guarantee both the principal and interest of Land Bank bonds, reporters asked if he would do the same for his new urban-mortgage company. Roosevelt said he hadn't thought about it yet, but "I think the chances are" that he would.[22] Eventually he did. By this time, despite sporadic efforts to support home mortgage investors, they had not attracted the administration's attention and interest.

Undercutting Housing

Not only did urban homes attract little interest in the early Roosevelt admin-istration, but many reforms in Roosevelt's first hundred days actually inhib-ited home building. The National Industrial Recovery Act of 1933, which tried to organize industries to ensure balanced production across different sectors, in practice tended to reduce competition and raise prices. Construction costs in particular rose more than almost any other under the new National Recovery Administration.[23] The lumber industry, two-thirds of whose product went into home building, was one of the "Big Six" industries that National Recovery administrator Hugh Johnson, the former leader of the price-parity movement, organized first. The resulting Lumber Code cut back hours worked by 25 percent and raised hourly wages by 45 percent.[24] It was one of the few codes that engaged directly in price fixing, establishing a number of minimum prices for lumber in different parts of the country. The Lumber Code Authority was also by far the most expensive to administer, at more than $4 million a year, almost twice the next most costly authority, and lumber sellers had to pay for it.[25]

New construction came under the Construction Code Authority, which forbade bids below a certain cost certified by the authority and prevented contractors from offering special rebates. The authority required complicated applications for projects and a fee as a percentage of the work performed, which funded this second-most-expensive authority in the system.[26] The administration also sanctioned new monopolistic cartels among both businesses and workers in construction trades. It organized groups of painters, paperhangers, bricklayers, carpenters, tile setters, plasterers, steamfitters, roofers, and other groups, each of which cut back production and raised prices.[27]

Many in and outside the administration became concerned about the resulting higher building costs.[28] One potential homebuyer wrote the administration that "I have plans ready for construction of a home for myself. . . . I will start my new home just as soon as this 'high-jacking' of prices of building materials has been corrected and not until then."[29] Tugwell wrote in his diary that although he once hoped the National Industrial Recovery Act would create "a balance in the price system which will enable each group to buy from every other," now he fretted that those "price disparities have been made worse by the [act]."[30]

Most of the reforms that limited home building in the first hundred days of the Roosevelt presidency affected the financial industry. Finance came under the National Industrial Recovery Act program, and the banking industry, too, used it to further restrict competition and raise prices.[31] B. Howell Griswold, the bond salesman whose Baltimore house had been the premier financier of the Federal Land Banks since their inception, wrote the Investment Bankers Code. While still negotiating with the Treasury on the sale of farm loan bonds (for which, the Treasury noted, Griswold's "firm receives special consideration in commissions, etc."), Griswold pushed for higher fees and more limited bond issues of all sorts.[32] The Investment Bankers Code required companies selling securities to maintain fixed prices without discounts and mandated large upfront down payments. At the code hearing, bankers noted the need to limit "excessive" offerings of new mortgage bonds in particular, which competed with older bond investments.[33] The B&L industry likewise celebrated that their code,

signed in December 1933, increased both the power and expense of B&L management. Its trade magazine stated that "management . . . should be compen-
sated more adequately. It looks as if the [B&L] Code has at last turned thoughts
in the right direction."[34]

The famed Glass-Steagall Banking Act, passed near the end of Roosevelt's
first hundred days, also inhibited some types of lending. This act, which sepa-
rated commercial and investment or short-term and long-term banking, would
seem to work against many of the recent moves by both Hoover and Roosevelt
to allow commercial banks to invest in longer-term assets, which is precisely
why Roosevelt himself did not favor it. (Roosevelt and one of the bill's sponsors, Senator Carter Glass, also opposed the act's Federal Deposit Insurance
Corporation, another implicitly guaranteed corporation to support banks.[35])
When the Federal Reserve Board received an early draft version of the bill,
which sharply limited national bank mortgage loans in particular, the board
argued that these mortgage prohibitions were "unreasonably severe."[36] The Federal Reserve's complaints at least caused the mortgage restrictions to be whit-
tled down by final passage, even as the act limited other types of long-term
investments.[37]

The final financial enactment of Roosevelt's first hundred days was a bill for
regulating stocks and bonds, an early version of what became the Securities and
Exchange Commission. It, too, seemed to inhibit long-term investments. After
its passage, Roosevelt's assistant Raymond Moley worried that many companies "felt that the [Securities] Act was excessively cumbersome. Whether or not
this was true was of less moment than the fact that corporations and bankers
believed that it was and consequently hesitated to float new issues."[38] Adolf Berle
agreed with this analysis, noting especially the dangers from fewer new mortgage bonds. In December 1933, he wrote to Roosevelt that in his private capacity
he was "working on a method of financing some of the major real estate"
bonds, which he hoped the administration would try to encourage as well.[39]
Roosevelt was already considering it.

New Ideas for a Housing Recovery

Despite or because of renewed roadblocks to home building, many thinkers in
the administration who once supported agriculture began to shift their focus
to residential construction. George F. Warren, the Cornell agricultural economist who had encouraged Roosevelt's gold inflation, wrote to Henry Morgenthau in October 1933 that the country now needed more activity in construction, especially home building. Warren argued "not until normal building is
resumed will we get to a normal amount of unemployment."[40] The Department
of Agriculture's top economist, Mordecai Ezekiel, who helped write the

agricultural allotment plan, also argued in October 1933 that because agriculture had largely recovered, the "degree of recovery and prices and activity from this time on will depend on how effectively the Government assumes its responsibility of providing all necessary forms of long term capital and stimulating its use." Most importantly, he argued, the "heart of unemployment is in the construction industries." He said they should get banker support for a new construction loan program and suggested a Lehman Brothers employee to run it.[41]

The administration did enlist bankers in a push for more urban mortgages.[42] In fact, the National Recovery Administration in November 1933 commissioned Alexander Sachs, a top official at Lehman Brothers, to write the "Program for the Stimulation of the Construction Industries to Promote Reemployment." In it, Sachs argued that the recovery wouldn't happen unless the government's "stimulus is transmitted to underlying capital goods industries, of which one of the important branches is the construction industry." He argued that "construction, as a capital production industry, must be revived to produce a balanced economy." He also suggested the federal government finance a home-modernization program, including loans for air conditioning and new washing machines, to improve the value of existing homes.[43]

Intellectuals outside the administration emphasized similar themes. O. M. W. Sprague, the professor of banking and money at Harvard, once a teacher of Roosevelt in his college days, and a recent Roosevelt adviser, began a much-discussed series in the *New York Times* in December 1933 on the "problems of recovery." His first article demanded the government lower building-material prices and finance more housing.[44] When one administration official privately asked Sprague how he would encourage recovery, Sprague replied, "I have told you many times. Spend Four Billion on houses."[45] John Maynard Keynes emphasized the importance of such financing in an open letter to Roosevelt that appeared in the *New York Times* just weeks after Sprague's missives. As a cure for continuing ills, Keynes advocated "the maintenance of cheap and abundant credit, in particular the reduction of the long-term rate of interest," which would spur mortgage lending most of all.[46]

The most important conduit for these views came through a Federal Reserve economist, a man who had long been a friend of Keynes and had already had a profound impact on mortgage policy during the Hoover years.[47] After Roosevelt came into office, Winfield Riefler became the guiding economic influence of the radical young lawyers at the famous "Little Red House" in Georgetown, whose inhabitants permeated the New Deal and drafted many of its bills. One of the house's residents, the attorney Frank Watson, later said, "We followed the economics of Winfield Riefler. . . . His philosophy was that we had a credit mechanism that had come to grinding halt and that it was necessary for us to get the whole mechanism going again." As another inhabitant said, Riefler was "extremely good in working with lawyers," who helped him in drafting new economic programs. The New Dealers also found "Win" a fun and enjoyable presence who lightened their interminable schedules.[48] With broad support in the administration, Roosevelt nominated the prodigious Riefler as the chief economist of his new National Executive Council in August 1933, and it was not long before Roosevelt was referring to Riefler publicly as "my economist."[49]

The Internal Struggle for Mortgages

The National Executive Council was Franklin Roosevelt's first attempt to coordinate the myriad credit agencies and public corporations created by both Hoover and himself. In this council, all of the new semi-independent corporations, such as the Federal Home Loan Banks and the RFC, got a seat at the table of power with the regular cabinet, demonstrating the radically increased importance of these corporations in American government. The council became what Roosevelt called a "super-Cabinet."[50] It was also, however, a recognition that some parts of Roosevelt's program were working at cross purposes.

The meeting of the National Executive Council on Wednesday, December 27, 1933, would begin a reorientation of the New Deal's policy toward home loans and home building. It would also inaugurate a six-month internal debate about which industries deserved government largesse. At that meeting, nineteen of the most powerful members of the administration were in attendance, including Henry Morgenthau as the acting secretary of the Treasury, Henry Wallace as head of the Department of Agriculture, William Myers as head of the FCA, and Winfield Riefler, who had earlier written his first memo to the group on the mortgage situation, which argued that an "expansion in construction activities may help to pull us out of the depression."[51] At the meeting, Riefler passed around a chart that showed that the price of building materials had increased more than almost any other product in the past year. All knew the danger this price rise portended for future home construction.[52] The meeting minutes noted that after some debate the president ordered the creation of a committee to come up with a plan to encourage more building, "to be confined, as far as possible, to the financial problem without government aid."[53]

Roosevelt's charge was limited, yet the ambit of the council's new mortgage committee expanded exponentially over the next six months. Against Roosevelt's original wishes, the committee and his administration would endorse a broad-reaching transformation of all mortgage debt that created a bewildering array of new government financial schemes.

The chair of the new committee was John Fahey, the chair of the Federal Home Loan Board, who took the counsel of the B&L power brokers who dominated that board, such as Morton Bodfish, the hard-charging head of the United States Building and Loan League.[54] On Friday, December 29, 1933, just two days after the Executive Council meeting, Bodfish presented a plan to Fahey and the Home Loan Board on how they could take Roosevelt's minor committee and expand it to accomplish some of their goals. Bodfish proposed a bill that "is intended to restore confidence in thrift and home-financing institutions." He wanted to create a Federal Savings and Loan Insurance Corporation (using the now-preferred term *savings and loans* for *buildings and loans*) to provide his institutions the same deposit protection that commercial banks received under the recent Glass-Steagall Banking Act. He also wanted the government to spend hundreds of millions of dollars on a publicity campaign for home repairs, which would protect the B&Ls' existing investments by improving their housing collateral. He then proposed a number of major and minor federal subventions to mortgage lenders.[55] In total, Bodfish's plan would provide $1.45 billion for the B&L industry, with only the thinnest sheen of public interest to justify it. It was an impossibly ambitious plan in a time when the entire federal budget was only $6 billion dollars and when Roosevelt himself had just asked for a housing plan that didn't require government aid.[56]

Yet B&Ls soon added other demands, such as allowing the government to charter any number of private but tax-exempt urban-mortgage-lending corporations, similar to those that "have proved successful abroad," such as the Credit Foncier in France. Fahey argued that through these "National Mortgage Associations'" ability to buy and hold mortgages, they would add even more liquidity to mortgage loans as well as create "a high-grade, safe, and liquid investment instrument" in the form of their tax-exempt bonds. Unlike the Federal Home Loan Banks, which just loaned money on B&Ls' mortgages, a National Mortgage Association would purchase them directly and give them a permanent, semipublic home.[57]

The other members of Roosevelt's mortgage committee tried to form a plan less focused on just the B&L industry, but this plan, too, went further than Roosevelt hoped. One reason was that another aggressive voice was added to the committee meetings. Marriner Eccles was a boisterous and liberal Mormon banker from Utah who had recently joined the administration as a Treasury adviser. Alexander Sachs of Lehman Brothers noted that Eccles's "mind is that of a crusader—a term which he applied to himself." Eccles told Sachs that he embodied the peculiarly American "feeling of every man that he has a right to look any other man in the face and tell him to go to hell."[58] Many found Eccles's persistence exhausting. John Maynard Keynes supposedly said, "No wonder that man is a Mormon. No single woman could stand him."[59]

It is no coincidence that urban real estate was of concern to Eccles. During his time at the Treasury, he remained president of a lumber company and a construction company, positions he retained for at least a decade.[60] He also ran a bank, which, as a federal bank examiner noted on February 10, 1934, had many "criticized" and failing loans in real estate. Eccles's bank had also loaned

7.1 Marriner Eccles at work, 1937.

Source: Library of Congress.

both of his brothers thousands of dollars, and a bank examiner had placed those loans in the "slow" or questionable category because of concerns about the brothers' solvency. The same bank examiner noted that a "Real Estate Finance Company," which was "owned 100% by Eccles Investment Company," received a $31,500 loan, now in default, from yet another Eccles bank. The mortgage bill Eccles helped prepare could very well have been a matter of life and death for his family's businesses.[61] While in the administration, Eccles told Alexander Sachs that he was a proud capitalist, "as selfish as the rest of them." Sachs noted that Eccles had a mischievous smile on his lips when he said it.[62] When administration officials asked Morgenthau about Eccles's connection to the bill, he said Eccles was "very much interested personally."[63]

Eccles later wrote in his memoirs that when he first went to the Treasury, Winfield Riefler "opened the sluice gates on my own thoughts about housing, and after a torrent of talk lasting many hours Riefler suggested that I become" part of the new housing committee. As Eccles said, before he joined the administration, he "could not at that time have had the faintest idea that I was to have the Treasury assume indirectly the role of mortgage guarantor."[64]

Riefler, with Eccles's assistance, now proposed what would become the Federal Housing Administration (FHA), which would guarantee banks' home mortgages for up to 80 percent of the value of a house and for loans of up to twenty years in exchange for a small fee, but only on newly built homes. Unlike previous government mortgage supports, this was a direct guarantee of a financial asset, which would make any home mortgage on a new house almost as good as a government bond. Riefler told the National Executive Council mortgage committee that although some other sectors of the economy were recovering, the "interests of a balanced recovery program" required more home building. He said the government "does not advance money under the plan but receive[s] money in a continuing trust fund. It, therefore, helps the financing problem of the Treasury during the immediate future"—that is, in the short-term. Any long-term costs of defaults would be borne by future generations.[65]

Over the following months, both the B&Ls' and Riefler's plans would be hashed out at numerous meetings of the new "super-Cabinet," the National Executive Council.[66] But the council also gave Roosevelt a chance to push back. At one meeting on January 23, 1934, Roosevelt raged against the expansion of guarantees. He said that people "should be told all the different things the government cannot do. That doesn't appear here at all. You know, we are getting requests practically to finance the entire United States." He worried that such demands "will become a habit with the country." All the banks and B&Ls wanting more support were "squawking. It is just too bad!" Secretary of Labor Frances Perkins stated, "We have come to the point where we all want to say no," but they also wanted a plan to support construction. Roosevelt acknowledged the need but asked the committee to carry on with a more circumspect vision.[67]

The mortgage committee presented a new version of the combined plan to the National Executive Council in mid-February. Roosevelt was not in attendance, which was for the best because, despite his pleas, the plan expanded government aid even further.[68] The bill added a new program to guarantee mortgages on existing housing, not just on new construction. The committee understood the provision would help garner the support of other financial industries burdened with bad old mortgages, especially the insurance industry, because it would provide those questionable older mortgages with a government guarantee. One member explained that "we are going to get very serious attention from the insurance people if you confine [the guarantee] to new construction."[69] Francis Perkins stated, "I thought we would have the insurance lobby on us" with the original bill, but with this change insurance companies seemed sympathetic. She placed the issue in the most obvious political terms: "It is a political choice as to which group you can best cope with," insurance companies or B&Ls. The B&Ls hated the guarantee on existing mortgages because they felt it allowed others to compete with their long-term loans on older workers' housing. For the moment, however, the overall housing committee went with the insurance industry, and the B&Ls retreated into opposition.[70]

This interindustry squabbling continued at an early May meeting of the National Executive Council until Roosevelt burst into the room with a quip, "Well, people, how many insurance companies have you organized so far?"[71] After hearing from all sides, Roosevelt summed up the situation, "Here is the point. This whole subject was started with the idea of putting people to work. . . . That was the original objective, starting what was called the heavy industries. Suppose we confine ourselves to that for the moment and get the legislation of that." When others in the administration refused to concede to new limits, Roosevelt allowed that some financial supports might be necessary but demanded that all groups had to approve a final plan. He told the leaders to get all the notables "in a room and tell them no lunch unless they agree!"[72]

Riefler and Eccles ceaselessly lobbied the B&Ls to support the final bill. Eccles offered a monetary limit on existing home guarantees and even offered to place the new FHA under the control of the Federal Home Loan Board, but they refused all his blandishments. As one assistant said, "We took John Fahey up on the mountaintop and showed him the kingdoms of the earth and he would have no part of it."[73] Finally, the group told the B&Ls that the government would agree to insure all of the B&Ls' deposits, which finally brought Fahey and the B&L lobby on board.[74] To conciliate a handful of advocates, the committee had given a government guarantee to an entire industry.

Negotiations with Congress before the plan's release succeeded in further expanding the scope of guarantees. Frank Watson, the Little Red House lawyer who drafted the law, said he went through "about sixty four drafts before all the congressmen and senators were finally satisfied." These congressmen, at the urging of a few major home-repair and lending companies, wanted one thing in particular. Instead of providing only advertising for a home-repair campaign, the FHA should guarantee loans on all home or commercial building improvements up to $5,000, with absolutely no cost to creditors, and to refund lenders for losses up to 20 percent of all these loans. It was a massive and uncompensated expansion of government support, to which the administration agreed.[75]

Heavy Industry and Finance Inside Congress

The hearings of the House and Senate Banking and Currency Committees in May 1934, which John Maynard Keynes visited behind the scenes, dramatized the importance of the proposed National Housing Act for heavy industry and the need to balance that sector with others.[76] Riefler told Congress that "the light industries, the consumption-goods industries, are now coming back to life" but that "these heavy industries are stagnant," and the "problem of further devel-opment and recovery lies in the heavy industries."[77] John Fahey noted that the goal of the bill was to "get the heavy construction industry back to work" because that was "the most important in our recovery, and it is the one that is most depressed."[78] Frances Perkins noted that the bill's goal was the "stimula-tion of capital-goods industries." She said, "These industries are commonly known as the "'durable goods' and 'capital goods' industries" and "are always the most difficult to bring about in recovery, as they recover after the consumption-goods industries."[79]

Not surprisingly, the owners of the heavy industries had similar feelings. Lewis Brown of the Johns-Manville Corporation, which made heating systems, was a member of the Durable-Goods Committee of the National Recovery Administration, and he must have shocked Congress when he said that "key to the unemployment problem is . . . in the stimulation of the durable-goods industries." He said that guarantee of home-repair lending was the greatest sin-gle thing that could be done for recovery. Brown did not mention that he, a representative of a home-repair company, had helped write that section of the bill.[80] (Ironically, Brown later founded the free-market American Enterprise Institute.) Henry I. Harriman, chair of the U.S. Chamber of Commerce who made his fortune in public utilities and railroads, claimed "that our industries are divided roughly into two classes, those of consumable goods and those of capital goods, permanent goods, or construction." He argued this bill "definitely is aimed at stimulating construction work, where there is today the recognized need for it rather than in consumable goods."[81] The focus on benefits to indus-try annoyed some in Congress. Representative John Hollister said that although the bill is called a "'housing bill[,]' [t]hat is really a misnomer. . . . [T]he main purpose of this bill is to pump money out, as soon as possible, into the build-ing industry, because [of] the general feeling of economists . . . that money is not being spent in the building industry and in the durable-goods industries[,] which rely to a great extent on building."[82]

Administration officials, however, also noted the incentives to financiers in the bill. One official told Congress that many companies, such as Brown's Johns-Manville Company and the General Motors Acceptance Corporation, had made intermediate loans for home improvements of up to three years. The new bill would encourage this type of financing and allow banks to get involved in it. The extending of government-protected intermediate-term loans for repairs almost perfectly mimicked the early Intermediate Credit Banks' extension of farm credit and had a similar impetus in filling out all parts of the lending market—rural and urban, short, intermediate, and long—with government guarantees.[83] One official said the federal government needed to protect banks against any losses in home lending because otherwise the average banker tended to "go along the line of least resistance and follow the custom of banking in the old fashion, with 90-day paper."[84] The final draft of the bill said that the goal of the home-improvement program was "to insure [sic] liquidity to financial institutions" in making new types of loans.[85]

Some congressmen worried about the many government advantages given to financiers, especially the proposed tax advantage and the attached government "instrumentality" language of the proposed National Mortgage Associations. One congressman claimed that after the chaos in the Federal Land Bank and Joint-Stock Land Bank systems, this new act was similarly "putting the seal of official Federal approval upon a private corporation. It has the potentialities for plunging us back to the depths from which we are now emerging."[86] Representative Robert Luce complained that "the land banks, by those instrumentalities, were enabled to hold themselves out to the public as Federal institutions." He thought that had been one of "the most calamitous things that the Congress had had to do with in our generation." He asked one supporter, "How can you ask us to repeat the scandals of the last few years?"[87] The bill, he argued, was "for the relief of certain financial interests instead of for the relief" of workers or home buyers.[88] (Luce had apparently forgotten his own essential part in making the Federal Home Loan Banks tax-exempt instrumentalities under the Hoover administration.) Eccles reluctantly endorsed such government benefits, arguing, "I personally would like to see all tax-exemptions of securities eliminated," but he thought the desperate need for more mortgages in this case necessitated the exemption.[89]

The National Housing Act, which finally passed Congress and was signed by the president on June 28, 1934, changed the face of American banking. It made mortgages in a bank as safe and liquid as a government bond. As *Millar's Housing Letter* explained to its subscribers, the act would "revolutionize the mortgage lending field" because "a so-called 'mortgage market' would be created." Now mortgages not only would be held by people and institutions but also could be bought and sold across the nation by people who could assume they all had the federal government's backing.[90] As one FHA official later told the *Bankers Magazine*, the "National Housing [A]ct was one of the most far-reaching pieces of banking legislation enacted since the passage of the Federal Reserve Act."[91]

The act's proponents had explained to Congress that it aimed to encourage industrial producers and financiers, not workers or consumers. This focus was affirmed after its passage by a new attempt to lower workers' incomes. An earlier version of the plan had demanded union construction labor reduce their wages, but the unions became alarmed when word of the reduction leaked in a *New York Times* story. The article described the administration's concern with the "unduly high scale for construction labor," which was "out of line with other labor costs." Because of union outrage, this early provision was removed.[92] Yet a month after the National Housing Act passed, an emergency declaration by

7.2 A symbol of B&Ls' success: Miss Jane Bondi of the Federal Home Loan Bank Board holds up a sign to be mailed to hundreds of B&Ls, reading "Safety of Your Investment Insured up to $5000," advertising the new government guarantee.

Source: Library of Congress.

the National Recovery Administration forced the lumber industry and other building materials industries to lower their minimum prices by 10 percent and to encourage cost savings in wages. The declaration was part of a new administration attack on both prices and wages in home building, an attack that would expand over the following years.[93]

Although Roosevelt at first struggled against extending more federal guarantees to urban builders and lenders, he eventually came to embrace such guarantees. In his fireside chat on the very day he signed the National Housing Act, he said he would describe a few of the major enactments of his New Deal to that point. He started with "the readjustment of the debt burden" through numerous credit and bankruptcy acts and moved to the act he had just signed "to encourage private capital in the rebuilding of the homes of the Nation." He said that he and his administration's central desideratum was to "seek the security of the men, women and children of the Nation. That security involves added means of providing better homes for the people of the Nation. That is the first principle of our future program."[94] The Housing Act was only the beginning of a new focus on housing.

CHAPTER 8

AN ECONOMY BALANCED BY MORTGAGES

In November 1937, something dire and unexpected was happening to the American economy. An onrushing economic downturn, soon to be known as the "Roosevelt recession," was causing businesses to close and millions of workers to be laid off. Many in President Franklin D. Roosevelt's administration worried that all the economic gains made during the past four years would be dissolved. Late on the night of November 3, Roosevelt's secretary of the Treasury, the sour Henry Morgenthau, phoned the Oval Office with troubling news. Morgenthau had been reviewing the incoming economic statistics and had "come to the conclusion that we are headed right into another Depression. . . . The question is, Mr. President—what are we going to do to stop it?"[1]

Roosevelt wasted no time finding out. The next morning he called an emergency meeting in the official Cabinet Room of the West Wing. The dreary subject was belied by the bright day and the cheery Rose Garden located directly outside the windows. All the members of the cabinet were seated when the president burst in with his usual smile and bonhomie, giving little indication of concern. Yet soon the president turned to his fraught-looking secretary of labor, Frances Perkins, and asked, "Well, Frances, anything on your mind?" Perkins pulled out a memorandum showing that employment had declined substantially and said that the "report shows the falling off is greatest in heavy industries." Postmaster General James Farley noted that "others chimed in with gloomy reports." Roosevelt's usual calm demeanor broke, and he thundered, "I am sick and tired of being told by the Cabinet, by Henry and by everybody else for the last two weeks what's the matter with the country and nobody suggests what I should do." His outburst met a stunned silence. Morgenthau later wrote in his diary that when he suggested some reassuring statements to business, Roosevelt "sneered at me" and through clenched teeth said, "You want me to turn the old record on."[2] Interior Secretary Harold Ickes noted that Morgenthau "looked and acted like a spanked child."[3]

The cabinet then suggested several solutions before the president finally stated his own, and with confidence, "There are a number of things which must be done. There's housing and railroads and utilities." In fact, Roosevelt focused on the housing issue and its connection to the other two.[4] He told his cabinet that the "speeding up of housing will go a long way toward adjusting the present business situation. An increase in construction will give considerable help to the industry itself, which has been in a bad way for a long time. Its stimulation will help, naturally enough, all industries engaged in supporting materials and also will help the transportation industry," which moved the materials.[5]

Ickes thought that encouraging housing was "the best thing that could possibly be done" for recovery, especially because "it would provide employment in the producers' goods industries." Perkins added her statistics, which showed that the country could easily build 600,000 homes a year, more than double the current rate, which would contribute to the heavy industries she thought most troubled.[6] Those who had long supported liberalized housing and mortgage policies beamed as their plans seemed to garner wide acceptance, no minor feat in an oft fractious cabinet. Ickes said that he had "never seen [Roosevelt] so eager for counsel from his Cabinet. Neither have I ever seen him so anxious."[7] The meeting lasted for an unprecedented two and a half hours, but at the end of it Roosevelt gave the cabinet marching orders to find some program for housing that he could propose to Congress, one that would allow financial companies once again to expand their investment in mortgages. He hoped the plan would especially encourage large-scale or mechanized housing production at low cost. Farley called the meeting "one of the most interesting Cabinet sessions during my years in office." Roosevelt told him he thought it was the best they ever had.[8]

Roosevelt's reaction to the recession of 1937, the third worst of the twentieth century, is often portrayed as his "coming to Keynes" moment, when he and the New Deal gave up lingering austere inclinations and embraced government deficits as the one route to recovery.[9] Roosevelt's actions are also said to be part of a New Deal move toward embracing increased consumer spending and income redistribution, as opposed to broader economic reforms, as its singular focus.[10] Roosevelt's interest in financing large-scale housing, however, suggests that his reaction to the recession was the culmination of his administration's ever-increasing interest in mortgages as the centerpiece of recovery, an interest that emerged first in farming, moved to housing, and continued throughout his presidency. The recession cemented the growing interest in the New Deal in using federal credit support and price reforms to bolster heavy industries in general and home construction in particular. And far from encouraging more consumer spending, the administration in this period attacked what it saw as excessive wage advances in some fields and tried to limit consumer goods in order to encourage building.

The New Deal's reaction to the recession, in fact, was the zenith of more than twenty years of federal mortgage reforms aimed at balancing the national economy. By the end of the recession, the New Deal had permanently transformed the nation's banking system to one devoted to mortgage lending with federal guarantees. Yet, like earlier reformers, officials in the administration were in the end frustrated that they had not transformed the "real" economy or balanced the sectors they thought would ensure recovery. The Roosevelt administration, like many before it, had achieved many of its financial reforms but then worried that the financiers were the only ones who benefitted.

The New Officials Behind Housing

When late in 1934 Henry Morgenthau offhandedly told Marriner Eccles during a conversation in the White House that Roosevelt was considering Eccles for the post of governor of the Federal Reserve Board, Eccles was taken aback: "For once in my life I was mum." For the garrulous, small-town Mormon banker to become the most powerful financial personage in Washington was something more than even he could have hoped.[11] Yet Eccles soon entered the position of governor just as the board was constructing a new, large neoclassical office building along Constitution Avenue in Washington, a symbol of its increasing power. The building would eventually be named after Eccles.[12]

Eccles brought to the Federal Reserve a particular concern with mortgages in the financial system inherited from his time as a banker with significant (and continuing) real estate investments and from his time drafting the seminal National Housing Act (see chapter 7). Eccles saw housing as essential for the whole economy, arguing that "a program of new home construction . . . would act as the wheel within the wheel to move the whole economic engine. It would affect everyone, from the manufacturer of lace curtains to the manufacturers of lumber, bricks, furniture, cement, and electrical appliances. The mere shipment of these supplies would affect the railroads, which in turn would need the produce of steel mills for rails, freight cars and so on."[13] Despite the Federal Reserve's continuing focus on short-term loans, Eccles would use his position to encourage more long-term lending and more mortgages. He found good company for his beliefs at the Federal Reserve. George Harrison, governor of the New York Federal Reserve Bank since early in Herbert Hoover's presidency and the second-most-powerful person in the system, said he was also "very strongly of the opinion that a general reopening of the mortgage market" was the only path to recovery.[14]

Roosevelt's "super-Cabinet," formerly the National Executive Council but now renamed the National Emergency Council, became a place where Eccles and Fed officials could push for expanded mortgages. The council's economist, formerly of the Federal Reserve, Winfield Riefler, used it as a platform to implement the National Housing Act, which he had just drafted. (At one National Emergency Council meeting, Eccles said, "We wanted Mr. Riefler back," to which Roosevelt replied, "We cannot let you have him back. We like him too much."[15]) Frank Walker, a wealthy former bond salesman, was chairman of the council and, as one official said, the ambassador to "men of means who might be persuaded to put up some money" for Roosevelt. Not surprisingly, Walker was a believer in encouraging private credit.[16] In October 1934, he gave his first official speech to the Mortgage Bankers' Association, which he said he could not refuse because "during the past year in Washington a greater proportion of my time and attention has been focused on the mortgage problem than on any other." He said federal mortgage support was essential because "unemployment is concentrated very heavily in the heavy industries, or in the dependent service industries, and particularly in the construction industry."[17] Meanwhile, even the Department of Agriculture wrote a report that same month to the National Emergency Council that the country had now reached the point where industrial recovery was the only means to spur more agriculture prosperity rather than the reverse. The department said that "federal housing financing offers the single most important stimulus" for industry.[18]

These pleas for increased federal mortgage support met with hearty banker approval. Leonard Ayres of the influential Cleveland Trust Company wrote a report for the American Bankers Association meeting in late 1934 where he argued that of those issues "chiefly responsible" for current banking problems, the largest was the "existing stagnation in privately financed building construction." The report celebrated the work done by the National Housing Act for helping banks finance these loans but demanded that work be expanded. These concerns were passed on, with approval, to Eccles by A. P. Giannini, head of the Bank of America.[19] Paul Mazur, the chief of Lehman Brothers, meanwhile wrote in early 1935 to the administration that "unquestionably the best opportunity in terms of economic and social need lies in a major rebuilding program," which he said would "stimulate heavy industry and thereby promote recovery" as well as "re-establish the flow of capital into mortgages and housing." He hoped, of course, that his own bank could help reestablish that flow.[20]

Lehman Brothers received clear indications that it and its financial brethren would find supporters in the new agencies. An internal memo by Lehman Brothers employee Alexander Sachs described a trip to the headquarters of the new Federal Housing Administration. He was delighted when government officials there told him the agency was "designed to insure [*sic*] a profit to all." Sachs said, "Naturally, the espousal of the profit motive was sweet music to my ears" because he knew that "some real possibility exists for Lehman Brothers to take an interest in the financing" of various projects under the Federal Housing Administration.[21] Albert Deane, the former president of the General Motors Acceptance Corporation who helped design the home-repair program under the National Housing Act and who became the FHA's deputy administrator, told Sachs, too, that the repair program "was inclined to favor existing financial institutions" over new competition and was "framed with the idea that no financial institution might take any loss." Sachs was delighted.[22]

Many independent professors and thinkers outside government trumpeted the need for more housing finance as well.[23] But the final and most important thinker in pushing the combined issues of mortgage reform and housing construction was a little-known recent graduate of Harvard University's economics program, Lauchlin Currie. He was quiet, studious, and wiry, with prematurely graying hair, but he would soon become a master memo writer and Eccles's éminence grise at the Federal Reserve.[24] Although often seen as the most prominent voice for "Keynesian" deficit spending and increasing consumer income in the New Deal, Currie in fact emphasized the need for balancing different sectors of the economy with cheap finance.

In his first memo to the administration in late 1934, "Comments on Pump Priming," Currie denied that pump priming had to do with bigger deficits or increased consumer spending. He wrote, "Pump priming may be described as a process of making it profitable to increase the production of durable goods." The administration's goal should be to restore "an approximate balance or equilibrium in the economy," as had occurred before the Depression, where the "production of producers' and consumers' goods were in amounts proper to a condition of balance." Since the start of the Depression, though, there had been relatively too much consumption. The "conditions [needed] for balance have not changed"; they just needed to be restored, and the best way was obvious: "The most desirable type of private expenditure that should be subsidized is housing" because it "is socially beneficial [and] will bring direct relief to the most depressed industries[,] . . . *provided* the incentive is substantial." As the final section of his memo stated, "The impasse is building."[25]

Soon after Eccles hired Currie at the Federal Reserve Board, Currie wrote his boss a letter arguing that he should have a larger salary and direct access to his new chief because "I'm a better monetary theorist than anyone on the staff and . . . my attitude and objectives are closer to yours."[26] The supremely

8.1 Lauchlin Currie testifying to Congress, May 16, 1939.

Source: Library of Congress.

confident Currie would become Eccles's favorite economist and eventually Roosevelt's as well. (Currie, however, would later be identified as a possible agent of Communist espionage, who procured secret government documents for the Soviet Union.[27]) For the moment, it seemed as if all the major players in the Roosevelt administration's struggle for recovery were united in one voice and one thought: the need to use housing to restore balance to the economy.

Ending the Real-Bills Doctrine

As the new governor of the Federal Reserve Board, Marriner Eccles had limited powers to influence mortgage policy. Despite emergency reforms during the Hoover years, which later expired, the system remained legally tied to the real-bills doctrine and thus could discount or make loans only on short-term debts backed by real goods. Its member banks, after all, were still called "commercial banks." The only other way, besides discounting, to push more Federal Reserve money into the banking system was through purchasing government debt directly, which became increasingly common as the Depression continued.[28]

Eccles hoped to widen the types of loans that commercial banks could make, and he thought the Federal Reserve System could help in that transformation. He understood the problem on a visceral level. During the early days of the Depression, Eccles had had to keep the knowledge of his own increasingly illiquid bank from the public and then engage in what he called a "daytime masquerade" of cheerfulness. But when he got home at night, he would slump forward on his table and pray for answers. Strangely, he beseeched the Almighty about how to balance the economy and make it liquid. "What was to be done when men on the farms and in the cities who needed each other's goods, were stranded on opposite river banks?" He asked the Lord, "What was to be done when the pressure on the banks to 'get liquid'" made the situation worse?[29] He apparently received an answer. He said that the reform to "which my own thoughts were drawn when I had fought to keep my banks open in the Depression . . . was a need to broaden the types of paper eligible for discount at the Federal Reserve Banks," so the Fed could loan on any asset whatsoever.[30] Eccles's new adviser, Currie, encouraged this focus. Currie's just-completed Harvard dissertation was an extended attack on the real-bills doctrine claim that banks should lend only on short terms. It argued that "there would seem to be no sound theoretical basis for distinction between paper that is eligible for rediscount and paper which is not," so the Federal Reserve should be allowed to discount long-term assets with the same conditions as all other loans.[31] Currie said such broad liberalization of lending "would cause an immediate easing of the long-term interest rates" and lead to "an increase of loans for fixed capital purposes[, which] is the very best way credit can be created in times of depression."[32] Eccles agreed that specifically allowing mortgage discounts at the Federal Reserve would help because with constant access to the Fed "the mortgages in the banks might be given the liquidity needed."[33]

Eccles knew that in advocating discounting for all assets, he was suggesting a profound transformation of the American banking system. He told the public in February 1935, "What we are proposing is that the problem of liquidity shall cease to be an individual concern and shall become the collective concern of the banking system"—or, more specifically, of the federal government through the Federal Reserve.[34] In effect, Eccles wanted to socialize "liquidity," to make the salability of all financial assets a government-guaranteed benefit, like other, more commonly known benefits granted by the New Deal. Adam Smith's liquid, real-bills bank would be no more. Every bank could invest in mortgages because mortgages would be "shiftable" to the government coffers at all times.

Eccles thought such socializing of liquidity was more important than deficit spending for recovery. He lamented that the Federal Reserve's current focus on buying government debt was actually due to the banking system's failure to lend on mortgages. "If, for instance, the banking system utilized in real estate loans and other long-term investments the savings and excess funds they possessed, bank business activity could be greatly stimulated and the government would then be able to withdraw rapidly from the lending field." He thought that of all the government debt issued during the New Deal, the "greater part of that debt was incurred in refinancing mortgages" through its numerous mortgage-support programs.[35] He thought new Fed lending could "short circuit the money from where it is to where it is needed, without going through a government bond, as is being done now. Make the mortgage in the banks as good as a Government bond in the bank."[36]

As a concomitant reform, Eccles proposed ending the law restricting mortgages to a limited percentage of national bank balance sheets. In one meeting in Eccles's office, the comptroller of the currency, the nation's top bank regulator, objected to this idea, saying, "The greatest trouble of the banks had been real estate loans and this [proposal] would put us right back" in the same situation as before the Depression. He noted that all of the worst banking areas in the country at that time "resulted from heavy real estate loans." Eccles, however, thought these reasons were precisely why more support for mortgages was necessary: only if banks and the federal government supported mortgages would their value be boosted.[37]

Eccles collaborated with Lauchlin Currie and the Federal Reserve counsel Chester Morrill to craft a Federal Reserve reform act. Their proposal also centralized power in the governor of the Federal Reserve Board (the position Eccles held) and took it away from the Fed "member banks" that once owned and ran the system. When Eccles presented Roosevelt with a preliminary version of his plan in the Oval Office, the president was alert and encouraging. Eccles said, "At last his powerful hands slapped down on the table as he said: 'Marriner, that's quite an action program you want. It will be a knock-down and drag-out fight to get it through, but we might as well undertake it now as at any other time.'"[38]

Eccles announced to the nation's bankers the opportunities his new Federal Reserve bill offered them. In a press conference on Friday, February 8, 1935, he said that the new act "would enable commercial banks to take an effective part in the reopening of the mortgage market, and to give their unstinted support, in a manner not now possible for them, to that branch of industry in which the opportunity for meeting both a social and an economic need is now the greatest."[39] In an address to the Ohio Banking Association a few days later, Eccles emphasized "the one proposal which I regard as the most important[;] . . . the provision permitting banks to make loans on improved real estate" would allow them to expand into new areas of business.[40]

Some bankers had clear personal interests in this plan. A. P. Giannini of the Bank of America was a persistent advocate for the bill. The *Nation* magazine pointed to his banks' large real estate holdings, which could be discounted under the bill, and said that "the bill might be called a Giannini bill."[41] Eccles noted that other regulations "would be liberalized to advantage the bankers." One that especially concerned him was a little noticed part of the Glass-Steagall Banking Act that required bank officers to pay back loans from their own banks. Eccles thought excising this clause would "give bankers relief from a harsh prospect" and enlist more of them in his cause.[42] Yet he had a personal interest in the change. A recent bank examiner report indicated that Eccles's two brothers, who were directors of his bank in Utah, had tens of thousands of dollars in loans from the bank that looked as if they were not going to be paid off anytime soon. This change would allow his brothers to stay on the board of the family bank.[43]

Many commentators recognized that Eccles's plan was a radical attempt to reshape the entire banking industry. It would bury the real-bills doctrine that had existed since the time of Adam Smith and remake all commercial banks in the image of mortgage banks. The *Bankers Magazine* said that once "the art of banking consisted in the ability to distinguish between a mortgage and a [real] bill of exchange. But should the pending banking bill become a law," this old-time distinction would evaporate. "If the door is opened to the rediscount at the Federal Reserve of mortgages, it will constitute . . . a revolutionary change."[44] A group of sixty-six conservative economists signed an open letter opposing the bill. They first attacked the bill's concentration of political power in the Federal Reserve Board and its governor, but their three other complaints decried the attempt to increase the number of mortgages in commercial banks, which they warned "will invite ultimate disaster for this country."[45]

On the whole, however, the banking world celebrated Eccles's mortgage revolution. Another article in the *Bankers Magazine* claimed "the last five years have made it clear that the methods of the more orthodox school of banking philosophy have broken down in their attempt to preserve banking liquidity" by keeping just to short-term loans. "The beginnings of this realization lay in the formation of the R.F.C. [Reconstruction Finance Corporation] and its development has led to the Eccles Bill." The article's author celebrated the rise of the "shiftability" theory behind loan changes at banks: "It seems evident that the preservation of banking liquidity in time of crisis involves the absorption by the public of assets formerly held by the banking system."[46]

When presenting his bill to Congress, Eccles argued that both the discount "eligibility feature of this legislation, and the real-estate feature, one of which is the corollary of the other," were essential. He told the members of Congress that only through these two reforms could they spur recovery.[47] Despite some staunch opposition from remaining real-bills believers, such as Carter Glass, Eccles's Banking Act of 1935 passed easily.[48]

After its passage, responsibility for the liquidity of the financial system was transferred largely to Eccles himself. The *Bankers Magazine* was soon urging its readers to "abandon liquidity fetish" for short-term loans. "Governor Marriner S. Eccles and the Federal Reserve officials have already done this" in their sphere; now the rest of the banks should follow through.[49] Eccles told attendees of the American Bankers Association annual meeting that, "speaking as a banker, business man and capitalist," he urged them to "put those funds in the long-term mortgage market."[50] The association's president claimed that with the new law "there is no longer need for the maintenance of too high a percentage of liquidity."[51] Eccles would soon assist this practice by ending the bank regulations that prohibited banks from making "slow" loans and by stating that bank regulators would focus on "intrinsic value rather than upon liquidity."[52] As one economist wrote a few years later, because of Eccles, "liquidity is therefore no longer a 'natural' or 'market' idea, but an institutional, legal, or conventional concept," subject to control by the government.[53]

The Federal Reserve amendments in the Banking Act and Eccles's efforts fundamentally transformed America's commercial banking system. They pushed banks into a system almost the opposite of the real-bills vision of many of America's early bankers and focused them ever more on long-term loans, mortgage debts, and government support.

The Housing Agencies' "Mess"

After the passage of the Federal Reserve reform bill, Eccles thought it was his foremost duty as Fed governor to push mortgages any way he could. Even when discussing normal Federal Reserve interest-rate policy a few years later, he said, "I favor relatively low interest rates as a continued encouragement to capital expenditures, including housing."[54] Eccles told his Federal Reserve staff in November 1935, "In view of the extent to which the lag in construction continues to be the chief factor in unemployment, and also the chief factor in retarding a more general recovery among the heavy industries . . . particularly in the field of residential building," they should proselytize the banks they oversaw to make more mortgages.[55] He advised other Federal Reserve Board members that they should encourage bank buy-in to the new FHA programs, including by helping to arrange meetings of bankers with the FHA.[56]

In response to demands made by Eccles and others, the administration replaced an early and unenergetic FHA chief with Stewart McDonald, a former St. Louis manufacturer and administrative wunderkind who expanded the size and scope of the agency.[57] McDonald also understood Eccles's vision of encouraging bank mortgages. He used publications directed at banks, such as the FHA's *Insured Mortgage Portfolio*, to tell them that FHA-insured mortgages were as good as cash and could be discounted by the Federal Reserve.[58] The FHA also tried to ensure banks of the "stability" of their mortgage investment by guaranteeing that "inharmonious" racial groups would not move into the new housing developments. They thus encouraged racially restrictive covenants against minority ownership in FHA-funded housing.[59] As Eccles recommended, the FHA also began "wholesale" operation at banks, placing its own staff in bank buildings and providing stenographic help and office equipment so banks could convert their old real estate loans to the new FHA-insured mortgage.[60]

After helping to establish and expand the FHA, Eccles turned his eye on the next largest source of government funds for housing, the Reconstruction Finance Corporation, now run by Texas millionaire builder Jesse Jones. The tall and commanding Jones, who had almost been ruined by collapsing real estate bonds early in the Depression and had been saved by having these bonds bought up by the RFC, understood on a personal level the need for government mortgage support.[61] Jones once claimed that "our nation's greatest single asset is real estate," and he believed it was his job to support it.[62] He and Eccles helped pass a bill in January 1935 that allowed the RFC to create its own mortgage company to make mortgage loans directly, what became the RFC Mortgage Company.[63] Financial interests were paramount there. The RFC Mortgage Company's head remained vice president at the Bowery Savings Banks, one of the largest institutions in the country specializing in mortgages.[64]

President Roosevelt at first let Eccles and his assistants fight the battle for more housing loans on their own, but he soon demonstrated his increasing fervor for the subject. In November 1934, one *New York Times* article described a press conference where Roosevelt made a "reiteration of his interest in the plans to stimulate" home construction, claiming that "low-cost housing has been made the spearhead of the renewed assault on the Depression."[65] As Eccles's and others' reforms picked up steam, Roosevelt could by March 1935 promise that the "American people will clearly see that the housing act provides the Nation a way back to recovery and prosperity." He said that now everything was in place "to make the program the fountain head of American prosperity."[66] With increased public propaganda for the FHA throughout the following year, the *Washington Post* claimed that "not since the Blue Eagle [of the National

8.2 and 8.3 The Economics and Statistical Division of the FHA, which made estimates of residential construction and "calculated the estimates of funds available for mortgages."

Source: Library of Congress.

Recovery Administration] strutted and soared across the country has any New Deal undertaking been subjected to so much ballyhoo as the Federal Housing Administration."[67]

Unfortunately for Roosevelt, the much-promised housing revival never happened. Part of the problem was that the vast majority of new RFC and FHA loans, like federal mortgage programs going back to the Federal Land Banks, simply refinanced existing mortgages, which helped banks but did not encourage more construction.[68] Commercial banks that Eccles had tried to encourage with his Federal Reserve reforms invested little in new mortgages. The Federal Reserve therefore discounted few mortgage loans even as it continued to absorb more and more government debt. It seemed that in the government's attempt to salvage the financial sector, little of the money was seeping out into the real economy the administration promised to balance.

The proliferating housing agencies also sometimes worked at cross-purposes. Roosevelt's uncle, the financier and urban planner Frederic Delano, created the Central Housing Committee to investigate the problem. Its report in May 1935 found that more than thirty-seven federal agencies dealt with housing issues. A horrified Roosevelt asked Delano to try and corral them and have them meet under his aegis.[69] Yet the Central Housing Committee itself only added to the confusion, merely becoming a thirty-eighth housing agency. Other officials sabotaged the committee's efforts. An FHA official said that his boss Stewart McDonald "referred to [the committee] as the Three Hours of Lost Motion Club, and left me to represent the FHA with instruction not to let anything happen."[70] At one point, McDonald was sharing a plane ride with another federal housing official when the official came over, tapped him on the knee, and asked, "Well, Stewart, how's everything in your shop?" McDonald gave him a mischievous eye and said, "Does Macy's tell Gimbel's?" It became a popular story across Washington about the administration's internal squabbles.[71] In March 1936, Roosevelt declared federal housing policy "to be in a mess," and the term *mess* was often repeated in both private and public.[72]

Nonetheless, the hope of a housing recovery remained. The Democratic Party platform of 1936 promised "every encouragement should be given to the building of new homes by private enterprise." After Roosevelt's landslide reelection, his State of the Union Address on January 6, 1937, gave attention to the need for new housing. The *New York Times* said that "housing bulks large in President Roosevelt's report to Congress on the state of the nation," noting that "in this particular field Recovery and Reform would be marching hand in hand," especially for "heavy industry."[73] In the president's Inaugural Address just two weeks later, he famously said that he saw one-third of the nation "ill-housed, ill-clad, ill-nourished." It was instructive that housing came first in the list.[74]

High Prices and a Housing Recession

Early in 1937, Eccles and his camp began to worry that forces besides agency squabbling were holding back housing. Although construction had picked up from its low of 200,000 new homes a year in 1933 to about 300,000 in 1937, the latter number was still 70 percent below the peak in the 1920s.[75] One common concern was that the costs of everything that went into homes, from lumber to cement to piping, were rising rapidly, faster than other prices in the economy. Many worried that more government financial support would only encourage this insidious cost inflation and exacerbate a cost imbalance with other sectors.[76]

Several administration allies raised new concerns about building costs. George F. Warren and Frank A. Pearson, the agricultural economists and Gold Dust Twins who once lamented low agricultural prices, now shifted their attention to high housing costs. They released a sequel of sorts to their magnum opus *Prices* (1933), which had focused on agriculture. *World Prices and the Building Industry* (1937) declared that agriculture was relatively stable due to a steady need for its products "and is therefore less important than building in certain fluctuations of business." But they worried that high prices in the building sector affected the entire economy and said that "full employment in production and distribution does not occur unless building is active."[77]

Lauchlin Currie was similarly concerned about building prices. In March 1937, he wrote a memo on fighting against "excessive wage advances" in this field and others. He discussed setting up a "National Balance Committee" to coordinate federal policy and prices across industries.[78] In another memo, "Our Common Responsibility for Economic Balance," Currie pointed to the "one field that perhaps more than those in any other threaten our prospects of achieving and maintaining a period of economic balance. I refer to the construction industry," which continued to have disproportionately high costs.[79] The danger for these thinkers, once again, was not low purchasing power overall but "imbalanced" power between different groups and high wages specifically in some unionized spheres such as construction.[80] Preliminary construction statistics in late 1937 confirmed these observers' worst fears, demonstrating that home building was again in decline. They now worried that the danger was not just a stalled recovery but a possible return to recession or worse.

In September 1937, just as the economy began to turn south again, Currie wrote the first draft of what would become his most famous memorandum, "The Causes of the Recession." Currie's memo has often been cited as the predominant cause of the Roosevelt administration's move from a focus on economic reform to a focus on Keynesian consumption spending. Alan Brinkley claims that for "the next six months, the memo served as a New Deal *samizdat*, continually revised and passed from agency to agency and official to official. It became the central document in the battle for new federal spending."[81] Yet a supposed focus on deficits and consumer purchasing power twists the thrust of Currie's ideas. Currie did not feel an attraction to the new deficit-spending ideas in John Maynard Keynes's *General Theory of Employment, Interest, and Money* (1936), which he reviewed unfavorably, but he remained enamored of Keynes's earlier work in *Treatise on Money*, which focused on financing costs and heavy industry as determining factors in the business cycle.[82]

Currie wrote his "Causes" memo originally to help Marriner Eccles as he was preparing new home-financing plans, and the original draft, titled "A Tentative Program to Meet the Business Recession," reflects that focus. The draft memo said that the "importance of securing a building revival next year cannot be overstressed. The continuation of recovery depends on it." Currie admitted that either deficit spending or building would help pull the nation out of recovery. Yet because he believed deficit spending posed dangers and difficulties in the foreseeable future, he argued that "we are by a process of elimination forced back to building as being the primary source on which we must depend for a reversal of the downward trend." He advocated increased attacks on high prices and on unions and told Eccles that the FHA should be reformed to focus on large-scale, mechanized housing production, which would increase the volume of building and lower the cost of labor at the same time. Currie's encouragement of mechanizing housing production with government support would prove to be the most consequential idea in his memo.[83] Currie's ideas had the support of Stewart McDonald, who said that "putting construction of homes on a wholesale basis" was a sort of holy grail of housing reform, "the inner-tomb of the housing pyramid," as he called it, because it would lower the high costs of building while it expanded production.[84]

Roosevelt began expressing similar concerns about the high costs in certain sectors and looking for ways to reduce them. He argued in one press conference in April 1937, "I am concerned—we are all concerned—over the price rise in certain materials that go into durable goods primarily." He called the rise a "danger sign" and said, "Now, that is history and I think almost all economists agreed on that."[85] For this reason, Senator Robert Wagner's Housing Act of August 1937, which provided federal loans to cities to construct public housing, received almost no support from Roosevelt. He worried that it would only encourage more price inflation and thus inhibit private housing. Despite praising the bill in general terms, Roosevelt asked that the authorization for public-housing loans be reduced one-fifth from what was originally proposed and, upon signing the Housing Act, said it should be at least a year before any building took place.[86]

During Roosevelt's Hyde Park sojourn in September 1937, he invited Marriner Eccles to talk with him about what he could do to save the endangered economy. Before the meeting, Currie emphasized to Eccles that Eccles had to "impress on him [Roosevelt] the possible seriousness of the decline in residential building."[87] Eccles told Roosevelt that the real danger was "the labor problem and the price rise that stopped our building . . . and got your economy out of balance." He said they had to find a way to encourage more financing and cheaper housing at the same time, without increasing costs. Otherwise, the economy, the administration, maybe even the nation would be at risk.[88]

A Mortgage Assault on Recession

After Roosevelt's seminal cabinet meeting on November 4, 1937, described earlier, Eccles submitted a new mortgage plan that hoped to square the circle of more building and lower prices. His draft bill claimed that the continued lag in construction work since 1933 was "the most deep-rooted retarding factor in national income, budget balancing, and full employment of labor." He demanded a new program "designed especially to encourage and facilitate large-scale operations in housing both for sale and rent." Eccles, like Currie, thought only large-scale or mechanized housing production could solve the housing dilemma.[89]

The new bill liberalized FHA loans, lowered mortgage interest rates to 5 percent, and allowed loans on some houses to go up to 90 percent of their value, with only a 10 percent down payment. The FHA, which originally had its guarantees limited in time and amount, was now promised an unlimited government guarantee for an unlimited amount of time. The bill also allowed more generous terms for large rental projects, especially those built on a mass scale for workers in urban areas. The National Mortgage Associations authorized by the National Housing Act of 1934, but never chartered would also get special tax exemptions to encourage their purchase of loans for large-scale housing projects.[90] The press afterward celebrated that "the New Deal is turning once more to private housing as a means of stimulating the lagging construction industry and through it industry in general"; in this, the government was "following a well-proved business rule: that construction, and particularly housing, should be the leader in business recovery."[91]

Roosevelt called Congress back into a special session on November 27 to deal with the recession. He told its members that "from the point of view of widespread and sustained economic recovery, housing constitutes the largest and most promising single field." He put the recent downturn almost entirely on housing, saying that decreased construction "was one of the principle reasons why general business failed to forge ahead during the latter part of the year" and that the increase in building prices in particular "was primarily responsible for the downturn in housing and thus recovery." Large-scale production to lower such costs, however, could be encouraged through large-scale federal mortgages.[92]

The bill faced a dire threat from the same labor groups many in the administration blamed for the recession. Senator Robert Bulkley of Ohio, once crucial in passing the Farm Loan Act and the Federal Home Loan Bank Act, was now the second-ranking Democratic member of the Senate Banking and Currency Committee, and he demanded that union wages be paid on all home construction insured by the FHA. Bulkley's plan would have unionized almost the entire construction industry in one swoop, and so almost every federal official opposed it.[93] When Steward McDonald of the FHA ran into Senator Bulkley in the corridor leading from the Senate to the House chamber, according to his assistant he "took [Bulkley] by the coat lapel . . . and said to him 'If you pass this amendment, you can kiss my ass in Macy's window and that will be the end of the FHA." Bulkley backed off. As the assistant said, "It was an example of McDonald's type of persuasion."[94]

Soon after the amendments to the National Housing Act passed on February 3, 1938, the only act to pass to that point in the special session Roosevelt called to deal with the recession, the government created its own mortgage association with RFC funds: the Federal National Mortgage Association, now better known by its nickname "Fannie Mae."[95] According to Jesse Jones, Fannie Mae would focus on efficient "large-scale" housing construction, which would "stimulate business, more perhaps than any other thing that can be done."[96]

As the act neared passage, Roosevelt received a letter that further cemented his belief in home building as the solution to the country's economic ills. John Maynard Keynes wrote to Roosevelt on February 1, 1938, to say that it was obvious what was needed to cure the continuing recession, "namely increased investment in durable goods such as housing, public utilities, and transport." Of course, as earlier, Keynes viewed the first issue as the most important. "Take housing. When I was with you three and a half years ago the necessity for effective new measures was evident. I remember vividly my conversations with Riefler at that time." He said, "Housing is by far the best aid to recovery. . . . I should advise putting most of your eggs in this basket, *caring* about this more than about anything, and making absolutely sure that they are being hatched without delay."[97] Roosevelt wrote back to Keynes that the "emphasis you put upon the need for stimulating housing construction is well placed," but he also noted that some obstacles remained in the way. "I hope that our efforts will be successful in removing the barriers to the revival of this industry."[98]

Price Barriers and the "Splending" Administration

On February 18, 1938, soon after the passage of the housing bill, Roosevelt gave a press conference in the Oval Office about what it meant for the economy. The press conference constituted perhaps his most extensive argument about economic balance since his campaign in 1932. Roosevelt told the press he had talked to all his top officials, including Wallace, Morgenthau, Perkins, Eccles, and "economists of various departments." Together "they worked up for me yesterday a statement on which they are all agreed. That is pretty good, to get six or eight different agencies of the Government to agree. It might be called noteworthy," especially for Roosevelt's often conflicted administration. He read to the assembled reporters the administration's statement, which argued that "prices of different groups of products must be brought into balanced relations to one another. Some prices and some costs are still too high to promote that balanced relationship between prices that is necessary for sustained recovery. . . . This is shown by our recent experience with housing[;] . . . all the major elements in housing costs advanced so sharply by the Spring of 1937 as to kill a promising expansion of activity in an industry whose restoration is vital to continued recovery." Roosevelt thus argued that "the decline in housing construction, laid much of the ground for the present recession."

Roosevelt brought out several charts for the reporters assembled around his Oval Office desk but started with one: "This chart is, I think, one of the most significant ones. It shows the price trends of certain building materials." The president of the United States then preceded to discuss at length such issues of national importance as the prices of "board and house paint," "plaster," and "prepared strip shingles" and tried to show how price rises in each had stymied housing. He said, "There are many elements in the recovery program which have already been directed toward a better balance of prices. That phrase, 'better balance of prices,' is the key to the whole thing."[99]

The administration began action on all fronts against the housing-cost menace. Morgenthau and the Treasury spent an almost unimaginable amount of time trying to use the power of government purchasing, including that of the War Department, the Navy Department, and the Veterans Administration, to force cement manufacturers to reduce prices. Their efforts soon spread to other building-trades areas. Morgenthau kept the president updated on studies of building prices and set up an interdepartmental group, the Committee on Certain Uneconomic Practices in the Building Industry.[100] The U.S. embassy in London, under Ambassador Joseph Kennedy, began reporting on how the British government fought "price rings" in the building trades. One embassy message on the vital issue of British lumber costs had in handwriting a note that it was "to be seen by the President."[101] Bankers rejoined this latest administration campaign. Winthrop Aldrich, chairman of the Chase National Bank, complained about the "failure of residential construction to respond to the stimulation of low interest rates. This failure is to be attributed to the increase in construction costs." He asked other industrialists to join him in the war against those costs.[102]

Despite the increased focus on housing costs, most histories of the New Deal point to a fundamental shift in the administration in April 1938. They argue that in that month Roosevelt and his administration, encouraged by Keynesian deficit spenders such as Eccles and Currie, buried any lingering attempts at reform and embraced deficit spending, mass consumption, and redistribution as the only solution to the ongoing recession.[103] Yet there was in fact no break with previous plans. Lauchlin Currie's final version of his famous "Causes of the Recession" memorandum, issued on April 1, 1938, lamented the perceived shortcomings of increased deficit spending and focused again on housing costs. Currie argued that much of the current deficit stimulus was not being spent, as demonstrated by "the lag in expenditures on durable goods such as houses." Although he thought more deficits could stimulate recovery, he also said "it is not necessary to stress the difficulties in such a course." He noted instead that the "petering out of the promising building revival that had gotten under way in 1936 appears to be associated with the advance in the price of new houses." He blamed "individual strategically-located unions" and said that there "is absolutely no assurance that another recovery will not be chocked off by excessive price and cost advances."[104] Far from a call for more federal spending, Currie's final memo was a demand for cost-and-wage control and again focused on home building.

When Roosevelt, after a meeting with his adviser Harry Hopkins and others at his Warm Springs retreat, unveiled a new recovery plan to his staff in Washington in April, it sounded more like Currie's plan than a modern Keynesian deficit program. In fact, most of his proposed programs did not spend money directly but increased government loans or guarantees to construction. The first part of his plan was to allow the new public-housing program to make $500 million in loan guarantees to local municipalities. Next, Roosevelt said, "Stewart McDonald was to build [that is, guarantee] 500 million dollars worth of housing for rent" through the FHA under the new Housing Act. At the same time, Ickes and the Interior Department would loan money to states and municipalities to fund public construction projects.[105] The goal was to use these federal loans to encourage efficient, large-scale production, while at the same time tackling high construction prices through government pressure.

These proposals were indicative of what the journalists Joseph Alsop and Robert Kintner at the time called Roosevelt's "splending" policy, or spending through lending.[106] In fact, just before his speech on recovery in April, Roosevelt had asked for and Congress had passed a bill that took most government loans out of the regular federal budget and counted them as expenditures only when the loans defaulted. The president would also later ask Congress to take all "self-liquidating" and semipublic corporation loans out of the budget.[107]

In Roosevelt's speech to Congress on his new program on April 14, 1938, he did not blame insufficient government spending for the recession but rather problems balancing spending different sectors. He said the recession arose because "the prices of many vital products had risen faster than was warranted. . . . In many lines of goods and materials, prices got so high that buyers and builders ceased to buy or to build." Thus, the economy had "got completely out of balance." Roosevelt told members of Congress that their job was "preserving the balance between all groups and all sections." More financing help by the government was central in restoring that balance. The first new measure he mentioned to Congress was not deficit spending but the making of more than $2 billion of additional bank reserves through gold sales and regulatory changes to banks, the vast majority of which would go to business lending and, he hoped, to construction loans. The other lending and construction programs followed.[108]

A few administration officials resigned after the April speech. Their issue was not "conservative" opposition to deficit spending but what they saw as misdirected spending. They worried that excessive government loans would further inflate housing costs and do nothing to control the menace of high prices. Winfield Riefler, long a stalwart of housing policy in the administration, submitted his resignation with a heavy heart. He said he supported more spending but "doubt[ed] the wisdom of directing public expenditures down construction channels during a depression that was brought about in an important measure by an utterly excessive rise in construction costs. Furthermore, partly as a result of the President's housing program, which constitutes by far the most effective action taken to date, we appear to be again at the start of a real residential building revival. It is extremely important that this revival be allowed to gather headway without again being choked by rising costs."[109]

After his recovery "splending" bills passed, Roosevelt tried to address the construction cost problem, an effort he saw as the necessary corollary to his new construction subsidies. When he presented his antitrust plans to Congress in his next speech on April 29, the high prices in the building trades was his focus. The president gave the example of when a "contractor pays more for materials; the home builder pays more for his house; the tenant pays more rent; and the worker pays in lost work." In fact, the president said, "our housing shortage is a perfect example of how ability to control prices interferes with the ability of private enterprise to fill the needs of the community and provide employment for capital and labor." He argued that attacks on certain high prices would "put our price structure into more workable balance and make the debt burden more tolerable." [110] Roosevelt's antitrust move was not merely an attack on large corporations, as described in many histories of his struggle against "administered prices."[111] High prices by labor and small building contractors were squarely in Roosevelt's sights.

Thurman Arnold, the new head of the Antitrust Division of the Justice Department, who as a Yale law instructor in 1933 once advocated reforming farm mortgages, embraced the new ideology. In fact, he launched an attack on the entire housing industry. In his later book *The Bottlenecks of Business* (1940), he questioned "why pump-priming on the housing market failed to start the pump" for the whole economy. His answer was that it failed because of housing combinations, monopolies, and unions.[112] Arnold said his building-price campaign was the first industry-wide prosecution in the history of antitrust. It took the work of two hundred lawyers and cost more than a million dollars, but he thought it was worth the effort.[113] The campaign led to more than two hundred indictments and lassoed several construction union officials, including one of the most powerful members of the American Federation of Labor. The use of antitrust laws against labor had been a liberal bugbear for half a century, but the Roosevelt administration was eager to use such prosecutions to encourage building.[114] The labor indictments, however, led to a later Supreme Court decision that once and for all exempted unions and their officials from the reach of antitrust attacks.[115] The attempts to break what Arnold and others called "bottlenecks" in the housing industry thus caused only more frustration.

Roosevelt made one final effort to publicize the danger of high housing costs and the necessity of more building. He convinced Congress to create the Temporary National Economic Commission (TNEC) to find an explanation for continued economic stagnation and establish a sort of official economic philosophy for the New Deal. The TNEC hearings have been declared the American "showcase for Keynesian economics," with Alvin Hansen from Harvard (soon to be known as the "American Keynes") recruited by Lauchlin Currie to be the "star witness."[116] Yet Hansen was a near fanatic on the need for more housing. As early as 1932, in his appropriately titled book *Economic Stabilization in an Unbalanced World*, Hansen had claimed that "housing is one of the most important aspects of economic life" and that "no industry affects more, or is affected more by, business-cycle fluctuations."[117] In his testimony to the TNEC, Hansen said that the prosperity of the 1920s relied on, "first, and this I regard as of quite extraordinary importance, . . . residential building which reached in this decade an all time high." More recently, the "most important single gap, and I would like to stress this, in the recovery of '36 and '37, was residential construction." When offering suggestions for the future, Hansen said that "residential building, everything considered, would appear to offer the most hopeful field." As he had for years, he advocated more FHA loans and mortgage support instead of deficit spending.[118]

The final report of the TNEC, written with Currie's assistance, repeated these housing nostrums. It said the fall-off in construction from 1929 on "explains in large part both the disastrous depression of 1929–1933 and the halting nature of the subsequent prosperity." It argued that the old issue of balance between producers and consumers goods was at the heart of contemporary stagnation, claiming that "prices of producers' goods have been uneconomically high levels since the early 1920s." It hoped that the "adjustment downward of various important producers' goods' prices . . . may open up favorable opportunities for investment. To mention one example, residential construction . . . offers considerable possibilities." The report specified that "the construction industry affords the largest single unexploited outlet for investment funds—outlets for which are so necessary to maintain a proper balance in our economic system."[119]

The report showed the essential continuity and comity between antitrust attacks and the stimulation of housing finance in Roosevelt's plans. Yet, unbeknownst to the TNEC, the New Deal's housing stimulus program had reached its conclusion.[120]

The looming war and its attendant defense buildup sabotaged any hopes for more private-housing investment, but the New Deal's consistency is noteworthy. From Roosevelt's nomination speech in Chicago in 1932, where he had trumpeted the small depositors and investors who tied the agricultural and industrial sectors together, to his desire to find a way to bridge the divide between investors and homebuilders, all as part of an economy that balanced agriculture and manufacturing as well as heavy and light industry, the New Deal's vision for the recovery of the American economy had been consistent. The means had changed, but the goals remained the same. In fact, the goals had remained basically the same ever since William Potter had formulated the idea of a land bank in the seventeenth century. He and his followers wanted to restore the prosperity of backward sectors of the economy and to make the land a more liquid part of the financial world.

In the end, however, Roosevelt and the long train of believers in economic balance before him would remain frustrated. The use of the term *balanced economy* peaked in the last year of Roosevelt's presidency and gradually declined as a concept and motivating force thereafter.[121] Because of the efforts of balanced-economy believers, however, the financial world had been completely reformed. Commercial banks, which had once eschewed mortgages entirely, enlarged their residential mortgage holdings from $2.1 billion at their Depression nadir in 1934 to almost $3 billion in 1940, an increase of almost 50 percent and higher even than their peak in the 1920s. Building-and-loan associations, insurance companies, and other financiers expanded their mortgage portfolios by 30 to 50 percent as well. The country was set for an even more astounding surge in mortgage debt after the war, with ever more of it in the hands of banks and B&Ls and ever more of it supported by the banks' new partner, the federal government.[122] The government was increasingly bolstering private banking debts and making them its own. Roosevelt's one-time adviser Raymond Moley bemoaned that "the government of the United States was being made the greatest investment and mortgage banker in the world."[123] It would remain so.

CONCLUSION

This book has traced the long history of an idea. That idea declared that mortgages, particular debts based on particular patches of land, could be made as easily tradable and liquid as cash and that through that transformation those parts of the economy that depended on mortgages and on land could be brought into some sort of balance with other parts that did not. The reforms inspired by this idea reshaped American government, politics, and economics.

The dream of liquid mortgages was touted by farmers, by bankers, by builders, by lobbyists, and by intellectuals, who allied together over decades to create a host of new government corporations and agencies. They succeeded beyond their wildest dreams. By 1939, government corporations and credit agencies owned or guaranteed more than $12 billion in financial assets, a larger dollar amount than the entire federal budget at the time, and the majority of these assets were based on mortgages.[1]

Yet even as the federal government reshaped the financial world to balance different industries, the financial sector reshaped the government and the public understanding of its role in the economy. The means of balancing the economy, cheap finance, often supplanted the supposed ends, supporting endangered sectors. Supporting financial stability and expansion, sometimes known as the "financialization" of the economy, became one of the federal government's premier duties. By the end of the New Deal, the government saw ensuring the stability and profitability of American finance as its raison d'être. The old dream of economic balance gradually receded into the mists of history, while the financial institutions and supports that it birthed became overweening aspects of modern American life.

In fact, as housing went from a depressed sector to a booming one, many intellectuals and economists lamented that mortgage subsidies were now threatening to create new and dangerous problems in the economy. They warned that supports provided to newly successful construction and banking industries only fueled economic *im*balances as well as general inflation. The interest groups that relied on these subsidies, such as builders and financiers, became divorced from many of their original intellectual allies and continued to demand ever greater subsidies.

Marriner Eccles at the Federal Reserve became convinced that government subsidies to mortgages were the root cause of the post–World War II inflation. At one Federal Reserve meeting in 1948, Eccles said that "one of the most inflationary factors in the expansion of bank credit for some time had been the growth in mortgage credit." He hoped that it could be reduced.[2] "Win" Riefler, who again became chief adviser and an éminence grise at the Federal Reserve after the war, also became concerned with inflation based on excess housing credit. He even formulated a new theory that demanded that the Federal Reserve purchase only short-term government bills, which became known as the "bills only" policy, a strange reemergence of the real-bills doctrine in a different form. Riefler hoped it would prevent undue amounts of long-term credit and especially mortgage debt.[3]

Yet Eccles, Riefler, and others understood that the growth of a housing lobby made the paring back of long-term credits difficult. The National Association of Home Builders, founded in 1942, as well as older groups such as the now pro-federal intervention Mortgage Bankers of America pushed for ever more federal guarantees. Besides preventing the imposing of capital constraints on housing during World War II, as was done in World War I, these groups prepared for more mortgage loans after the war. Howard Russell, who helped create the Home Owners Loan Corporation for the building-and-loan industry, almost single-handedly crafted the provision of the GI Bill that provided a 100 percent guarantee to banks providing mortgage loans to veterans, inaugurating the famous Veterans Administration housing program. Despite opposition from the Federal Reserve and others to expanding more mortgage credit, the lending and building industries won out over their erstwhile intellectual allies.[4]

After the war, housing groups further extended mortgage guarantees. Attempts by President Dwight Eisenhower and his administration in the 1950s to slow down housing credit in order to stanch inflation ran into this lobbying gauntlet and were reversed.[5] The administration now faced what the *New York Times* called the "housing bloc" in Congress. The *Times* noted this "powerful Congressional bloc is rated by students of such phenomena as at least a full cut, in terms of efficiency, above such log-rolling groups of the past," including, of course, the Agricultural Bloc.[6] The housing bloc was part of what the *Times* called a "bloc-dominated Capitol."[7] A *Wall Street Journal* page-one report in 1959 titled "The Housing Lobby" said the lobby represented "a fundamental shift in the historic custom of trying to influence Congress. From a haphazard, often crude practice, lobbying has been transformed over the years into a calculated, sophisticated science." The housing lobby, according to one unnamed senator, "is one of the most potent around" and was in fact "a cluster of lobbies within lobbies," including everything from bankers to builders to heavy-industry groups.[8]

The federal agencies that reformers created also became powerful lobbyists for more mortgages and allied with these housing groups against older proponents of balance. The *New York Times* noted that the FHA "conceives of its role, in part, as that of a 'representative' within the Government of the segment of the economy it serves." In 1957, despite a booming economy and housing sector, the FHA pushed Congress to lower down payments on its guaranteed mortgages. The *Times* said the "agency fought hard . . . and finally won out over opposition in the Treasury, Federal Reserve, and Council of Economic Advisers." Winfield Riefler railed against the change, arguing that down payments should be increased and the number of housing loans decreased during a boom such as the one then in progress.[9]

Yet paring back housing subsidies when reformers thought them unnecessary was easier said than done. Such attempts to fine-tune and balance the economy ran into the logrolling politics that the balance ideologues had once relied upon to create the new mortgage institutions. Now the reformers who had celebrated the original changes had lost control of them. As a presidential candidate, John F. Kennedy promised to roll back Riefler's "bills-only" ideas at the Fed and to increase long-term credit and mortgages again, and he succeeded in doing so.[10] From this point on, there would be no more attempts at balance, only a continual increase of subsidies for mortgage credit. The reformers and believers in balance had created a golem, far too powerful for them to command or control.[11]

If the government had spent the first half of the twentieth century sowing the wind with its mortgage supports, it wasn't until the 1980s that it began to reap the whirlwind. The implicit pledge once given by the government to support financiers finally "died" or came due, in the old terminology of the mortgage.

Under the encompassing protection of the federal government, the financial sector and especially the mortgage market grew in size and scope in the postwar years, nearly doubling its proportion of the total economy.[12] One sector in particular attained prominence. From the end of the war to the end of the 1970s, the savings-and-loan (S&L) industry (formerly known as the building-and-loan industry) grew by more than 600 percent and came to provide more than half of all mortgages in the United States.[13] The support of the Federal Home Loan Bank system, Fannie Mae and Freddie Mac (the Federal Home Loan Mortgage Corporation, a Fannie Mae spinoff created in 1970 specifically to assist S&Ls), and the Federal Savings and Loan Insurance Corporation (FSLIC, or more colloquially "Fizz Slick") had shepherded this industry into prominence.

Yet the S&Ls, which still used short-term deposits to fund long-term mortgage, suffered under the combination of high inflation and high interest rates in the late 1970s. In this period, S&Ls held many vintage mortgages of the 1960s and 1970s that were paying them just 4 or 5 percent interest a year and whose value was depreciating by the day under high inflation. Yet new higher interest rates meant the S&Ls had to pay their short-term depositors 7 or 8 percent a year. Every day that passed the S&Ls were losing more and more money. The dangers of short-term deposits supporting long-term loans, which theorists going back to Adam Smith had recognized, were still apparent. Now they had a new name: economists began worrying about the danger of "maturity mismatch" on the S&Ls' balance sheets.[14]

The federal government's reaction to the S&Ls' predicament should have been predictable. In 1980 and 1982, Congress expanded the powers of the S&L industry and allowed the S&Ls to invest in a wider array of assets. Congress hoped riskier loans would help the S&Ls recoup some of their past losses. At the same time, it expanded federal protection of the banks, increasing the limit on guaranteed deposits at FSLIC from $40,000 to $100,000 per customer. In another maneuver that was familiar from the 1920s and 1930s, the federal government also began hiding how bad the situation at the S&Ls had become. Federal Home Loan Bank Board examiners, who supervised the industry, were told to be generous in accounting for losses. They began using special Regulatory Accounting Standards, which conjured billions of dollars in nonexistent "goodwill" assets that would somehow keep the S&Ls afloat. When S&Ls owners realized that they were effectively bankrupt but that the government was allowing them to stay open with guarantees and obfuscations, they decided to bet the house, so to speak. They engaged in ever-riskier loans and speculations, all in the hope that they could revive their industry, with the government taking all of the downside.[15]

As in the Great Depression, obfuscations could hide the problems for only so long. By the end of the 1980s, the Home Loan Bank Board had been forced to close more than two hundred S&Ls. Some S&Ls were not unwilling to bribe examiners or congressmembers to avoid the ax. The Speaker of the House, Representative Jim Wright of Texas, at the behest of a real estate mogul who had put Wright and his wife on a retainer, tried to get the new hard-charging deputy director of FSLIC fired even as he lobbied for more leniency from the Federal Home Loan Bank Board. This incident and the exposure of other ethical peccadillos led Speaker Wright to resign from the House. Even more damning to Congress were the charges faced by the "Keating Five," five senators who asked for the Home Loan Bank Board to keep Charles Keating's Lincoln Savings and Loan open after he donated to their political campaigns. Three senators were sanctioned by the Senate and forced to leave at the end of their terms. Outsiders could no longer doubt the influence of the housing and finance bloc on Congress.[16]

In 1989, a chastened Congress recognized that FSLIC and the entire S&L industry were bankrupt and needed a bailout. So what did it do but create the Resolution Trust Corporation, a new federal corporation that would pay off former depositors and buy up failed S&L assets. In effect, it tried to wind down the whole industry and sell off its mountain of foreclosed properties. Through this new corporation, the U.S. government became the owner of thousands of Americans homes as well as wind-swept shopping malls and empty commercial office buildings. By the time the Resolution Trust Corporation wound itself down years later, it had cost taxpayers more than $130 billion.[17]

The S&L bailout was so massive that few recognized that the Federal Land Banks, which had been struck by the simultaneous farm crisis of the 1980s, were also bailed out again. Congress's solution to the Land Banks' problems was the creation of yet another federally sponsored corporation, "Farmer Mac" (formally the Federal Agricultural Mortgage Corporation), with $4 billion provided by the taxpayers. No commentators at the time recognized this action as a repetition of the Land Banks' earlier bailout.[18]

For commercial banks, however, the implosion of the S&Ls represented a new opportunity to capture the mortgage market. They soon became the biggest mortgage lenders in the country and went from having about 25 percent of their loans as mortgages in 1980 to 60 percent in the early 2000s. Loans by commercial banks to industrial and mercantile companies, once the entire reason for these banks' existence, dropped to less than 20 percent of their portfolios.[19] By the early 2000s, government assistance had made the "commercial" bank a complete inversion of its previous self. Although such banks were once defined by their opposition to mortgage debts, they were now defined precisely by their focus on such mortgages.

At the same time, Fannie Mae and Freddie Mac helped commercial banks expand by creating and selling a new type of mortgage asset. These government-sponsored enterprises, as they were now officially known, began buying bank mortgages and transforming them into "mortgage-backed securities," or bonds backed by hundreds or thousands of individual mortgages, with the bonds paying different amounts to different investors depending on how much risk they wanted to take. By the early 2000s, Fannie and Freddie backed almost 50 percent of mortgages issued by banks and other financiers. These enterprises also expanded their already considerable political influence through Fannie Mae

Foundation grants to special congressional districts, VIP loans to politicians and friends, and increasing numbers of mortgages to borderline borrowers, as demanded by federal dictates.[20]

Fannie and Freddie's success with mortgage bonds inspired banks to issue their own "private-label" mortgage-backed securities. Investors began treating both Fannie and Freddie and private mortgage bonds as if they contained no risk. When a bank needed money for a bit, it packaged some of its own mortgages together and sold them off to another bank with the promise to "repurchase," or "repo," them in a few days. Banks traded mortgage bonds back and forth with each other as if these bonds were the safest and most liquid assets in the world.[21] At the same time, the assumption that the government would bail out banks that had taken on excessively risky mortgages, an assumption that had proven accurate in the past, encouraged these banks to expand their risky mortgage bond portfolios.[22]

The fact that mortgages, the most-illiquid and opaque of assets, had become the effective equivalent of cash or government debt demonstrates what proliferating government support had done to the industry. Although no one would at the time put it this way, by the early 2000s the land bankers' old dream had become a reality: the American banking system was based on mortgages, and mortgages were treated like money.

The problems with the government support for illiquid mortgages became apparent once again in the global financial crisis of the 2000s. As the housing market began to turn south around 2006, many banks realized that the value of their mortgages and mortgage-backed bonds was *not* fully guaranteed by the government. The mortgages that they had treated like cash suddenly became suspect, and the banks stopped trading them with each other. Banks that had offered each other loans based on their mortgage debts demanded cash instead. In effect, there was a giant bank run, but it was banks running on each other, pulling apart the intricate web of mortgages and repo loans they had used to keep one another afloat. As mortgages lost their liquidity, they declined in value, which in turn hurt the banks' balance sheets. The construction sector, starved of both demand and funds, soon declined by 60 percent.[23]

At first, the government dithered on how much support to give mortgages and the banks. It went back and forth before deciding in March 2008 to bail out the fifth-largest investment bank in the country, Bear Stearns, with $30 billion in taxpayer and Federal Reserve funds. On September 7, 2008, the government decided to bail out two corporations that few could deny demanded government support, Fannie Mae and Freddie Mac. In the previous two years, Fannie and Freddie had bought and guaranteed just about every mortgage they could get their hand on in a bid to salvage both the financial sector and the home-building industry. By 2008, they guaranteed more than 65 percent of the mortgage market and had expanded into increasingly questionable assets. Just as the Federal Land Banks had helped support both politicians and the banking system in the 1920s and 1930s and then needed to be bailed out, Fannie and Freddie walked the same path. The bailout of Fannie and Freddie required more than $180 billion in government money.[24]

Yet on September 15, 2008, just a week after the Fannie and Freddie bailout, the government decided against saving Lehman Brothers, the fourth-largest investment bank in the country. The decision was ironic considering Lehman Brothers' efforts to create many of the government mortgage guarantees in the 1930s. To that point, it was the largest bankruptcy in American history, and it stunned the banking world. The government's refusal to bail out a major bank sparked panic in the stock markets and soon the greatest financial crisis since the Great Depression.[25]

The political class came to rue its failure to bail out every bank and support every mortgage and so quickly reversed course. Its new bailouts took predictable forms but went further than any in the past. First, within two weeks of Lehman's failure, Congress passed the Toxic Asset Relief Program, or TARP, to buy up bad, largely mortgage, assets. President George W. Bush's administration reformed the program to also give capital to banks that were in danger of failing. TARP would disburse more than $450 billion dollars before it wound down years later at a loss to taxpayers of about $30 billion.[26] Second, Fannie and Freddie, now under federal conservatorship and with federal backing, continued to prop up the market and kept their mortgage market share above its precrisis level. Other Roosevelt-era programs, such as the Federal Housing Administration and the Veterans Administration, increased their mortgage support. Together the FHA and the Veterans Administration came to insure 25 percent of all mortgages, a substantial jump from less than 5 percent just a few years earlier.[27] The Federal Reserve, just as in the Great Depression, expanded its balance sheet to buy up mortgages as well. At the expansion's peak in the mid-2010s, almost 40 percent of all Fed assets were mortgage-backed securities, largely issued by Fannie and Freddie. The Federal Reserve had almost achieved Marriner Eccles's dream of backing U.S. money directly with mortgages. It also created a host of new "facilities" to purchase bad or illiquid long-term assets from banks, such as the Term Auctions Facility and the Term Securities Lending Facilities.[28]

With these proliferating and overlapping mortgage and financials supports, the banking system began to regain profitability starting in 2009. The nonfinancial sector, however, endured one of the longest and slowest recoveries on record.[29]

Even this recovery was interrupted by the devastating COVID-19 recession of 2020. In this new crisis, the federal government offered trillions of dollars in bailouts to businesses, but, as in earlier decades, one reason for these bailouts was to allow those businesses to pay back their lenders. The largest lending program passed by Congress, the Payment Protection Program, was merely a guarantee for bank loans to businesses. Banks earned billions in fees on these essentially risk-free loans. The Federal Reserve also offered trillions of dollars of new loans to financiers, bankers, and mortgage holders, with almost no public debate. Bailouts of every possible industry and every possible lender had become almost second nature.[30]

One of the surprising aspects of the recent banking bailouts is that almost no one related them to the bailouts of the 1930s or to the proliferating government guarantees of finance that arose beginning in the 1910s. Even many experts on the Great Depression, including former Federal Reserve chairman Ben Bernanke, claimed that the failure to bail out banks in the Great Depression was a mistake that had to be rectified during the 2008 crisis.[31] In reality, one could find remarkable similarities in both the explanations of and the government response to the Great Depression and the Great Recession. In both cases, many leading thinkers blamed the financial collapse on the proliferation of illiquid mortgages and the resulting collapse in construction.[32] In both cases, the government expanded old forms of mortgage support and created new ones. During the more recent coronavirus crisis, such bailouts were extended to every conceivable business and lender.

One difference between the Great Depression and the recent crises, however, is rhetorical. No one in the latter crises talked about the need for a "balanced economy." Economists in 2008 and 2020 talked about the need to restore aggregate demand and purchasing power and to revive consumer spending, all the supposedly "Keynesian" ideas that have become part of the economic lexicon. The old ideal of a "balanced economy," which Keynes himself once embraced, had been long forgotten.

In practice, the ideal of a balanced economy was always a mirage. A stable balance between all sectors is impossible, with the balance changing as technologies and demands change. Yet the idea of a balanced economy did have an effect, as mistaken ideas often do. The idea and the people, both self-interested and disinterested, who trumpeted it created our modern financial system, one in which mortgages are cheaper and more easily tradable than ever. But the idea also created a financial system that relies on the federal government's constant solicitude for support. We live in the world that the balanced economy theorists and politicians of the early twentieth century created, even if we can be confident that all of them might not be thrilled with how that world looks. In many ways, both subtle and unsubtle, we are still paying a price to achieve their forgotten dream.

NOTES

Introduction

1. Willa Cather, *O Pioneers!* (Boston: Houghton Mifflin, 1913), 66.
2. See Elizabeth Sanders, *Roots of Reform: Farmers, Workers, and the American State, 1877–1917* (Chicago: University of Chicago Press, 1999).
3. Richard Hofstader, *Age of Reform* (New York: Knopf, 1955). See note 5 on historiography.
4. Henry Edmiston and Gunhild Anderson, "United States Government Corporations and Credit Agencies in 1940," *Federal Reserve Bulletin*, April 1941, 299; Office of Management and Budget, *Fiscal Year 2013 Historical Tables* (Washington, DC: US Government Printing Office, 2012), 21.
5. The literature on the "ideologies" of the Progressive Era and New Deal is one of the most substantial and enduring in the historical literature, and although this book does not hope to supplant it, it does hope to make a contribution and corrective to it. The issue of class legislation has become increasingly important in the field of legal history, but only one article that I am aware of describes class legislation as a subject of political debate in this period. Only two works that I am aware of study the ideology of "economic balance" in this period; both focus exclusively on the New Deal and ignore the centrality of farming and mortgages in their analysis. For a taste of the literature on the ideologies of this period, see Daniel Rodgers, *Atlantic Crossings: Social Politics in a Progressive Age* (Cambridge, MA: Belknap Press of Harvard University Press, 1998); Jackson Lears, *Rebirth of a Nation: The Making of Modern America, 1877–1920* (New York: Harper Perennial, 2010); Ira Katznelson, *Fear Itself: The New Deal and the Origins of Our Time* (New York: Liveright, 2013). For discussions of "class legislation," see Howard Gillman, *The Constitution Besieged: The Rise and Demise of Lochner Era Police Powers Jurisprudence* (Durham, NC: Duke University Press, 1993);

Howard Gillman, "The Constitution Besieged: T. R., Taft, and Wilson on the Virtue of a Faction-Free Republic," *Presidential Studies Quarterly* 19 (Winter 1989): 179–201. For works that discuss "economic balance," see Michael Bernstein, *The Great Depression: Delayed Recovery and Economic Change in America, 1929–1939* (New York: Cambridge University Press, 1987); Thomas Ferguson, "Industrial Conflict and the Coming of the New Deal: The Triumph of Multinational Liberalism in America," in *The Rise and Fall of the New Deal Order*, ed. Steve Fraser and Gary Gerstle (Princeton, NJ: Princeton University Press, 1989), 3–31. And for some discussion of price "balance," see Ellis Hawley, *The New Deal and the Problem of Monopoly: A Study in Economic Ambivalence* (1966; reprint, Princeton, NJ: Princeton University Press, 2016). Other such sources are referenced when relevant.

6. As late as 1973, however, Wassily Leontief won the Nobel Prize in Economics for his analysis of how inputs and outputs of different sectors affect overall output, an analysis similar to the one discussed here. For the basis of this work, see Wassily Leontief, *Structure of the American Economy, 1919–1929* (Cambridge, MA: Harvard University Press, 1941).

7. It should be noted that in this book I do not attempt to divine the "correct" way to analyze the U.S. economy in the early twentieth century. I try not to comment on the wisdom of particular reforms or economic ideas, such as the reasons for agricultural decline or the importance of mortgage defaults in causing the Great Depression. Although I occasionally reference modern works of economic history that do engage with these issues, my main goal is to portray how policy makers and reformers conceived of the economy and how their reforms reshaped it.

8. Many historians have placed the mortgage reforms described in this book into a history of either agricultural policy or urban and suburban development. They have thus ignored the essential financial nature of these reforms and how agricultural and urban financial policies shared similar motivations and methods over these decades. It should also be noted that agricultural ideologies of balance were distinct from ideologies that claimed agriculture was always and everywhere the foundation of prosperity, an ideology known as "agricultural fundamentalism," which balance proponents argued against. For agricultural-policy history, see David E. Hamilton, *From New Day to New Deal: American Farm Policy from Hoover to Roosevelt, 1928–1933* (Chapel Hill: University of North Carolina Press, 1991); Adam Sheingate, *The Rise of the Agricultural Welfare State: Institutions and Interest Group Power in the United States, France, and Japan* (Princeton, NJ: Princeton University Press, 2001). For "agricultural fundamentalism," see Joseph Davis, "Agricultural Fundamentalism," in *On Agricultural Policy* (Stanford, CA: Food Research Institute, 1939), 24–43. For typical urban and suburban interpretations of these policies and ideologies, see Kenneth T. Jackson, *Crabgrass Frontier: The Suburbanization of the United States* (New York: Oxford University Press, 1985); Marc A. Weiss, *The Rise of the Community Builders: The American Real Estate Industry and Urban Land Use Planning* (New York: Columbia University Press, 1987); David Freund, *Colored Property: State Policy and White Racial Politics in Suburban America* (Chicago: University of Chicago Press, 2007). For an argument against the "suburban" motivation of federal housing policy, which argues instead that housing policy focused on the needs of urban areas, see Judge Glock, "How the Federal Housing Administration Tried to Save America's Cities, 1934–1960," *Journal of Policy History* 28, no. 2 (2016): 290–317.

9. The rise of explicit industry lobbying groups in this period—for farmers, builders, bankers, and other groups—has been the subject of recent research. The self-interested

bureaucrats described here, however, are closest to what Daniel Carpenter has called "bureaucratic entrepreneurs," although just as often they were entrepreneurs who happened to be bureaucrats or bankers who happened to be politicians. For interest-group politics, see Elisabeth Clemens, *The People's Lobby: Organization Innovation and the Rise of Interest Group Politics in the United States, 1890–1925* (Chicago: University of Chicago Press, 1997). For bureaucratic entrepreneurs, see Daniel P. Carpenter, *The Forging of Bureaucratic Autonomy: Reputations, Networks, and Policy Innovation in Executive Agencies, 1862–1928* (Princeton, NJ: Princeton University Press, 2001).

10. For the preeminent examples of this literature, see Alan Brinkley, *The End of Reform: New Deal Liberalism in Recession and War* (New York: Vintage, 1995); Meg Jacobs, *Pocketbook Politics: Economic Citizenship in Twentieth Century America* (Princeton, NJ: Princeton University Press, 2005); Monica Prasad, *The Land of Too Much: American Abundance and the Paradox of Poverty* (Cambridge, MA: Harvard University Press, 2012).

11. The literature on the history of economic thought has come largely from economics departments and has made little headway into the broader studies of history or politics. With this book, I hope to elucidate some of the connections among these fields. The historian of economic thought who comes closest to my ideas in this work is Perry Mehrling, who describes institutionalist financial ideas and the importance of creating more "liquid" financial assets. For histories of economic thought that influenced this book, see David Laidler, *Fabricating the Keynesian Revolution: Studies of the Interwar Literature on Money, the Cycle, and Unemployment* (Cambridge: Cambridge University Press, 1999); Perry Mehrling, *The Money Interest and the Public Interest: American Monetary Thought, 1920–1970* (Cambridge, MA: Harvard University Press, 1998); Perry Mehrling, *The New Lombard Street: How the Fed Became the Dealer of Last Resort* (Princeton, NJ: Princeton University Press, 2011), 30–50. For some recent historical work, see Eli Cook, *The Pricing of Progress: Economic Indicators and the Capitalization of American Life* (Cambridge, MA: Harvard University Press, 2017).

12. Although earlier state-building literature focused on the growth of the bureaucracy, recent literature has shown how the state expanded its influence by contracting out and engaging with private groups. By focusing in particular on how the government expanded its power by expanding guarantees and supports for private finance, I hope this book will contribute to this type of analysis, especially in its description of the rise of a new type of government-guaranteed, semipublic corporation, now known as a government-sponsored enterprise, as an addition to the purely publicly funded corporations identified by Gail Radford as an essential innovation of this era. For older literature, see Stephen Skowronek, *Building the American State: The Expansion of National Administrative Capacities, 1877–1920* (Cambridge: Cambridge University Press, 1982); Theda Skocpol, *Protecting Soldiers and Mothers: The Political Origins of Social Policy in the United States* (Cambridge, MA: Harvard University Press, 1992). For newer literature, see Kimberley S. Johnson, *Governing the American State: Congress and the New Federalism, 1877–1929* (Princeton, NJ: Princeton University Press, 2007); Gail Radford, *The Rise of the Public Authority: Statebuilding and Economic Development in Twentieth-Century America* (Chicago: Chicago University Press, 2013); Brian Balogh, *The Associational State: American Governance in the Twentieth Century* (Philadelphia: University of Pennsylvania Press, 2015).

13. A few histories have described how the government encouraged the rise of particular financial industries, such as credit unions and building-and-loan associations. In recent years, there has been an increased focus on the "too big to fail" phenomena and

bailouts in banking history, but my intention is to explain why the government worked to save many types and sizes of financial institutions, not just those dubbed systematically important, and how these supports were often tied to the expansion of mortgage debt. This work also draws on the massive literature on the Federal Reserve, which, however, tends to ignore the simultaneous debate about mortgage debt and government-sponsored enterprise surrounding it. For particular industries, see J. Carroll Moody and Gilbert C. Fite, *The Credit Union Movement: Origins and Development, 1850–1970* (Lincoln: University of Nebraska Press, 1971); and David L. Mason, *From Building and Loans to Bail-outs: A History of the American Savings and Loan Industry, 1831–1995* (Cambridge: Cambridge University Press, 2004). For an overview of consumer debt, see James Grant, *Money of the Mind: Borrowing and Lending in America from the Civil War to Michael Milken* (New York: Farrar Straus Giroux, 1992). For too-big-to-fail analyses, see Benton E. Gup, ed., *Too Big to Fail: Policies and Practices in Government Bailouts* (Westport, CT: Praeger, 2004). For histories of bank failures in the era discussed, see David C. Wheelock, "Government Policy and Banking Market Structure in the 1920s," *Journal of Economic History* 53, no. 4 (December 1993): 857–79; Lee Alston, Wayne A. Grove, and David C. Wheelock, "Why Do Banks Fail? Evidence from the 1920s," *Explorations in Economic History* 31 (1994): 409–31. In his comprehensive work *A History of the Federal Reserve*, vol. 1: *1913–1951* (Chicago: University of Chicago Press, 2003), Allan H. Meltzer does not discuss mortgage policy. For some work on mortgage history, see Kenneth Snowden, "Mortgage Securitization in the United States: Twentieth Century Developments in Historical Perspective," in *Anglo-American Financial Systems: Institutions and Markets in the Twentieth Century*, ed. Michael Bordo and Eugene Silva (New York: New York University Salomon Center, 1995), 260–98.

14. Many recent histories of capitalism have focused on finance but not on the transformation of the banking industry or the attempts to use new government powers to simultaneously bail out banks and support certain industries. They have also tended to focus on the expansion of consumer debt as a sort of ersatz version of redistribution as opposed to debt extended to producers. If these histories describe mortgage loans, they categorize them as consumer loans, though economists then and now consider them investment loans, which create a durable good or "fixed-capital" asset. See, for instance, U.S. Bureau of Labor Statistics, "How the CPI Measures Price Change of Owners' Equivalent Rent of Primary Residence (OER) and Rent of Primary Residence (Rent)," April 2009, https://www.bls.gov/cpi/factsheets/owners-equivalent-rent-and-rent.pdf ("Houses and other residential structures are not consumption items.... All buildings and structures are capital goods"). For recent histories of financial capitalism, see Louis Hyman, *Debtor Nation: The History of America in Red Ink* (Princeton, NJ: Princeton University Press, 2011); Julia Ott, *When Wall Street Met Main Street: The Quest for an Investors' Democracy* (Cambridge, MA: Harvard University Press, 2011); Scott Reynolds Nelson, *A Nation of Deadbeats: An Uncommon History of America's Financial Disasters* (New York: Knopf, 2012); Greta Krippner, *Capitalizing on Crisis: The Political Origins of the Rise of Finance* (Cambridge, MA: Harvard University Press, 2012); Prasad, *The Land of Too Much*, and Sarah Quinn, *American Bonds: How Credit Markets Shaped a Nation* (Princeton, NJ: Princeton University Press, 2019). For a discussion on how some of the reforms described in this book also "democratized" finance in this period, see Christopher Shaw, *Money, Power, and the People: The American Struggle to Make Banking Democratic* (Chicago: University of Chicago, 2019). These writers deal much more thoroughly than I could here with the

important racial and gender implications of the new federal credit, which in the overwhelmingly white and male world of banks and large producers that I focus on was less salient than in the consumer sphere. For more discussion of the racial implications of early federal mortgage programs, see Glock, "How the Federal Housing Administration Tried to Save America's Cities," 304–8.

15. A brief note on terminology is warranted. Although this book examines the history of banking and finance and is intended to be of some service to those interested in that history, it also tries to communicate with a wider audience interested in political, business, and intellectual history. Unfortunately, the use of some financial terms uncommon in these other fields is inevitable. In the text, I try to describe these terms as they arise and what they meant to contemporaries. A wary reader can perhaps be comforted that the precise meaning of terms such as *liquidity* and *capital* can bedevil even experts in the field and that the reader needs to understand only how they work in context of this book. As far as some institutional terminology goes, I have tried to keep it consistent throughout. For instance, I use designations such as "governor of the Federal Reserve Board," though in later years this position became known as the "chair of the Board of Governors of the Federal Reserve System."

16. Today close to a majority of so-called commercial bank assets are actually mortgages, which typically carry numerous government guarantees and subsidies originating in the period discussed in this book. See Alex J. Pollack, "'Commercial' Bank Is a Misnomer. 'Real Estate' Bank Is More Apt," *American Banker*, August 8, 2016.

17. Total bank assets also expanded in this period. The ratio of commercial bank assets to gross domestic product rose from 30 percent in 1900 to around 50 percent in the New Deal 1930s and then expanded more quickly after World War II under the impetus of government guarantees. The assets of noncommercial mortgage banks, such as "building and loans," which focused on mortgages, expanded more than 3,700 percent from 1900 to 1940. See Richard Grossman, *Unsettled Account: The Evolution of Banking in the Industrialized World Since 1800* (Princeton, NJ: Princeton University Press, 2010), 25; and Louis Winnick, "The Burden of Residential Mortgage Debt," *Journal of Finance* 11, no. 2 (May 1956): 166.

18. Murray Shipley Wildman, "Independent Treasury and the Banks," in *Banking Problems* (Philadelphia: American Academy of Political and Social Sciences, 1910), 108.

1. Making the Land Liquid: The Roots of Land Banking

1. Tyler Beck Goodspeed, *Legislating Instability: Adam Smith, Free Banking, and the Financial Crisis of 1772* (Cambridge, MA: Harvard University Press, 2016), 135. The bank is alternately called the "Air Bank" or "Ayr Bank" in the literature. For histories of the bank, see Douglas, Heron, and Company, *The Precipitation and Fall of Mess. Douglas, Heron, and Company, Late Bankers in Air, with Causes of Their Distress and Ruin, Investigated . . .* (Edinburgh: Douglas, Heron, 1778); and Paul Kostemos, "The Winding-Up of the Ayr Bank, 1772–1827," *Financial History Review* 21, no. 2 (August 2014): 165–90.

2. Quoted in Antoin Murphy, *The Genesis of Macroeconomics: New Ideas from Sir William Petty to Henry Thornton* (New York: Oxford University Press, 2009), 176.

3. Quoted in Richard Saville, *The Bank of Scotland: A History, 1695–1995* (Edinburgh: Edinburgh University Press, 1996), 163.

4. Adam Smith, *An Inquiry Into the Nature and Causes of the Wealth of Nations* (1776; reprint, New York: Random House, 1994), 341.

5. Smith, *An Inquiry*, 334–35. Smith used the full phrase "real bills of exchange," but later writers would shorten it to "real bills." For background of the phrase, see Lloyd Mints, *A History of Banking Theory in Great Britain and the United States* (Chicago: University of Chicago Press, 1945), 9, 207.

6. Smith, *An Inquiry*, 334–35.

7. Smith, *An Inquiry*, 334, 331.

8. In another metaphysical metaphor and perhaps an allusion to the bank's name, Smith said that a bank's credit was always "suspended upon the Daedelian wings of paper money" and was thus always in danger of crashing to earth (quoted in Goodspeed, *Legislating Instability*, 6).

9. William Playfair, *A Letter to Sir William Pulteney* (London: Crosby, 1797), 16–17. William Playfair acquired his greatest fame as inventor of the pie and bar graphs. See Cara Giaimo, "The Scottish Scoundrel Who Changed How We See Data," *Atlas Obscura*, June 28, 2016, https://www.atlasobscura.com/articles/the-scottish-scoundrel-who-changed-how-we-see-data.

10. Charles Dunbar, *The Theory and History of Banking* (1891; reprint, New York: Putnam's, 1922), 29–30.

11. Much of the history of land banks focuses on a few isolated banks or periods, usually in the seventeenth or eighteenth centuries. Most histories of banking in the nineteenth or early twentieth centuries mention mortgages only tangentially. Histories of later land-banking ideas usually subsume them under general histories of agricultural cooperation without examining the special financial nature of the reforms. For early discussions of land banks, see Carl Wennerlind, *Casualties of Credit: The English Financial Revolution, 1620–1720* (Cambridge, MA: Harvard University Press, 2011); Margaret Ellen Newell, *From Dependency to Independence: Economic Revolution in Colonial New England* (Ithaca, NY: Cornell University Press, 1998), 213–36; Daniel Rodgers, *Atlantic Crossings: Social Politics in a Progressive Age* (Cambridge, MA: Belknap Press of Harvard University Press, 1998), 318–34.

12. Arthur R. Hogue, *Origins of the Common Law* (Indianapolis: Indiana University Press, 1966), 112–13. See also Theodore F. T. Plunkett, *A Concise History of the Common Law* (New York: Little, Brown 1956), 177; and Lynn M. Fisher, "Renegotiation in the Common Law Mortgage and the Impact of Equitable Redemption," *Journal of Real Estate Finance and Economics* 32, no. 1 (2006): 63.

13. *Oxford English Dictionary*, s.v. "mortgage."

14. See Henry Roseveare, *Financial Revolution, 1660–1750* (New York: Routledge, 1991).

15. Quoted in Roseveare, *Financial Revolution*, 17. See also Peter Temin and Hans-Joachin Voth, *Prometheus Shackled: Goldsmith Banks and England's Financial Revolution After 1700* (Oxford: Oxford University Press, 2012).

16. Wennerlind, *Casualties of Credit*, 60.

17. William Potter, *The Key of Wealth: Or a New Way for Improving Trade, Lawfull, Easie, Safe, and Effectuall* (London: R.A., 1650), 1, 8, 24.

18. Wennerlind, *Casualties of Credit*, 68.

19. Cheney Culpeper, *An Essay Upon Master W. Potters Design* (London: n.p., 1653) 33; see also Wennerlind, *Casualties of Credit*, 67–75.

20. For opposition to governments, see Wennerlind, *Casualties of Credit*, 78.

21. Wennerlind, *Casualties of Credit*, 114.

22. Hugh Chamberlen, *A Proposal for Erecting a General Bank, Which May Be Fitly Called the Land Bank of England* (London: E. Whitlock, 1695), not paginated.

23. Richard Kleer, "'Fictitious Cash': England Public Finance and Paper Money, 1689–97," in *Money, Power, and Print: Interdisciplinary Studies on the Financial Revolution in the British Isles*, ed. Charles McGrath and Chris Fauske (Newark: University of Delaware Press, 2008), 90–96; John Briscoe, *A Short Scheme or Proposals for a National Land-Bank* (London: n.p., c. 1695).

24. Wennerlind, *Casualties of Credit*, 120–21. The pattern of a new central commercial bank followed by a new land bank would be repeated centuries later in the United States.

25. Bernard Bailyn, *The Ideological Origins of the American Revolution* (Cambridge, MA: Harvard University Press, 1992).

26. Quoted in Newell, *From Dependency to Independence*, 124.

27. Theodore Thayer, "The Land Bank System in the American Colonies," *Journal of Economic History* 13, no. 2 (Spring 1953): 145–59. On the Massachusetts battle, see *A Projection for Erecting a Bank of Credit in Boston, New-England. Founded on Landed Security* (Boston: n.p., 1714). For more liberal American land laws, which encouraged the commercialization and therefore the financialization of land, see Claire Priest, "Creating an American Property Law: Alienability and Its Limits in American History," *Harvard Law Review* 120, no. 2 (December 2006): 387–458.

28. Donald Kemmerer, "The Colonial Loan-Office System in New Jersey," *Journal of Political Economy* 47, no. 6 (December 1939): 870.

29. Farley Grubb, *Benjamin Franklin and the Birth of a Paper Money Economy* (Philadelphia: Federal Reserve Bank of Philadelphia, 2007), 5.

30. Newell, *From Dependency to Independence*, 228.

31. Gary Nash, *The Urban Crucible: The Northern Seaports and the Origins of the American Revolution* (Cambridge, MA: Harvard University Press, 1986), 134, 140. See also Samuel Adams, *The Manufactory Scheme*, pamphlet (Boston: n.p., c. 1744).

32. Grubb, *Benjamin Franklin*, 5–8.

33. Edmund Burke, *Reflections on the Revolution in France* (1790; reprint, London: Methuen, 1905), 189–91, emphasis in original.

34. See Michael D. Bordo and Eugene White, "A Tale of Two Currencies: British and French Finance During the Napoleonic Wars," *Journal of Economic History* 51, no. 2 (June 1991): 303–16.

35. Bray Hammond, "Long and Short Term Credit in Early American Banking," *Quarterly Journal of Economics* 49, no. 1 (1934): 81–82.

36. Philadelphiensis, "Omnis Homines," *Freeman's Journal*, March 3, 1785, 3, emphasis in original.

37. Hammond, "Long and Short Term Credit," 83; Alexander Hamilton to John Barker Church, March 10, 1784, in *The Works of Alexander Hamilton*, ed. Henry Cabot Lodge (New York: Putnam's, 1886), 159. Hamilton said it was his duty to oppose land bank schemes "for the sake of the commercial interests of the State."

38. Hammond, "Long and Short Term Credit," 85.

39. Numerous states supported agricultural land banks but usually as part of a more competitive banking system and without legal-tender status for their notes. Unlike the earlier land banks, these agricultural land banks also kept coins as reserves behind their notes, meaning that land was not the only recourse. Some people at the time differentiated them from earlier "land banks" by calling them "mortgage

banks." Most collapsed after the Panic of 1837. See Howard Bodenhorn, *State Banking in Early America: A New Economic History* (New York: Oxford University Press, 2003), 250–60.

40. "An Act to Authorize the Business of Banking," April 18, 1838, in *Laws of the State of New York Passed at the 61st Session of the Legislature* (Albany, NY: E. Croswell, 1838), 245–53.

41. "Capital Needed for Agricultural Improvement," *Monthly Journal of Agriculture* 1, no. 8 (February 1846): 406.

42. "The General Banking Law of the State of New York," *United States Magazine and Democratic Review* 5, no. 17 (May 1839): 427. See also Charles McCurdy, *The Anti-rent Era in New York Law and Politics, 1839–1865* (Chapel Hill: University of North Carolina Press, 2006), 81.

43. Hammond, "Long and Short Term Credit," 97–100. The deposits and the capital of a bank are known as its "liabilities"—namely, what the banking corporation owes to others—whereas a bank's loans and other investments are known as its "assets," what the bank owns or can earn money on.

44. John Denis Haeger, "Eastern Financiers and Institutional Change: The Origins of the New York Life Insurance Trust Company and the Ohio Life Insurance Trust Company," *Journal of Economic History* 1979, 259–60.

45. Haeger, "Eastern Financiers and Institutional Change," 270.

46. "The Failure of the Ohio Life and Trust Company," *Chicago Daily Tribune*, August 26, 1857. See also Charles W. Calomiris and Larry Schweikart, "The Panic of 1857: Origins, Transmission, and Containment," *Journal of Economic History* 51, no. 4 (December 1991): 807–34; Charles Clifford Huntington, "A History of Banking and Currency in Ohio Before the Civil War," PhD diss., Cornell University, 1915, 242–44.

47. John Sherman, *Recollections of Forty Years in the House, Senate, and Cabinet: An Autobiography* (Chicago: Werner, 1896), 258–59.

48. For the debate on the national banking system and national currency, see Cong. Globe, 37th Cong., 3rd sess. (1863), 820.

49. *An Act to Provide a National Currency*, Pub. L. 84, 37th Cong., 3d sess. (February 25, 1863), 668–69.

50. Sherman, *Recollections*, 237.

51. For an attempt to ban mortgages, see Cong. Globe, 38th Cong., 1st sess. (1864), 1338–339.

52. William Graham Sumner, *A History of Banking in All the Leading Nations* (New York: Journal of Commerce and Commercial Bulletin, 1896), 423.

53. Cong. Globe, 38th Cong., 1st sess. (1864), 1871, 2019, 2450. The confusing clause forbade banks to hold any real estate unless for non-real estate "debts previously contracted," which meant that they could not contract for new debts on real estate and thus in turn that they could not make new mortgages. In the debates, Sherman elided the importance of this clause and insinuated that it was only continuing the previous law forbidding banks to hold real estate.

54. See the chapter "Abolishment of the State Banks" in Sherman, *Recollections*, 284. The House of Representatives soon formed the Banking and Currency Committee to manage the national banks.

55. Dunbar, *The Theory and History of Banking*, 29–30.

56. Charles A. Conant, "The Principles of a Banking Currency: The Necessity for Liquid Assets," *Bankers Magazine* 58, no. 6 (June 1899): 819.

57. Kenneth Snowden, "The Evolution of Interregional Mortgage Lending Channels, 1870–1940: The Life Insurance–Mortgage Company Connection," in *Coordination and*

Information: Historical Perspectives on the Organization of Enterprise, ed. Naomi Lamoreaux and Daniel M. G. Raff (Chicago: University of Chicago Press, 1995), 221; U.S. Census Office, *Report on Real Estate Mortgages* (Washington, DC: U.S. Government Printing Office, 1895); Susan Carter, Scott Sigmund Gartner, Michael R. Haines, Alan L. Olmstead, Richard Sutch, and Gavin Wright, eds., *Historical Statistics of the United States: Earliest Times to the Present*, millennial ed. (New York: Cambridge University Press, 2006), tables Dc903–28. See also *Report on Farms and Homes: Proprietorship and Indebtedness in the United States at the Eleventh Census: 1890* (Washington, DC: U.S. Government Printing Office, 1896).

58. D. M. Frederiksen, "Mortgage Banking in America," *Journal of Political Economy* 2, no. 2 (March 1894): 210.

59. For early discussion of the communal banks' background and the anti-Semitic tropes that motivated them, see Henry William Wolff, *People's Banks: A Record of Social and Economic Success*, 2nd ed. (London: King, 1896), esp. 65–67.

60. See the background on building-and-loan associations in David Mason, *From Building and Loans to Bail-outs: A History of the American Savings and Loan Industry, 1831–1995* (Cambridge: Cambridge University Press, 2004).

61. H. Peers Brewer, "Eastern Money and Western Mortgages in the 1870s," *Business History Review* 50, no. 3 (Autumn 1976): 358, 373. For state requirements on investing life insurance funds in mortgages, see Sharon Ann Murphy, *Investing in Life: Insurance in Antebellum America* (Baltimore: John Hopkins University Press, 2010), 118–19.

62. For debate on what caused the high rates in the South and the West, whether it was higher risk or lack of access to capital, see Barry Eichengreen, "Interest Rates in the Populist Era," *American Economic Review* 74, no. 5 (1984): 995–1015; and Kenneth Snowden, "Mortgage Rates and American Capital Market Development in the Late Nineteenth Century," *Journal of Economic History* 47, no. 3 (1987): 671–91.

63. E. W. Kemmerer, "Agricultural Credit in the United States," *American Economic Review* 2, no. 4 (December 1912): 852.

64. E. U. Cook, *The First Mortgage* (Chicago: Rhodes & McClure, 1901), 27, 164–65.

65. Quoted in Studs Terkel, *Hard Times: An Oral History of the Great Depression* (New York: Pantheon Books, 1970), 213, recounting earlier "hard times."

66. Frank M. Drew, "The Present Farmers' Movement," *Political Science Quarterly* 6, no. 2 (June 1891): 291, 295; S. M. Scott, *The Sub-Treasury Plan and the Land and Loan System* (Topeka, KS: Hamilton, 1891). Charles Postel only briefly mentions land loans in *The Populist Vision* (New York: Oxford University Press, 2007), 154. California senator Leland Stanford proposed such a bill in Congress, and it was taken up by others, such as Populist senator William Peffer of Kansas. See Leland Stanford, *Government Loans on Real Estate* (Washington, DC: U.S. Government Printing Office, March 10, 1890); Benjamin Tucker, "Leland Stanford's Land Bank Plan," *Liberty*, June 7, 1890; William Peffer, "Government Control of Money," in *The Farmers Alliance History and Agricultural Digest*, ed. N. A. Dunning (Washington, DC: National Alliance, 1891), 266–67; William Peffer, *The Farmer's Side: His Troubles and Their Remedy* (New York: Appleton, 1891), 34–42; William Peffer, *The Land Loan Bill, Remarks in the Senate, January 21, 1892* (Washington, DC: U.S. Government Printing Office, 1892); William Peffer, *Populism: Its Rise and Fall*, ed. and with an introduction by Peter Argersinger (1899; reprint, Topeka: University of Kansas Press, 1991). The more conservative National Grange, however, refused to endorse such a plan; see John Trimble, ed., *Journal of Proceedings, Twenty-Sixth Session of the National Grange, 1892*

(Philadelphia: J. A. Wagenseller, 1892), 180–82 (these and other cited Grange proceedings are usually organized by each day within the session).

67. "Populist Party Platform of 1892," July 4, 1892, American Presidency Project, https://www.presidency.ucsb.edu/documents/populist-party-platform-1892.

68. Fabian Franklin, *Cost of Living* (Garden City, NY: Doubleday, Page, 1916), 110–11. For Bryan on high-priced mortgages and the need for inflation, see William Jennings Bryan, *The First Battle: A Story of the Campaign of 1896* (Chicago: W. B. Conkey, 1896), 81, 98, 146, 241, 551, 562, 572, 587.

69. Jonathan Levy, " 'The Mortgage Worked the Hardest': The Fate of Landed Independence in Nineteenth-Century America," in *Capitalism Takes Command: The Social Transformation of Nineteenth-Century America*, ed. Gary J. Kornblith and Michael Zakim (Chicago: University of Chicago Press, 2012), 39–67.

70. Sumner, *A History of Banking*, 111–13; Patrick Camiller, *Haussmann: His Life and Times, and the Making of Modern Paris*, trans. Michael Carmona (Chicago: Ivan R. Dee, 2020), 267–68. The only other institution that mimicked these "semipublic" attributes was the Banque de France, the country's central bank. Central banks always had a special relationship to their governments, and most were later nationalized.

71. U.S. Bureau of Insular Affairs, "Laws and Regulations Relating to the Hungarian Boden-Kredit Institute," in *Report of the Chief of the Division of the Currency to the Treasurer of the Philippines Islands* (Washington, DC: US. Government Printing Office, 1906), 95–96; Alice Teichova, "Banking in Austria," in *Handbook on the History of European Banks*, ed. Manfred Pohl (Aldershot, U.K.: Edward Elgar, 1994), 4.

72. Manfred Pohl, "Deutsche Centralbodenkredit-Aktiengesellschaft," in *Handbook on the History of European Banks*, ed. Pohl, 389; D. M. Frederiksen, "Mortgage Banking in Germany," *Quarterly Journal of Economics* 9, no. 1 (October 1894): 47–76; Joseph Louis Cohen, *The Mortgage Bank: A Study in Investment Banking* (London: Pittman, 1931), 146.

73. Chief of the Division of the Currency, U.S. Bureau of Insular Affairs, *Advisability of Establishing a Government Agricultural Bank in the Philippines* (Washington, DC: U.S. Government Printing Office, 1906), 8.

74. Niall Ferguson, *House of Rothschild: The World's Banker, 1849–1999*, vol. 2 (New York: Penguin, 1998), 182. For interest in America regarding the German land bank project, see Frederiksen, "Mortgage Banking in Germany."

75. Emily Rosenberg, *Financial Missionaries to the World: The Politics and Culture of Dollar Diplomacy* (Durham, NC: Duke University Press, 2004), 15–23.

76. Subcommittee of the Senate Committee on the Philippines, *Hearings on a System of Currency for the Philippine Islands*, 57th Cong., 1st sess. (1902), 84.

77. Charles Conant, *A Special Report on Coinage and Banking in the Philippines Islands* (Washington, DC: U.S. Government Printing Office, 1901), 56–62.

78. Subcommittee on the Philippines, *Hearings on a System of Currency*, 533, testimony by Charles Conant.

79. See Paul Drake, *The Money Doctor in the Andes: The Kemmerer Missions, 1923–1933* (Durham, NC: Duke University Press, 1989), 9.

80. Chief of the Division of the Currency, *Advisability of Establishing a Government Agricultural Bank*, 8–12.

81. Chief of the Division of the Currency, *Advisability of Establishing a Government Agricultural Bank*, 8.

82. Chief of the Division of the Currency, *Advisability of Establishing a Government Agricultural Bank*, 489.

83. Chief of the Division of the Currency, *Advisability of Establishing a Government Agricultural Bank*, 496.

84. U.S. Secretary of War, *Report of the Taft Philippine Commission* (Washington, DC: U.S. Government Printing Office, 1901), 109. For similar government encouragement of Philippine investment, see Colin D. Moore, "State Building Through Partnership: Delegation, Public–Private Partnerships, and the Political Development of American Imperialism, 1898–1916," *Studies in American Political Development* 25 (April 2011): 27–55.

85. Christopher Morrison, "A World of Empires: United States Rule in the Philippines, 1898–1913," PhD diss., Georgetown University, 2009, 181.

86. House Committee on Insular Affairs, "Railroads and Agricultural Bank in the Philippine Islands," 59th Cong., 2d sess. (1907), 41.

87. House Committee on Insular Affairs, "Railroads and Agricultural Bank in the Philippine Islands," 64–65.

88. 41 Cong. Rec. 4551 (March 3, 1907).

89. Jeremiah Jenks, "The Agricultural Bank for the Philippine Islands," *Annals of the American Academy of Political and Social Sciences* 30 (July 1907): 38. The importance that the famous money doctors placed on such land banks here and elsewhere has been ignored in much of the literature on U.S. imperialism. See also E. W. Kemmerer, "An Agricultural Bank for the Philippines," *Yale Review*, November 1907, 262; and Rosenberg, *Financial Missionaries*.

90. U.S. War Department, *Annual Report of the Philippine Commission*, vol. 3 (Washington, DC: U.S. Government Printing Office, 1908), 14.

91. Yoshiko Nagano, "The Agricultural Bank of the Philippine Government, 1908–1916," *Journal of Southeast Asian Studies* 28, no. 2 (September 1997): 301–23.

92. See G. Scott-Dalgleish, "The Agricultural Bank of Egypt and Its Success in Suppressing Usury, Also the Reasons Why It Failed to Maintain the Confidence It Had Built Up Among the Fellaheen," *Journal of the American Bankers Association* 8, no. 11 (May 1916): 976–80.

93. Kingman Nott Robins, *The Farm Mortgage Handbook* (Garden City, NY: Doubleday, Page, 1916), 3.

94. T. Bentley Mott, *Myron Herrick: Friend of France, an Autobiographical Biography* (Garden City, NY: Doubleday, Doran, 1929).

95. "High Price Cure Is Cheap Farm Loan," *Cleveland Plain Dealer*, November 2, 1911, File 3002, Reel 438, William Howard Taft Presidential Papers, Library of Congress, Washington, DC.

96. Myron Herrick and R. Ingalls, *How to Finance the Farmer: Private Enterprise—Not State Aid* (Cleveland: Ohio State Committee on Rural Credit, 1915).

97. Mott, *Myron Herrick*, chap. 15; "Republican Party Platform of 1912," June 18, 1912, American Presidency Project, https://www.presidency.ucsb.edu/documents/republican-party-platform-1912.

98. For "sacred pledge," see "A Review of the World," *Current Literature* 53, no. 6 (December 1912): 1.

99. *Report of the Country Life Commission*, 60th Cong., 2nd sess., S. Doc. 705 (1909), 56, 59.

100. "Progressive Party Platform of 1912," June 25, 1912, American Presidency Project, https://www.presidency.ucsb.edu/documents/progressive-party-platform-1912.

101. William Roscoe Thayer, "A Recollection of David Lubin," in Olivia Rossetti Agresti, *David Lubin: A Study in Practical Idealism* (Boston: Little, Brown, 1922), v–vi.

102. Chief of the Division of the Currency, *Advisability of Establishing a Government Agricultural Bank*, 75–76. The historian Daniel Rodgers, for instance, says such *Landschaften* "were not true cooperative associations. Rooted in the corporatist past, with the state as their managing patron," they did not aim at the self-supported cooperative goals of other groups (*Atlantic Crossings*, 337).

103. David Lubin, *The Landschaften System of Rural Credits*, 63d Cong., 1st sess., S. Doc. 123 (1913), 4–5. Lubin denied that the government would directly guarantee the bonds, but his advocacy for the government's "safeguards" and its management implied a responsibility for them.

104. U.S. Congress, *Statement of David Lubin on H.J. Res No. 344 by Request of Hon. William Kent, March 3, 1915* (Washington, DC: U.S. Government Printing Office, 1915).

105. David Lubin to O. D. Anderson, April 27, 1915, Reel 183, Woodrow Wilson Presidential Papers, Library of Congress.

106. "Fletcher Praises Convention's Work," *Washington Herald*, April 18, 1912.

107. See "Democratic Party Platform," June 25, 1912, American Presidency Project, https://www.presidency.ucsb.edu/documents/1912-democratic-party-platform. The platform also mentioned that "we also favor legislation permitting national banks to loan a reasonable proportion of their funds on real estate security," which would become part of the Federal Reserve Act of 1913.

108. Joint Subcommittees of the Committees on Banking and Currency, *Investigation of Rural Credits*, 63rd Cong., 2d sess. (1914), 3–4.

109. For public discussion of the mortgage issue in 1912, see "Loans to Saxon Farmers," *New York Times*, August 4, 1912; "Co-operation Among Farmers: Makes Germany and Other European Countries Prosperous," *Richmond Times Dispatch*, August 25, 1912; "Farmers' Banks," *Washington Post*, July 4, 1912.

110. Huntington Wilson to Charles D. Ellis, July 6, 1912, Series 3002, Reel 438, Taft Presidential Papers.

111. William Taft, foreword to Myron Herrick, *Preliminary Report on Land and Agricultural Credit in Europe* (Washington, DC: U.S. Government Printing Office, 1912), 7; "Taft Warns Farmer," *Washington Post*, October 25, 1912.

112. "Taft to Discuss Rural Credit Plan," *Washington Herald*, November 18, 1912. The race also involved the Socialist Party, which attained its popular-vote peak in this election, but at only 6 percent of the total. The party advocated the total nationalization of land. See "The Socialist Party Platform of 1912," Labor History Links, http://www.laborhistorylinks.org/PDF%20Files/Socialist%20Party%20Platform%201912.pdf.

113. "Would Aid Farmers," *Washington Post*, December 7, 1912; "Blease Scorns Laws," *Washington Post*, December 6, 1912.

114. "Report [Transcript] of a Conference Held on the Subject of Rural Credit, in the East Room of the White House, December 7, 1912," Reel 372, Taft Presidential Papers.

115. "Want Farm Loan," *Washington Post*, December 8, 1912.

116. 49 Cong. Rec. 2499 (February, 3, 1913).

117. "Bill for 'Rural Credits'" *Washington Post*, January 5, 1913.

118. 49 Cong. Rec. 4651 (March 3, 1913); *An Act Making Appropriations for the Department of Agriculture*, Pub. L. 62, 62nd Cong., 3rd sess. (March 4, 1913), 855.

119. 49 Cong. Rec. 4755 (March 3, 1913); 49 Cong. Rec. 4842 (March 4, 1913).

120. Rodgers, *Atlantic Crossings*, 337.

121. See David Lubin to Irwin Laughlin, London chargé d'affaires, April 10, 1913, Box 2, Lillian Correspondence, Record Group 103, National Archives, College Park, MD.

2. The Special Privileges of the Federal Banks

1. Andrew Jackson, "Veto of the Bank Bill," in *The Evolving Presidency: Landmark Documents, 1787–2010*, ed. Michael Nelson (Washington, DC: CQ College Press, 2011), 92.

2. William Leggett, "The True Functions of Government," *New York Evening Post*, November 21, 1834, in *Democratick Editorials*, ed. Lawrence White (Indianapolis, Ind.: Liberty Fund, 1984), 3.

3. Gerald Leonard, *The Invention of Party Politics: Federalism, Popular Sovereignty, and Constitutional Development in Jacksonian Illinois* (Chapel Hill: University of North Carolina Press, 2002), 183.

4. See, for example, Howard Gillman, *The Constitution Besieged: The Rise and Demise of Lochner Era Police Powers Jurisprudence* (Durham, NC: Duke University Press, 1993); V. F. Nourse and Sarah Maguire, "The Lost History of Governance and Equal Protection," *Duke Law Journal* 58, no. 6 (March 2009): 955–1012. For one article on political implications of these ideas, see Howard Gillman, "The Constitution Besieged: T. R., Taft, and Wilson on the Virtue of a Faction-Free Republic," *Presidential Studies Quarterly* 19 (Winter 1989): 179–201.

5. As early as 1915, the *New Republic* began asking if Wilson was undergoing a "radical reversal" because his program now "seems to contradict every principle of the party which enacted it." See "An Unseen Reversal," *New Republic* 1, no. 10 (January 9, 1915): 7–8.

6. For a typical discussion of shift, see John Milton Cooper, *Woodrow Wilson: A Biography* (New York: Knopf, 2009), 234. For histories of the era that ignore the issue of class legislation, see Arthur Link, *Wilson: The New Freedom* (Princeton, NJ: Princeton University Press, 1956), 241–43, 264; and David Sarasohn, *The Party of Reform: Democrats in the Progressive Era* (Jackson: University Press of Mississippi, 1989). The historiography on the passage of the Federal Reserve Act is extensive, but there is almost no mention in this literature about class legislation or the connection to the mortgage and rural-credits debates. See Richard T. McCulley, *Banks and Politics During the Progressive Era: The Origins of the Federal Reserve System, 1897–1913* (New York: Garland, 1992); Roger Lowenstein, *America's Bank: The Epic Struggle to Create the Federal Reserve* (New York: Penguin, 2015), 228. The historiography on the passage of the Federal Farm Loan Act sees it largely as the result of agricultural activism and ignores its connections to financial-reform debates, the ideology of "balance," and the innovative use of the implicit guarantee for the Federal Land Banks. See Gail Radford, *The Rise of the Public Authority: State-building and Economic Development in Twentieth-Century America* (Chicago: University of Chicago Press, 2013), 41–69; Elizabeth Sanders, *Roots of Reform: Farmers, Workers, and the American State, 1877–1917* (Chicago: University of Chicago Press, 1999), 259–61; Daniel Rodgers, *Atlantic Crossings: Social Politics in a Progressive Age* (Cambridge, MA: Belknap Press of Harvard University Press, 1998), 318–34. For discussion of the Federal Reserve and Land Banks as tools for democratizing finance, see Christopher Shaw, *Money, Power, and the People: The American Struggle to Make Banking Democratic* (Chicago: University of Chicago Press, 2019), 87–108.

7. Of course, Democrats denied that the idea of "equal protection" applied to the "race question" and even claimed that "race agitation" was based on a plea for special privileges. See "1904 Democratic Party Platform," July 6, 1904, American Presidency Project, https://www.presidency.ucsb.edu/documents/1904-democratic-party-platform.

8. "Democratic Party Platform of 1840," quoted in Joel H. Sibley, *The American Political Nation, 1838–1893* (Stanford, CA: Stanford University Press, 1991), 82.

9. George Vest, "The Hopes of the Democratic Party," *North American Review* 149, no. 396 (November 1889): 545.

10. "1892 Democratic Party Platform," June 21, 1892, American Presidency Project, https://www.presidency.ucsb.edu/documents/1892-democratic-party-platform; "Democratic Party Platform of 1896," July 7, 1896, American Presidency Project, https://www.presidency.ucsb.edu/documents/1896-democratic-party-platform.

11. *National Association of Democratic Clubs* (New York: Journal Job Print, 1900), 5, 20.

12. *The Campaign Text Book of the Democratic Party of the United States, 1904* (New York: Democratic National Committee, 1904), title page, 76; *Democratic Campaign Book Congressional Election* (Baltimore: Sun Job and Printing Office, 1906), title page. For other examples, see Thomas Nelson Page, "The Democratic Opportunity," *North American Review* 193, no. 663 (February 1911): 193–205.

13. *Democratic Campaign Book for 1910* (Washington, DC: National Democratic Congressional Committee, 1910), 286.

14. According to Google N-Gram (https://books.google.com/ngrams), use of the term *class legislation* as a percentage of all printed terms increased almost fivefold from 1880 to the 1910s and peaked in the latter decade.

15. John Trimble, ed., *Journal of Proceedings of the National Grange, 1898* (Concord, New Hampshire: Rumford Press, 1898), 164.

16. Frank M. Drew, "The Present Farmers' Movement," *Political Science Quarterly* 6, no. 2 (June 1891); 289; Trimble, *Journal of Proceedings of the National Grange, 1898*, 164.

17. Joint Subcommittees of the House and Senate Banking and Currency Committees, *Investigation of Rural Credits*, 63rd Cong., 2nd sess. (1914), 263.

18. William Jennings Bryan, "Letter Accepting Democratic Nomination," September 9, 1896, in *The Life and Speeches of Honorable William Jennings Bryan* (Baltimore: R. H. Woodward, 1900), 358.

19. James K. Polk, "The President's Message," December 5, 1848, in *Abridgement of the Debates of Congress*, vol. 16 (New York: D. Appleton, 1861), 275.

20. Sigmund Freud and William C. Bullitt, *Woodrow Wilson: A Psychological Study* (1966; reprint, New Brunswick, NJ: Transaction, 1999), 6.

21. Quoted in John M. Mulder, *Woodrow Wilson: The Years of Preparation* (Princeton, NJ: Princeton University Press, 1978), 76–77.

22. Woodrow Wilson, *Congressional Government* (1885; reprint, New York: Putnam's, 1900), dedication.

23. See Woodrow Wilson, *Mere Literature, and Other Essays* (Boston: Houghton Mifflin, 1896), 155.

24. Wilson, *Mere Literature*, 155. Wilson tended to speak more in the language of "interests" than of classes, and his focus on executive administration as opposed to legislation meant he rarely used the term *class legislation*, though many of his supporters did. For other quotes from Wilson, see Gillman, "The Constitution Besieged," 192.

25. Woodrow Wilson, *The New Freedom: A Call for the Emancipation of the Generous Energies of the People* (Garden City, NY: Doubleday, Page, 1921), 199, 288. It is important to differentiate Wilson's stance from "mossback" conservatism. As president, Wilson supported a purely government-owned shipping corporation to support exports. He defended the idea by saying that "private capital" would not do the job "without asking for the very kind of government backing and support to which I feel the deepest objection on principle." To Wilson, direct government intervention was worthy as

long as the government did not give explicit support and subsidies to one economic group. Wilson likewise signed a bill that provided direct government construction of a railroad in the territory of Alaska, which he contrasted favorably with subsidies to transcontinental railroads by Republicans in the previous century. See Woodrow Wilson to O. G. Villard, September 4, 1914, in *The Papers of Woodrow Wilson*, vol. 30: *May 6–September 5, 1914*, ed. Arthur Link (Princeton, NJ: Princeton University Press, 1980), 479; Richard Sicotte, "Economic Crisis and Political Response: The Political Economy of the Shipping Act of 1916," *Journal of Economic History* 59, no. 4 (December 1999): 871; Gail Radford, "William Gibbs McAdoo, the Emergency Fleet Corporation, and the Origins of the Public-Authority Model of Government Action," *Journal of Policy History* 11, no. 1 (January 1999): 59–88; Woodrow Wilson, "Second Annual Message," December 8, 1914, American Presidency Project, https://www.presidency.ucsb.edu/documents/second-annual-message-19.

26. David Greenberg, *Republic of Spin: An Inside History of the American Presidency* (New York: Norton, 2016), 79–82.

27. Woodrow Wilson, "Address to a Joint Session of Congress on Tariff Reform," April 8, 1913, American Presidency Project, https://www.presidency.ucsb.edu/documents/address-joint-session-congress-tariff-reform. This speech mimicked speeches Wilson gave during the campaign on the tariff, which were collected in a chapter entitled "The Tariff, 'Protection' or Special Privilege?," in Wilson, *New Freedom*, 136–62.

28. For Wilson's feelings on party leadership, see Woodrow Wilson, *Constitutional Government in the United States* (1908; reprint, New York: Columbia University Press, 1921), 198–222.

29. C. M. Freedman, ed., *Journal of Proceedings of the National Grange, 1913* (Concord, NH: Rumford Press, 1913), 122.

30. Carter Glass, *An Adventure in Constructive Finance* (New York: Doubleday, Page, 1927), 60, 62.

31. Carter Glass, "Financial Freedom Under Woodrow Wilson," speech, April 13, 1916, Box 21, Carter Glass Papers, University of Virginia Special Collections, Charlottesville.

32. Rixey Smith and Norman Beasley, *Carter Glass: A Biography* (New York: Longmans, Green, 1939), 403.

33. Glass, *Adventure*, 63.

34. The Federal Reserve Bank notes would not be legal tender until the Gold Reserve Act of 1934, which slipped the legal-tender clause into a subsection discussing definitions. See *Gold Reserve Act of 1934*, Pub. L. 87, 73rd Cong., 2nd sess. (January 30, 1934), 8.

35. Glass, *Adventure*, 81–82, 91–92.

36. H. P. Willis, *The Federal Reserve System: Legislation, Organization, and Operation* (New York: Ronald Press, 1923), 225–26.

37. Link, *Wilson*, 209.

38. Link, *Wilson*, 113.

39. "Here Is the New Currency Bill," *New York Times*, June 191, 1913; *New York Sun*, June 21, 1913, quoted in Link, *Wilson*, 216.

40. Glass, *Adventure*, 124–25, 199, emphasis in original.

41. John Lauritz Larson, *Internal Improvements: National Public Works and the Promise of Popular Government in the Early United States* (Chapel Hill: University of North Carolina Press, 2001), 190–91.

42. Glass, *Adventure*, 116–18. I have not seen any history of the rise of such "advisory councils" or of how the Federal Reserve's council represented the first iteration of this trend. The government did not attempt to organize these councils and corral their

growing power until 1972 with the Federal Advisory Committee Act (https://www.gsa
.gov/cdnstatic/FACA-Statute-2013.pdf).

43. Willis, *Federal Reserve System*, 217, 233, 314–15.

44. Glass, *Adventure*, 67–68.

45. William Blake, *The Marriage of Heaven and Hell* (Boston: John W. Luce, 1906), 42.

46. Robert Inklaar, Marcel P. Timmer, Bart van Ark, Wendy Carlin, and Jonathan Temple, "Market Services Productivity Across Europe and the U.S.," *Economic Policy* 23, no. 53 (January 2008): 139–94. At the same time, the urban population grew until it almost surpassed the rural population by the 1910 census (William Learner, ed., *Historical Statistics of the United States, Colonial Times to 1970, Bicentennial Edition* [Washington, DC: U.S. Government Printing Office, 1975], series A, 73–81, 12).

47. James. J. Hill, "The Nation's Future," in *Addresses of James J. Hill* (N.p.: privately printed), 26, 29; "Go Back to the Land, Says James J. Hill," *New York Times*, September 4, 1906.

48. James J. Hill, "National Wealth and the Farm," in *Addresses of James J. Hill*, 17, 8.

49. "Farms or Famine," *Washington Post*, October 30, 1909. See also Eric Rauchway, "The High Cost of Living in the Progressives' Economy," *Journal of American History* 88, no. 3 (December 2001): 909.

50. "Report of the Country Life Commission," 60th Cong., 2nd sess., S. Doc. 705 (1909), 56, 59.

51. House Committee on Agriculture, *Hearings on Miscellaneous Bills and Other Matters*, 62nd Cong., 2nd sess. (1912), 130.

52. Joint Subcommittees, *Investigation of Rural Credits*, 243. James Hill pointed to the imbalance of England and Rome as warnings for America (Hill, "National Wealth and the Farm," 8–10).

53. Charles Simon Barrett, *The Mission, History, and Times of the Farmers' Union* (Nashville, TN: Marshall & Bruce, 1909), 98, 101.

54. Murray R. Benedict, *Farm Policies of the United States,1790–1950: A Study of Their Origins and Development* (New York: Twentieth Century Fund, 1953), 134–35.

55. One member of the Farmers Union told Congress that James Hill was right that the cities were in danger of collapsing because of the declining number of farmers and reduced production of food. He argued that the farm-population decline was happening because "as far as financial matters are concerned [the farmer] is the biggest slave that walks the earth" (Subcommittee of House Banking and Currency Committee, *Rural Credits Hearings*, 63rd Cong., 2nd sess. [1913], 188).

56. Quoted in James C. Milligan, *Oklahoma Farmers Union: A History of the First 91 Years* (Oklahoma City: Cottonwood Publications, 1997), 11.

57. Thomas Cushing Davis, *The High Cost of Living: Cause—Remedy* (Washington, DC: Monetary Educational Bureau, 1912), 10, 13, 20, emphasis in original.

58. Subcommittee of the House Banking and Currency Committee, *Hearing on Rural Credits*, 63rd Cong., 2nd sess. (1914), 191.

59. Stuart William Shulman, "The Origin of the Federal Farm Loan Act: Agenda-Setting in the Progressive Era Print Press," PhD diss., University of Oregon, 1999, 42–43.

60. "A Farmer's Credit: How the Bankers and the Farmers May Get Together on Loans," *New York Times*, September 29, 1912; James Gardner, "Banking and Farming," *Bankers Magazine* 85, no. 5 (1912): 507.

61. Charles Conant, "Land and Agricultural Credit," in *Proceedings of the Thirty-Eighth Annual Convention of the American Bankers Association* (New York: Trow Press, 1912), 192, 201–3.

62. House Committee on Agriculture, *Hearings on Miscellaneous Bills*, 130.

63. Besides farmers and bankers, the next most important source of criticism of the idea of "class legislation" in this period came from the labor movement, which wanted special exemptions from antitrust laws. See Melvyn Dubofsky, *The State and Labor in Modern America* (Chapel Hill: University of North Carolina Press, 1994), 56–58.

64. Quoted in George Galloway, *History of the House of Representatives* (New York: Thomas Y. Crowell, 1961), vii.

65. 52 Cong. Rec. 4994 (March 1, 1915).

66. House Committee on Veterans Affairs, "History of the Cannon House Office Building," 1988, https://archives-veterans.house.gov/about/history-chob.

67. Wilson, *Congressional Government*, xiii.

68. Wilder H. Haines, "The Congressional Caucus of Today," *American Political Science Association* 9, no. 1 (February 1915): 696. See also Richard Bolling, *Power in the House: A History of the Leadership of the House of Representatives* (New York: Dutton, 1968), 96.

69. Quoted in Claude Bowers, *The Life of John Worth Kern* (Indianapolis, IN: Hollenbeck Press, 1918), 293. Just days into Wilson's presidency, the Senate caucus also said, "We propose that this great body shall be democratic not only in name, but in particular reality" and would no longer be "controlled by a few men." See Senate Democratic Caucus Minutes, March 15, 1913, Record Group (RG) 46, Records of the U.S. Senate, National Archives, Washington, DC (NARA I).

70. Galloway, *History of the House of Representatives*, 138–39; Senate Democratic Caucus Minutes, May 28, 1913, RG 46, NARA I.

71. Cordell Hull, *The Memoirs of Cordell Hull*, vol. 1 (New York: MacMillan, 1948), 62–63.

72. Glass, *Adventure*, 133, 136.

73. "Currency Bill Thorns in the Democratic Caucus," *Wall Street Journal*, August 20, 1913.

74. Willis, *Federal Reserve System*, 906.

75. 53 Cong. Rec. 7073 (April 29, 1916).

76. Glass, *Adventure*, 136.

77. Carter Glass to Oscar Underwood, January 16, 1914, Box 21, Glass Papers.

78. Lowenstein, *America's Bank*, 228.

79. 53 Cong. Rec. 7073 (April 29, 1916), reprinting Robert Bulkley to James Byrnes, June 29, 1914; see also Willis, *Federal Reserve System*, 1604.

80. Quoted in "Change Money Bill: Democrats Make 'Farm Paper' Equal of Any Other," *Washington Post*, August 26, 1913.

81. Willis, *Federal Reserve System*, 1625.

82. Willis, *Federal Reserve System*, 1531–553.

83. House Banking and Currency Committee, *Banking and Currency, Part 9*, 62nd Cong., 3rd. sess. (1913), 516.

84. For increased interest at the time in banks' ability to provide mortgage loans, see James Gardner, "Banking and Farming," *Bankers Magazine* 85, no. 5 (November 1912): 505.

85. House Banking and Currency Committee, *Banking and Currency, Part 10*, 62nd Cong., 3rd. sess. (1913), 603–4.

86. House Banking and Currency Committee, *Banking and Currency, Part 10*, 500.

87. "1912 Democratic Party Platform," June 25, 1912, American Presidency Project, https://www.presidency.ucsb.edu/documents/1912-democratic-party-platform.

88. Revised draft of Glass bill, May 1, 1913, in Willis, *Federal Reserve System*, 1572. The loans were limited to 25 percent of the bank's capital and not allowed in certain major cities.

89. Senate Banking and Currency Committee, *Hearing on Consolidation of National Banking Associations*, 68th Cong., 2nd. sess. (1925), 105.

90. 53 Cong. Rec. 7885–886 (May 12, 1916) (Murray discussing previous caucus and reprinting caucus minutes); and Marvin Jones Oral History, 1970, 541, Columbia University Archives, New York.

91. Woodrow Wilson, "A Statement with Regard to Rural Credits," August 13, 1913, in *The Papers of Woodrow Wilson*, vol. 29: *December 2, 1913 to May 5, 1914*, ed. Arthur Link (Princeton, NJ: Princeton University Press, 1979), 146–48.

92. 50 Cong. Rec. 4846 (July 12, 1913); Glass, *Adventure*, 141.

93. Lowenstein, *America's Bank*, 227.

94. Woodrow Wilson, "First Annual Message," December 2, 1913, American Presidency Project, https://www.presidency.ucsb.edu/documents/first-annual-message-18; Wilson devoted almost a fourth of his speech to the topic. He partially incorporated a letter he had received from Horace Plunkett, where Plunkett argued against government support for rural credits (Sir Horace Plunkett to Edward Mundell House, October 28, 1913, in Woodrow Wilson, *The Papers of Woodrow Wilson*, vol. 28: *1913*, ed. Arthur Link [Princeton, NJ: Princeton University Press, 1979], 115–17).

95. 50 Cong. Rec. 4769 (September 11, 1913).

96. Joint Subcommittees, *Investigation of Rural Credits*, 62, 71. The final recommended legislation was remarkably like the regular national banking system before the Federal Reserve Act and, according to Moss, was "modeled after" it.

97. "Memorandum with Regard to the Relation Between Guy Huston and the Guy Huston Company and Various Joint Stock Land Banks," Box 51, RG 56, Records of the Secretary of the Treasury, National Archives, College Park, MD (NARA II).

98. Joint Subcommittees, *Investigation of Rural Credits*, 83.

99. Woodrow Wilson (WW) to Oscar Underwood, January 23, 1914, in Wilson, *The Papers of Woodrow Wilson*, 29:163–64.

100. Joint Subcommittees, *Investigation of Rural Credits*, 97–98.

101. Joint Subcommittees, *Investigation of Rural Credits*, 97–98.

102. Joint Subcommittees, *Investigation of Rural Credits*, 44.

103. In his most famous act, Hollis in 1917 sponsored the amendment to make charitable donations deductible from income taxes, a definite type of "special privilege" and "class legislation" (Link, *Wilson*, 438).

104. Joint Subcommittees, *Investigation of Rural Credits*, 44.

105. 53 Cong. Rec. 7311 (May 3, 1916).

106. 51 Cong. Rec. 15615 (September 24, 1914).

107. 53 Cong. Rec. 7022 (April 29, 1916).

108. "Von Engelken—Maxfield," *Ocala Banner*, February 9, 1906; Joint Subcommittees, *Investigation of Rural Credits*, 341–42, 344–45, 381.

109. Joint Subcommittees, *Investigation of Rural Credits*, 620, 638.

110. Joint Subcommittees, *Investigation of Rural Credits*, 623.

111. Joint Subcommittees, *Investigation of Rural Credits*, 221. Scuder also suggested mandated investment of government postal trust funds in the banks' bonds.

112. "Land Bank Schemes," *Bankers Magazine* 88, no. 4 (April 1914): 438. The magazine noted that the Savings Bank Section of the American Bankers Association submitted a report in 1914 that called for the "organization of land credit" through a "large central bank with a Federal charter."

113. Joint Subcommittees, *Investigation of Rural Credits*, 410.

114. Joint Subcommittees, *Investigation of Rural Credits*, 393.

115. Herbert Myrick to Senator Henry Hollis, July 14, 1916, Reel 183, Woodrow Wilson Presidential Papers, Library of Congress, Washington, DC.

116. 51 Cong. Rec. 15615 (September 24, 1914). See financial interests in Robert J. Bulkley to H. P. Willis, April 2, 1914, Box 3, H. Parker Willis Papers, Columbia University Archives.

117. Joint Subcommittees, *Investigation of Rural Credits*, 328–29.

118. 53 Cong. Rec. 7134 (May 1, 1916).

119. "Rural Credit Plan Shelved: President Angers Joint Sub-committee by Ignoring Request," *New York Times*, May 13, 1914.

120. "Pass Trust Bills by July 1," *New York Times*, May 5, 1914.

121. Joint Subcommittees, *Investigation of Rural Credits*, 883.

122. H. H. Schenk et al., "Petition," 1914, Box 442, RG 233, Records of the U.S. House of Representatives, NARA I.

123. Grant Youmans, "Rural Credit Bills," c. 1914, Box 34, RG 233, NARA I.

124. WW to Carter Glass, May 9, 1914, in *The Papers of Woodrow Wilson*, 30:10.

125. WW to Carter Glass, May 12, 1914, in *The Papers of Woodrow Wilson*, 30:24.

126. "Antitrust Bills Alone to Be Passed," *New York Times*, May 13, 1914; "Rural Credit Plan Shelved."

127. "House Filibuster Over Rural Credits," *New York Times*, May 15, 1914.

128. WW to William McAdoo, November 17, 1914, reprinted in *Wall Street Journal*, November 19, 1914. For progressive reaction to this statement, see "Presidential Complacency," *New Republic* 1, no. 3 (November 21, 1914): 7.

129. Woodrow Wilson, "Second Annual Message," December 8, 1914, American Presidency Project, https://www.presidency.ucsb.edu/documents/second-annual-message-19.

130. Freedman, *Journal of Proceedings of the National Grange, 1913*, 152–54.

131. "Fight Over Rural Credits: 60,000 Letters to Be Sent to Farmers Throughout the Country," *New York Times*, January 31, 1914; Joint Subcommittees, *Investigation of Rural Credits*, 103, 382.

132. Nathan Exley and Evelyn Hall to George McLean, March 6, 1914, Box 124, RG 46, NARA I.

133. J. D. Covington et al., "Petition for Hollis-Bulkley Rural Credits Bill," c. 1915, Box 442, RG 233, NARA I.

134. Herbert Myrick to WW, November 10, 1914, Doc. 86, Reel 183, Wilson Presidential Papers.

135. Duncan Fletcher to WW, December 18, 1914, Doc. 94, Reel 183, Wilson Presidential Papers.

136. "Farm Mortgage Men Organize," *New York Times*, May 8, 1914; "Organization—Original Purposes—Brief Review of its Accomplishments," in *Proceedings of the Fourth Annual Convention of the Farm Mortgage Bankers of America, September 11–13, 1917*, ed. H. M. Hanson (Chicago: Farm Mortgage Bankers Association of America, 1917), 11–18.

137. See "Uncle Sam's Rural Credits Measure—and Some Talks About Credit," *Banker Farmer* 3, no. 10 (September 1916): 5–6; and "The Federal Farm Loan Act," *Bankers Magazine* 93, no. 4 (October 1916): 299, which, despite some concerns, celebrated the "standardizing of the farm mortgage and of the bonds . . . so that these securities would have the widest possible market at the most favorable prices."

138. *Annual Report of the Secretary of the Treasury, 1914* (Washington, DC: U.S. Government Printing Office, 1914), 50–53; "Revision of Printing Laws," 63rd Cong., 2nd sess., S. Rept., 438 (1914), 5.

139. 51 Cong. Rec. 367 (December 6, 1913).

140. Duncan Fletcher to WW, December 18, 1914, Doc. 94, Reel 183, Wilson Presidential Papers.

141. 51 Cong. Rec. 11135 (June 25, 1914).

142. 50 Cong. Rec. 5701 (October 20, 1913); 50 Cong. Rec. 5906, 5935 (November 17, 1913). See also "Waste in Public Printing," *New York Times*, May 3, 1914.

143. 51 Cong. Rec. 13765 (August 15, 1914).

144. 51 Cong. Rec. 15615 (September 24, 1914).

145. 51 Cong. Rec. 11135 (June 25, 1914).

146. See Duncan Fletcher to WW, April 6, 1915, Reel 183, Wilson Presidential Papers.

147. That same year, 1916, Congress would pass the first federal Highway Act, which was also based on similar concerns about rural-population loss. Oklahoma senator Robert Owen argued, for instance, that "bad roads mean loss of population" (53 Cong. Rec. 7291 [May 3, 1916]).

148. "Report of the Joint Committee on Rural Credits," 64th Cong., 1st sess., H. Doc. 494 (1916), 21–22.

149. See Link, *Wilson*, 347–48.

150. "Report to Accompany S. 2986, Rural Credits," 64th Cong., 1st sess., S. Rep. 144 (1916), 32.

151. 53 Cong. Rec. 6794 (April 25, 1916).

152. 53 Cong. Rec. 7383, 7388 (May 4, 1916).

153. 53 Cong. Rec. 6696 (April 24, 1916).

154. 53 Cong. Rec. 7820–821, 7823, 7826 (May 11, 1916). Wilson, who had remained conspicuously silent after the introduction of the Senate bill, wrote to thank the authors of the original House bill, which had pared back support for investors, for having "perfected" the measure. See WW to Ralph Moss, May 10, 1916; WW to Michael Phelan, May 10, 1916; WW to Jousett Shouse, May 10, 1916, all on Reel 183, Wilson Presidential Papers.

155. 53 Cong. Rec. 7827, 7385 (May 11, 1916).

156. 53 Cong. Rec. 7829 (May 11, 1916).

157. 53 Cong. Rec. 7833 (May 11, 1916).

158. WW to Joseph Tumulty, n.d., Reel 183, Wilson Presidential Papers.

3. The Federal Land Banks and Financial Distress, 1916–1926

1. Owen Wister, foreword to George Norris, *Ended Episodes* (Philadelphia: John C. Winston, 1937), vi, and Norris, *Ended Episodes*, 130–31; William McAdoo to Woodrow Wilson (WW), July 27, 1916, Reel 183, Woodrow Wilson Presidential Papers, Library of Congress, Washington, DC. Norris was no relation to the famous Nebraska senator of the same name.

2. Despite years of scholarship documenting reformist movements in the 1920s, the overwhelmingly majority of surveys of the era argue for a sharp shift between a Progressive Woodrow Wilson and standpatist Republican eras. See Robert Leuchtenburg, *The Perils of Prosperity, 1914–1932*, 2nd ed. (Chicago: University of Chicago Press, 1993); Eugene Trani and David Wilson, *The Presidency of Warren G. Harding* (Topeka: University Press of Kansas, 1977); Robert Sobol, *Coolidge: An American Enigma* (Washington, DC: Regnery, 1998); Daniel Rodgers, *Atlantic Crossings: Social Politics in*

a Progressive Age (Cambridge, MA: Belknap Press of Harvard University Press, 1998), 296–317. The so-called persistence-of-progressivism historiography does focus on continued reforms to the farm economy, but this literature does not focus on continuities in financial policies or support for rural banks. See James H. Shideler, *Farm Crisis, 1919–1923* (Berkeley: University of California Press, 1957); Donald L. Winters, "The Persistence of Progressivism: Henry Cantwell Wallace and the Movement for Agricultural Economics," *Agricultural History* 41, no. 2 (April 1967): 109–20. The Federal Land Banks receive almost no attention in the literature on reforms either during World War I or in the early 1920s. David Kennedy and Douglas Craig have no discussion of the Federal Land Banks in their books. See David Kennedy, *Over Here: The First World War and American Society* (Oxford: Oxford University Press, 2003), esp. 93–143; and Douglas B. Craig, *Progressives at War: William G. McAdoo and Newton D. Baker, 1863–1941* (Baltimore: John Hopkins University Press, 2013). Most works that examine financial policy in the 1920s look at state-level banking decisions or focus on econometric explanations for bank failure but do not discuss the Land Bank issue. See, for example, Lee Alston, Wayne A. Grove, and David C. Wheelock, "Why Do Banks Fail? Evidence from the 1920s," *Explorations in Economic History* 31 (1994): 409–31.

3. Norris, *Ended Episodes*, 149–50; see also William McAdoo to WW, July 27, 1916, Reel 183, Wilson Presidential Papers.

4. H. M. Hanson, ed., *Proceedings of the Fourth Annual Convention of the Farm Mortgage Bankers of America, September 11–13, 1917* (Chicago: Farm Mortgage Bankers Association of America, 1917), 48.

5. William McAdoo to WW, July 27, 1916, Reel 183, Wilson Presidential Papers.

6. Norris, *Ended Episodes*, 167.

7. Jordan A. Schwartz, *The New Dealers: Power Politics in the Age of Roosevelt* (New York: Knopf, 1993), 5–6.

8. Woodrow Wilson, *Congressional Government* (1885; reprint, New York: Putnam's, 1900), vii.

9. See O. M. W. Sprague, *Crises Under the National Banking System* (Washington, DC: U.S. Government Printing Office, 1910), 40–42, 135–39, 230–32, 316–18; and "Treasury Aid to Check Panic," *New York Times*, March 15, 1907.

10. Wilson, *Congressional Government*, vii–viii.

11. William Silber, *When Washington Shut Down Wall Street: The Great Financial Crisis of 1914 and the Origins of America's Monetary Supremacy* (Princeton, NJ: Princeton University Press, 2008), 123, 70.

12. Silber, *When Washington Shut Down Wall Street*, 147.

13. *Annual Report of the Secretary of the Treasury, 1914* (Washington, DC: U.S. Government Printing Office, 1915), 25–26.

14. "Transcript of Hearings, Augusta, Maine August 21, 1916," 9, Box 1, Entry 4, Records of Federal Farm Loan Board, Minutes of Hearings, 1916, Record Group (RG) 103, Records of the Farm Credit Administration, National Archives, College Park, MD (NARA II).

15. "Transcript of Hearings, Springfield, Mass., August 23, 1916," 3–4, Box 5, Entry 4, Records of Federal Farm Loan Board, Minutes of Hearings, 1916, RG 103, NARA II.

16. "Transcript of Hearings, Augusta, Maine August 21, 1916," 5–6.

17. Petersburg Land Bank Committee, *Argument Presented to the Federal Farm Loan Board* (Petersburg, VA: Petersburg Chamber of Commerce, 1916), 9–10, 48, Box 2, Entry

5, Correspondence Re: Location of Federal Land Banks, 1916–1917, Alabama to New England, RG 103, NARA II.

18. "Columbia, South Carolina Call for Federal Land Bank," October 25, 1916, Box 2, Entry 5, Correspondence Re: Location of Federal Land Banks, 1916–1917, Alabama to New England, RG 103, NARA II.

19. Norris, *Ended Episodes*, 149–50; Senate Banking and Currency Committee, *Hearings on Sale of Farm Loan Bonds*, 67th Cong., 2nd sess. (1922), 63.

20. See, for example, Carter Glass to William McAdoo, September 27, 1918, Box 125, Carter Glass Papers, University of Virginia Special Collections, Charlottesville.

21. W. S. A. Smith to R. H. Welch (Registrar of Columbia Federal Land Bank), July 12, 1917, Box 1, Correspondence Concerning the Federal Land Banks, 1916–1926, RG 103, NARA II. See also Norris, *Ended Episodes*, 150–51.

22. Norris, *Ended Episodes*, 150; F. J. H. Engelken to W. S. A. Smith, June 11 and 14, 1917, Box 2, Correspondence Concerning the Federal Land Banks, 1916–1926, RG 103, NARA II.

23. George W. Norris to Walter Howell, April 4, 1917, Box 51, Correspondence Concerning the Federal Land Banks, 1916–1926, RG 103, NARA II.

24. Walter Howell to George W. Norris, April 7, 1917, Box 51, Correspondence Concerning the Federal Land Banks, 1916–1926, RG 103, NARA II.

25. Quoted in "90 Loans Made by Farm Bank," *Berkeley Daily Gazette*, August 16, 1917.

26. Norris, *Ended Episodes*, 168–69.

27. "Benjamin Howell Griswold," in *Baltimore: Its History and Its People*, vol. 2: *Biography* (New York: Lewis Historical, 1912), 179–81; Norris, *Ended Episodes*, 169.

28. Subcommittee of the Senate Banking and Currency Committee, *To Strengthen the Capital Structure of the Federal Land Banks*, 72nd Cong., 1st sess. (1931), 20; Norris, *Ended Episodes*, 169–73; "Investment Houses Will Market Farm Loan Bonds," *Wall Street Journal*, June 22, 1917.

29. George W. Norris to A. S. Burleson, March 9, 1917, Box 1, Correspondence Concerning the Federal Land Banks, RG 103, NARA II.

30. "Thrift Stamp Notes Ineligible for Rediscounts: National Banks May Lend on Farm Loan Bonds Without Infringing Real Estate Restriction," *Wall Street Journal*, July 18, 1918.

31. "Farm Loan Board Moves for State Legislation," *Wall Street Journal*, March 19, 1918.

32. Norris, *Ended Episodes*, 179–81.

33. "Farm Loan Board Moves for State Legislation."

34. Norris, *Ended Episodes*, 171–72.

35. Subcommittee of the Senate Banking and Currency Committee, *To Strengthen the Capital Structure of the Federal Land Banks*, 21.

36. Quoted in Norris, *Ended Episodes*, 137.

37. "Minutes [Transcript] of the Meeting of the Presidents of the Twelve Federal Land Banks and the Farm Loan Board Held at Washington March 15–17, 1917," Box 51, Correspondence Concerning the Federal Land Banks, RG 103, NARA II.

38. Kennedy, *Over Here*, 105.

39. William G. McAdoo, *Crowded Years: The Reminiscences of William G. McAdoo* (Boston: Houghton Mifflin, 1931), 374, 378.

40. See Julia Ott, *When Wall Street Met Main Street: The Quest for an Investors' Democracy* (Cambridge, MA: Harvard University Press, 2011).

41. Quoted in Vern McKinley, *Financing Failure: A Century of Bailouts* (Oakland, CA: Independent Institute, 2011), 48.

42. Quoted in "War Finance Corporation Bill in Senate," *Commercial and Financial Chronicle* 109 (March 2, 1918): 869–70.

43. "Government Money in Federal Land Banks," *Wall Street Journal*, November 14, 1917; "Federal Land Bank Deposits," *Wall Street Journal*, December 5, 1917.

44. George Norris to William McAdoo, December 4, 1917, Box 237, General Correspondence, RG 103, NARA II.

45. Norris, *Ended Episodes*, 175.

46. Woodrow Wilson, "Address to a Joint Session of Congress on Government Administration of Railways," January 4, 1918, American Presidency Project, https://www.presidency.ucsb.edu/documents/address-joint-session-congress-government-administration-railways.

47. 56 Cong. Rec. 592 (January 4, 1918).

48. *An Act Amending Section Thirty-Two, Federal Farm Loan Act*, Pub. L. 95, 65th Cong., 2nd sess. (January 18, 1918), 431–32.

49. "Why U.S. Land Bank Bonds Are Booming," *New York Sun*, July 14, 1918.

50. George H. Putnam, "Recent Developments in the Federal Farm Loan System," *American Economic Review* 11, no. 3 (September 1921): 427.

51. "Claims Tax-Free Farm Loan Bonds Unjust," *Wall Street Journal*, January 22, 1919.

52. "Claim Land Banks Privileged and Exclusive," *Wall Street Journal*, September 13, 1919.

53. "Tax Exempt Loan Bonds Favor Rich Investors," *Wall Street Journal*, March 20, 1919.

54. "M'Adoo out of Cabinet: Tells Wilson He Must Retire to Increase His Personal Income," *New York Times*, November 23, 1918.

55. McAdoo, *Crowded Years*, 440.

56. "Transcript of Record, Supreme Court of the United States, October Term, 1920, No. 199, *Charles E. Smith Versus Kansas City Title & Trust Company*," U.S. Supreme Court Library, HeinOnline, 34, https://home.heinonline.org/content/u-s-supreme-court-library/. McAdoo, Wickersham, and Hughes were faced in court by William Marshall Bullitt, Taft's former solicitor general, for the mortgage brokers. See "Appellee's Brief, Chicago Joint Stock Land Bank," in "Transcript of Record," 33–34.

57. W. M. Heckler, "Bulletin to Farm Mortgage Bankers' Association of America Members," May 12, 1920, reprinted in 59 Cong. Rec. 7293 (May 19, 1920).

58. 59 Cong. Rec. 7257–259, 7292 (May 19, 1920).

59. George S. Mornin to Carter Glass, February 15, 1921, Box 224, Glass Papers.

60. *Smith v. Kansas Title and Trust Company* 255 U.S. 180 (1921).

61. For purchases and later sales of federal farm loan bonds in this period, see Judge Glock, "The Rise and Fall of the First Government-Sponsored Enterprise: The Federal Land Banks, 1916–1932," *Business History Review* 90, no. 4 (Winter 2016): 623–45.

62. See Treasury Secretary McAdoo's early complaints about Hoover's imperial ambitions in William McAdoo to WW, January 22, 1918, 68–69, Reel 2, Russell Leffingwell Letterbooks, Library of Congress. For more on the effects of the Land Banks during the war and its aftermath, see Sara M. Gregg, "From Breadbasket to Dust Bowel: Rural Credit, the World War I Plow-Up, and the Transformation of American Agriculture," *Great Plains Quarterly* 35, no. 2 (2015): 129–66.

63. Shideler, *Farm Crisis*, 46–58.

64. Quoted in Gilbert C. Fite, *George N. Peek and the Fight for Farm Parity* (Norman: University of Oklahoma Press, 1954), 3.

65. Although some Republicans adhered to anti-class-legislation ideals, Republican progressives embraced the balance ideology even before the Democrats did. Republican

Herbert Croly, founder of the *New Republic* magazine, for instance, argued that "it is not too much to say that substantially all the industrial legislation, demanded by the 'people' both here and abroad and passed in the public interest, has been based essentially on class discrimination" and that Republicans should embrace such discrimination (Herbert Croly, *The Promise of American Life* [1909; reprint, New York: MacMillan, 1914], 191).

66. Winters, "The Persistence of Progressivism," 115.

67. Shideler, *Farm Crisis*, 34; "Republican Party Platform of 1920," June 8, 1920, American Presidency Project, https://www.presidency.ucsb.edu/documents/republican-party-platform-1920.

68. Warren G. Harding, "First Annual Message to Congress," December 6, 1921, American Presidency Project, https://www.presidency.ucsb.edu/documents/first-annual-message-19.

69. O. M. W. Sprague and Randolph Burgess, "Money and Credit and Their Effects on Business," in Committee on Recent Economic Changes, *Recent Economic Changes in the United States*, vol. 2 (New York: McGraw-Hill, 1929), 693–94.

70. Sprague and Burgess, "Money and Credit," 693–94.

71. For the argument that the Land Banks helped inflate the land boom, see Maureen O'Hara, "Tax-Exempt Financing: Some Lessons from History," *Journal of Money, Credit, and Banking* 15 (November 1983): 425–41.

72. House Banking and Currency Committee, *Hearings on Amendment to the Farm Loan Act*, 67th Cong., 1st sess. (1921), 3–5.

73. House Banking and Currency Committee, *Hearings on Amendment to the Farm Loan Act*, 39; "Will Aid Land Banks," *Washington Times*, June 3, 1921.

74. "Time Congress Did Something: J. H. Allen of Des Moines 'Talks Turkey' to Senate Committee on Banking and Currency," *Lake Benton News* (Lake Benton, MN), April 28, 1920.

75. House Banking and Currency Committee, *Hearings on Amendment to the Farm Loan Act*, 26, 30–31.

76. Thomas Clark Atkeson, "Pioneering in Agriculture: Legislative Work in Washington," *Country Gentlemen*, February 23, 1925, 12, Box 2, Thomas Clark Atkeson Papers, West Virginia University Archives, Morgantown. Louis Taber, later master of the Grange, lamented that if the Grange had set up a Washington lobbying office two years earlier, the American Farm Bureau Federation would never have arisen (Louis Taber Oral History, 1952, 86, Columbia University Archives, New York).

77. Robert Howard, *James R. Howard and the Farm Bureau* (Ames: Iowa State University Press, 1983), 131–32; W. S. Kenyon to Gray Silver, January 5, 1921; Herbert Hoover to Gray Silver, October 11, 1923; Bernard Baruch to Gray Silver, October 15, 1923; Calvin Coolidge to Gray Silver, October 26, 1923, all in Box 6, Gray Silver Papers, West Virginia University Archives.

78. Murray Benedict, *Farm Policies of the United States: A Study of Their Origins and Development* (New York: Twentieth Century Fund, 1953), 181; John Mark Hansen, *Gaining Access: Congress and the Farm Lobby, 1919–1981* (Chicago: University of Chicago Press, 1991), 31.

79. Daniel Carpenter, *The Forging of Bureaucratic Autonomy: Reputations, Networks, and Policy Innovation in Executive Agencies, 1862–1928* (Princeton, NJ: Princeton University Press, 2001), 301–5. For more on the rise of farmer interest groups, see Elisabeth Clemens, *The People's Lobby: Organization Innovation and the Rise of Interest Group Politics in the United States, 1890–1925* (Chicago: University of Chicago Press, 1997).

80. Arthur Capper, *The Agricultural Bloc* (New York: Harcourt, Brace, 1922), 23–24, 166, 57; see also 4, 11, 107, 110.

81. Herbert Myrick, *Rural Credits System for the United States* (New York: Orange Judd, 1922), 62.

82. Gray Silver to E. L. Coblentz, June 7, 1921, Box 2, Silver Papers.

83. Shideler, *Farm Crisis*, 158–65; Capper, *Agricultural Bloc*, 66.

84. James Grant, *Bernard M. Baruch: The Adventures of a Wall Street Legend* (New York: Wiley, 1997), 188.

85. House Banking and Currency Committee, *Hearings on War Finance Corporation*, 67th Cong., 1st sess. (1921), 28.

86. [Clinton Gilbert], *Behind the Mirrors: The Psychology of Disintegration in Washington* (New York: Putnam's, 1922), 230, 221, 211.

87. Chicago Joint-Stock Land Bank Receipt, April 15, 1924, and Gray Silver to I. D. Van Metre, April 1, 1924, Box 7, Silver Papers. The *Baltimore Evening Sun* also reported that Silver "hold[s] the whip" in Congress; see "Seen as Big Power in Congress Session," *Baltimore Evening Sun*, December 4, 1923, Box 6, Silver Papers.

88. George Rothwell Brown, *The Leadership of Congress* (Indianapolis, IN: Bobbs-Merrill, 1922), 266–67.

89. Grover Clark, "The New Road to Equality," *Atlantic Monthly*, July 1921.

90. "Farm Bloc Forming to Fight in Albany," *New York Times*, February 9, 1922.

91. Gilbert C. Fite, "South Dakota's Rural Credit System, a Venture in State Socialism, 1917–1946," *Agricultural History* 21, no. 4 (October 1947): 239–49.

92. *Annual Report of the Federal Farm Loan Board, 1930* (Washington, DC: U.S. Government Printing Office, 1931), 144–45.

93. Charles Lobdell to Andrew Mellon, June 10, 1922, Box 238, General Correspondence, RG 103, NARA II.

94. "Report of the Real Estate Securities Committee," in *Proceedings of the Eleventh Annual Convention of the Investment Bankers Association of America, October 9–12, 1922*, ed. Frederick Fenton (Chicago: Lakeside Press, 1922), 116.

95. House Banking and Currency Committee, *Hearings on Amendment to the Farm Loan Act*, 30.

96. Anna Schwartz, "The Misuse of the Fed's Discount Window," *Federal Reserve Bank of St. Louis Review*, September–October 1992, 58. Many of these banks would subsequently fail.

97. House Banking and Currency Committee, *Hearings on Farm Organizations*, 66th Cong., 3rd sess. (1921), 34.

98. "Board of Directors of Federal Reserve Bank of Atlanta Resolutions," April 29, 1921, Box 83, General Correspondence, RG 103, NARA II.

99. Joseph Hirsch, "Report of the Agricultural Commission," *Journal of the American Bankers Association* 13, no. 5 (November 1920): 274–75.

100. "Country Bankers and Farm Finance," *Journal of the American Bankers Association* 14, no. 10 (April 1922): 693–702.

101. Senate Banking and Currency Committee, *Federal Farm Loan Board: Hearings on Nominations of Members of Board*, 68th Cong., 1st sess. (1924), 8.

102. *Annual Report of the Federal Farm Loan Board, 1922*, 67th Cong., 4th sess., H. Doc. 560 (1923), 4.

103. Hanson, *Proceedings of the Fourth Annual Convention of the Farm Mortgage Bankers of America, September 11–13, 1917*, 62–63, 90, 154–58, 206.

104. Senate Banking and Currency Committee, *Hearings to Amend the Federal Farm Loan Act*, 67th Cong., 4th sess. (1921), 49.

105. *Des Moines Joint Stock Land Bank of Des Moines, Iowa v. Allen et. all*, 261 N.W. 912, 220 Iowa 448, July 17, 1935; "To Educate the Farmer as to the Merits of the Amortized Loan," *The Economist* (Chicago) 68, no. 9 (August 26, 1922): 472.

106. "Leaves Farm Loan Board: Asbury F. Lever Will Head New Land Bank," *New York Times*, April 16, 1922.

107. Drew Pearson and Robert Allen, *More Washington Merry-Go-Round* (New York: Horace Liverlight, 1932), 341; "New Land Bank Organized: Senator Robinson of Arkansas Interested in Little Rock Institution," *New York Times*, May 12, 1926.

108. M. L. Corey to Gerard Winston, March 18, 1925, and Winston to Corey, March 19, 1925, Box 238, General Correspondence, RG 103, NARA II.

109. Taber Oral History, 160–63.

110. Senate Banking and Currency Committee, *Hearings to Amend the Federal Farm Loan Act*, 103.

111. Senate Banking and Currency Committee, *Hearings to Amend the Federal Farm Loan Act*, 34.

112. "How About That Maturing Mortgage—Advertisement," *Logan Republican* (Utah), May 14, 1918.

113. John E. Miller, *Becoming Laura Ingalls Wilder: The Woman Behind the Legend* (Columbia: University of Missouri Press, 1998), 163. The fact that Wilder had helped organize the Missouri farm loan association indicates that she most likely received a federally subsidized mortgage from it as well.

114. Senate Banking and Currency Committee, *Hearings to Amend the Federal Farm Loan Act*, 108. W. S. A. Smith of the Farm Loan Board in fact admitted that due to the cooperative nature of the local associations, "in some localities prejudice of white farmers to admit colored farmers might have prevented" the black farmers from receiving loans. "But this is a condition over which this Bureau has no control whatever" (quoted in "Federal Farm Loan Bureau Member Denies Prejudice," *New York Age*, June 10, 1922). Yet the Farm Loan Board could have sanctioned other farm associations instead.

115. See H. R. Ellis to W. W. Flannagan, September 29, 1919; W. W. Flannagan to Vuloska Vaiden, president, Federal Land Bank of Baltimore, October 2, 1919; and C. R. Titlow to Flannagan, October 4, 1919, all in Farm Credit History Archive, http://www.farmcredit.com/node/4654.

116. Senate Banking and Currency Committee, *Hearings to Amend the Federal Farm Loan Act*, 19, 20.

117. Gray Silver to E. L. Jody, April 8, 1929, Box 13, Silver Papers.

118. House Banking and Currency Committee, *Hearings on Bill to Provide Credit Facilities to the Agricultural and Live-stock Industries*, 67th Cong., 3rd sess. (1922), 1–2.

119. Howard, *James R. Howard*, 188–89.

120. "State Banks Committee," *Banker Farmer* 9, no. 5 (June 1922): 8.

121. The bill also raised the maximum loan from $10,000 to $25,000, a long-term goal of the farm lobby, and extended the justifications available for requesting loans from the Land Banks. See American Farm Bureau Federation, *The Loan Limit of the Federal Land Banks Should Be Increased to $25,000.00* (Chicago: American Farm Bureau Federation, 1922); and "Law Department: Agricultural Credits Act of 1923," *Federal Reserve Bulletin*, March 1923, 303–16.

122. Grant, *Bernard M. Baruch*, 188.

123. Silver to Jody, April 8, 1929, Box 8, Silver Papers.

124. Gray Silver to George Starring, South Dakota Banking Association, January 1, 1926, Box 8, Silver Papers.

125. "Discounting Agricultural and Cattle Paper, Before Group 7, C.B.A.," March 14, 1925, Box 201, General Correspondence, RG 103, NARA II.

126. *Annual Report of the Secretary of the Treasury, 1923* (Washington, DC: U.S. Government Printing Office, 1924), 2.

127. Senate Banking and Currency Committee, *Federal Farm Loan Board: Hearings on Nominations*, 216–17. In a recent biography of Mellon, David Cannadine demonstrates that Mellon, too, his vigorous protestations to the contrary, remained intimately involved in his previous banking and business activities while secretary of the Treasury (*Mellon: An American Life* [New York: Knopf, 2006], 296–98).

128. Senate Banking and Currency Committee, *Federal Farm Loan Board: Hearings on Nominations*, 398.

129. Eugene Meyer Memoir Manuscript, 1952, not paginated, Box 167, Eugene Meyer Papers, Library of Congress.

130. Harold Moulton, *The Financial Organization of Society* (Chicago: University of Chicago Press, 1921), 688–89.

131. Quoted in "Calls for a Halt in Government Tax-Exemption Policy," *The Annalist*, November 10, 1919. For the tax situation, see M. Susan Murname, "Selling Scientific Taxation: The Treasury Department's Campaign for Tax Reform in the 1920s," *Law and Social Inquiry* 29, no. 4 (2004): 819–56.

132. 65 Cong. Rec. 2090 (February 8, 1924).

133. 65 Cong. Rec. 2106 (February 8, 1924).

134. "Bond Amendment Is Defeated in House: Lacks Seven Votes," *Washington Post*, February 9, 1924.

135. Unlike the broad-based ownership of government bonds after World War I, which turned America into a "nation of bondholders," as described by Julia Ott in *When Wall Street Met Main Street*, these tax-exempt securities were usually held by the wealthy. But the political pull of these bondholders was no less powerful for that fact.

136. "Federal Land Banks: Loans by Federal Land Banks and Land Bank Commissioner to Congressmen and Relatives of Congressmen," July 19, 1935, Box 2, Investigations of Irregularities, RG 103, NARA II.

137. Spunk County National Farm Loan Association to Carter Glass, February 23, 1922, Box 224, Glass Papers.

138. Calvin Coolidge, "Second Annual Message to Congress," December 3, 1924, American Presidency Project, https://www.presidency.ucsb.edu/documents/second-annual -message-18.

139. "Republican Party Platform of 1924," June 10, 1924, American Presidency Project, https://www.presidency.ucsb.edu/documents/republican-party-platform-1924.

140. *Annual Report of the Federal Reserve Board, 1923* (Washington, DC: U.S. Government Printing Office, 1924), 1.

141. Quoted in William Allen White, *Puritan in Babylon: The Story of Calvin Coolidge* (New York: MacMillan, 1938), 343–44. This quote comes from a letter sent by R. A. Cooper to White personally in September 1936.

142. White, *Puritan in Babylon*, 21. White noted that in Coolidge's hometown the only relief from hardship was that "the farmer's thrift had bought for him a few Iowa and Kansas mortgages" (51).

143. Senator Frank R. Gooding to Andrew W. Mellon, Secretary of the Treasury, February 1, 1922; Mellon to Senator Gooding, March 9, 1922; Mellon to Charles Lobdell, March 23, 1922, all in Box 237, General Correspondence, RG 103, NARA II. For more problems with the Land Banks in this period, see Glock, "Rise and Fall of the First Government-Sponsored Enterprise."

144. *Annual Report of the Secretary of the Treasury, 1924* (Washington, DC: U.S. Government Printing Office, 1924), 72.

145. Harry O'Brien, "Credits Thaw Out in Northwest," *Country Gentleman* 90, no. 2 (January 10, 1925), 9, Box 1, AM 1126, Atkeson Papers.

146. "Farmers: Private Cooperation," *Time* magazine, February 18, 1924.

147. O'Brien, "Credits Thaw Out in Northwest," 9.

148. "Minutes of Third Joint District Meeting, April 23, 1926," 10, Box 5, Investigations of Irregularities, RG 103, NARA II.

149. Chairman Spokane Commission to Federal Farm Loan Board, July 20, 1925, Box 5, Investigations of Irregularities, RG 103, NARA II.

150. "1925 Report of the Spokane Commission," 1925 (no specific date provided), Box 5, Investigations of Irregularities, RG 103, NARA II.

151. "1925 Report of the Spokane Commission," 4–5.

152. "Call of Conference," Spokane Commission, c. September 1926, Box 5, Investigations of Irregularities, RG 103, NARA II.

153. "Memorandum with Regard to the Relation Between Guy Huston . . . ," Box 51, RG 56, Records of the Secretary of the Treasury, NARA II.

154. Humphrey of Kissel, Kinnicurtt & Co. to Andrew Mellon, November 19, 1926, Box 51, RG 56, NARA II.

155. *U.S.A. Plaintiff vs. W. H. Gold, et. al.*, R. A. Cooper testimony taken November 11, 1927, at 2549, Box 59, RG 56, NARA II.

156. *U.S.A. Plaintiff vs. W.H Gold, et. al.*, Cooper testimony at 2549.

157. Minot, Kendall & Co. Inc. to Andrew Mellon, October 27, 1926, Box 51, RG 56, NARA II.

158. Andrew Mellon to CC, June 16, 1926, Box 51, RG 56, NARA II.

159. Mellon to CC, June 16, 1926.

160. R. A. Cooper to CC, June 16, 1926, and CC to Cooper, June 16, 1926, Box 51, RG 56, NARA II.

161. *Annual Report of the Federal Farm Loan Board, 1928* (Washington, DC: U.S. Government Printing Office, 1928), 14; *Annual Report of the Federal Farm Loan Board* (Washington, DC: U.S. Government Printing Office, 1929), 135–36. Huston's sentence would later be overturned on appeal.

162. "Suicide of One Employee Who Had Embezzled a Large Amount of Bank Funds," *Berkeley Daily Gazette*, April 15, 1926.

163. House Banking and Currency Committee, *Hearing on Accounting and Examinations Under the Federal Farm Loan Act*, 69th Cong., 2nd sess. (1927), 107.

164. The North Dakota collapse led to the first successful recall elections in U.S. history, of Lemke and Governor Lynn Frazier (both of whom would later be elected to Congress and help pass the Frazier–Lemke Act for a nationwide mortgage moratorium in the New Deal; see chapter 6). See Merlin E. Nelson, "Recalling the First Recall," *New York Times*, August 23, 2003.

4. Falling Prices and Mortgage Crisis, 1926–1933

1. George F. Warren and Frank A. Pearson, *Prices* (New York: Wiley, 1933), 4–5.

2. Susan Carter, Scott Sigmund Gartner, Michael R. Haines, Alan L. Olmstead, Richard Sutch, and Gavin Wright, eds., *Historical Statistics of the United States: Earliest Times*

to the Present, millennial ed. (New York: Cambridge University Press, 2006), tables Da693–706 and Da717–29.

3. There is surprisingly little history on the "price-parity" campaign, despite its being one of the most significant political movements of the 1920s and 1930s. Gilbert C. Fite wrote one of the few comprehensive works on the subject, although he provided no discussion of the Land Banks and no discussion of a wider ideology of balance. See Gilbert C. Fite, *George N. Peek and the Fight for Farm Parity* (Norman: University of Oklahoma Press, 1954). Most modern historians argue that agricultural-reform movements of the 1920s were "minimalist" and had little impact. See, for example, Robert Paarlberg and Don Paarlberg, "Agricultural Policy in the Twentieth Century," *Agricultural History* 47, no. 2 (Spring 2000): 136–61. The most comprehensive analysis of Hoover's farm plans can be found in David Hamilton's work, which acknowledges significant continuity with Franklin Roosevelt's later plans, but Hamilton, too, focuses on the failure of "associationalism" instead of on finance. See, for example, David E. Hamilton, *From New Day to New Deal: American Farm Policy from Hoover to Roosevelt, 1928–1933* (Chapel Hill: University of North Carolina Press, 1991). The modern literature likewise ignores how the price-parity campaign conflicted with other demands for increasing consumer "purchasing power" or for redistribution. See Meg Jacobs, *Pocketbook Politics: Economic Citizenship in Twentieth-Century America* (Princeton, NJ: Princeton University Press, 2005), 75–92. For a look at the public debate on price movements more generally in this era, however, see Eli Cook, "The Neoclassical Club: Irving Fisher and the Progressive Origins of Neoliberalism," *Journal of the Gilded Age and the Progressive Era* 15, no. 3 (July 2016): 246–62. The literature on Herbert Hoover's overall economic policies dwells on his "associational" and technocratic vision and does not discuss balancing ideology or the place of agriculture in this ideology. See, for example, William J. Barber, *From New Era to New Deal: Herbert Hoover, the Economists, and American Economic Policy, 1921–1933* (Cambridge: Cambridge University Press, 1985); and Patrick D. Reagan, *Designing a New America: The Origins of New Deal Planning, 1890–1943* (Amherst: University of Massachusetts Press, 1999).

4. Fite, *George N. Peek*, 21.

5. "He Risked Disgrace to Speed the Draft," *New York Times*, June 9, 1918.

6. George Peek and Hugh Johnson, *Equality for Agriculture* (Moline, IL: H. W. Harrington, 1922), 10, 25.

7. Hugh S. Johnson, *The Blue Eagle from Egg to Earth* (Garden City, NY: Doubleday, Doran, 1935), 161–62.

8. Peek and Johnson, *Equality for Agriculture*, 7.

9. Bernard Baruch, "Some Aspects of the Farmers' Problems," *Atlantic Monthly*, July 1921, emphasis in original.

10. Jordon A. Scwhartz, *The New Dealers: Power Politics in the Age of Roosevelt* (New York: Knopf, 1993), 37; Fite, *George N. Peek*, 147.

11. Louis Taber, "Worthy Master Address," in *Journal of the Proceedings of the National Grange, 1927*, ed. C. M. Freedman (Springfield, MA: National Grange Monthly, 1927), 10–14.

12. Quoted in Robert Howard, *James R. Howard and the Farm Bureau* (Ames: Iowa State University Press, 1983), 170.

13. Henry A. Wallace, *Agricultural Prices* (Des Moines: Wallace, 1920), 17.

14. "Report of the National Agricultural Conference," January 23–27, 1922, 67th Cong., 2nd sess., H. Doc. 195 (1922), 137.

15. Quoted in William Allen White, *A Puritan in Babylon: The Story of Calvin Coolidge* (New York: MacMillan, 1938), 344.

16. Theodore Salotus, *The American Farmer and the New Deal* (Ames: Iowa State University Press, 1982), 21; "Farm Prosperity—Business Profits," *Wallace's Farmer* 42, no. 11 (March 16, 1917): 481.

17. Jacobs, *Pocketbook Politics*, 3.

18. See Anna Youngman, "A Popular Theory of Credit," *American Economic Review* 12, no. 3 (September 1922): 430, 423.

19. See, for example, Paul A. Eke, "The Price and Purchasing Power of Farm Land," *Journal of Farm Economics* 7, no. 4 (October 1925): 437–38; A. B. Genung, "The Purchasing Power of the Farmer's Dollar from 1913 to Date," *Annals of the American Academy of Political and Social Science* 117 (January 1925): 22–26.

20. Quoted in Fite, *George N. Peek*, 51.

21. *Annual Report of the Secretary of the Treasury, 1923* (Washington, DC: U.S. Government Printing Office, 1924), 2.

22. "Senate Rejects Fess Farm Measure by 26 to 54 Vote," *New York Times*, June 30, 1926.

23. "State Banks Committee," *Banker Farmer* 9, no. 5 (June 1922): 8.

24. Evans Clark, "The Farm Issue Moves Toward a Climax," *New York Times*, January 2, 1927.

25. Oliver McKee Jr., "Lobbying for Good or Evil," *North American Review* 227, no. 3 (March 1929): 343.

26. "Text of the President's Message Vetoing the McNary-Haugen Farm Bill," *New York Times*, February 26, 1927.

27. Eugene Meyer Memoir Manuscript, 1952, 23, Box 167, Eugene Meyer Papers, Library of Congress, Washington, DC.

28. Merlo Pusey, *Eugene Meyer* (New York: Knopf, 1974), 68–77.

29. Pusey, *Eugene Meyer*, 27, 136–37. See also Drew Pearson and Robert Allen, *More Washington Merry-Go-Round* (New York: Horace Liveright, 1932), 122.

30. Eugene Meyer, "We've Learned the Lesson: Agriculture Is Truly Basis of Prosperity," *Banker Farmer* 9, no. 9 (September 1922): 2.

31. Eugene Meyer, "Eugene Meyer on Co-operative Marketing Legislation," *Commercial and Financial Chronicle* 115 (December 23, 1922): 2741.

32. Chester Morrill Oral History, 1952, 121, Columbia University Archives, New York.

33. Walter Wyatt Oral History, 1970, 2, Columbia University Archives.

34. Agnes Meyer Diary, March 4, 1931, Box 18, Agnes Meyer Papers, Library of Congress. For more family background from the Meyers' famous daughter, who later owned the *Washington Post*, see Katherine Graham, *Personal History* (New York: Vintage Books, 1997).

35. E. Meyer Memoir Manuscript, unnumbered page.

36. E. Meyer Memoir Manuscript, 26.

37. Morrill Oral History, 42. The *Washington Post* reported accurately in "War Finance Group Now on Farm Board," May 6, 1927, Box 59, Record Group (RG) 56, Records of the Secretary of the Treasury, National Archives, College Park, MD (NARA II).

38. Morrill Oral History, 145, 146–47.

39. Senate Banking and Currency Committee, *Hearing on Confirmation of Members of the Federal Farm Loan Board*, 70th Cong., 1st sess. (1927), 9; E. Meyer Memoir Manuscript, 12; "Memorandum for Board FLB Columbia," June 28, 1928, Box 2, Records of Irregularities, RG 103, Records of the Farm Credit Administration, NARA II. See also the list of all resignations for the first seven months in Senate Banking and Currency Committee, *Hearing on Confirmation*, 36.

40. Senate Banking and Currency Committee, *Hearing on Confirmation*, 89.

41. Senate Banking and Currency Committee, *Hearing on Confirmation*, 97.
42. "Reorganized Farm Board Works Well," *Wall Street Journal*, May 22, 1928.
43. "Twelfth Annual Report of the Federal Farm Loan Board, 1928," 70th Cong., 2nd sess., H. Doc. 382 (1929), 14–15.
44. Senate Banking and Currency Committee, *Hearing on Confirmation*, 39.
45. Senate Banking and Currency Committee, *Hearing on Confirmation*, 44, 64; Calvin Coolidge, "Fifth Annual Message," December 6, 1927, American Presidency Project, https://www.presidency.ucsb.edu/documents/fifth-annual-message-5.
46. "Farm Board Changes Displease Fletcher," *New York Journal of Commerce*, May 23, 1927.
47. See Senate Banking and Currency Committee, *Hearing on Confirmation*, 74.
48. Carl Williams to Eugene Meyer, January 12, 1928, Box 72, E. Meyer Papers.
49. Subcommittee of the Senate Banking and Currency Committee, *Hearings on Nomination of Eugene Meyer to Be a Member of the Federal Reserve Board*, 71st Cong., 3rd sess. (1931), 100 (Meyer discussed the Farm Loan Board appointment hearing at the Federal Reserve Board appointment hearing).
50. Subcommittee of the Senate Banking and Currency Committee, *Hearings on Nomination of Eugene Meyer*, 105–6.
51. *Annual Report of the Federal Farm Loan Board, 1927* (Washington, DC: U.S. Government Printing Office, 1928), 80–81, 84–85.
52. L. H. Paulger, Special Examiner, to Mr. Meyer, memorandum, Re: Federal Land Bank, Columbia, SC, October 29, 1927, Box 2, Investigations of Irregularities, RG 103, NARA II.
53. Memorandum for Board Federal Land Bank, Columbia, SC, June 28, 1928, Box 2, Investigations of Irregularities, RG 103, NARA II. For more examples of problems in the banks and their loans as well as statistics on their failures, see Judge Glock, "The Rise and Fall of the First Government-Sponsored Enterprise: The Federal Land Banks, 1916–1932," *Business History Review* 90, no. 4 (Winter 2016): 623–45.
54. "Report on Sale of Bonds by the Federal Land Banks for Delivery June 29, 1928," Box 1, Entry 7, Report on Sale of Bonds, 1928, RG 103, NARA II.
55. *Annual Report of the Federal Farm Loan Board, 1928* (Washington, DC: U.S. Government Printing Office, 1929), 48.
56. See, for example, "U.S. Farm Loan System Gained," *Wall Street Journal*, March 9, 1929.
57. Herbert Hoover (HH) to Eugene Meyer, April 29, 1929, released to the public on May 1, 1929, in *Herbert Hoover: 1929: Containing the Public Messages, Speeches, and Statements of the President, March 4 to December 31, 1929* (Ann Arbor: University of Michigan Library, 2005), 129.
58. Herbert Hoover, "Some Notes on Agricultural Readjustment and High Cost of Living," *Saturday Evening Post*, April 10, 1920, reprinted independently.
59. Arthur Burns, *The Frontiers of Economic Knowledge* (Princeton, NJ: Princeton University Press, 1954), 62.
60. Committee on Recent Economic Changes, *Recent Economic Changes in the United States*, vol. 1 (New York: McGraw-Hill, 1929), xx. Some historians claim that the report was focused on balancing consumption and production, but in fact it noted that the balance of consumption and production was already in effect. Imbalances between types of production were of greatest concern (xxi). See also Guy Alchon, *The Invisible Hand of Planning: Capitalism, Social Science, and the State in the 1920s* (Princeton, NJ: Princeton University Press, 1985), 149–50.
61. Committee on Recent Economic Changes, *Recent Economic Changes*, xxi. The final section of the report's introduction was originally titled "Economic Equilibrium," but

Hoover in his draft copy crossed out the title and wrote in "Economic Balance," and this subhead was retained in the final report (xxii). For this change, see Edwin F. Gay, "Recent Economic Changes: Confidential," Box 135, Herbert Hoover Presidential Papers, Herbert Hoover Presidential Library, West Branch, IA.

62. Gay, "Recent Economic Changes."

63. Herbert Hoover, *The Memoirs of Herbert Hoover*, vol. 2: *The Cabinet and the Presidency, 1920–1933* (New York: MacMillan, 1952), 253.

64. Ogden Mills, "Speech at Annual Dinner Meeting of the American Association of Advertising Agencies, May 15, 1930," Box 52, Hoover Presidential Papers.

65. Ogden Mills, "Speech to Be Delivered by Undersecretary of the Treasury at the Annual Dinner Meeting of the American Association of Advertising Agencies," May 15, 1930, Box 52, Treasury Correspondence, Hoover Presidential Papers.

66. Harris Gaylord Warren, *Herbert Hoover and the Great Depression* (New York: Oxford University Press, 1959), 150.

67. Andrew Volstead to Gray Silver, T. C. Atkeson, et al., March 4, 1922, Box 3, Gray Silver Papers, West Virginia University Archives, Morgantown; "Summary of Farm Bureau Support for Cooperative Credit," c. 1928, Box 13, Silver Papers; Freedman, *Journal of Proceedings of the National Grange, 1927*, 147; Thomas Clark Atkeson, *Outlines of Grange History* (Washington, DC: Farm Press News, 1928), 27, Box 2, Thomas Clark Atkeson Papers, West Virginia University Archives.

68. Howard, *James R. Howard*, 155–56.

69. Hamilton, *From New Day to New Deal*, 43; Franklin W. Fort, "The Decline in the Purchasing Power of American Farmers Since 1900," *Proceedings of the Academy of Political Science in the City of New York* 12, no. 3 (July 1927): 43–47.

70. Hoover, *Memoirs*, 2:253. For another example of the administration discussing the benefits to banks of the new Federal Farm Board system, see "Legge Advises Farmers to Go to Local Banks," *Chicago Daily Tribune*, July 18, 1929.

71. Legge had also negotiated on behalf of life insurers and mortgage companies to receive loans from Meyer's War Finance Corporation. See "Harold M'Cormick Quits as President of Harvest Firm," *New York Times*, June 3, 1923; Alex Legge to HH, March 6, 1924, Box 155, Herbert Hoover Cabinet Papers, Herbert Hoover Presidential Library.

72. Quoted in "Legge, 'Mad,' Lauds Farm Board's Work," *New York Times*, April 7, 1931.

73. "Farm Board Holds 189,656,187 Bushels of 81-Cent Wheat," *New York Times*, November 25, 1931 (describing actions of the previous year). See also "Why Farm Board Pegged Wheat," *Wall Street Journal*, December 16, 1930; "Farm Board's Vision Lauded," *Los Angeles Times*, June 13, 1931; "Stone Defends Farm Policies," *Wall Street Journal*, May 2, 1931.

74. *Annual Report of the Federal Farm Board, 1931* (Washington, DC: U.S. Government Printing Office, 1931), 40. Hoover later argued that if the board had not stepped in, "a thousand country banks would likely be closed and a general panic was possible" (Herbert Hoover, "Address at the Coliseum in Des Moines, Iowa, October 4, 1932," American Presidency Project, https://www.presidency.ucsb.edu/documents/address-the-coliseum-des-moines-iowa).

75. "Holds Farm Board Averted Disaster: Fort Says Its Stabilization Plans Prevented Ruin of Banking and Business Structure," *New York Times*, May 17, 1931.

76. "Farm Board Closes Deal on Storing Huge Cotton Stock," *New York Times*, November 23, 1931.

77. "Stone to Address Mortgage Bankers," *Washington Post*, September 24, 1932; "Mortgage Bankers Will Discuss Home Loans," *New York Times*, September 24, 1932, 19.

78. Carter et al., *Historical Statistics*, tables Da693–706, Da717–29.

79. *Annual Report of the Federal Farm Board, 1932* (Washington, DC: U.S. Government Printing Office, 1932), 2.

80. Herbert Hoover, *Memoirs of Herbert Hoover*, vol. 1: *Years of Adventure, 1874–1920* (New York: MacMillan, 1952), 6.

81. Warren, *Herbert Hoover and the Great Depression*, 20.

82. HH to Eugene Meyer, April 29, 1929, in Herbert Hoover, *Public Papers of Herbert Hoover* (Washington, DC: U.S. Government Printing Office, 1974), 129–30. The Republican Party platform of 1928 had also celebrated the land bank system and its enlarged "one billion eight hundred fifty millions of dollars for loaning purposes at a low rate of interest" ("Republican Party Platform of 1928," June 12, 1928, American Presidency Project, https://www.presidency.ucsb.edu/documents/republican-party-plat form-1928).

83. "Farm Loan Liability Bill," *Wall Street Journal*, February 21, 1930. For banker support of this proposal, see "Aid for Land Banks," *Wall Street Journal*, March 7, 1930.

84. House Banking and Currency Committee, *Receivership of Joint-Stock Land Banks*, 71st Cong., 2nd sess. (1930), 12, 56–60; A. F. Lever to Henry Rainey, July 23, 1928, Box 3, Henry Rainey Papers, Library of Congress; Statement of the First Carolinas Joint-Stock Land Bank of Columbia, SC, as of June 30, 1928, Box 3, Rainey Papers. Rainey was also very close with disgraced Joint-Stock Land Bank mogul Guy Huston. See Guy Huston to Henry Rainey, December 20, 1929, and April 27, 1931, Box 3, Rainey Papers.

85. Subcommittee of Senate Committee on Agriculture and Forestry, *To Establish an Efficient Agricultural Credit System*, 72nd Cong., 1st sess. (1932), 37. After his stint in government, Bestor would go on to make farm mortgage loans at the Prudential Insurance Company, the largest private farm mortgage lender (*Newark Evening News*, February 9, 1944).

86. Minutes of the Meeting of the Federal Farm Loan Board, May 19, 1930, 241–68, Box 36, RG 103, NARA II.

87. For farm leaders' meetings with Hoover, see Louis Taber Oral History, 1952, 162–63, Columbia University Archives.

88. Walter H. Newton, "Memorandum" and handwritten notes, June 2, 1930, dictated May 31, 1930, Box 58, Hoover Presidential Papers.

89. See Herbert Hoover Daily Calendar for 1930 and 1931, Hoover Library Online, http://www.ecommcode2.com/hoover/calendar/search_results.cfm. Several additional meetings that appear to have taken place, as noted in correspondence, are not recorded in the daily calendar.

90. "Federal Land Banks, Delinquencies, June 1931," Box 58, Hoover Presidential Papers.

91. Raymond Goldsmith, *The Changing Structure of American Banking* (London: Routledge, 1933), 106, quoted in Milton Friedman and Anna Schwartz, *A Monetary History of the United States, 1867–1960* (Princeton, NJ: Princeton University Press, 1963), 355.

92. Combined, Federal Land Bank and Joint-Stock Land Bank bonds caused the banks to lose more money than from all other bonds except textile bonds and telephone and telegraph bonds. See Federal Reserve Branch, Chain and Group Banking Committee, "225 Bank Suspensions: Case Histories from Examiners' Reports," 1938, 153, Federal Reserve Archival System for Economic Research (FRASER), Library of Congress, https://fraser.stlouisfed.org. For discussion of how decline in bond prices exacerbated banking collapse, see Eugene White, "A Reinterpretation of the Banking Crisis of 1930," *Journal of Economic History* 44, no. 1 (March 1984): 119–38.

93. Paul Bestor to the President, September 17, 1931, Box 58, Hoover Presidential Papers. For public discussion at the time about government support for "quasi-public" banks, see Joseph Cohen, *The Mortgage Bank: A Study in Investment Banking* (New York: Pitman, 1931), 124.

94. Both of these actions, however, were reported at the time with banner headlines. See, for example, "Hoover Urges $500,000,000 Pool to Aid Banks, with Enlarged Federal Farm Loan System," *New York Times*, October 7, 1931.

95. "Bond Prices Rise in New Confidence," *New York Times*, October 8, 1931.

96. Subcommittee of the Senate Banking and Currency Committee, *To Strengthen the Capital Structure of the Federal Land Banks*, 72nd Cong., 1st sess. (1931), 10.

97. "New Capital Lifts Land Banks' Bonds," *New York Times*, January 24, 1932.

98. Walter H. Newton, File Memo, January 26 and 27, 1932, Box 280, Reconstruction Finance Corporation, Hoover Presidential Papers.

99. Raymond B. Vickers, *Panic in the Loop: Chicago's Banking Crisis of 1932* (Lanham, MD: Lexington Books, 2011), 91.

100. Everett Sanders to Walter H. Newton, August 20, 1932, Box 279, Reconstruction Finance Corporation, Hoover Presidential Papers.

101. Everett Sanders, *The Government's Obligation to the Joint Stock Land Banks and Their Farmer Borrowers*, pamphlet, October 26, 1931, Box 53, Entry 191, RG 56, NARA II.

102. See Eugene Meyer to HH, July 5, 1932, Box 283, RG 56, NARA II; and "Report of Reconstruction Finance Corporation," *Federal Reserve Bulletin* 18, no. 8 (August 1932): 481.

103. See "Detailed Federal Reserve Statistics," *Federal Reserve Bulletin* 18, no. 3 (March 1932): 182; "Resources and Liabilities of Federal Reserve Banks in Detail," *Federal Reserve Bulletin* 18, no. 5 (May 1932): 293; "Resources and Liabilities of Federal Reserve Banks in Detail," *Federal Reserve Bulletin* 18, no. 6 (June 1932): 353.

104. Lee Alston, "Farm Foreclosures in the United States During the Interwar Period," *Journal of Economic History* 43, no. 4 (December 1983): 885–903; Carrie A. Meyer, *Days on the Family Farm: From the Golden Age Through the Great Depression* (Washington, DC: George Mason University Press, 2007), 152.

105. John H. Bosch, "Recollections of Rural Revolt" (interview), ed. David L. Nass, *Minnesota History*, Winter 1975, 305.

106. Studs Terkel, *Hard Times: An Oral History of the Great Depression* (New York: Pantheon Books, 1970), 94 (Slim Collier).

107. Terkel, *Hard Times*, 215 (Harry Terrell).

108. Marvin Jones Oral History, 1953, 599, Columbia University Archives.

109. R. Bosch Oral History, 1962, 9, Farm Holiday Association Oral Histories, Columbia University Archives.

110. John L. Shover, *Cornbelt Rebellion* (Urbana: University of Illinois Press, 1965), 78.

111. Quoted in "Farm Mortgage Aid Urged to Avert Serious Crisis," *Los Angeles Times*, February 4, 1933.

112. Quoted in "Warn on Urgency of Farm Relief," *New York Times*, February 12, 1933.

113. John A. Filter and Derek S. Hof, *Fighting Foreclosure: The Blaisdell Case, the Contract Clause, and the Great Depression* (Lawrence: University of Kansas Press, 2012), 60.

114. Shover, *Cornbelt Rebellion*, 81; Langer quoted in Si Sheppard, *The Buying of the Presidency? Franklin D. Roosevelt, the New Deal, and the Election of 1936* (Santa Barbara, CA: Praeger, 2014), 8.

115. Quoted in "Reno Says President Spoke 'Half-Truths," *New York Times*, September 30, 1935.

116. Homer Hush Oral History, 1953, 35–37, Columbia University Archives. See "'Penny' Farm Bids Face Court Action," *New York Times*, February 7, 1933.

117. Owen P. White, "Helping the Farmer Out," *Collier's*, October 8, 1932. The White House was so concerned about the *Collier's* story that it telegraphed Bestor while he was on a railroad trip to ask him to counteract it. A Pullman conductor flagged Bestor down at the next stop and handed him the emergency telegram. Bestor immediately turned around to travel to the *Collier's* New York office to demand an apology for what he called a "despicable" attack on the land bank system. Bestor also criticized the "implications of the cartoons" that the banks were focused on foreclosures. The editor refused to change anything but at least revealed that his principal source for the story was Democratic congressman Henry Steagall of Alabama. See Paul Bestor to Richey (full name not given), October 8, 1932; Paul Bestor to William L. Chenery, Editor, *Collier's*, October 7, 1932; Walter H. Newton to Paul Bestor, October 1, 1932; and White House memo, October 1, 1932, 11:25 a.m., all in Box 58, Hoover Presidential Papers.

118. J. C. Hanrahan, assistant to Gardner Cowles, to Walter Newton, August 26, 1932, Box 279, Reconstruction Finance Corporation, Hoover Presidential Papers.

119. Governor Dan W. Turner to HH, September 27, 1932, Box 58, Hoover Presidential Papers.

120. HH to Paul Bestor, October 29, 1931, with draft, Box 58, Hoover Presidential Papers.

121. "Begin Drive to Aid Mortgaged Farmer," *New York Times*, October 1, 1932.

122. Donald R. Murphy Oral History, 1962, 21, Farm Holiday Association Oral Histories, Columbia University Archives.

123. Herbert Hoover, "Address at the Coliseum in Des Moines, Iowa, October 4, 1932," American Presidency Project, https://www.presidency.ucsb.edu/documents/address -the-coliseum-des-moines-iowa.

124. Herbert Hoover, *The Memoirs of Herbert Hoover*, vol. 3: *The Great Depression, 1929– 1941* (New York: MacMillan, 1952), 265–66.

125. John Bosch Oral History, 1962, 41–43, Farm Holiday Association Oral Histories, Columbia University Archives.

126. Filter and Hof, *Fighting Foreclosure*, 64, 62; Christopher Shaw, *Money, Power, and the People: The American Struggle to Make Banking Democratic* (Chicago: University of Chicago, 2019), 4.

5. Herbert Hoover and the Urban-Mortgage Crisis in the Great Depression

1. Herbert Hoover (HH) to Roy A. Young, March 24, 1930, Box 180, Herbert Hoover Presidential Papers, Herbert Hoover Presidential Library, West Branch, IA.

2. HH to Young, March 24, 1930. See also William J. Barber, *New Era to New Deal: Herbert Hoover, the Economists, and American Economic Policy* (Cambridge: Cambridge University Press, 1985), 96–97.

3. See the discussion of the real-bills doctrine in Lloyd Mints, *A History of Banking Theory in Great Britain and the United States* (Chicago: University of Chicago Press, 1945), 9, 207.

4. This consensus has been embraced on all sides of the ideological spectrum. See Milton Friedman and Anna Jacobson Schwartz, *A Monetary History of the United States 1867–1960* (Princeton, NJ: Princeton University Press, 1963), 299–419; Ben Bernanke, "Nonmonetary Effects of the Financial Crisis in the Propagation of the Great

Depression," *American Economic Review* 73, no. 3 (June 1983): 257–76; Christina Romer, "What Ended the Great Depression?," *Journal of Economic History* 52, no. 4 (December 1992): 757–78; Barry Eichengreen, *Golden Fetters: The Gold Standard and the Great Depression* (Oxford: Oxford University Press, 1992). Those writers who focus on Hoover's mortgage reforms tend to discuss just the Federal Home Loan Banks and usually tie them to Hoover's supposed moral case for homeownership instead of to an attempt to bail out the financial sector. For typical examples, see Kenneth Jackson, *Crabgrass Frontier: The Suburbanization of the United States* (New York: Oxford University Press, 1987), 193–95; and David Freund, *Colored Property: State Policy and White Racial Politics in Suburban America* (Chicago: University of Chicago Press, 2007), 103–11. There is no discussion about how these reforms emerged out of the example of the Federal Land Banks. David Mason discusses the financial impacts of the Federal Home Loan Banks, but he does not root them in Hoover's economic ideas or in his other reforms of the financial sector. See David Mason, *From Building and Loans to Bail-outs* (Cambridge: Cambridge University Press, 2004), 74–89.

5. Elmus Wicker and Natacha Postel-Viney have shown how many of the banking collapses of the Midwest were exacerbated by real estate loans. Others have shown that the real estate price increases of the 1920s were consistent with a "bubble" that damaged the economy. In contrast, writers such as Eugene White have shown that real estate loans cannot explain much of the banking collapse. Although in this chapter I hope to emphasize some moments in the Depression in which real estate was a substantial cause of banking failures and economic troubles, my main purpose is to analyze how contemporary policy makers viewed the importance of mortgages in explaining the collapse, which has received little attention. Those writers who focus on Herbert Hoover's and the Federal Reserve's responses to the Depression almost never analyze mortgages. For connection between mortgages and the banking panic, see Elmus Wicker, *Banking Panics of the Great Depression* (Cambridge: Cambridge University Press, 1996), 15–16; Natacha Postel-Viney, "What Caused Chicago Bank Failures in the Great Depression? A Look at the 1920s," *Journal of Economic History* 76, no. 2 (2016): 478–519; Eugene White, "Lessons from the Great American Real Estate Boom and Bust of the 1920s," in *Housing and Mortgage Markets in Historical Perspective*, ed. Eugene White, Kenneth Snowden, and Price Fishback (Chicago: University of Chicago Press, 2014), 115–61. For older writings about Hoover's response to the Depression, see Jordon A. Schwartz, *The Interregnum of Despair: Hoover, Congress, and the Depression* (Chicago: University of Illinois Press, 1970); and James Stuart Olson, *Herbert Hoover and the Reconstruction Finance Corporation* (Ames: Iowa State University Press, 1977).

6. S. W. Straus, "What You Should Know About Lending and Borrowing Money on Mortgages," *American Magazine* 93 (January 1922): 118.

7. Upton Sinclair, *The Jungle* (1906; reprint, Chicago: Upton Sinclair, 1920), 205–18.

8. U.S. Census Office, *Twelfth Census of the United States—1900*, vol. 1 (Washington, DC: U.S. Government Printing Office, 1902), 663, 670.

9. For a later dolorous history of land contracts in Chicago, see Beryl Satter, *Family Properties: Race, Real Estate, and the Exploitation of Black Urban America* (New York: Metropolitan Books, 2009).

10. U.S. Census Office, *Report on Farms and Homes: Proprietorship and Indebtedness in the United States at the Eleventh Census: 1890* (Washington, DC: U.S. Government Printing Office, 1896); Susan Carter, Scott Sigmund Gartner, Michael R. Haines, Alan L.

Olmstead, Richard Sutch, and Gavin Wright, eds., *Historical Statistics of the United States: Earliest Times to the Present*, millennial ed. (New York: Cambridge University Press, 2006), tables Dc903–28. Life insurance companies, some commercial banks, and "other institutional lenders" divided up 15 percent of mortgages (Carter et. al., *Historical Statistics*, tables Dc903–28).

11. 53 Cong. Rec. 7744 (May 6, 1916); "William Schley Howard," in *Biographical Directory of the United States Congress*, n.d., http://bioguide.congress.gov/scripts/biodisplay.pl ?index=H000849. See also 52 Cong. Rec. 406 (December 19, 1914).

12. See, though, Federal Reserve support for renewing one-year mortgages indefinitely in "Regulation G, Series of 1917," *Federal Reserve Bulletin* 3, no. 7 (July 1917): 546.

13. By contrast, farm mortgages received special privileges during World War I. See "Restrictions on Farm Mortgage Removed by U.S.," *Chicago Daily Tribune*, October 10, 1918.

14. See H. F. Cellarius, "Building and Loan Legislations and Federal Legislation: An Historical Review," in *History of Building and Loan in the United States*, ed. H. Morton Bodfish (Chicago: U.S. Building and Loan League, 1931), 186–88; Mason, *From Building and Loans to Bail-outs*, 76.

15. Daniel Roland Fusfeld, *The Economic Thought of Franklin D. Roosevelt and the Origins of the New Deal* (New York: Columbia University Press, 1954), 74; "1920 Democratic Party Platform," June 28, 1920, American Presidency Project, https://www .presidency.ucsb.edu/documents/1920-democratic-party-platform. A similar extension of the Federal Farm Loan Act to home builders was incorporated in the Progressive Party platform of 1924, November 4, 1924, American Presidency Project, https://www .presidency.ucsb.edu/documents/progressive-party-platform-1924.

16. Herbert Hoover, *The Memoirs of Herbert Hoover*, vol. 2: *The Cabinet and the Presidency, 1920–1933* (New York: MacMillan, 1951), 92, 48.

17. "Federal Activity in Promotion of Better Housing Conditions and Home Ownership," c. 1921, Box 63, Commerce Department Papers, Hoover Presidential Library.

18. Herbert Hoover, foreword to *Seasonal Operation in the Construction Industries* (Washington, DC: U.S. Government Printing Office, 1924), vi.

19. Herbert Hoover, chairman, *Report of the President's Conference on Unemployment, September 26 to October 13, 1921* (Washington, DC: U.S. Government Printing Office, 1921), 21.

20. Hoover, *Report of the President's Conference on Unemployment*, 22.

21. See "F. D. Roosevelt to Be Building Arbiter: Chosen to Direct Industry as Hays and Landis Run Motion Pictures and Baseball," *New York Times*, May 15, 1922; "Hoover and Roosevelt Back American Council," *Building Supply News* 11, no. 11 (May 23, 1922): 773.

22. Franklin D. Roosevelt (FDR) to HH, May 29, 1922, in *Herbert Hoover and FDR: A Documentary History*, ed. Dwight Miller and Timothy Walch (Westport, CT: Greenwood Press, 1998), 10–11.

23. Herbert Hoover, *The Memoirs of Herbert Hoover*, vol. 1: *Years of Adventure, 1874–1920* (New York: MacMillan, 1951), 6. See also the previous chapter.

24. "Department of Commerce Press Release, in Response to a Request by the President in Connection with Senator King's Suggestion for a National Conference on Housing," February 9, 1922, Box 63, Commerce Department Papers, Hoover Presidential Library.

25. Hoover worried in particular about burdensome second mortgages: "To my mind the center point of economic home building is to find a method of handling the second

mortgage margin on home construction." He thus believed local building and loans, with their low down payments, provided the best hope for cheaper mortgages. See HH to D. E. McAvoy, February 10, 1922, Box 63, Commerce Department Papers; "Is Housing a 'Local Issue,'" *Brooklyn Eagle*, February 10, 1922, Box 63, Commerce Department Papers; "Federal Aid on Homes For U.S. Workers Seen," *Washington Post*, May 1, 1925, Box 64, Commerce Department Papers.

26. HH to Senator William Calder, August 12, 1921, Box 67, Commerce Department Papers.

27. John H. Gray and George W. Terborgh, *First Mortgages in Urban Real Estate Finance* (Washington, DC: Brookings Institution Press, 1929), foreword. For Moulton at Brookings, see James A. Smith, *The Idea Brokers: Think Tanks and the Rise of the New Policy Elite* (New York: Free Press, 1994), 59–62.

28. White, "Lessons from the Great American Real Estate Boom," 115.

29. White, "Lessons from the Great American Real Estate Boom," 144. These loans equaled 23 percent of banks' capital, right below the legal limit of 25 percent of capital to mortgages. Insurance companies took mortgages from 36 percent of all their assets in 1922 to 43 percent in 1926 (White, "Lessons from the Great American Real Estate Boom," 146). See also Wicker, *Banking Panics of the Great Depression*, 16.

30. Cellarius, "The Financial Growth of Building and Loan," 136.

31. Straus, "What You Should Know," 120.

32. White, "Lessons from the Great American Real Estate Boom," 139; Sarah Quinn, *American Bonds: How Credit Markets Shaped a Nation* (Princeton, NJ: Princeton University Press, 2019), 109. One report noticed the "curious phenomenon of the 'moral guarantee'" of even private mortgage bonds (Gray and Terborgh, *First Mortgages in Urban Real Estate Finance*, 27).

33. Quinn, *American Bonds*, 113–14; Frederick Fenton, ed., *Proceedings of the Eleventh Annual Convention of the Investment Bankers Association of America, Held October 9–12, 1922* (Chicago: Lakeside Press, 1922), 115–44.

34. Carter et al., *Historical Statistics*, table Dc128; "Federal Activity in Promotion of Better Housing Conditions and Home Ownership," c. 1922, Box 63, Commerce Department Papers; Hoover, *Memoirs*, 2:95.

35. On Louis McFadden, see "The Case of the Hon. Mr. McFadden Vs. the Hon. Mr. Williams," *New York Tribune*, May 25, 1919.

36. See "Minutes of Federal Reserve Board Meeting," December 5, 1927, 427, Minutes of the Board of Governors of the Federal Reserve System, Federal Reserve Archival System for Economic Research (FRASER), https://fraser.stlouisfed.org/. The McFadden Act more famously expanded the right of national banks to create branches, but Representative Louis McFadden claimed the second most important part of the bill dealt with real estate mortgages in national banks. Glass's assistant, H. P. Willis, attacked in particular the liberalizing real estate provisions of the McFadden Act, and in his book *Contemporary Banking* argued that "the fact still remains that real estate is not a desirable type of security" (H. P. Willis, J. M. Chapman, and R. W. Robey, *Contemporary Banking* [New York: Harper and Row, 1933], 443).

37. Subcommittee of the Senate Banking and Currency Committee, *Hearing on Consolidation of National Banking Associations*, 69th Cong., 1st sess. (1926), 21.

38. 68 Cong. Rec. 2170 (January 24, 1927).

39. Lawrence Eillman, "What Is a Marketable Real Estate Security?," *Bankers Magazine* 114, no. 6 (June 1927): 817.

40. "Preliminary Memorandum of the Chairman of the Open Market Investment Committee," January 12, 1928, 169–70, Open Market Investment Policy: Excerpts: 1923–1928, FRASER.

41. Carter et al., *Historical Statistics*, tables Dc510–30.

42. For further background, see Judge Glock, "The 'Riefler-Keynes' Doctrine and Federal Reserve Policy in the Great Depression," *History of Political Economy* 51, no. 2 (April 2019): 297–327.

43. Wesley Clair Mitchell, *Business Cycles* (Berkeley: University of California Press, 1913), 489.

44. Mitchell, *Business Cycles*, 489–90, 499, 503, 558.

45. Mitchell's work was soon complimented by that of the institutionalist John Maurice Clark, who argued that changes in fixed investment created an "accelerator effect," leading ups and downs in other sectors and thus leading the business cycle. See John Maurice Clark, "Business Acceleration and the Law of Demand: A Technical Factor in Economic Cycles," *Journal of Political Economy* 25, no. 3 (1917): 217–35.

46. Malcolm Rutherford, *The Institutionalist Movement in American Economics, 1918–1947: Science and Social Control* (Cambridge: Cambridge University Press, 2011), 16.

47. H. G. Moulton, *Principles of Money and Banking: A Series of Selected Materials, with Explanatory Introductions* (Chicago: University of Chicago Press, 1916), xv–xvii.

48. H. G. Moulton, "Commercial Banking and Capital Formation: III," *Journal of Political Economy* 26, no. 7 (July 1918): 729. For public reception of Moulton's articles, see Joseph Dorfman, *The Economic Mind in American Civilization, 1918–1933*, vol. 4 (New York: Kelley, 1969), 335.

49. Harold Moulton, *The Financial Organization of Society* (Chicago: University of Chicago Press, 1921), 752–53.

50. For the work of another prominent monetary theorist who understood the logical extensions of Moulton's ideas but who received insufficient attention for her contributions both in that period and in the present, see Anna Youngman, "The Efficacy of Changes in the Discount Rates of the Federal Reserve Banks," *American Economic Review* 11 no. 3 (1921): 466–85, and "A Popular Theory of Credit Applied to Credit Policy," *American Economic Review* 12, no. 3 (1922): 417–46.

51. Waldo Mitchell, "The Institutional Basis for the Shiftability Theory of Bank Liquidity," *University Journal of Business* 1, no. 3 (May 1923): 352; Waldo F. Mitchell, "The Attack Upon the Theory of the Liquidity of Bank Earning Assets," *Journal of Political Economy* 31, no. 2 (April 1923): 259, emphasis in original.

52. W. F. Mitchell, "Interest Rates as Factors in Business Cycles," *American Economic Review* 18, no. 1 (March 1928): 217–30.

53. Rutherford, *Institutionalist Movement in American Economics*, 152, 165.

54. Winfield Riefler, *Money Rates and Money Markets in the United States* (New York: Harper, 1930), 120, 119, xv.

55. If Riefler is famous for anything today, however, it is for his supposed part in crafting what Allan Meltzer calls the "Riefler–Burgess doctrine," the idea that the Federal Reserve was basically impotent in the face of banks' reluctance to borrow and lend during the Depression (*A History of the Federal Reserve*, vol. 1: *1913–1951* [Chicago: University of Chicago Press, 2003], 398).

56. Winfield Riefler to Adolph Miller, "Economics of Equilibrium," August 25, 1932, Box 1, Winfield Riefler Papers, National Archives, College Park, MD (NARA II).

57. "Preliminary Memorandum for the Open Market Investment Committee," November 14, 1928, Open Market Investment Policy: Excerpts: 1923–1928, 248–49, FRASER. For recent analysis of the stock-market boom and bust, see Julia Ott, "What Was the Great Bull Market? Value, Valuation, and Financial History," in *American Capitalism: New Histories*, ed. Sven Beckert and Christine Desan (New York: Columbia University Press, 2018), 63–95.

58. "Preliminary Memorandum for the Open Market Investment Committee," April 1, 1929, Open Market Investment Policy: Excerpts: 1929–Mid-1931, 287, FRASER.

59. "Letter from Harrison to Board on Committee Action," September 30, 1929, Open Market Investment Policy: Excerpts: 1929–Mid-1931, 352, FRASER.

60. "Letter from Harrison Explaining Open Market Actions," November 27, 1929, Open Market Investment Policy: Excerpts: 1929–Mid-1931, 380, FRASER. See also R. W. Goldsmith, *Changing Structure of American Banking* (New York: Routledge, 1933), 106.

61. "Preliminary Memorandum to the Open Market Investment Committee," January 28, 1930, Open Market Investment Policy: Excerpts: 1929–Mid-1931, 402, FRASER.

62. "Minutes of the Open Market Investment Committee," March 24, 1930, Minutes of the Meetings of the Open Market Investment Committee, 1923–1930, 419, FRASER.

63. "Meeting Minutes of Federal Reserve Board," April 15, 1930, Minutes of the Board of Governors of the Federal Reserve System, vol. 17, part 2, 351, FRASER. Harrison noted that "although their efforts must necessarily be directed to the short term money market, . . . [t]he maintenance of reasonable rates for short time money will gradually affect the long time investment market."

64. Herbert Hoover, "Address to the American Bankers Association in Cleveland, Ohio," October 2, 1930, American Presidency Project, https://www.presidency.ucsb.edu /documents/address-the-american-bankers-association-cleveland-ohio.

65. Eugene Meyer Oral History, 1953, 603, Columbia University Archives, New York; Theodore Joslin Diary, August 27, 1931, Hoover Presidential Library.

66. Herbert Hoover, "Statement on the National Business and Economic Situation," October 25, 1929, American Presidency Project, https://www.presidency.ucsb.edu/documents /statement-the-national-business-and-economic-situation. For a typical quote of just the first part of Hoover's statement, see Joel Seligman, *The Transformation of Wall Street: A History of the Securities and Exchange Commission and Modern Corporate Finance*, 3rd ed. (New York: Aspen, 2003), 4.

67. Herbert Hoover, "The President's News Conference," November 5, 1929, American Presidency Project, https://www.presidency.ucsb.edu/documents/the-presidents-news -conference-843.

68. Herbert Hoover, "The President's News Conference," March 7, 1930, American Presidency Project, https://www.presidency.ucsb.edu/documents/the-presidents-news -conference-707.

69. Quoted in Barber, *From New Era to New Deal*, 87.

70. John Maynard Keynes, *A Treatise on Money*, vol. 2: *The Applied Theory of Money* (London: MacMillan, 1930), 352–55, 347. Keynes also made some unacknowledged borrowings from Harold Moulton and his "shiftability" theories. For another theorist who influenced Keynes and had similar ideas about the importance of durable goods and housing, see D. H. Robertson, *Banking Policy and the Price Level* (London: King, 1926), 5–12. For discussion of those who influenced Keynes's book, see Robert Skidelsky, *John Maynard Keynes: The Economist as Saviour, 1920–1937* (New York: Penguin Books, 1995), 272–80.

71. Quoted in Skidelsky, *John Maynard Keynes*, 364.

72. Keynes, *Treatise on Money*, 2:98.
73. John Maynard Keynes, "Lecture at Royal Institution: The Internal Mechanics of the Trade Slump," February, 6, 1930, in *The Collected Writings of John Maynard Keynes*, vol. 20: *Activities, 1929–1931*, ed. Donald Moggridge (Cambridge: Cambridge University Press, 2012), 480.
74. Eleanor Lansing Dulles, "Review: *The Theory of Monetary Policy*, by Bhalchandra P. Adarkar," *Journal of the American Statistical Association* 31, no. 195 (September 1935): 634.
75. Eugene Meyer (EM) to HH, July 2, 1930, Box 180, Hoover Presidential Papers.
76. See EM to E. A. Goldenweiser, February 3, 1930, and EM to Mark Sullivan, March 3, 1930, Box 72, Hoover Presidential Papers.
77. EM to HH, March 14, 1930, and May 13, 1930, Box 72, Hoover Presidential Papers.
78. E. Meyer Oral History, 618.
79. Merlo Pusey, *Eugene Meyer* (New York: Knopf, 1974), 200–203.
80. Andrew W. Mellon to HH, August 29, 1930, Box 180, Hoover Presidential Papers; see also Glock, "Riefler-Keynes," 310–11.
81. Lawrence Richey to Ray Lyman Wilbur, July 29, 1929, Box 180, Hoover Presidential Papers.
82. Quoted in Pusey, *Eugene Meyer*, 204. Pusey insists, however, that the two previous retirements of Young and the other Federal Reserve Board member had nothing to do with Meyer taking the job. The evidence in Hoover's library contradicts this claim.
83. Quoted in Agnes Meyer Diary, February 13, 1932, Box 18, Agnes Meyer Papers, Library of Congress, Washington, DC.
84. Charles Hamlin Diaries, November 5, 1931, 180, and Hamlin Diaries index, 54, Charles Hamlin Papers, Library of Congress. See also Francis Gloyd Awalt, "Recollections of the Banking Crisis in 1933," *Business History Review* 43, no. 3 (Autumn 1969): 367–68.
85. Walter Wyatt Oral History, 1970, 11, Columbia University Archives.
86. George Norris, *Ended Episodes* (Philadelphia: Winston, 1937), 199.
87. Julian Klein to EM, March 25, 1931, and John R. Riggleman, Senior Economist, Division of Building and Housing, Department of Commerce, to EM, March 19, 1931, Box 115, Eugene Meyer Papers, Library of Congress. See also E. Meyer Oral History, 545.
88. EM to Alfred Harcourt, Harcourt, Brace, and Co., December 2, 1930, Box 117, E. Meyer Papers.
89. "Meeting of the Board of Directors," April 23, 1931, Box 23, George Harrison Papers, Columbia University Archives; Meltzer, *History of the Federal Reserve*, 1:330. Meltzer does not pursue Meyer's thinking on this topic.
90. E. Meyer Oral History, 604.
91. E. Meyer Oral History, 606, emphasis in original. Years after the Depression, Meyer was still shocked that despite the chaos in the housing market helping to bring down the economy, "nobody has ever really written up the real estate aspects of that period" (608).
92. Goldsmith, *Changing Structure of American Banking*, 83, 242.
93. E. Meyer Oral History, 549–50. The Bank of United States was an odd example of the private market taking on some of the implicit and moral guarantees that had proliferated in government in the previous decade.
94. Kenneth S. Davis, *FDR: The New York Years, 1928–1933* (New York: Random House, 1979), 223–25.
95. J. H. Case, Federal Reserve Bank of New York, to EM, November 29 and December 4, 1930, Box 117, E. Meyer Papers; EM to J. H. Case, December 1 and 6, 1930, Box 117, E.

Meyer Papers; "Consolidated Report of Four Banks," November 29 and December 4, 1930, Box 117, E. Meyer Papers.

96. E. Meyer Oral History, 548, 604–6; Davis, *FDR*, 226–27. See also "Red Plot to Start Bank Run Revealed by Broderick Aides," *New York Times*, December 26, 1930.

97. See, for example, Friedman and Schwartz, *Monetary History of the United States*, 309–11. For an analysis of the collapse of the Bank of United States, see Joseph Lucia, "The Failure of the Bank of United States: A Reappraisal," *Explorations in Economic History* 22, no. 4 (October 1985): 402–16.

98. Quoted in Milton Esbitt, "Bank Portfolios and Bank Failures During the Great Depression: Chicago," *Journal of Economic History* 46, no. 2 (June 1986): 457.

99. "Minutes of the Open Market Policy Conference," July 22, 1931, FRASER.

100. In 1933, an economist published an update of Riefler's specific series showing the break. See Edward C. Simmons, "Mr. Keynes's Control Scheme," *American Economic Review* 23, no. 2 (June 1933): 264–73.

101. Friedman and Schwartz, *Monetary History of the United States*, 304–5.

102. Carter et al., *Historical Statistics*, tables Dc510–30.

103. John Maynard Keynes, "Report of the Committee on Finance and Industry—Addendum I," 1930, in *Collected Writings*, 20:396.

104. John Maynard Keynes, "Comments on Mr. Brand's Memorandum on the Need for a Bridging Chapter," April 7, 1931, in *Collected Writings*, 20:273.

105. John Maynard Keynes, "Do We Want Prices to Rise?," July 15, 1931, in *Collected Writings*, 20:544, 553.

106. John Maynard Keynes, "Economic Advisory Council, Committee on Economists—Draft Report I," 1930, in *Collected Writings*, 20:562, 572.

107. See Herbert Stein, *The Fiscal Revolution in America* (Chicago: University of Chicago Press, 1969), 18–19, and White, "Lessons from the Great American Real Estate Boom."

108. HH to Young, March 24, 1930.

109. "Text of President's Speech," *New York Times*, May 2, 1930; "Text of Hoover's Speech Before Commerce Group," *Washington Post*, May 2, 1930. This call was partially reproduced in a prospectus for a "National Real Estate Salvage Corporation," Box 183, Hoover Presidential Papers.

110. Winfield Riefler, "Mortgage Loan Situation," April 5, 1930, Box 1, Riefler Papers.

111. Riefler later told the Federal Reserve Board that "construction is our largest industry" and that it had to be boosted to restore the economy (Winfield Riefler to Adolph Miller, January 14, 1931, Box 1, Riefler Papers).

112. Herbert Hoover, "The President's News Conference," August 1, 1930, American Presidency Project, https://www.presidency.ucsb.edu/documents/the-presidents-news-conference-775. See also "Announcement of White House Conference on Housing," August 1, 1930, Box 90, Hoover Presidential Papers. One housing reformer complained that "criticism has been made to me from several sources that this conference may be merely an effort to tone up the building industry and improve home ownership financing," with little interest in homeownership per se (Alfred K. Stern to French Strother, September 17, 1930, Box 90, Hoover Presidential Papers).

113. Herbert Hoover, "Remarks to the Planning Committee of the White House Conference on Home Building and Home Ownership," September 24, 1930, American Presidency Project, https://www.presidency.ucsb.edu/documents/remarks-the-planning-committee-the-white-house-conference-home-building-and-home-ownership.

114. William Chadbourne to HH, May 18, 1931, Box 183, Hoover Presidential Papers.

115. HH to Thomas Watts, August 31, 1931, Box 191, Hoover Presidential Papers.

116. HH to Henry Bruere, September 17, 1931, Box 191, Hoover Presidential Papers.

117. Mortgage bonds had found a broad market among small investors, however; see Quinn, *American Bonds*, 107–23.

118. "Bankers Plan Relief of Frozen Realty Assets," *New York Herald Tribune*, September 1, 1931; and "Bankers Draft Aid to Holders of Building Bonds," *New York Herald Tribune*, September 2, 1931, both in Box 191, Hoover Presidential Papers.

119. Charles G. Edwards to HH, September 3, 1931; Edgar Rickard to Theodore G. Joslin, September 17, 1931; and HH to Otis Glenn, September 14, 1931, all in Box 191, Hoover Presidential Papers. See also Hoover's daily calendar, September 17, 1931, Herbert Hoover Presidential Library and Museum, http://www.ecommcode2.com/hoover /calendar/home.cfm.

120. Wicker, *Banking Panics*, 72–74.

121. Henry Bruere to HH, September 22, 1931, Box 191, Hoover Presidential Papers; Ray Lyman Wilbur and Arthur Hyde, *The Hoover Policies* (New York: Scribner's, 1937), 415–16.

122. As described, for instance, in Olson, *Herbert Hoover and the Reconstruction Finance Corporation*, 24–25.

123. Eugene Meyer Memoir Manuscript, 1952, 25–26, 35–36, Box 167, E. Meyer Papers; E. Meyer Oral History, 614.

124. Herbert Hoover, *The Memoirs of Herbert Hoover*, vol. 3:*The Great Depression, 1929–1941* (New York: MacMillan, 1952), 88, 93.

125. Wicker, *Banking Panics*, 109, 158; Olson, *Herbert Hoover and the Reconstruction Finance Corporation*, 28–29, 31–32; "Review of the Month," *Federal Reserve Bulletin* 17, no. 10 (October 1931): 551–52.

126. Olson, *Herbert Hoover and the Reconstruction Finance Corporation*, 29.

127. Herbert Hoover, "Annual Message to Congress on the State of the Union," December 7, 1931, American Presidency Project, https://www.presidency.ucsb.edu/documents /annual-message-the-congress-the-state-the-union-24.

128. E. Meyer Oral History, 627.

129. Chester Morrill Oral History, 1952, 170–71, Columbia University Archives; E. Meyer Oral History, 612. On borrowing personnel from already established agencies, see House Banking and Currency Committee, *Hearings on Reconstruction Finance Corporation*, 72nd Cong., 1st sess. (December 18, 1931), 11. Many historians have connected the RFC's program with Meyer's previous work on the War Finance Corporation but surprisingly have not discussed his stint as head of the Federal Land Banks. For previous historians' discussions of Meyer's work with the War Finance Corporation, see, for example, Olson, *Herbert Hoover and the Reconstruction Finance Corporation*, 42.

130. E. Meyer Oral History, 617.

131. House Banking and Currency Committee, *Hearings on Reconstruction Finance Corporation*, 12.

132. Quoted in Olson, *Herbert Hoover and the Reconstruction Finance Corporation*, 35.

133. House Banking and Currency Committee, *Hearings on Reconstruction Finance Corporation*, 16.

134. House Banking and Currency Committee, *Hearings on Reconstruction Finance Corporation*, 16–17. Meyer placed the RFC's potential contribution to the railroad industry, often emphasized in the literature, as secondary to its contribution to construction. He did, however, affirm that the RFC could support the farm loan system (House Banking and Currency Committee, *Hearings on Reconstruction Finance Corporation*, 8, 13–14, 39–42, 54–57).

135. House Banking and Currency Committee, *Hearings on Reconstruction Finance Corporation*, 20.

136. HH to EM, December 3, 1931, Box 181, Federal Reserve System, Board of Governors: Collection, 1917–1947, Hoover Presidential Papers.

137. James MacLafferty Diary, February 11, 1932, Hoover Presidential Papers. For Glass's earlier attempt to restrict instead of expand real estate and long-term lending, see Emanuel Goldenweiser and Randolph Burgess to Carter Glass, February 7, 1932, Box 10, H. Parker Willis Papers, Columbia University Archives.

138. Emanuel Goldenweiser, *American Monetary Policy* (New York: McGraw-Hill, 1951), 124.

139. House Banking and Currency Committee, *Hearings on Liberalizing the Credit Facilities of the Federal Reserve System*, 72nd Cong., 1st sess. (1932), 9–10.

140. Morrill Oral History, 175–77, 200–201; Joslin Diary, February 14, 1932.

141. As MacLafferty wrote in his diary the day the conference report on the bill with the new amendments was released, "I knew, of course, before I saw the President this morning that this is not what he wanted" (MacLafferty Diary, February 25, 1932).

142. MacLafferty Diary, February 2, 1925.

143. E. Meyer Oral History, 554.

144. Raymond B. Vickers, *Panic in the Loop: Chicago's Banking Crisis of 1932* (Lanham, MD: Lexington Books, 2011), 120–21.

145. Joslin Diary, May 4, 1932.

146. Joslin Diary March 16, 1932; E. Meyer Oral History, 638.

147. Hoover, *Memoirs*, 2:100.

148. HH to Carter Glass, November 13, 1931, Box 4, Carter Glass Papers, University of Virginia Special Collections, Charlottesville.

149. Gries wrote the bill creating the Federal Home Loan Banks, along with Senator Robert Bulkley and some real estate groups. Gries noted, "I have examined both the Farm Loan Act and certain features of the Act creating the Federal Reserve Board. In practically all cases, we have followed the Farm Loan Act" (John Gries to Theodore Joslin, October 13, 1931, Box 90, Hoover Presidential Papers; see also "Home Loan Rediscount Bank Bill Skeleton Outline," October 13, 1931, Box 90, Hoover Presidential Papers). Despite the current consensus that the act aimed to create more single-family suburbs, Gries wrote that he was against rapid suburbanization: "Any uncontrolled movements toward suburbs should be discouraged as they result in the leaving behind of blighted districts with a resultant waste in already installed municipal facilities" (John Gries to Harold Buttenheim, January 11, 1932, Box 1, White House Conference on Home Building and Home Ownership, Hoover Presidential Library).

150. Herbert Hoover, "Annual Message to Congress on the State of the Union," December 8, 1931, American Presidency Project, https://www.presidency.ucsb.edu/documents/annual-message-the-congress-the-state-the-union-24.

151. Hoover explained to his secretary of labor why the preparation for the conference was more important than the conference itself (HH to Secretary of Labor, n.d., Box 89, Hoover Presidential Papers).

152. See "President's Final Message to Home Ownership Conference," Box 89, Hoover Presidential Papers.

153. Herbert Hoover, "The President's News Conference," July 22, 1932, American Presidency Project, https://www.presidency.ucsb.edu/documents/the-presidents-news-conference-880.

154. Morrill Oral History, 218; Robert Luce, *Congress: An Explanation* (Cambridge, MA: Harvard University Press, 1926); Robert Luce, *Legislative Principles: The History and*

Theory of Lawmaking by Representative Government (Boston: Houghton Mifflin, 1930).

155. Subcommittee of the House Banking and Currency Committee, *Hearings on Creation of a System of Federal Home Loan Banks*, 72nd Cong., 1st sess. (1932), 14, 46–47.

156. James Watson, *As I Knew Them: Memoirs of James E. Watson, Former United States Senator from Indiana* (Indianapolis, IN: Bobbs-Merrill, 1936), 273; 75 Cong. Rec. 14453 (July 1, 1932); "If You Can't Lick 'Em, Jine 'Em," Bartleby.com, n.d., http://www.bartleby.com/73/257.html. Couzen was quoted to similar affect in Drew Pearson and Robert Allen, *More Washington Merry-Go-Round* (New York: Liveright, 1932), 331–32.

157. Subcommittee of the Senate Banking and Currency Committee, *Hearings on Creation of a System of Federal Home Loan Banks, Part I*, 72nd Cong., 1st sess. (1932), 17–19, 31–32.

158. Quoted in Alonzo L. Hamby, *For the Survival of Democracy: Franklin Roosevelt and the World Crisis of the 1930s* (New York: Free Press, 2004), 88.

159. House Banking and Currency Committee, *Hearings on National Housing Act*, 73rd Cong., 2nd sess. (1934), 74.

160. Subcommittee of the House Banking and Currency Committee, *Hearings on Creation of a System of Federal Home Loan Banks*, 14.

161. National Association of Real Estate Boards, press release, February 2, 1932, Box 167, Hoover Presidential Papers; Real Estate Boards "Not for Release Report," February 4, 1932, Box 167, Hoover Presidential Papers.

162. Subcommittee of the Senate Banking and Currency Committee, *Hearings on Creation of a System of Federal Home Loan Banks, Part IV*, 667.

163. Hoover, *Memoirs*, 3:113.

164. Mason, *Building and Loans to Bail-outs*, 78–86.

165. "Federal Reserve: Emergency Lending," Congressional Research Service, March 27, 2020, https://fas.org/sgp/crs/misc/R44185.pdf.

166. Norris, *Ended Episodes*, 211. Norris had long been interested in housing issues. He had earlier helped pass a state housing code in Pennsylvania. See Norris, *Ended Episodes*, 118.

167. Esbitt, "Bank Portfolios and Bank Failures"; Postel-Vinay, "What Caused Chicago Bank Failures?."

168. House building dropped much more rapidly than other types of construction spending in this period (Carter et al., *Historical Statistics*, tables Dc510–30, Dc869–78).

169. Goldsmith, *Changing Structure of American Banking*, 262, 83.

170. E. Meyer Oral History, 678.

171. Senate Banking and Currency Committee, *Hearings on Stock Exchange Practices, Part IX*, 73rd Cong,. 1st sess. (1933), 4248. The Guardian Detroit Union group also had an important Joint-Stock Land Bank affiliate that had collapsed in the general rout of the land bank system.

172. Wicker, *Banking Panics*, 118.

173. A. Meyer Diary, March 6, 1933.

6. A New Deal for Farm Mortgages

1. Raymond Moley, *After Seven Years* (New York: Harper, 1939), 2–5.

2. Rexford Tugwell to Felix Morley, Brookings Institution, September 15, 1931, and Rexford Tugwell to Henry Goddard Leach, the Forum, September 11, 1930, Boxes 4 and 5, Rexford Tugwell Papers, Franklin Delano Roosevelt (FDR) Library, Hyde Park, NY.

3. Rexford Tugwell, *The Brains Trust* (New York: Viking, 1968), 12–13.

4. Tugwell, *The Brains Trust*, 12–13, 16–17.

5. Rexford Tugwell, *The Roosevelt Revolution* (New York: MacMillan, 1977), xv, 32; Rexford Tugwell Diary, December 28, 1932, Box 30, Tugwell Papers.

6. Studs Terkel, *Hard Times: An Oral History of the Great Depression* (New York: Pantheon Books, 1970), 251 (Raymond Moley).

7. Tugwell, *Brains Trust*, 17. Modern economists are less sympathetic to this theory (see, for example, Giovanni Federico, "Not Guilty? Agriculture in the 1920s and the Great Depression," *Journal of Economic History* 65, no. 4 [December 2005]: 949–76), but some have shown the benefits of improving agriculture in the period to spur recovery (see, for example, Joshua Hausman, Paul W. Rhode, and Johannes Wieland, "Recovery from the Great Depression: The Farm Channel in Spring 1933," *American Economic Review* 109, no. 2 [February 2019]: 427–72).

8. Only a few histories discuss "economic balance" as a part of New Deal ideology. Michael Bernstein describes Rexford Tugwell's embrace of that ideology yet does not try to trace how or where this ideology was applied through policy or how it developed beyond Tugwell. The only other work to take balance seriously is Thomas Ferguson's article on sectoral politics, but Ferguson views the balance ideology only as an ideological superstructure emerging from new heavy-industry interest groups aligned with the New Deal. (I elaborate on the importance of heavy industry in the New Deal's ideology in chapter 7.) Ferguson does not try to explain how this ideology emerged and does not deal with the importance of agriculture in it. The concept of economic balance is also broached in Eliot Rosen's work on the Brains Trust and in Ellis Hawley's on prices, but it is secondary to supposed concerns about abstract "planning." See Michael Bernstein, *The Great Depression: Delayed Recovery and Economic Change in America, 1929–1939* (New York: Cambridge University Press, 1987); Thomas Ferguson, "Industrial Conflict and the Coming of the New Deal: The Triumph of Multinational Liberalism in America," in *The Rise and Fall of the New Deal Order*, ed. Steve Fraser and Gary Gerstle (Princeton, NJ: Princeton University Press, 1989), 3–31; Eliot A. Rosen, *Hoover, Roosevelt, and the Brains Trust: From Depression to New Deal* (New York: Columbia University Press, 1977); and Ellis Hawley, *The New Deal and the Problem of Monopoly: A Study in Economic Ambivalence* (1966; reprint, Princeton, NJ: Princeton University Press, 2016). For typical histories that focus on increasing consumer purchasing power or deficit spending, see Meg Jacobs, *Pocketbook Politics: Economic Citizenship in Twentieth Century America* (Princeton, NJ: Princeton University Press, 2005); William J. Barber, *Designs Within Disorder: Franklin D. Roosevelt, the Economists, and the Shaping of American Economic Policy, 1933–1945* (Cambridge: Cambridge University Press, 1996); David M. Kennedy, *Freedom from Fear: The American People in Depression and War, 1929–1945* (New York: Oxford University Press, 1999); Patrick D. Reagan, *Designing a New America: The Origins of New Deal Planning* (Amherst: University of Massachusetts Press, 1999). Books on Roosevelt's earliest policies also tend to ignore farm politics and balance. See Anthony J. Badger, *FDR: The First Hundred Days* (New York: Hill and Wang, 2008); Adam Cohen, *Nothing to Fear: FDR's Inner Circle and the Hundred Days That Created Modern America* (New York: Penguin Press, 2009). Typical books on New Deal agricultural policy have at best a few stray mentions of banking or farm credit policy. See, for example, Richard S. Kirkendall, *Social Scientists and Farm Politics in the Age of Roosevelt* (Columbia: University of Missouri Press, 1966); and Theodore Saloutos, *The American Farmer and the New Deal* (Ames: Iowa State University Press, 1982). One of the few

books that discusses farm finance is Donald Slaybaugh's biography of William Myers, *William I. Myers and the Modernization of American Agriculture* (Ames: Iowa State University Press, 1996), though he focuses largely on Myers own work as head of the FCA and does not place agricultural credit policy as a central component of the New Deal. Modern international historians are beginning to grapple with the surprising importance of agriculture reform in many of the economic ideologies of this era. See, for example, Adam Tooze, *The Wages of Destruction: The Making and Breaking of the Nazi War Machine* (New York: Penguin Books, 2008); Robert Allen, *Farm to Factory: A Reinterpretation of the Soviet Industrial Revolution* (Princeton, NJ: Princeton University Press, 2009). For Tugwell's celebration of the Soviet Union's "really ingenious Land Bank system" and its work in creating "a balanced industrial system," see Rexford Tugwell, "Experimental Control in Russian Industry," *Political Science Quarterly* 43, no. 2 (June 1928): 171, 184–87.

9. Federal Land Bank loans totaled $2.3 billion, more than all of the other forms of loans combined (data provided by Price Fishback, personal communication with the author, February 2014).

10. Quoted in W. M. Kiplinger, *Washington Is Like That* (New York: Harper, 1942), 456.

11. Quoted in Herbert Hovenkamp, *Enterprise and American Law, 1836–1937* (Cambridge, MA: Harvard University Press, 1991), 360.

12. Adolf Berle and Gardiner Means, *The Modern Corporation and Private Property* (New York: Harcourt, Brace, 1932), 286.

13. Berle and Means, *The Modern Corporation*, 331, 40–42. Although many today recall Berle's book from 1932, few today recall his next work, cowritten with Victoria J. Pederson, *Liquid Claims and National Wealth* (New York: MacMillan, 1934), which explained how ever-increasing liquidity in the banking system was both an increasing part of economic development and a potential danger to it.

14. Adolf Berle Oral History, 1967, 169, 174–75, Columbia University Archives, New York.

15. Adolf Berle, "The Nature of the Difficulty" (May 1932), in *Navigating the Rapids, 1918–1971: From the Papers of Adolf A. Berle*, ed. Beatrice Bishop Berle and Travis Beal Jacobs (New York: Harcourt Brace, 1973), 32–41. The other two credit groups were municipal bonds and railroad bonds. Berle noted that the former were tied up in the health of urban mortgages and homes and that the latter were in decent shape (Berle, "The Nature of the Difficulty," 32–41).

16. Berle Oral History, 176.

17. Berle, "The Nature of the Difficulty," 48. Indeed, Berle cited Harold Moulton's work as "a concise and relatively complete statement of the shiftability theory" (Berle and Pederson, *Liquid Claims*, 20, 225).

18. Berle Oral History, 170.

19. Beatrice B. Berle Diary, October 6, 1932, in *Navigating the Rapids*, ed. Berle and Jacobs, 50–51.

20. Hugh S. Johnson, *The Blue Eagle from Egg to Earth* (Garden City, NY: Doubleday, Doran, 1935), 114, emphasis in original.

21. "A Proclamation, by Muscleinny, Dictator Pro Tem," June 20, 1932, reprinted in Johnson, *Blue Eagle from Egg to Earth*, 123–32.

22. Kenneth Davis, *FDR: The Beckoning of Destiny, 1882–1928* (New York: Putnam's, 1971), 808.

23. Jean Edward Smith, *FDR* (New York: Random House, 2007), 184–85 (Roosevelt quotation); "F. D. Roosevelt's New Post," *New York Times*, December 21, 1920.

24. Kenneth S. Davis, *FDR: The New York Years, 1928–1933* (New York: Random House, 1979), 223.

25. Franklin Delano Roosevelt (FDR) to Colonel Edward House, November 21, 1933, in Franklin D. Roosevelt, *F.D.R.: His Personal Letters 1928–1945*, vol. 1, ed. Elliot Roosevelt (New York: Duell, Sloan, and Pearce, 1950), 373.

26. Rosen, *Hoover, Roosevelt, and the Brains Trust*, 137.

27. FDR to Secretary of the Treasury, October 9, 1933, Box 77, Presidential Subject Files, FDR Library.

28. For Roosevelt, these efforts to extend and support credit had the additional benefit that they did not immediately involve increased federal expenditures, which Roosevelt, despite his liberal reputation, remained opposed to in principle in his campaign and for much of his presidency. See Julian Zelizer, "The Forgotten Legacy of the New Deal: Fiscal Conservatism and the Roosevelt Administration," *Presidential Studies Quarterly* 30, no. 2 (June 2000): 331–58.

29. See, for example, William Leuchtenburg, *Franklin D. Roosevelt and the New Deal, 1932–1940* (New York: Harper Perennial, 1963), 10–12.

30. Moley, *After Seven Years*, 15–16. Moley also said that it was the political adviser "Louis Howe's cardinal principle to concentrate on farmers in planning a campaign" (16).

31. Lee Alston, "Farm Foreclosures in the United States During the Interwar Period," *Journal of Economic History* 43, no. 4 (December 1983): 885–903.

32. Franklin D. Roosevelt, "Radio Address from Albany, New York: 'The "Forgotten Man" Speech,'" April 7, 1932, American Presidency Project, https://www.presidency.ucsb.edu/documents/radio-address-from-albany-new-york-the-forgotten-man-speech.

33. Franklin D. Roosevelt, "Address Accepting the Presidential Nomination at the Democratic National Convention in Chicago," July 2, 1932, American Presidency Project, https://www.presidency.ucsb.edu/documents/address-accepting-the-presidential-nomination-the-democratic-national-convention-chicago-1.

34. Franklin D. Roosevelt, "Campaign Address in Topeka, Kansas, on the Farm Problem," September 14, 1932, American Presidency Project, https://www.presidency.ucsb.edu/documents/campaign-address-topeka-kansas-the-farm-problem.

35. Franklin D. Roosevelt, "Campaign Address on a Program for Unemployment and Long-Range Planning at Boston, Massachusetts," October 31, 1932, American Presidency Project, https://www.presidency.ucsb.edu/documents/campaign-address-program-for-unemployment-and-long-range-planning-boston-massachusetts. Moley said later that "the Boston speech of October 31st completed the program of the New Deal" (*After Seven Years*, 63).

36. Franklin D. Roosevelt, "Radio Address to the Business and Professional Men's League Throughout the Nation," October 6, 1932, American Presidency Project, https://www.presidency.ucsb.edu/documents/radio-address-the-business-and-professional-mens-league-throughout-the-nation.

37. Franklin D. Roosevelt, "Campaign Address on Agriculture and Tariffs at Sioux City, Iowa," September 29, 1932, American Presidency Project, https://www.presidency.ucsb.edu/documents/campaign-address-agriculture-and-tariffs-sioux-city-iowa.

38. Tugwell Diary, January 12, 1933, Tugwell Papers.

39. Franklin D. Roosevelt, "Campaign Address on Farm Mortgages at Springfield, Illinois," October 21, 1932, American Presidency Project, https://www.presidency.ucsb.edu/documents/campaign-address-farm-mortgages-springfield-illinois.

40. See Peter Grimm Oral History, 1972, 62, Columbia University Archives.

41. Grace Tully, *F.D.R. My Boss* (New York: Scribner's, 1949), 192–93.

42. "Program: Laying Corner Stone of Agricultural Economics Building," May 23, 1932, Box 37, William Myers Papers, Cornell University Archives, Ithaca, NY.

43. William I. Myers Oral History, 1975, 1–2, 16–17, 41, Columbia University Archives.

44. "Memorandum on Conference in Washington, D.C.: Conference on Agricultural Credit," December 22–23, 1932, Box 44, Myers Papers.

45. Slaybaugh, *William I. Myers*, 104–12.

46. William I. Myers, "Important Issues in Future Farm Credit Administration Policy," *Journal of Farm Economics* 19, no. 1 (February 1937): 92.

47. See the "balanced-economy" argument for domestic allotment in Tugwell Diary, January 1933; and "Woodin Advocate of Sound Money," *New York Times*, February 22, 1933.

48. Mordecai Ezekiel to M. L. Wilson, February 13, 1933, Box 1, Mordecai Ezekiel Papers, FDR Library.

49. Rexford Tugwell Oral History, 1950, 9, Columbia University Archives; Rexford Tugwell, *The Diary of Rexford Tugwell: The New Deal, 1932–1935*, ed. Michael V. Namorato (Westport, CT: Greenwood Press, 1992), January 6, 1933, 52. See also Richard Tanner Johnson, *Managing the White House: An Intimate Study of the Presidency* (New York: Harper and Row, 1974), 5–6.

50. Tugwell Diary, January 12, 1933, Tugwell Papers.

51. Winthrop Aldrich, *The Causes of the Present Depression and Possible Remedies* (N.p.: n.p., 1933), 10, 18–19.

52. Tugwell, *The Diary of Rexford Tugwell*, February 1932, 68.

53. James A. Hagerty, "Roosevelt Confers on Federal Budget Looking to March 4," *New York Times*, December 2, 1932; Eric Rauchway, *The Money Makers: How Roosevelt and Keynes Ended the Depression, Defeated Fascism, and Secured a Prosperous Peace* (New York: Basic Books, 2015), 28–29.

54. Franklin D. Roosevelt, "Inaugural Address," March 4, 1933, American Presidency Project, https://www.presidency.ucsb.edu/documents/inaugural-address-8.

55. For the implicit guarantee of bank debts, see William Silber, "Why Did FDR's Bank Holiday Succeed?," *Federal Reserve Board of New York Economic Policy Review*, July 2009, 19–30. For internal banker requests for such a guarantee, see Adolf Berle, "Memorandum of Treasury Conference," March 5, 1933, Box 17, Adolf Berle Papers, FDR Library.

56. Franklin Roosevelt, "Fireside Chat on Banking," March 12, 1933, American Presidency Project, https://www.presidency.ucsb.edu/documents/fireside-chat-banking. Roosevelt also emphasized that he liberalized Federal Reserve loans so that they could be made on all "good assets," which would demonstrate to people that the government was standing behind the banks.

57. Jordan A. Schwartz, *The New Dealers: Power Politics in the Age of Roosevelt* (New York: Vintage, 1994), 70–71.

58. Scott Sumner, *The Midas Paradox: Financial Markets, Government Policy Shocks, and the Great Depression* (Oakland, CA: Independent Institute, 2015), 175.

59. Rauchway, *Money Makers*, 58; Francis Gloyd Awalt, "Recollections of the Banking Crisis in 1933," *Business History Review* 43, no. 3 (Autumn 1969): 368–69.

60. "Confidential Memorandum of Conferences in Washington D.C.," January 7, 1933, Box 44, Myers Papers.

61. "Mortgage Aid Plan Approved by Roosevelt: Program Intended to Help Farmers," *Chicago Tribune*, March 24, 1933, quoting the report; Franklin Roosevelt, "Message to Congress on Farm Mortgage Foreclosures," April 3, 1933, American Presidency

Project, https://www.presidency.ucsb.edu/documents/message-congress-farm-mort gage-foreclosures; Henry Morgenthau Jr. to Marvin McIntrye, April 3, 1933, Box 1, Franklin Roosevelt Official Files 27, Farm Credit Administration, FDR Library.

62. Marvin Jones, *Marvin Jones Memoirs 1917–1973: Fifty Years of Continuing Service in All Three Branches of the Federal Government*, ed. Joseph Ray (El Paso: Texas Western University Press, 1973), 5–6, 641–42. In his oral history for Columbia University, Jones spent more time talking about the mortgage refinancing and credit plans than about the significantly more famous allotment plans (Marvin Jones Oral History, 1953, Columbia University Archives).

63. "Memorandum of Conferences in Washington D.C. on Emergency Farm Credit Legislation," January 23, 1933, Box 44, Myers Papers.

64. "Memorandum of Conferences in Washington D.C. on Emergency Farm Credit Legislation," February 1, 1933, Box 44, Myers Papers.

65. "Aid for Rural Banks Nearer," *Wall Street Journal*, April 14, 1933.

66. "Tentative Program of Federal Legislation to Meet Emergency Credit Situation of Agriculture," January 11, 1933, Box 44, Myers Papers.

67. "Confidential Memorandum on Conferences in Connection with Emergency Credit Legislation," January 12–17, 1933, Box 44, Myers Papers.

68. "Confidential Memorandum on Conferences in Connection with Emergency Credit Legislation," January 26, 1933, Box 44, Myers Papers.

69. Jones Oral History, 609–10.

70. Franklin D. Roosevelt, "Message to Congress on the Agricultural Adjustment Act," March 16, 1933, https://www.presidency.ucsb.edu/documents/message-congress-the -agricultural-adjustment-act; Franklin D. Roosevelt, "Second Fireside Chat," May 7, 1933, American Presidency Project, https://www.presidency.ucsb.edu/documents /second-fireside-chat.

71. See, for example, "What the Farm Bill Will Do: Measure to Lower Interest Rates on Farm Mortgages," *Wallace's Farmer* 58, no. 8 (April 15, 1933): 163; this article spends almost three times as much space discussing the mortgage changes as the price-policy changes.

72. *An Act to Encourage National Industrial Recovery*, Pub. L. 67, 73rd Cong., 1st sess. (June 16, 1933), 205–6.

73. Franklin D. Roosevelt, "Fireside Chat (Recovery Program)," July 24, 1933, American Presidency Project, https://www.presidency.ucsb.edu/documents/fireside-chat-recovery -program.

74. "Aid for Rural Banks Nearer," *Wall Street Journal*, April 14, 1933.

75. "Refinancing of Farm Mortgages," *Bankers Magazine* 127, no. 6 (December 1933): 648.

76. "Bank Mortgage Relief Decided," *Wall Street Journal*, September 15, 1933.

77. "Federal Credit Agencies and Postal Savings System Report 4, Federal Land Banks and Federal Farm Mortgage Corporation," November 13, 1933, Box 64, Walter Wyatt Papers, University of Virginia Special Collections, Charlottesville.

78. Henry A. Wallace, *Agricultural Prices* (Des Moines, IA: Wallace, 1920).

79. G. F. Warren, "Causes of the Depression, Speech to Rotary and Kiwanis Clubs of Auburn, New York," April 5, 1933, Box 28, George Warren Papers, Cornell University Archives.

80. Franklin D. Roosevelt, "Fireside Chat," October 22, 1933, American Presidency Project, https://www.presidency.ucsb.edu/documents/fireside-chat-22. For more on Roosevelt's focus on agriculture in increasing prices, see Sebastian Edward, *American*

Default: The Untold Story of FDR, the Supreme Court, and the Battle Over Gold (Princeton, NJ: Princeton University Press, 2018).

81. FDR to Edward House, November 21, 1933, in Roosevelt, *F.D.R.: His Personal Letters*, 1:371–73.
82. Henry Morgenthau Jr. (HMJ) Diaries, August 16, 1933, Farm Credit Diary, 58, Library of Congress, Washington, DC.
83. "Personnel Strength of District Units," Box 48, Myers Papers.
84. "Morgenthau Made Farm Aid Records," *New York Times*, January 2, 1934.
85. HMJ Diaries, June 12, 1933, Farm Credit Diary, p. 43.
86. "$150,000,000 for Land Banks," *Wall Street Journal*, September 19, 1933.
87. Unsigned letter to the president, with corrections, February 10, 1934, Box 3, Official Files 27, Farm Credit Administration. The language of the letter and the situation it refers to indicate that it was likely written by Morgenthau.
88. FDR Press Conference no. 85, January 5, 1934, 4:03 p.m., 42–46, Press Conferences January 1 to January 10, 1934, Press Conferences of President Franklin D. Roosevelt, 1933–1945, FDR Library.
89. "To Concentrate on Debt Erasure: Administration Plans Center First on Farm and Home Mortgage," *Wall Street Journal*, January 8, 1934.
90. Franklin D. Roosevelt, "Annual Message to Congress," January 3, 1934, American Presidency Project, https://www.presidency.ucsb.edu/documents/annual-message-con gress-4.
91. John A. Filter and Derek S. Hof, *Fighting Foreclosure: The* Blaisdell *Case, the Contract Clause, and the Great Depression* (Lawrence: University of Kansas Press, 2012), 89–91.
92. Filter and Hof, *Fighting Foreclosure*, 130–39; *Blaisdell v. Home Owners Loan Association*, 290 U.S. 398, 442, 467.
93. Filter and Hof, *Fighting Foreclosure*, 160–61.
94. Filter and Hof, *Fighting Foreclosure*, 144.
95. Stephen Early to FDR, April 9, 1934, in Roosevelt, *F.D.R.: His Personal Letters*, 1:395–97.
96. "Roosevelt Signs Farm, Rail Bills," *New York Times*, July 1, 1934. Unlike the state mortgage moratorium, Frazier–Lemke would be struck down by the Supreme Court in a nine–zero decision as part of the Court's famous "Black Monday" in May 1935. The case against the law was brought by a Joint-Stock Land Bank: *Louisville Joint Stock Land Bank v. Radford*, 295 U.S. 555 (1935).
97. Leuchtenburg, *Franklin D. Roosevelt and the New Deal*, 51.
98. William I. Myers, "The Program of the Farm Credit Administration," *Journal of Farm Economics* 16, no. 1 (January 1934): 32.
99. HMJ Diaries, November 13, 1933, book 1, p. 100.

7. Housing, Heavy Industry, and the Forgotten New Deal Banking Act

1. Frances Perkins, *The Roosevelt I Knew* (1946; reprint, New York: Penguin, 2011), 215–16.
2. For modern argument against this once-common view of Keynes's lack of influence, see Eric Rauchway, *The Money Makers: How Roosevelt and Keynes Ended the Depression, Defeated Fascism, and Secured a Prosperous Peace* (New York: Basic Books, 2015).

3. John Maynard Keynes to Franklin Roosevelt, February 1, 1938, FDR Library Online, http://www.fdrlibrary.marist.edu/aboutfdr/pdfs/smFDR-Keynes_1938.pdf. In his letter, Keynes also reiterated that "housing is by far the best aid to recovery because of the large and continuing scale of potential demand."

4. Winfield Riefler to John Maynard Keynes, June 6, 1934, in *The Collected Writings of John Maynard Keynes*, vol. 21, *Activities 1931–1939: World Crises and Policies in Britain and America*, ed. Elizabeth Johnson and Donald Moggridge (Cambridge: Cambridge University Press, 2012), 320–21. Keynes's biographer Robert Skidelsky mentions this meeting in one sentence but attributes Riefler's enthusiasm to the fact that Keynes "was once more credited with magical powers over the New Deal" (*John Maynard Keynes: The Economist as Saviour, 1920–1937* [New York: Penguin Books, 1995], 508).

5. See, for instance, Eliot A. Rosen, *Roosevelt, the Great Depression, and the Economics of Recovery* (Charlottesville: University of Virginia Press, 2005), 186.

6. For urban historiography, see Kenneth Jackson, *Crabgrass Frontier: The Suburbanization of the United States* (New York: Oxford University Press, 1987); Marc A. Weiss, *The Rise of the Community Builders: The American Real Estate Industry and Urban Land Use Planning* (New York: Columbia University Press, 1987); David Freund, *Colored Property: State Policy and White Racial Politics in Suburban America* (Chicago: University of Chicago Press, 2007). For argument against the "suburban" interpretation of the Federal Housing Administration, see Judge Glock, "How the Federal Housing Administration Tried to Save America's Cities, 1934–1960," *Journal of Policy History* 28, no. 2 (2016): 290–317. In fact, the National Association of Real Estate Boards tried to expand the National Housing Act to focus on real estate "other than owner-occupied homes." Most interest groups had no particular reason to focus on homeownership per se. See Senate Banking and Currency Committee, *Hearings on National Housing Act*, 73rd Cong., 2nd sess. (1934), 280–81.

7. Louis Hyman, *Debtor Nation: The History of America in Red Ink* (Princeton, NJ: Princeton University Press, 2012), 49; Susan Carter, Scott Sigmund Gartner, Michael R. Haines, Alan L. Olmstead, Richard Sutch, and Gavin Wright, eds., *Historical Statistics of the United States: Earliest Times to the Present*, millennial ed. (New York: Cambridge University Press, 2006), tables Dc1255–270.

8. See Benjamin Roth, *The Great Depression: A Diary*, ed. James Ledbetter and Daniel B. Roth (New York: PublicAffairs), 44, 67, 79.

9. Jared Day, *Urban Castles: Tenement Housing and Landlord Activism in New York City, 1890–1943* (New York: Columbia University Press, 1999), 179–86.

10. Arthur Schlesinger, *The Coming of the New Deal* (Boston: Houghton Mifflin, 1958), 298.

11. Jordan A. Schwartz, *The New Dealers: Power Politics in the Age of Roosevelt* (New York: Vintage, 1994), 86. See more agreement in Robert S. McElvaine, *The Great Depression: America, 1929–1941* (New York: Times Books, 1984), 162.

12. Horace Russell, *Savings and Loan Associations* (Albany, NY: Matthew Bender, 1956), 52. See also "President Asks Mortgage Relief; Home Aid Later," *New York Times*, April 4, 1933.

13. Russell, *Savings and Loan Associations*, 52. For other early influences on the bill, see William Myers to Stephen Early, April 5, 1933, Box 1, Franklin Roosevelt Official Files 27, Farm Credit Administration, Franklin Delano Roosevelt (FDR) Library, Hyde Park, NY.

14. Russell, *Savings and Loan Associations*, 52–55.

15. T. J. Coolidge to Secretary of the Treasury, April 16, 1935, Box 1, Thomas Jefferson Coolidge Papers, FDR Library.

16. Leon Keyserling, interview, in *The Making of the New Deal: The Insiders Speak*, ed. Kate Louchheim (Cambridge, MA: Harvard University Press, 1983), 197. For one example of a B&L that was able to offload tens of thousands of dollars of questionable mortgages in exchange for Home Owners Loan Corporation bonds, see Minutes Books of the Monogohalia Building and Loan Association, 1932–1951, Box 5, ASM 2339, Monogohalia Building and Loan Association Papers, University of West Virginia Archives, Morgantown.

17. A. Scott Henderson, *Housing and the Democratic Ideal: The Life and Thought of Charles Abrams* (New York: Columbia University Press, 2000), 105–6. See also Franklin D. Roosevelt, "Message to Congress on Small Home Mortgage Foreclosures," April 13, 1933, American Presidency Project, https://www.presidency.ucsb.edu/documents/message-congress-small-home-mortgage-foreclosures.

18. Carter et al., *Historical Statistics*, tables Dc1255–270. For the benefits of the Home Owners Loan Act, however, see Price Fishback, Jonathan Rose, and Kenneth Snowden, *Well Worth Saving: How the New Deal Safeguarded Homeownership* (Chicago: University of Chicago Press, 2013).

19. Franklin D. Roosevelt, "Campaign Address on Progressive Government," September 23, 1932, American Presidency Project, https://www.presidency.ucsb.edu/documents/campaign-address-progressive-government-the-commonwealth-club-san-francisco-california.

20. Franklin D. Roosevelt (FDR) to Marie Thies, November 3, 1933, Box 1, Franklin Roosevelt Official Files 242, Securities and Exchange Act, FDR Library.

21. "Bank Mortgage Relief Decided," *Wall Street Journal*, September 15, 1933.

22. FDR Press Conference no. 85, January 5, 1934, 4:03 p.m., Press Conferences January 1 to January 10, 1934, 44, Press Conferences of President Franklin D. Roosevelt, 1933–1945, FDR Library.

23. In designing the National Industrial Recovery Act, Raymond Moley asked Roosevelt, "You realize then, that you're taking an enormous step away from the philosophy of equalitarianism . . . ?" To which Roosevelt said: "I never felt surer of anything in my life" (Raymond Moley, *After Seven Years* [New York: Harper & Brothers, 1939], 187, ellipses indicating omission). It is worthwhile to note that "equalitarianism" here obviously does not mean "egalitarianism" but rather the principle that the government should treat all groups equally and eschew special privileges.

24. Peter H. Irons, *The New Deal Lawyers* (Princeton, NJ: Princeton University Press, 1982), 31; David Townsend Mason, Executive Officer, the Lumber Code Authority, *The Lumber Code: An Address* (New Haven, CT: Yale University, 1935), 11–12.

25. Senate Finance Committee, *Investigation of the National Recovery Administration*, 74th Cong., 1st sess. (1935), 2341.

26. J. M. Hadley, Consumers Advisory Board, "The Effect of Price Control and Price Stabilization on the Construction Industry," January 9, 1935, in Senate Finance Committee, *Investigation of the National Recovery Administration*, 889. The National Association of Real Estate Boards labored hard to remove all construction from the code, which it claimed was "formulated by a group of architects and contractors" and inhibited home building (Senate Finance Committee, *Investigation of the National Recovery Administration*, 2137–139).

27. R. D. Winstead, "Preliminary Report on the Construction Industry," June 1935, Box 3, Leon Henderson Papers, FDR Library. For analysis of the National Recovery Act, see Jason E. Taylor, *Deconstructing the Monolith: The Microeconomics of the National Recovery Act* (Chicago: University of Chicago Press, 2019).

28. One administrator in the Lumber Dealers Authority noted that the authority was "interested in finding out how much of a change in prices has been experienced as a result of our mode mark-up procedure." See Paul Collier, Northeastern Retail Lumbermen's Association Administering Agency, *Official Code Bulletin* 9 (February 27, 1934), Box 66, Miscellaneous Records, Builders Supply of Lumber, Record Group (RG) 9, National Recovery Administration, National Archives, College Park, MD (NARA II).

29. M. Hadley, Consumers Advisory Board, "The Effect of Price Control and Price Stabilization on the Construction Industry," January 9, 1935, in Senate Finance Committee, *Investigation of the National Recovery Administration*, 889.

30. Rexford Tugwell Diary, April 13, 1934, Box 31, Rexford Tugwell Papers, FDR Library.

31. National Recovery Administration, *Codes of Fair Competition, Nos. 1–57, as Approved by President Roosevelt, June 16–October 11, 1933* (Washington, DC: U.S. Government Printing Office, 1933), 580–81.

32. T. J. Coolidge Memorandum, December 3, 1934, Box 1, Coolidge Papers. When one sale went off without Griswold, the Treasury undersecretary wrote to assuage Griswold's hurt feelings: "I feel that Farm Credit should not have acted as they did, and have told them so" (T. J Coolidge to Secretary of Treasury, January 24, March 2, and March 26, 1935, Box 1, Coolidge Papers).

33. Investment Bankers Code Committee, *Code of Fair Competition for Investment Bankers* (Washington, DC: Investment Bankers Code Committee, 1934), 16–25, 37–41, 62. Griswold would go on to lead this group into the late 1930s and discuss new regulations with the Securities and Exchange Commission (James Landis to B. Howell Griswold, June 29, 1936, Securities and Exchange Commission Historical Website, http://www.sechistorical.org/).

34. Edward J. Fyfe, "Beneficent Results of the NRA Code Beginning to Be Felt," *American Building Association News*, August 1934, 369–70.

35. Helen Burns, *The American Banking Community and the New Deal Banking Reform, 1933–1935* (Westport, CT: Greenwood Press, 1974), xi; George Benston, *The Separation of Commercial and Investment Banking: The Glass–Steagall Act Revisited and Reconsidered* (Oxford: Oxford University Press, 1990), 136–38. The Federal Deposit Insurance Corporation remains only implicitly guaranteed. See Alex J. Pollock, "Deposits Guaranteed Up to $250,000—Maybe," *Wall Street Journal*, May 28, 2013.

36. Walter Wyatt, "Preliminary Analysis of Senate Bill 3215," January 24, 1932, and Walter Wyatt, "S. 4412, Introduced April 18, 1932, Provision of This Bill Compared with S. 4115," 15–16, Walter Wyatt Papers, University of Virginia Special Collections, Charlottesville. For more on Glass–Steagall, see Burns, *American Banking Community*, 88–93, and Susan Estabrook Kennedy, *The Banking Crisis of 1933* (Lexington: University Press of Kentucky, 1973), 214–15.

37. See Benston, *The Separation of Commercial and Investment Banking*.

38. Moley, *After Seven Years*, 176–83.

39. Adolf Berle to FDR, December 9, 1933, in *Navigating the Rapids, 1918–1971: From the Papers of Adolf A. Berle*, ed. Beatrice Bishop Berle and Travis Beal Jacobs (New York: Harcourt Brace Jovanovich, 1973), 90–91; "Corporate Financing Lags," *Los Angeles Times*, October 10, 1933, 14. The *Washington Post* noted that the administration tried to prepare a plan for the country's banks, "a giant liquidation medium for frozen assets, notably real estate mortgages." Jesse Jones of the RFC tried to organize "substantial mortgage companies in each community" to assist with the recovery, but noted that there was already one in New York, probably referring to Berle's work. See "Three

Bankers Give Counsel to Roosevelt," *Washington Post*, October 15, 1933; and "Glass Thinks Bank Guaranty Might Be Changed," *Chicago Tribune*, December 2, 1933.

40. G. F. Warren to Henry Morgenthau, October 16, 1933, and G. F. Warren, "How to Raise Prices," October 21, 1933, Box 28, George Warren Papers, Cornell University Archives, Ithaca, NY.

41. Mordekai Ezekiel, "Memorandum for the Secretary, Means of Implementing the President's Monetary Policy," October 27, 1933, Box 1, Mordecai Ezekiel Papers, FDR Library.

42. See, for instance, Henry Bruere, "Interview with the President," November 16, 1933, Box 1, Franklin Roosevelt Official Files 21, Department of the Treasury, FDR Library.

43. Alexander Sachs, "Program for the Stimulation of the Construction Industries to Promote Reemployment," November 1933, Box 3, Henderson Papers. Sachs also suggested that the "real property inventory," then just starting in Cleveland, be expanded.

44. O. M. W. Sprague, "Problems of Recovery," *New York Times*, December 1, 1933.

45. George Warren Diary, January 4, 1934, Box 28, Warren Papers. Warren also noted in his diary that Roosevelt read all of Sprague's articles and that "Sprague repeated his idea of building middle class houses" for "needed capital investment. His chief idea of recovery seems to be middle class houses" (November 17, 1933). See also Sprague's later call for more mortgage loans by banks in Subcommittee of the Senate Banking and Currency Committee, *Hearings on the Banking Act of 1935*, 74th Cong, 1st sess. (1935), 214–15, as well as Gardiner Means, "Program for Reorganization of Capital and Credit Markets and Stimulation of Employment and Activity in the Heavy Industries Depending on These Markets for Financing," September 20, 1933, Box 1, Gardiner Means Papers, FDR Library.

46. John Maynard Keynes to FDR, December 30, 1933, in Keynes, *Collected Writings*, 21:293, 297.

47. In December 1932, after Roosevelt's election, Winfield Riefler wrote a memorandum titled "Easy Money in Its Relation to Construction," where he noted the need to bring down long-term rates. See Winfield Riefler, "Easy Money in Its Relation to Construction," December 1932, Box 1, Winfield Riefler Papers, NARA II, also in Federal Reserve Archival System for Archival Research (FRASER), www.fraser.stlouis.org.

48. Frank Watson, interview, in *The Making of the New Deal*, ed. Louchheim, 110; Paul A. Freund, oral history interview, October 18, 1982, Louie B. Nunn Center for Oral History, University of Kentucky Libraries, https://kentuckyoralhistory.org/catalog /xt72fq9q2q2s.

49. E. R. Black to Winfield Riefler, August 4, 1933, and Executive Order, "Central Statistical Board," August 3, 1933, Box 1, Riefler Papers; Joseph Alsop and Robert Kintner, *Men Around the President* (New York: Doubleday, Doran, 1939), 64.

50. Rexford Tugwell, *The Roosevelt Revolution* (New York: MacMillan, 1977), 120, 127–33.

51. Winfield Riefler, "Mortgage Situation," September 1933, Box 1, Riefler Papers.

52. "Prices in Wholesale Markets," December 27, 1933, Box 4, Records of Executive Council, RG 44, Office of Government Reports, NARA II. The only other area that was closer to the "1926 Price Level" was "Hides and Leather."

53. "Minutes of a Meeting of the Executive Council of the United States," December 27, 1933, Box 4, Records of Executive Council, RG 44, NARA II.

54. For John Fahey's background as Chamber of Commerce organizer, see Robert Wiebe, *Businessmen and Reform: A Study of the Progressive Movement* (Cambridge, MA: Harvard University Press, 1962), 35–40. See also Morton Bodfish, "FIGHT! You Building and Loan Men, We've Been Waiting Long Enough," *American Building Association*

News 53, no. 5 (May 1933): 206; Morton Bodfish, "Defense of the Legislative Branch of Our Federal Government," *American Building Association News* 54, no. 2 (February 1934): 55.

55. Minutes of the 131st Meeting of the Home Owners Loan Corporation, 8–12, Box 2, Home Owners Loan Corporation Minutes, RG 195, Federal Home Loan Board, NARA II. See also "Subject of Modernization," *American Building Association News* 53, no. 1 (January 1933): 5.

56. Office of Management and Budget, Historical Tables, table 1.1: "Summary of Receipts, Outlays, and Surpluses or Deficits: 1789–2025," https://www.whitehouse.gov/omb /historical-tables/.

57. John Fahey to Frank Walker, "The Residential Construction Problem," February 14, 1934, Box 561, Records of the Better Housing Division, RG 44, NARA II.

58. Alexander Sachs, memorandum, November 28, 1934, Box 21, Alexander Sachs Papers, FDR Library.

59. Quoted in Peter Conti-Brown, *The Power and the Independence of the Federal Reserve* (Princeton, NJ: Princeton University Press, 2016), 26.

60. Senate Finance Committee, *Investigation of Economic Problems*, 72nd Cong., 2nd sess. (1933), 703–4; Sterling D. Sessions and Gene A. Sessions, *A History of Utah International: From Construction to Mining* (Salt Lake City: University of Utah Press, 2005), 44.

61. "Examination Report Summaries from First National Bank of Ogden and First Security Bank of Utah, from September 12, 1929 to August 13, 1934," Marriner S. Eccles Papers, FRASER.

62. Sachs, memorandum, November 28, 1934.

63. Morgenthau Press Conference, April 12, 1934, Morgenthau Press Conferences, vol. 2, 34, FDR Library Online, http://www.fdrlibrary.marist.edu/archives/collections /franklin/index.php?p=collections/findingaid&id=536. Eccles was similar to Roosevelt in that he remained wary of deficits and debt, claiming that he "felt that in a depression that proper role of government should be that of generating a maximum degree of private spending through a minimum amount of public spending" (Marriner Eccles, *Beckoning Frontiers: Public and Personal Recollections* [New York: Knopf, 1951], 147–49).

64. Eccles, *Beckoning Frontiers*, 146.

65. Winfield Riefler, "Program to Stimulate New Home Mortgage Financing," January 18, 1934, Box 1, Riefler Papers.

66. The council changed its name to the National Emergency Council, but I keep the nomenclature consistent in this chapter for clarity's sake, switching to "National Emergency Council" in chapter 8.

67. National Emergency Council, Meeting 3, Tuesday, January 23, 1934, 2:00 p.m., in *New Deal Mosaic: Roosevelt Confers with His National Emergency Council: 1933–1936*, ed. Lester G. Seligman and Elmer E. Cornwell Jr. (Eugene: University of Oregon Books, 1965), 75–76, 77–78.

68. Morgenthau Press Conference, April 12, 1934, 2:34; Minutes of the Conference on Housing, February 12 and 14, 1934, Box 561, Records of the Better Housing Division, RG 44, NARA II.

69. This explanation was made at a future meeting. See National Emergency Council, Meeting 9, Tuesday, May 1, 1934, 2:25 p.m., in *New Deal Mosaic*, ed. Seligman and Cornwell, 213.

70. National Emergency Council, Meeting 9, Tuesday, May 1, 1934, 2:25 p.m., 213.

71. National Emergency Council, Meeting 9, Tuesday, May 1, 1934, 2:25 p.m., 208.

72. National Emergency Council, Meeting 9, Tuesday, May 1, 1934, 2:25 p.m., 217–18.

73. Quoted in Miles Colean, *A Backward Glance: An Oral History* (New York: Columbia University Press, 1975), 31.

74. Eccles, *Beckoning Frontiers*, 153–54.

75. Watson, interview, 108–9.

76. Franklin Roosevelt, "Message to Congress Recommending Legislation on Assistance for Home Repair and Construction," May 14, 1934, American Presidency Project, https://www.presidency.ucsb.edu/documents/message-congress-recommending -legislation-assistance-for-home-repair-and-construction.

77. Senate Banking and Currency Committee, *Hearings on National Housing Act*, 21–22, 49. FDR's National Executive Council housing committee chair Frank Walker told the committee that although light industry had improved, "we found a great lagging in the capital goods industry. We also found insofar as the mortgage market was concerned that it was in a frozen condition" (House Banking and Currency Committee, *Hearings on National Housing Act*, 73nd Cong., 2nd sess. [1934], 3).

78. House Banking and Currency Committee, *Hearings on National Housing Act*, 38.

79. House Banking and Currency Committee, *Hearings on National Housing Act*, 65–66.

80. Senate Banking and Currency Committee, *Hearings on National Housing Act*, 287; Lewis Brown, "Housing Shortage in Nation Is Seen," *New York Times*, May 27, 1934; "Heavy Industry Held Work Key," *Wall Street Journal*, May 21, 1934; Watson, interview, 108–9.

81. House Banking and Currency Committee, *Hearings on National Housing Act*, 122–23; "Harriman Puts O.K. on Federal Housing Scheme," *Chicago Tribune*, May 19, 1934.

82. 78 Cong. Rec. 11189 (June 12, 1934).

83. Senate Banking and Currency Committee, *Hearings on National Housing Act*, 24, 29.

84. Senate Banking and Currency Committee, *Hearings on National Housing Act*, 27. The bill also allowed commercial banks to make loans for the construction of homes and to treat such loans as commercial paper, eligible for discount at the Federal Reserve. See House Banking and Currency Committee, *Hearings on National Housing Act*, 2, 69.

85. House Banking and Currency Committee, *Hearings on National Housing Act*, 10.

86. 78 Cong. Rec. 11201 (June 12, 1934). The Congressman was Everett Dirksen, later the Republican minority leader in the 1960s.

87. House Banking and Currency Committee, *Hearings on National Housing Act*, 163.

88. 78 Cong. Rec. 11209 (June 12, 1934).

89. House Banking and Currency Committee, *Hearings on National Housing Act*, 175.

90. "Victory," *Millar's Housing Letter*, June 25, 1934, 2, Box 1, Franklin Roosevelt Official Files 63, Housing, FDR Library.

91. Quoted in "Insured Mortgages as Bank Investments," *Bankers Magazine* 134, no. 4 (April 1937): 321.

92. Arthur Krock, "Ask Cut Rate Plan to Improve Homes," *New York Times*, March 2, 1934. For Walker as the possible source of the leak, see Arthur Krock to Frank Walker, March 12, 1934, Box 562, Records of the Better Housing Division, RG 44, NARA II.

93. Senate Finance Committee, *Investigation of the National Recovery Administration*, 891.

94. Franklin D. Roosevelt, "Fireside Chat," June 28, 1934, American Presidency Project, https://www.presidency.ucsb.edu/documents/fireside-chat-21.

8. An Economy Balanced by Mortgages

1. Henry Morgenthau Jr. to Franklin Delano Roosevelt (FDR), November 4, 1937, and diary entry, November 4, 1937, both in Henry Morgenthau Jr. (HMJ) Diaries, book 94, pp. 48, 49, Library of Congress, Washington, DC.
2. HMJ Diaries, November 4, 1937, book 94, p. 52.
3. Harold Ickes, *The Secret Diary of Harold L. Ickes*, vol. 2: *The Inside Struggle, 1936–1939* (New York: Simon and Schuster, 1954), 240.
4. The previous night Roosevelt had asked Morgenthau to look at a memo on housing and economic recovery prepared by Federal Reserve chair Marriner Eccles (phone conversation transcript, HMJ and Marriner Eccles, November 4, 1937, 10:48 a.m., HMJ Diaries, book 94, pp. 54–55, describing previous night's conversation with the president).
5. Quoted in Ickes, *Secret Diary*, 2:240.
6. Ickes, *Secret Diary*, 2:240; Susan Carter, Scott Sigmund Gartner, Michael R. Haines, Alan L. Olmstead, Richard Sutch, and Gavin Wright, eds., *Historical Statistics of the United States: Earliest Times to the Present*, millennial ed. (New York: Cambridge University Press, 2006), tables Dc510–30.
7. Ickes, *Secret Diary*, 2:242.
8. James Farley, *Jim Farley's Story* (New York: Whittlesay House, 1948), 103–7; Ickes, *Secret Diary*, 2:240.
9. William Leuchtenburg, *Franklin D. Roosevelt and the New Deal, 1932–1940* (New York: Harper, 1963); Herbert Stein, *The Fiscal Revolution in America* (Chicago: University of Chicago Press, 1969); William J. Barber, *Designs Within Disorder: Franklin D. Roosevelt, the Economists, and the Shaping of American Economic Policy, 1933–1945* (Cambridge: Cambridge University Press, 1996).
10. Alan Brinkley, *The End of Reform: New Deal Liberalism in Recession and War* (New York: Vintage Books, 1995); Meg Jacobs, *Pocketbook Politics: Economic Citizenship in Twentieth Century America* (Princeton, NJ: Princeton University Press, 2005).
11. Marriner Eccles, *Beckoning Frontiers: Public and Personal Recollections* (New York: Knopf, 1951), 165.
12. See, for example, FDR to Governor Black, July 1, 1934, and FDR to Harold Ickes, July 13, 1934, Franklin Roosevelt Official Files 90, Federal Reserve Board, Franklin Delano Roosevelt (FDR) Presidential Library, Hyde Park, NY. Morgenthau complained when the building was going up that "there isn't a street car or lunch counter within a mile" (HMJ Press Conference, October 15, 1934, Press Conferences of Henry Morgenthau, September 4, 1934, to April 22, 1935, vol. 3, p. 94, FDR Library Online, http://www.fdrlibrary.marist.edu/archives/collections/franklin/index.php?p=collections/findingaid&id=536).
13. Eccles, *Beckoning Frontiers*, 145–46.
14. J. M. Daiger to Governor Eccles, December 7, 1934, Marriner S. Eccles Papers, Federal Reserve System for Economic Research (FRASER), https://fraser.stlouisfed.org/. Harrison, however, remained opposed to many of Eccles's other reforms, and they fought often. See Allan Meltzer, *A History of the Federal Reserve*, vol. 1: *1913–1951* (Chicago: University of Chicago Press, 2003), 471–72.
15. National Emergency Council meeting, December 11, 1934, transcript, in *New Deal Mosaic: Roosevelt Confers with His National Emergency Council, 1933–1936*, ed. Lester G. Seligman and Elmer E. Cornwell Jr. (Eugene: University of Oregon Books, 1965), 377.

16. W. M. Kiplinger, *Washington Is Like That* (New York: Harper & Brothers, 1942), 437.

17. Winfield Riefler, "The Federal Housing Program: A Proposed Draft of an Address by Frank C. Walker Before the National Mortgage Bankers Association, Chicago, October 4, 1934," September 29, 1934, Box 1, Winfield Riefler Papers, National Archives, College Park, MD (NARA II).

18. Henry C. Wallace (but likely written by Mordecai Ezekiel), "Report of the Department of Agriculture to the Executive Council," October 2, 1934, Box 2, Mordecai Ezekiel Papers, FDR Presidential Library.

19. A. P. Giannini to Leonard Ayres, "Suggestions for Report of Economic Policy Commission of the American Bankers Association, Washington Meeting—1934," September 15, 1934; Giannini to Ayres, September 22, 1934; Giannini to Marriner Eccles, September 15, 1934; Eccles to Giannini, October 12, 1934, all in Box 9, Eccles Papers.

20. Paul Mazur, "Expenditures in Relation to Recovery," January 31, 1935, and Marriner Eccles to Harold Ickes, February 7, 1935, Box 24, Eccles Papers. The B&L bankers, including Morton Bodfish, opposed this move of commercial banks into their territory of home financing. See "Mortgage Lending by Banks Opposed," *New York Times*, May 31, 1935.

21. E. B. Kapp, memorandum, re: Housing Administration, September 20, 1934, Box 97, Alexander Sachs Papers, FDR Presidential Library.

22. E. B. Kapp, memorandum, re: Housing Administration, September 8, 1934, Box 97, Sachs Papers.

23. Other outside professors supported the increased housing focus. Adolf Berle at Columbia University wrote a memo saying housing construction should come first in the recovery. And the Columbia economist John Maurice Clark wrote a book that claimed that of all indicators of a recession "the largest and some of the most clearly prevailing leads are found in the construction industry." He said controlling such fluctuations was part of the "the meaning and requirements of balance." Construction was also the first factor dealt with in the book. See Adolf Berle, "Memorandum on Phases," September 18, 1934, 8, Presidential Subject Files, Treasury Department Files, 1933-1936, FDR Presidential Library; and John Maurice Clark, *Strategic Factors in Business Cycles* (New York: National Bureau of Economic Research, 1935), 27, 32-33.

24. Kiplinger, *Washington Is Like That*, 448. Lauchlin Currie had also written a seminal book, *The Supply and Control of Money in the United States* (Cambridge, MA: Harvard University Press, 1934), claiming that the Depression was caused by the Federal Reserve's failure to act more aggressively. See also Lauchlin Currie, "Lauchlin Currie's Memoirs," *Journal of Economic Studies* 31, no. 3 (2004): "Chapter III: The New Deal," 203.

25. Lauchlin Currie, "Comments on Pump Priming," memorandum, November 30, 1934, Eccles Papers. Roger Sandiland, William Barber, and other commentators usually expain away Currie's seemingly anachronistic focus on certain sectors, especially building, as just one part of a broader interest in "active fiscal policy" or "compensatory budgets" instead of as part of a distinct ideology of economic balance. See Roger J. Sandiland, *The Life and Political Eocnomy of Lauchlin Currie: New Dealer, Presidential Adviser, and Development Economist* (Durham, NC: Duke University Press, 1990); Barber, *Designs Within Disorder*; Brinkley, *End of Reform*; Byrd L. Jones, "Lauchlin Currie and the Causes of the 1937 Recession," *History of Political Economy* 12, no. 3 (1980): 303-15.

26. Lauchlin Currie to Marriner Eccles, November 17, 1934, Eccles Papers. This letter is misdated in the files as 1943.

27. John Earl Haynes, Harvey Klehr, and Alexander Vassiliev, *Spies: The Rise and Fall of the KGB in America* (New Haven, CT: Yale University Press, 2009), 262–68, which uses new evidence against Roger J. Sandilands's argument that Currie did not spy in his article "Guilt by Association? Lauchlin Currie's Alleged Involvement with Washington Economists in Soviet Espionage," *History of Political Economy* 32, no. 3 (2000): 473–515.

28. For more on the Federal Reserve's transition to ending the real-bills doctrine, see Judge Glock, "The 'Riefler-Keynes' Doctrine and Federal Reserve Policy in the Great Depression," *History of Political Economy* 51, no. 2 (April 2019): 297–327.

29. Eccles, *Beckoning Frontiers*, 54–55. Eccles's interest in the balanced-economy idea continued throughout his career. In 1940, while still at the Federal Reserve, he published the book *Economic Balance and a Balanced Budget* (New York: Harper Brothers, 1940).

30. Eccles, *Beckoning Frontiers*, 171.

31. Lauchlin Currie, "PhD Thesis," *Journal of Economic Studies* 31, no. 3 (2004 [1931]): chap. 12, "Conclusion," 257–59. It is also no coincidence that just as Eccles assumed the helm, a Federal Reserve researcher, Bray Hammond, who would eventually write a Pulitzer Prize–winning book on banking in American history, published an article on how bankers going back to the eighteenth century "ignored the fundamental legitimacy of the demand for long term credit" (Bray Hammond, "Long and Short Credit in Early American Banking," *Quarterly Journal of Economics* 49, no. 1 [November 1934]: 102–3). For approval by a majority of the Federal Reserve Board for the publication of this article, see Mr. Carpenter to Mr. Smead, September 15, 1934, and Smead to Federal Reserve Board, September 15, 1934, Box 424, RG 82, Federal Reserve Central Subject Files, NARA II.

32. Currie, "PhD Thesis," chap. 9, "Bank Assets and the Business Cycle," 253, 247. The *anti-consumer-spending* thrust of Currie's theory is made clear in the next line, where he states, "What is needed is that consumers' incomes should be increased with no corresponding immediate increase in finished consumption goods."

33. Minutes of the Subcommittee on Housing of Interdepartmental Loan Committee, January 3, 1935, HMJ Diaries, book 3, p. 90.

34. Federal Reserve Board, Statement for the Press, "Address by Marriner S. Eccles, at the Mid-winter Meeting of the Ohio Bankers Association," February 12, 1935, Box 2, Franklin Roosevelt Official Files 90, Federal Reserve Board.

35. Eccles, *Beckoning Frontiers*, 171–72.

36. Minutes of the Subcommittee on Housing of Interdepartmental Loan Committee, January 3, 1935, HMJ Diaries, book 3, p. 90.

37. Minutes of the Subcommittee on Housing of Interdepartmental Loan Committee, January 3, 1935, HMJ Diaries, book 3, p. 90.

38. Eccles, *Beckoning Frontiers*, 174–75. For a failed attempt in Congress to change eligibility and real estate rules before Eccles's tenure, see Chester Morrill to Senator Duncan Fletcher, April 28, 1934, Box 143, RG 82, NARA II.

39. Marriner Eccles, "Press Conference of February 8, 1935," Eccles Papers.

40. Marriner Eccles, "Monetary Problems of Recovery," Annual Midwinter Meeting of the Ohio Banking Association, February 12, 1935, Eccles Papers.

41. Quoted in Mark Wayne Nelson, *Jumping the Abyss: Marriner Eccles and the New Deal, 1933–1940* (Salt Lake City: University of Utah Press, 2017), 204.

42. Eccles, *Beckoning Frontiers*, 196–97.

43. Examiners Reports, 1934, Eccles Investment Company, Eccles Papers.

44. "The Liquefaction of Ice," *Bankers Magazine* 130, no. 3 (March 1935): 296.

45. "Memorandum to Congress by the Economists' National Committee on Monetary Policy," March 7, 1935, reprinted in House Committee on Banking and Currency, *Government Ownership of the Twelve Federal Reserve Banks*, 75th Cong., 3rd sess. (1938), 319–23.

46. Charles Ashley Wright, "Bank Liquidity and the Eccles Bill," *Bankers Magazine* 130, no. 5 (May 1935): 527.

47. House Banking and Currency Committee, *Hearings on the Banking Act of 1935*, 74th Cong., 1st sess. (1935), 179, 184, 224–26, 240, 258–70.

48. "Report on Banking Act of 1935," 74th Cong., 1st sess., H. Rpt. 742 (1935), 14–15. For letters between Eccles and Giannini celebrating passage of the act, especially "the real-estate provisions," see Marquis James and Bessie James, *The Story of Bank of America: Biography of a Bank* (Washington, DC: Beard Books, 2002), 389.

49. Walter A. Morton, "Abandon Liquidity Fetish," *Bankers Magazine* (May 1939): 449 (volume and issue numbers not listed).

50. Marriner Eccles, "Address Before the American Bankers' Association Convention in New Orleans," November 14, 1935, Box 5, Howard Babcock Papers, Cornell University Archives, Ithaca, NY.

51. Robert Fleming, "A Broader Field for Banking," *Insured Mortgage Portfolio* 1, no. 3 (September 1936): 3–4.

52. Nelson, *Jumping the Abyss*, 333.

53. Walter A. Morton, "Liquidity and Solvency," *American Economic Review* 29, no. 2 (June 1939): 272.

54. Marriner Eccles, "Address at the 25th Anniversary of the Opening of the Federal Reserve Bank of St. Louis," November 9, 1939, Box 218, Thomas G. Corcoran Papers, Library of Congress.

55. Marriner Eccles to Messrs. Clayton, Thurston, Smeed, Perry, Chester Morrill, Walter Wyatt, Leo Paulger, Emanuel Goldenweiser, "Housing and Mortgage Matters," November 6, 1935, Eccles Papers.

56. "Excerpt from the Minutes of the Meeting of the Executive Committee of the Federal Reserve Board Held November 8, 1934," Eccles Papers.

57. Miles Colean, *A Backward Glance: An Oral History* (New York: Columbia University Press, 1975), 38.

58. Miles Colean, "Bond Issues for Large-Scale Housing," *Insured Mortgage Portfolio* 1, no. 4 (October 1936): 9–11; Miles Colean, "Markets for Insured Mortgages," *Insured Mortgage Portfolio* 1, no. 2 (August 1935): 16–17.

59. For discussion not only of how early FHA programs encouraged such racist practices but also of how later FHA programs worked against them, see Judge Glock, "How the Federal Housing Administration Tried to Save America's Cities, 1934–1960," *Journal of Policy History* 28, no. 2 (2016): 290–317.

60. W. D. Flanders, "Recasting Mortgage Portfolios," *Insured Mortgage Portfolio* 1, no. 5 (November 1936): 13–14.

61. Raymond B. Vickers, *Panic in the Loop: Chicago's Banking Crisis of 1932* (Lanham, MD: Lexington Books, 2011), 104–16.

62. Quoted in "RFC Will Buy Trust Company Stock, Notes," *Chicago Daily Tribune*, September 28, 1934.

63. Raymond Carl to RFC Mortgage Company, August 6, 1935, Box 4, Entry 130, RG 234, Records of the Reconstruction Finance Corporation, 1935–1948, NARA II.

64. "Earl Shwulst, Banker, Dies at 90," *New York Times*, July 19, 1987.

65. "Roosevelt Scores Mortgage Usury," *New York Times*, November 3, 1934.

66. Quoted in "Housing Seen Business Spur by President," *Washington Post*, March 14, 1935, Box 1, RG 234, NARA II.

67. "Castles in the Air: FHA Insured Loans Go Mostly to Refinancing; Hope Expressed New RFC Company Will Help Bring Construction Upturn," *Washington Post*, October 28, 1936. See also RFC Mortgage Company Loan Authorizations, March 14, 1935, to March 31, 1936, Box 8, RG 234, NARA II.

68. "Castles in the Air," *Washington Post*, October 28, 1936. This article was the fifth in a series investigating the housing problem.

69. "Report of the Committee on Coordination of Housing Activities of the Federal Government," May 27, 1935, Box 3, Entry 1, RG 207, Records of the Department of Housing and Urban Development, NARA II.

70. Colean, *Backward Glance*, 43; J. M. Daiger to Peter Grimm, "Housing Construction," February 29, 1936, Eccles Papers.

71. Colean, *Backward Glance*, 43.

72. "Housing Aid 'Mess' Balks President," *New York Times*, March 11, 1936.

73. "1936 Democratic Party Platform," June 23, 1936, American Presidency Project, https://www.presidency.ucsb.edu/documents/1936-democratic-party-platform; Franklin D. Roosevelt, "Annual Message to Congress," January 6, 1937, American Presidency Project, https://www.presidency.ucsb.edu/documents/annual-message-congress-1; "Topics of the Times," *New York Times*, January 9, 1937.

74. Franklin D. Roosevelt, "Inaugural Address," January 20, 1937, American Presidency Project, https://www.presidency.ucsb.edu/documents/inaugural-address-7.

75. Carter et al., *Historical Statistics*, tables Dc510–30.

76. Unlike those historians who emphasize the supposed conflict between antitrusters who were concerned about "administered prices" and Keynesians who were concerned about spending, this chapter hopes to show the essential unity in these two approaches, which were usually carried on simultaneously by the same people and which often involved opposition to labor as well as to corporations. See, by contrast, Brinkley, *End of Reform*; and Theodore Rosenof, *Economics in the Long Run: New Deal Theorists and Their Legacies, 1933–1993* (Chapel Hill: University of North Carolina Press, 1997).

77. George F. Warren and Frank A. Pearson, *World Prices and the Building Industry* (New York: Wiley, 1937), 97, 132, 143–44. Warren, still an agricultural economist at Cornell, declared in a public speech that "building is our most important urban industry" (quoted in "Boom in Building in 1936 Held Likely," *New York Times*, July 17, 1935).

78. Lauchlin Currie, "The Rise of Prices and the Problem of Maintaining an Orderly Revival," March 10, 1937, Eccles Papers.

79. Lauchlin Currie, "Our Common Responsibility for Economic Balance," August 11, 1937, Eccles Papers. One historian describes Leon Henderson, a close friend of Currie, as worried about a "real danger of runaway prices," "particularly those producing materials for the construction industry . . . [that] might put a brake on capital spending." See William Barber, "Government as a Laboratory for Economic Learning in the Years of the Democratic Roosevelt," in *The State and Economic Knowledge: The American and British Experiences*, ed. Mary Furner and Barry Supple (Cambridge: Cambridge University Press, 1990), 112. See also Currie, "Lauchlin Currie's Memoirs," 209. Even Henry Wallace at the Department of Agriculture worried at this time that a "major danger spot is the housing industry" (Henry A. Wallace, "Technology, Corporations, and the General Welfare," June 24, 1937, Eccles Papers).

80. Marriner Eccles, "Statement of Chairman Eccles with Reference to His Position on Credit and Monetary Problems," March 15, 1937, Box 2, Franklin Roosevelt Official Files

90, Federal Reserve Board. Eccles stated that "increased wages and shorter hours when they limit or actually reduce production are not at this time in the interest of the public" and that these higher wages "result in throwing the buying power of the various groups in the entire economy out of balance."

81. Brinkley, *End of Reform*, 97.

82. See chapter 5 and Jones, "Lauchlin Currie," 307. In the *General Theory*, Keynes did not focus on financing and building as he did in *Treatise*, but he described "the most important class of very long-term investments, namely buildings," and continued to focus overwhelmingly on the importance of long-term interest rates for recovery. See John Maynard Keynes, *The Collected Writings of John Maynard Keynes*, vol. 7: *The General Theory of Employment, Interest, and Money*, ed. Elizabeth Johnson and Donald Moggridge (London: MacMillan, 1978), 163 (in a chapter titled "The State of Long-Term Expectation"). For a description of Keynes's focus on long-term interest rates, see Axel Leijonhufvud, *On Keynesianism and Keynesian Economics* (New York: Oxford University Press, 1968).

83. L. B. Currie, "A Tentative Program to Meet the Business Recession," October 13, 1937, Eccles Papers. See also Lauchlin Currie, "Federal Income-Increasing Expenditures, 1932–1935," c. November 1935, *Journal of Economic Studies* 31, no. 3 (2004): 289–93.

84. Stewart McDonald to Winfield Riefler, May 17, 1938 and Winfield Riefler, "Outline of a Plan to Interest Private Capital in the Construction of Low-Cost Housing," c. October 4, 1937, both in Box 1, Folder 6, Riefler Papers.

85. Franklin D. Roosevelt, "Excerpts from the Press Conference," April 2, 1937, American Presidency Project, http://www.presidency.ucsb.edu/ws/?pid=15383.

86. D. Bradford Hunt, *Blueprint for Disaster: The Unraveling of Chicago Public Housing* (Chicago: Chicago University Press, 2009), 15–34; Roosevelt, "Excerpts from the Press Conference," April 2, 1937. FDR had similar concerns about Senator Robert Wagner's National Labor Relations Act of 1935, which encouraged union organizing and would thus increase prices. FDR originally refused to endorse it and voiced qualms about its scope. In classic Rooseveltian fashion, he switched to support it only after passage looked inevitable. See J. Joseph Huthmacher, *Senator Robert F. Wagner and the Rise of Urban Liberalism* (New York: Atheneum, 1968), 190; and Peter H. Irons, *The New Deal Lawyers* (Princeton, NJ: Princeton University Press, 1982), 213–14, 230–31.

87. Currie, "Lauchlin Currie Memoirs," 212.

88. Henry Morgenthau and Marriner Eccles, phone conversation, 10:48 a.m., November 4, 1937, transcript, HMJ Diaries, book 94, pp. 54–60. See also Eccles, *Beckoning Frontiers*, 302–3.

89. "Immediate Measures to Stimulate Housing Construction," November 10, 1937, Eccles Papers.

90. "Immediate Measures to Stimulate Housing Construction."

91. Delbart Clark, "Housing Viewed as Key to Recovery," *New York Times*, November 14, 1937. Most modern explanations of the recession, by contrast, point to a tightening of both monetary and fiscal policy. See Francois R. Velde, "The Recession of 1937—a Cautionary Tale," *Economic Perspectives*, Fourth Quarter, 2009, 16–37. The bill was supported by, among others, the American Construction Council, the organization Hoover and Roosevelt had led in the 1920s. See "Federal Mortgage Aid and Tax Relief Called Key to Construction Revival," *New York Times*, November 23, 1937.

92. Franklin Roosevelt, "Message to Congress on Legislation for Private Construction of Housing," November 27, 1937, American Presidency Project, https://www.presidency

.ucsb.edu/documents/message-congress-legislation-for-private-construction
-housing. Eccles presented the plan to Congress as an attempt at balance. He said that
if the government could encourage more cheap construction, "then we would get a
balance between our various elements in our economy, instead of high costs maintained by organized groups, both in business and labor." In the present situation, "we
get a disequilibrium, so that one group of the population is unable to exchange its
goods and services with the other groups. That is essential. That is at the bottom of
our present difficulties today" (Senate Banking and Currency Committee, *Hearing to
Amend the National Housing Act*, 75th Cong., 2nd sess. [1937], 174).

93. Franklin Roosevelt, "Annual Message to Congress," January 3, 1938, American Presidency Project, https://www.presidency.ucsb.edu/documents/annual-message-con
gress-0.

94. Colean, *Backward Glance*, 40. Colean, perhaps ironically, said McDonald's "forte was
his way of handling Congress" (38). On similar strong-arm tactics in the House, see
J. M. Daiger, "Statement on the Lodge Amendment," confidential notes for January 10,
1938, Meeting of House and Senate Conferees, Eccles Papers.

95. Eccles told Congress he wanted to revive the National Mortgage Associations of the
original National Housing Act by restoring their tax exemption, which he called the
"most important feature" of his proposed bill. When Senator Wagner objected to
exemptions for proposed private corporations, Eccles said that these associations "are
instrumentalities of the Government, even though they are privately owned," and thus
deserved tax benefits (Senate Banking and Currency Committee, *Hearing to Amend
the National Housing Act*, 168, 191).

96. Eccles, *Beckoning Frontiers*, 307; "Housing Loan Body Is Set Up by RFC," *New York
Times*, February 11, 1938. Widespread hopes at this time are indicated by "Home Build-
ing May Lead U.S. out of 'Slump': Building Industry Hopes to Repeat Role of 'Moses'
Played in 1921," *Washington Post*, April 10, 1938.

97. John Maynard Keynes to FDR, February 1, 1938, emphasis in original, FDR Library
Online, http://www.fdrlibrary.marist.edu/aboutfdr/pdfs/smFDR-Keynes_1938.pdf.

98. FDR to John Maynard Keynes, March 3, 1938, FDR Library Online, http://www
.fdrlibrary.marist.edu/aboutfdr/pdfs/smFDR-Keynes_1938.pdf..

99. FDR Press Conference no. 435, February 18, 1938, 10:40 a.m., Press Conferences February 18, 1938, to March 4, 1938, 159–69, 174, Press Conferences of President Franklin D.
Roosevelt, 1933–1945, FDR Library. In his talk, in fact, Roosevelt further elevated housing to the same level as the other three great sectors of the economy he had long tried
to balance. "Our program seeks a balanced system of prices such as will promote a
balanced expansion of production. . . . Our agricultural, industrial, housing and monetary programs have been and will be directed toward this end" (161). The influence
of Currie in this conference is clear from the president's discussion of the rise in copper prices, which Currie had been studying because copper was used in homes for
wiring, flashing, and piping. See Lauchlin Currie to Marriner Eccles, March 23, 1937,
and Currie to Eccles, "The Copper Situation," April 19, 1937, Eccles Papers.

100. HMJ Diaries, February 25, 1938, book 1, Presidential Diaries, p. 4. Economists identified cement as the building material with the highest "relative stickiness" of prices and
therefore the one that demanded the greatest adjustment. See W. D. Conklin, "Building Costs in the Business Cycle," *Journal of Political Economy* 43, no. 3 (June 1935): 391.

101. Johnson (full name not given) to Cordell Hull, February 28, 1938, HMJ Diaries, book
112, p. 209.

102. Winthrop Aldrich, "Business Recession in Relation to Government Policy," *Bankers Magazine* 136, no. 2 (February 1938): 120.

103. See, for example, William Leuchtenburg, *Franklin D. Roosevelt and the New Deal, 1932–1940* (New York: Harper Perennial, 1963), 256–57; and Brinkley, *End of Reform*.

104. Lauchlin Currie, "Causes of the Recession," April 1, 1938, Eccles Papers.

105. Morgenthau Presidential Book 1, HMJ Diaries, April 11, 1938, book 1, Presidential Diaries, p. 5; HMJ Diaries, April 12, 1938, book 118, pp. 343–48.

106. Joseph Alsop and Robert Kintner, *Men Around the President* (New York: Doubleday, Doran, 1939).

107. Franklin Roosevelt, "Annual Budget Message," January 3, 1940, American Presidency Project, https://presidency.ucsb.edu/documents/annual-budget-message-3.

108. Frank Roosevelt, "Message to Congress on Stimulating Recovery," April 14, 1938, American Presidency Project, https://www.presidency.ucsb.edu/documents/message-congress-stimulating-recovery. In regards to spending, Roosevelt's biggest announcement was that he hoped to "keep the Government expenditures for work relief and similar purposes during the coming fiscal year at the same rate of expenditure as at present." See also Franklin Roosevelt, "Fireside Chat," April 14, 1938, American Presidency Project, https://www.presidency.ucsb.edu/documents/fireside-chat-15. The total recommendations, if one takes account of all increased authorizations to loan, would be $1.95 billion in loans and $1.06 billion in "increased" expenditures, with the latter largely a continuation of previous "emergency spending levels." For the law that largely mimicked these recommendations, see "Joint Resolution: Making Appropriation for Work Relief," Public Resolution 122, 75th Cong., 3rd sess. (June 21, 1938), 809.

109. Winfield Riefler to HMJ, April 21, 1938, and "Notes on the Recent Fiscal and Monetary Program" April 21, 1938, HMJ Diaries, book 120, pp. 268–71.

110. Franklin Roosevelt, "Message to Congress on Curbing Monopolies," April 29, 1938, American Presidency Project, https://www.presidency.ucsb.edu/documents/message-congress-curbing-monopolies. In a throwback to his old house-divided metaphor, Roosevelt claimed that business could not stand "half regimented and half competitive, half-slave and half-free."

111. See Ellis Hawley, *The New Deal and the Problem of Monopoly: A Study in Economic Ambivalence* (New York: Fordham University Press, 1995).

112. Thurman W. Arnold, *The Bottlenecks of Business* (New York: Reynal and Hitchcock, 1940), 13–18, 36–37, 45.

113. Brinkley, *End of Reform*, 112.

114. "Suits to Cut Cost of Housing Likely to Hit Union Labor," *New York Times*, July 3, 1939; "Maps Trust Drive in Building Trades," *New York Times*, July 8, 1939; David M. Hart, *Forged Consensus: Science, Technology, and Economic Policy in the United States, 1921–1933* (Princeton, NJ: Princeton University Press, 2010), 110–13.

115. *United States v. Hutcheson*, 312 U.S. 219 (1941) (Frankfurter, J.)

116. Stein, *Fiscal Revolution*, 167–68; James Tobin, "Hansen and Public Policy," *Quarterly Journal of Economics* 90, no. 1 (February 1976): 33–34.

117. Alvin Hansen, *Economic Stabilization in an Unbalanced World* (New York: Harcourt, Brace 1932), 335.

118. Temporary National Economic Committee, *Investigation of Concentration of Economic Power, Part 9: Savings and Investment*, 76th Cong., 1st sess. (1939), 3512, 3514–515, 3527, also 39–50, 96–97, 101. In his later famous essay predicting a long period of "secular stagnation," Hansen attributed low investment largely to low population growth, which

"affects capital formation most directly in the field of construction, especially residential building" (Alvin Hansen, "Economic Progress and Declining Population Growth," *American Economic Review* 29, no. 1 [March 1939]: 1–15).

119. Temporary National Economic Committee, *Investigation of Concentration of Economic Power: Temporary National Economic Committee, Monograph No. 8, Toward More Housing*, 76th Cong., 1st sess. (1939), xv–xvi. See also Hart, *Forged Consensus*, 98.

120. For continued search for new housing finance plans in late 1938, see FDR Press Conference no. 496, November 1, 1938, 201–3, Press Conferences October 14, 1938, to November 1, 1938, Press Conferences of President Franklin D. Roosevelt, 1933–1945.

121. The term *economic balance* had a similar peak at the time, though there was some revival of that term in the 1950s, before it permanently fell into desuetude. For use of the two terms, see Google Ngram, https://books.google.com/ngrams/graph?content =balanced+economy&year_start=1800&year_end=2000&corpus=15&smoothing=1 &share=&direct_url=t1%3B%2Cbalanced%20economy%3B%2Cco and https://books .google.com/ngrams/graph?content=economic+balance&year_start=1800&year _end=2000&corpus=15&smoothing=3&share=&direct_url=t1%3B%2Ceconomic%20 balance%3B%2Cco.

122. Carter et al., *Historical Statistics*, tables Dc903–28. By 1952, total urban mortgage debt would increase almost 270 percent from its mid-1930s low.

123. Raymond Moley, *After Seven Years* (New York: Harper, 1939), 193.

Conclusion

1. Henry Edmiston and Gunhild Anderson, "United States Government Corporations and Credit Agencies in 1940," *Federal Reserve Bulletin*, April 1941, 299; Office of Management and Budget, *Fiscal Year 2013 Historical Tables* (Washington, DC: U.S. Government Printing Office, 2012), 21.

2. "Minutes of the Federal Open Market Committee," February 27, 1948, 14, Federal Open Market Committee Papers, Federal Reserve System for Economic Research (FRASER), https://fraser.stlouisfed.org/.

3. Stephen Axilrod, *Inside the Fed: Monetary Policy and Its Management, Martin Through Greenspan to Bernanke* (Cambridge, MA: MIT Press, 2014), 37–38; Robert Bermner, *Chairman of the Fed: William McChesney Martin Jr. and the Creation of the Modern American Financial System* (New Haven, CT: Yale University Press, 2004), 99–103.

4. Horace Russell, *Savings and Loan Associations* (Albany, NY: Matthew Bender, 1956), 101–3.

5. "Housing Agencies Prevail on Stimulus to Building," *New York Times*, August 11, 1957; "Reserve Board Official Opposes Cut in Down Payments Set by FHA," *Wall Street Journal*, March 5, 1957.

6. "Housing Economics: A Study of Building Field's Role as Both Stimulus and Stabilizer," *New York Times*, April 20, 1959.

7. Quoted in Allan Seymour Everest, *Morgenthau, the New Deal, and Silver: A Story of Pressure Politics* (New York: King's Crown Press, 1950), 137.

8. "The Housing Lobby: Its Tactics Point Up Growing Sophistication of Big Pressure Groups," *Wall Street Journal*, April 3, 1959.

9. "Housing Agencies Prevail on Stimulus to Building: Lower Down Payments on New Homes Will Be a Mild Boost for Inflation," *New York Times*, August 11, 1957.

10. President John F. Kennedy told Congress less than a month after his inauguration that they needed to increase financing "for residential construction. To increase the flow of credit for these purposes, long-term interest rates should decline." He tasked the Federal Reserve with lowering such rates directly through buying long-term bonds. He also demanded even lower down payments for federal mortgages "to make sure that general expansion of long-term credit is effective in stimulating residential construction" (John F. Kennedy, "Special Message to Congress," February 2, 1961, American Presidency Project, https://www.presidency.ucsb.edu/documents/special-message -the-congress-program-for-economic-recovery-and-growth; see also John F. Kennedy, "The President's News Conference," February 1, 1961, American Presidency Project, https://www.presidency.ucsb.edu/documents/the-presidents-news-conference-214). These actions would become the basis of the administration's Operation Twist. The housing motive behind Operation Twist has not, to the best of my knowledge, been discussed by previous historians or economists. See also Walter Heller, "Monetary Policy and Debt Management: Draft for Message, for Discussion," January 25, 1961, Walter Heller Papers, John F. Kennedy Presidential Library, Box 19, FRASER; "President Offers Multi-point Program to 'Restore Momentum' to the Economy," *Wall Street Journal*, February 3, 1961.

11. One example of the mortgage industry's continuing power was the enactment of the mortgage-interest tax deduction in 1986. Before then, all interest was tax deductible on the assumption that the investors had already paid taxes on the interest received. During the tax reform of 1986, all other forms of interest deduction were removed, yet housing groups succeeded in keeping their deduction and even acquired new tax advantages such as the Low Income Housing Tax Credit. See Roger Lowenstein, "Who Needs the Mortgage Interest Deduction?," *New York Times*, March 6, 2006.

12. Thomas Phillippon, "Has the U.S. Finance Industry Become Less Efficient? On the Theory and Measurement of Financial Intermediation," *American Economic Review* 105, no. 4 (April 2015): 1416–418.

13. Peter Rose and Richard L. Haney, "The Players in the Primary Mortgage Market," *Journal of Housing Research* 1, no. 1 (1989): 93; Federal Reserve Bank of St. Louis, "L.1 Credit Market Debt Outstanding, Savings Institution, 1949–1980," Federal Reserve Economic Data, https://fred.stlouisfed.org/series/SITCMAHDFS.

14. See the discussion of maturity mismatch in Federal Home Loan Bank of San Francisco, "New Sources of Capital for the Savings and Loan Industry," in *Proceedings of the Fifth Annual Conference, December 6–7, 1979* (San Francisco: Federal Home Loan Bank of San Francisco, 1980), 103.

15. Gary Hector, "S&Ls: Where Did All Those Billions Go?," *Fortune*, September 10, 1990; David L. Mason, *From Building and Loans to Bail-outs: A History of the American Savings and Loan Industry, 1831–1995* (Cambridge: Cambridge University Press, 2004), 213–65.

16. Mason, *From Building and Loans to Bail-outs*, 230–31; L. William Seidman, *Full Faith and Credit: The Great S&L Debacle and Other Washington Sagas* (New York: Times Books, 1993), 229–35.

17. Richard W. Stevenson, "G.A.O Puts Cost of S&L Bailout at Half a Trillion Dollars," *New York Times*, July 13, 1996. That cost to taxpayers was placed at $130 billion.

18. Farmer Mac was assisted by the Farm Credit System Financial Assistance Corporation, the Farm Credit System Insurance Corporation, and the Federal Farm Credit Banks Funding Corporation—all new federal financial corporations created in the bailout. See C. Nash Nathaniel, "Plan for Farm Loans Studied," *New York Times*,

February 2, 1987; "Fannie Mae, Meet Farmer Mac," *New York Times*, October 3, 1987. For more recent scandals, see Alison Leigh Cowan, "Big-City Paydays at 'Farmer Mac,'" *New York Times*, April 28, 2002.

19. Alex J. Pollack, " 'Commercial' Bank Is a Misnomer: 'Real Estate' Bank Is More Apt," *American Banker*, August 8, 2016. Banks have retreated somewhat from making direct mortgage loans in more recent years, even though they often provide funding to the "nonbank lenders" making such loans. See Michele Lerner, "The Mortgage Market Is Now Dominated by Non-bank Lenders," *Washington Post*, February 23, 2017.

20. Gretchen Morgenstern and Joshua Rosner, *Reckless Endangerment: How Outsized Ambition, Greed, and Corruption Created the Worst Financial Crisis of Our Time* (New York: St. Martin's Griffin, 2012).

21. See Gary Gorton, *Slapped by the Invisible Hand: The Panic of 2007* (Oxford: Oxford University Press, 2010).

22. Bryan Kelly, Hanno Lustig, and Stijn Van Nieuwerburgh, "Too Systematic-to-Fail: What Option Markets Imply About Sector-Wide Government Guarantees," *American Economic Review* 106, no. 6 (June 2016): 1278–319; W. Scott Frame, Andreas Fuster, Joseph Tracey, and James Vickery, "Evaluating the Rescue of Fannie Mae and Freddie Mac," Liberty Street Economics, Federal Reserve Bank of New York, October 15, 2015, https://libertystreeteconomics.newyorkfed.org/2015/10/evaluating-the-rescue-of-fannie-mae-and-freddie-mac.html.

23. Gorton, *Slapped by the Invisible Hand*; Federal Reserve Bank of St. Louis, "Total Construction Spending: Residential, 2005–2009," Federal Reserve Economic Data, n.d., https://fred.stlouisfed.org/series/MBST.

24. This money was "paid back" by the earnings of the government-sponsored enterprises over the next ten years, partially due to tax write-offs of previous losses. These government-sponsored enterprises stayed on the government books, however, and the government became officially responsible for any future losses. See Joe Light, "Will Fannie and Freddie Need Another Bailout?," *Wall Street Journal*, May 24, 2016.

25. For the well-supported argument that Lehman was solvent and that the government could have "saved" it just through normal Federal Reserve operations, see Laurence Ball, *The Fed and Lehman Brothers: Setting the Record Straight* (Cambridge: Cambridge University Press, 2018).

26. Congressional Budget Office, *Report on the Troubled Asset Relief Program—March 2018* (Washington, DC: Congressional Budget Office, 2018), https://www.cbo.gov/system/files/115th-congress-2017-2018/reports/53617-tarp-march2018.pdf.

27. Housing Finance Policy Center, *Housing Finance at a Glance: A Monthly Chartbook* (Washington, DC: Urban Institute, April 2019), 8; Lerner, "The Mortgage Market Is Now Dominated by Non-bank lenders."

28. Federal Reserve Bank of St. Louis, "Securities, Loans, and Other Assets & Liabilities Held by Fed, Mortgage Backed Securities Held by the Federal Reserve 2008–2020," n.d., Federal Reserve Economic Data, https://fred.stlouisfed.org/series/MBST.

29. John B. Taylor, "Causes of the Financial Crisis and the Slow Recovery: A Ten-Year Perspective," Stanford Working Papers, December 2013; Federal Reserve Bank of St. Louis, "Current Population Survey, Unemployment Rate, 2006–2020," n.d., Federal Reserve Economic Data, https://fred.stlouisfed.org/series/UNRATE/.

30. Vadim Elenev, Tim Landvoigt, and Stijn Van Nieuwerburgh, *Can the Covid Bailouts Save the Economy?*, Working Paper no. w2707 (Cambridge, MA: National Bureau of Economic Research, May 2020) (the authors argue that the funds spent on corporate bailouts "would otherwise have been spent on [financial] intermediary bailouts" due

to defaulting corporate debt); Kathryn Judge, "The Truth About the COVID-19 Bail-outs," *Forbes,* April 15, 2020, https://forbes.com/sites/kathrynjudge/2020/04/15/the -covid-19-bailouts; Carl Gibson, "Workers Are Getting the Short End of the Stick from the Cares Act," *Barron's,* April 15, 2020. For combination of regulatory forbear-ance and federal support for mortgage borrowers, see Diana Olick, "Regulators Ease Restrictions on Homeowners in Coronavirus Mortgage Bailouts Program," CNBC, May 19, 2020, https://www.cnbc.com/2020/05/19/coronavirus-bailout-regulators-ease -restrictions-on-mortgage-program.html.

31. See, for example, Ben Bernanke, *Courage to Act: A Memoir of the Crisis and Its After-math* (New York: Norton, 2015), 33–36.

32. For an explanation of the need for housing subsidies during the housing crisis, see Edward E. Leamer, "Housing Cycle is the Business Cycle," in *Proceedings—Economic Policy Symposium—Jackson Hole* (Kansas City: Federal Reserve Bank of Kansas City, 2007), 149–233.

REFERENCES

This book has relied on a number of published primary and secondary books and articles, which are cited in the chapter notes. Almost all of these sources were garnered from the Rutgers University, University of Virginia, and West Virginia University libraries during my time as either a graduate student or a professor. I cannot thank the librarians at these institutions enough. This book has also relied on significant research into archival and document collections. I provide an overview of those collections here. The archivists at these institutions were invariably helpful and generous with their time, and I only regret that I cannot thank them by name. I would, however, especially like to thank the Herbert Hoover and Franklin Delano Roosevelt Presidential Libraries for their generous grants to conduct research in their collections.

Manuscript Collections

Columbia University Archives, New York

Berle, Adolf. Oral History.
Farmers Holiday Association Oral Histories.
Grimm, Peter. Oral History.
Harrison, George. Papers.
Hush, Homer. Oral History.
Jones, Marvin. Oral History.
Lubin, Isador. Oral History.
Meyer, Eugene. Oral History.
Morrill, Chester. Oral History.
Myers, William I. Oral History.
Taber, Louis. Oral History.

Tugwell, Rexford. Oral History.
Willis, H. Parker. Papers.
Wyatt, Walter. Oral History.

Cornell University Archives, Ithaca, NY

Babcock, Howard. Papers.
Myers, William. Papers.
Warren, George W.. Papers.

Federal Reserve System for Economic Research (FRASER)

Eccles, Marriner S. Papers.
Federal Open Market Committee Papers.
Heller, Walter. Papers.

Franklin Delano Roosevelt Presidential Library, Hyde Park, NY

Berle, Adolf. Papers.
Coolidge, Thomas Jefferson. Papers.
Ezekiel, Mordecai. Papers.
Fahey, John H.. Papers.
Henderson, Leon. Papers.
Howe, Louis McHenry. Papers.
Means, Gardiner. Papers.
Presidential Subject Files.
Press Conferences of President Franklin D. Roosevelt, 1933–1945.
Roosevelt, Franklin. Official Files.
Sachs, Alexander. Papers.
Treasury Department Files, 1933–1936.
Tugwell, Rexford. Papers.

Herbert Hoover Presidential Library, West Branch, IA

Ballantine, Arthur A.. Papers, 1900–1960.
Commerce Department Papers.
Federal Farm Board, Minutes, July 1929–May 1933.
Federal Reserve System, Board of Governors: Collection, 1917–1947.
Hoover, Herbert. Cabinet Papers.
Hoover, Herbert. Presidential Papers.
Joslin, Theodore. Diary.
MacLafferty, James. Diary.
White House Conference on Home Building and Home Ownership.

Library of Congress, Manuscript Division, Washington, DC

Coolidge, Calvin. Presidential Papers.
Corcoran, Thomas. Papers.
Hamlin, Charles. Papers.

Harding, Warren G. Presidential Papers.
Leffingwell, Russell. Letterbooks.
Meyer, Agnes. Papers.
Meyer, Eugene. Papers.
Morgenthau, Henry, Jr. Diaries.
Rainey, Henry. Papers.
Taft, William Howard. Presidential Papers.
Wilson, Woodrow. Presidential Papers.

National Archives, College Park, MD

Record Group 9: National Recovery Administration.
Record Group 31: Records of the Federal Housing Administration.
Record Group 44: Office of Government Reports.
Record Group 56: Records of the Secretary of the Treasury.
Record Group 82: Federal Reserve Central Subject Files
Record Group 103: Records of the Farm Credit Administration.
Record Group 195: Federal Home Loan Board.
Record Group 207: Records of the Department of Housing and Urban Development.
Record Group 234: Records of the Reconstruction Finance Corporation.
Record Group 294: Records of the Federal National Mortgage Association.
Riefler, Winfield. Papers.

National Archives, Washington, DC

Record Group 46: Records of the U.S. Senate.
Record Group 233: Records of the U.S. House of Representatives.

University of Virginia, Special Collections, Charlottesville

Glass, Carter. Papers.
Wyatt, Walter. Papers.

West Virginia University Archives, Morgantown

Atkeson, Thomas Clark. Papers.
Monogohalia Building and Loan Association Papers.
Silver, Gray. Papers.

INDEX

Adams, John, 18, 36
"Age of Reform," 4
Agricultural Adjustment Administration, 148
Agricultural Credit Corporation, 82
Agricultural Credits Act (1923), 79, 228n121
agricultural fundamentalism, 204n8
Agricultural Marketing Act of (1929), 98
Agriculture Prices (H. A. Wallace), 89
agriculture reform, 248n8
Aguinaldo, Emilio, 26
Air Bank, 12, 207n1
American Bankers Association, 41–42, 44, 55, 79, 90–91, 114–15, 221n137
American Farm Bureau Federation, 76, 88, 94, 98, 147, 226n76; Silver and, 73–74, 79, 227n87
American Revolution, 18
amortization, 22, 113, 141
anti-Semitism, 22, 24, 29
antitrust, 49, 98, 191–92, 219n63, 276n110
Arnold, Thurman, 191–92

bailouts, 57; balanced economy and, 11; of banks, 9; as corporate or financial, 270n30; of Fannie Mae, 10; of farmers, 73–74; of Federal Land Banks, 10, 87, 100–102, 198, 236n94, 237n117, 269n18; Federal Reserve and, 133, 200–201; first U.S., 99–102; of FSLIC, 10, 198; by Hoover, 237n4; of industry support, 4, 8; of investors, 9; mortgages paid by, 8, 75, 98, 152, 200–201; RFC for bank, 145; urban mortgages and bank, 157–58
balanced economy, 4, 9, 80; against agricultural fundamentalism, 204n8; class legislation vs., 5–6, 203n5; Congress on, 44; consumption and, 138; Coolidge on, 81; Currie on, 176; domestic allotment for, 144; Eccles on, 262n29, 265n92; economic balance as, 192–93, 268n121; end of, 201; equal protection and, 33, 215n5; farmers in, 2, 75; Federal Farm Board and, 215n6; as financial, 8, 11; by government, 1–2, 5, 61; Hoover on, 3, 87, 96–97, 157–59, 233nn60–61; investments restoring, 138–39; light industries and, 193; mortgages for, 172, 174, 194; mortgages threatening, 195; New Deal policy and, 136–37, 248n8; politics on, 2, 6; price-parity movement in, 10, 87–88; product prices in, 86–87; Republicans embracing, 71–72, 225n65; Riefler on,

COLUMBIA STUDIES IN THE HISTORY OF U.S. CAPITALISM

Series Editors: Devin Fergus, Louis Hyman, Bethany Moreton, and Julia Ott

Capital of Capital: Money, Banking, and Power in New York City, 1784–2012, by Steven H. Jaffe and Jessica Lautin

From Head Shops to Whole Foods: The Rise and Fall of Activist Entrepreneurs, by Joshua Clark Davis

Creditworthy: A History of Consumer Surveillance and Financial Identity in America, by Josh Lauer

American Capitalism: New Histories, edited by Sven Beckert and Christine Desan

Buying Gay: How Physique Entrepreneurs Sparked a Movement, by David K. Johnson

City of Workers, City of Struggle: How Labor Movements Changed New York, edited by Joshua B. Freeman

Banking on Freedom: Black Women in U.S. Finance Before the New Deal, by Shennette Garrett-Scott

Threatening Property: Race, Class, and Campaigns to Legislate Jim Crow Neighborhoods, by Elizabeth A. Herbin-Triant

How the Suburbs Were Segregated: Developers and the Business of Exclusionary Housing, 1890–1960, by Paige Glotzer

Brain Magnet: Research Triangle Park and the Idea of the Idea Economy, by Alex Sayf Cummings

Histories of Racial Capitalism, edited by Destin Jenkins and Justin Leroy